SPECIAL OPERATIONS IN NORWAY

SPECIAL OPERATIONS IN NORWAY

SOE and Resistance in World War II

Ian Herrington

BLOOMSBURY ACADEMIC
LONDON • NEW YORK • OXFORD • NEW DELHI • SYDNEY

BLOOMSBURY ACADEMIC
Bloomsbury Publishing Plc
50 Bedford Square, London, WC1B 3DP, UK
1385 Broadway, New York, NY 10018, USA
29 Earlsfort Terrace, Dublin 2, Ireland

BLOOMSBURY, BLOOMSBURY ACADEMIC and the Diana logo
are trademarks of Bloomsbury Publishing Plc

First published in Great Britain 2019 by I. B. Tauris
This paperback edition published in 2021

Copyright © Ian Herrington, 2019

Ian Herrington has asserted his right under the Copyright,
Designs and Patents Act, 1988, to be identified as Author of this work.

For legal purposes the Acknowledgements on p. vii constitute
an extension of this copyright page.

All rights reserved. No part of this publication may be reproduced or
transmitted in any form or by any means, electronic or mechanical,
including photocopying, recording, or any information storage or retrieval
system, without prior permission in writing from the publishers.

Bloomsbury Publishing Plc does not have any control over, or responsibility for,
any third-party websites referred to or in this book. All internet addresses given
in this book were correct at the time of going to press. The author and publisher
regret any inconvenience caused if addresses have changed or sites have
ceased to exist, but can accept no responsibility for any such changes.

A catalogue record for this book is available from the British Library.

A catalog record for this book is available from the Library of Congress.

ISBN: HB: 978-1-78831-262-2
PB: 978-1-35019-264-5
ePDF: 978-1-78673-564-5
eBook: 978-1-78672-564-6

International Library of War Studies

Typeset by Newgen KnowledgeWorks Pvt. Ltd., Chennai, India

To find out more about our authors and books visit
www.bloomsbury.com and sign up for our newsletters.

CONTENTS

Acknowledgements	vii
List of Abbreviations	ix
Maps	xiii
INTRODUCTION	1

Chapter 1
THE FORMATION OF SOE AND ITS SCANDINAVIAN
SECTION: A NEW STRATEGIC TOOL AND A NORDIC
OPPORTUNITY   7

Chapter 2
SOE POLICY IN NORWAY, 1940–5: THE COMBINATION OF
SHORT- AND LONG-TERM OBJECTIVES   29

Chapter 3
SOE AND THE NORWEGIAN GOVERNMENT AND MILITARY
AUTHORITIES, 1940–5: CONTROL THROUGH COLLABORATION   49

Chapter 4
SOE AND THE MILITARY RESISTANCE IN NORWAY, 1940–5:
DIRECTION, SEPARATION AND FINALLY PARTNERSHIP   71

Chapter 5
SOE AND THE OTHER NEW ORGANIZATIONS OPERATING
IN NORWAY, 1940–5: A MILITARY ALLIANCE   93

Chapter 6
SOE AND THE MILITARY AND INTELLIGENCE
ESTABLISHMENT OPERATING IN NORWAY, 1940–5: AN
UNEXPECTED PARTNERSHIP   119

Chapter 7
SOE OPERATIONS IN NORWAY, 1940–4: THE COMBINATION
OF SABOTAGE AND THE ORGANIZATION OF A
CLANDESTINE ARMY   145

Chapter 8
SOE AND THE LIBERATION OF NORWAY, 1944–5:
OPERATIONS IN THE SHADOW OF OVERLORD   171

CONCLUSION   195

Appendix A: SOE *coup de main* operations in Norway, 1940–4   207
Appendix B: Sea-borne operations instigated by or involving
   SOE along the Norwegian seaboard, 1940–5   219
Appendix C: SOE long-term and miscellaneous operations in
   Norway, 1940–5   229
Notes   281
Bibliography   351
Index   369

ACKNOWLEDGEMENTS

My decision to examine special operations in Norway was prompted by not just my interest in the history of the country during the Second World War but also by Professor Patrick Salmon then at Newcastle University, now chief historian at the Foreign and Commonwealth Office, who took the time to reply to my correspondence and suggested that it was a topic that required and deserved attention.

A large part of my time was originally spent working on the extensive SOE material at *Norges Hjemmefrontmuseum* (the Resistance Museum) in Oslo. During that time, I received unstinting support from Ivar Kraglund, Frode Færøy, Arnfinn Moland and especially Anne Karin Sønsteby, who always with a smile responded to my requests for files and helped me locate important material. Working at the museum gave me the opportunity to meet several Norwegian resistance figures including the late Gunnar Sønsteby, with whom I had several enjoyable conversations. It also gave me the chance to encounter other Norwegian researchers and historians, such as Berit Nøkleby who regularly responded to my enquiries and kindly supplied me with some valuable material, including her excellent study of SIS. I would like to extend my thanks to all of these people. I must also mention my family in Norway, who regularly helped by bringing over to Britain many of the key Norwegian publications that have been so important for my work and which are sadly often unavailable in this country.

At the time of my research, I was ably supported by Mark Seaman, once SOE historian at the Imperial War Museum. Mark's knowledge and his willingness to answer my questions and to take the time to discuss and debate issues was a great help. Duncan Stuart, who was the SOE advisor at the Foreign and Commonwealth Office, also assisted by providing me with important documents and detail from SOE's personal files, which at the time of my research were just being released into the National Archives at Kew. My two PhD supervisors, Professor David Ryan and Dr H. P. Willmott were also of great support, not just through reading my work but also by putting forward valuable thoughts and insights that helped in its development.

Finally, I would like to thank those Norwegian historians who have enthusiastically encouraged me to get my original PhD published along with my wife and daughter who have provided unstinting support especially through the difficult times.

ABBREVIATIONS

ACAS (ops)	Assistant Chief of the Air Staff (Operations)
ACNS (H)	Assistant Chief of Naval Staff (Home)
ACO	Advisor on Combined Operations
ACOS	Admiral Commanding the Orkneys and Shetlands
AI	air intelligence (London)
AI 10	cover name for SOE
ALFN	Allied Land Forces Norway
ANCC	Anglo-Norwegian Collaboration Committee
AL	air liaison section in SOE
AT	*Arbeidstjenesten* (The Labour Services) in Norway
B.org	*Bedriftsorganisasjonen* (The Industrial Organization), a resistance organization in occupied Norway
BSS	Bayswater security section
C	head of SIS
CCS	Combined Chiefs of Staff
CCO	Chief of Combined Operations
CEO	Chief Executive Officer
CIGS	Chief of the Imperial General Staff
COHQ	Combined Operations headquarters
COS	Chiefs of Staff
COSSAC	Chief of Staff to the Supreme Allied Commander (Designate)
CS	Sir Campbell Stuart's propaganda department, part of the Foreign Office
D	sabotage section of SIS
DCO	Directorate of Combined Operations
DDOD(I)	Deputy Director, Operations Division (Irregular) at the Admiralty
D/F	direction finding, the action of using an aerial to determine the direction of incoming radio waves
DK	*Distriktskommandoer* (District Commanders)
DKN	*Distriktskommando Nord* (the District Commander for northern Norway)
DKT	*Distrikstkommando Trøndelag* (the District Commander for the county of Trøndelag)
DKØ	*Districtskommando Øst* (the District Commander for eastern Norway)
DMI	Director of Military Intelligence
DNA	*Det norske arbeiderparti* (the Norwegian Labour Party)

DNI	Director of Naval Intelligence
DSIR	Department for Scientific and Industrial Research
DZ	dropping zone
EH	Electra House, the propaganda department under Sir Cambell Stuart
FA	*Forsvarsstabens krigstidsarkiv* 1940–5, Oslo (the Defence Staff war archives)
FANY	First Aid Nursing Yeomanry
FD	*Forsvarsdepartementet* (the Norwegian Ministry of Defence)
FD/E	*Forsvarsdepartementet Etterretningskontor* (the Norwegian Ministry of Defence Intelligence Office)
FFK	*Flyvåpnenes Felleskommando* (the Royal Norwegian Air Force Joint Command)
FO	Foreign Office
FO	*Forsvarets Overkommando* (The Norwegian Defence High Command)
FO II	The Norwegian Defence High Command Intelligence Department
FO IV	The Norwegian Defence High Command, Department no. IV
FO-H	The Norwegian Defence High Command, Home Front Office
FO, Rapport	report on the Norwegian High Command's Activities outside Norway, 1942–5
Gestapo	*die Geheime Staatspolizei*
GC and CS	Government Code and Cipher School (Bletchley Park, Buckinghamshire)
Grepo	*Det norske (NS) Grensepoliti under okkupasjonen* (the Norwegian Border Police during the occupation)
GS (R)	General Staff (Research), department in the War Office responsible for researching aspects of tactics and operations
HHI	*Hjemmefrontens Historieinstitutts arkiv* (The Home Fronts Historical Archive, Oslo, Norway)
HL	*Hjemmefrontens Ledelse* (The Home Front Leadership in Norway)
HOK	*Hærens Overkommando* (The Royal Norwegian Army High Command)
HS	*Hjemmestyrkene* (The Home Forces)
Innst.	*Instilling fra Undersøkelseskommisjonen av 1945, utgitt av Stortinget* (report of the fact-finding commission of 1945, published by the Norwegian Parliament)
Inst.	*Universitetets historiske institutt, Oslo* (The University of Oslo Historical Institute)
ISRB	Inter-Services Research Bureau (cover name for SOE)
ISSU	Inter-Services Signals Unit (cover name for SOE)

JCS	Joint Chiefs of Staff	
JIC	Joint Intelligence Committee	
JP	Joint Planning Committee	
KK	*Koordinasjonskomitéen* (the Co-ordination Committee)	
	Kompani Linge the Linge Company	
Kripo	*die Kriminalpolizei* (The German Criminal Police)	
LCS	London Controlling Section (responsible for deception)	
MEW	Ministry of Economic Warfare	
MGB	motor gunboat	
MI	Military Intelligence, [London], specifically:	
MI5	responsible for home security	
MI6	responsible for intelligence	
MI9	responsible for escape	
Milorg	*Militærorganisasjonen* (the military resistance organization in Norway)	
Mi II	*Militærkontoret II* (the Military Office at the Royal Norwegian Legation in Stockholm responsible for matters of intelligence)	
Mi IV	*Militærkontoret IV* (the Military Office at the Royal Norwegian Legation in Stockholm responsible for contact with Milorg and SOE)	
MI (R)	Military Intelligence (Research), department of the War Office	
MO1(SP)	cover name for SOE	
MOI	Ministry of Information	
MTB	motor torpedo boat	
NHM	*Norges hjemmefrontmuseum* (Norway's Resistance Museum, Oslo, Norway)	
NIC (1)	The Norwegian Independent Company no. 1	
NID	Naval Intelligence Department	
NID(C)	cover name for the Navy Section of SIS, which was also in form part of NID	
NID(Q)	cover name for the Navy Section of SOE, which was in form part of NID	
NKP	*Norges kommunistiske parti* (the Norwegian Communist Party)	
Notraship	Norwegian Shipping and Trade Mission	
NRK	*Norsk Rikskringkasting* (the Norwegian State Broadcasting Corporation)	
NS	*Nasjonal Samling* (the Norwegian Nazi Party)	
OKW	*das Oberkommando der Wehrmacht* (the German Military High Command)	
OSS	Office of Strategic Services, United States	

PWE	Political Warfare Executive
RAF	Royal Air Force
RNorN	Royal Norwegian Navy
RNVR	Royal Naval Volunteer Reserve
RN	Royal Navy
ROH	*Regjeringen og hjemmefronten under krigen, aktstykker utgitt av Stortinget* (correspondence between the government and Home Front during the occupation published by the Norwegian parliament in 1948)
Rådet	Milorg's central council
SAS	Special Air Service
SCAEF	Supreme Commander, Allied expeditionary Force
Scotco	Scottish Command
SD	*der Sicherheitsdienst* (the German Security Service)
SFHQ	Special Force Headquarters
SHAEF	Supreme Headquarters, Allied Expeditionary Force
Sipo	*Sicherheitspolizei* (the German Security Police)
SOK	*Sjøforsvarets Overkommando* (the Royal Norwegian Navy High Command)
Sipo u. SD	*die Sicherheitspolizei und der Sicherheitsdienst* (the German Security Police and Security Service)
SIS	the Secret Intelligence Service, an alternative name for MI6
SL	*Sentralledelsen i Milorg* (the Central Leadership of Milorg)
SOE	the Special Operations Executive
SO	Special Operations section of OSS, the United States' equivalent of SOE
SO2	the department of SOE responsible for operations prior to the summer of 1941
SOE/SO	mixed SOE/OSS group working in north-west Europe
Stapo	*det Norske (NS) Statspoliti* (the Norwegian Nazi Party State Police)
STS	special training school
2A	Norwegian underground intelligence organization
U-boat	German submarine (*Unterseeboat*)
UK 1945	*Undersøkelseskommisjonen av 1945* (the Norwegian Parliamentary fact-finding commission of 1945)
USAAF	United States of America Air Force
VCNS	Vice Chief of Naval Staff
W/T	wireless telegraphy
XU	Norwegian underground intelligence organization

MAPS

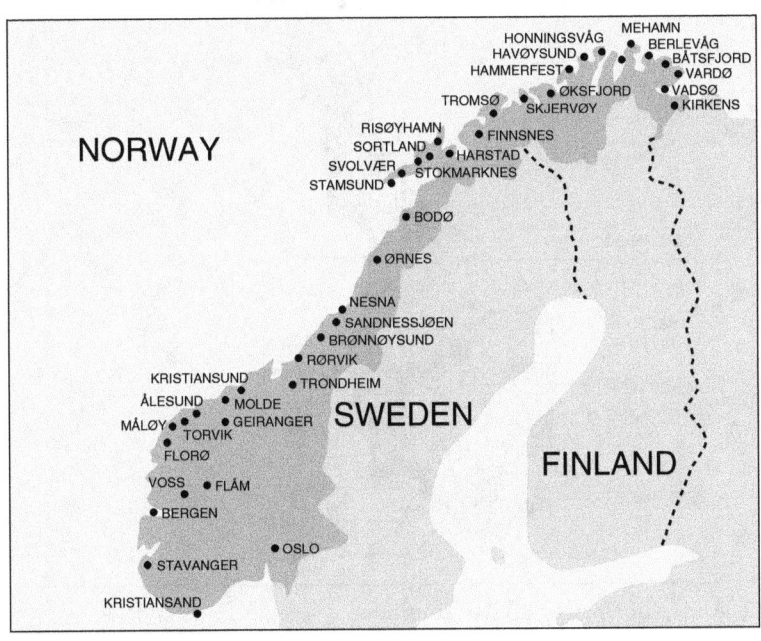

1 Major towns in Norway

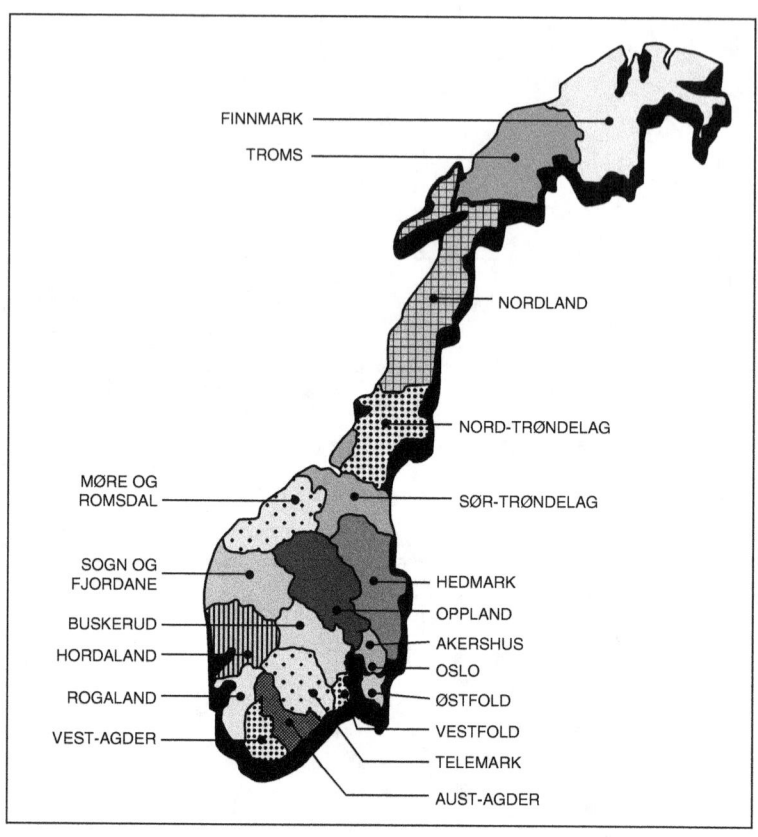

2 A map of Norway's fylke (counties)

INTRODUCTION

From the early hours of 9 April 1940, German forces gradually occupied a number of strategically important towns along the Norwegian coast from Narvik in the north to Oslo in the south. Allied land forces began arriving in Norway from the middle of April, but what turned out to be a disastrous campaign was quickly over when the last Allied troops left Narvik on 8 June and the Norwegian units that remained in the country capitulated two days later. This left Norway occupied for the next five years by enemy forces that at the time of the German surrender in May 1945 included eleven divisions and totalled over 350,000 military and civilian personnel.[1] The Norwegian government arrived in Britain on 10 June 1940 where according to Johan Nygaardsvold, the prime minister, it would continue the fight 'to regain Norway's independence',[2] and as Norway's constitutional and legitimate authority the government in exile spent the next five years endeavouring to mobilize all possible resources, including those of its allies, to win back the freedom of its country.[3] On 7 June 1945, King Haakon VII, Norway's first monarch after its separation from Sweden in 1905, arrived home exactly five years after departing into exile with the Norwegian government.

Although the brief Allied sojourn in Norway in the spring of 1940 was a failure, it did not result in Britain turning its back on the country, either strategically or militarily. Between 1940 and 1945, the Royal Navy (RN), Royal Air Force (RAF), Combined Operations and the Secret Intelligence Service (SIS) were all active in this theatre. Moreover, soon after its conception in July 1940, a new organization also began to take an interest in the country – this was the Special Operations Executive (henceforward SOE). SOE was set up, according to its founding charter approved by the War Cabinet on 22 July, 'to co-ordinate all action, by way of subversion and sabotage, against the enemy overseas', and therefore over the coming months it gradually subsumed those organizations, such as Section D and MI (R), which had previously been responsible for such activities.[4] Responsible to the Minister for Economic Warfare, over the next five years SOE sent over 500 agents into Norway, of which only three were British nationals and none were women. It also planned, attempted or carried out almost 200 operations that included *coup de main* attacks, sabotage, assassination and efforts to organize an underground guerrilla army.[5]

This is an examination of SOE's plans and operations in Norway between 1940 and 1945 within the context of the major strategic and political influences that shaped them. It uses archival material from both Britain and Norway, including SOE files at The National Archives in Kew, West London, which from 1993 have been gradually opened up to researchers. Unlike with France or the Low Countries,[6] a specific scholarly history of SOE in Norway has not as yet been published. The closest is Charles Cruickshank's rather slim 'official' history of SOE in Scandinavia, which includes Norway, Sweden and Denmark. It is based almost entirely on the use of British archives and, with the exception of a chapter on the development of secret armies, is largely a narrative of some of the organization's operations in Norway. Reflecting his reliance on British sources, the author does not examine the emergence and development of resistance in Norway within the wider context of the occupation. According to Cruickshank, the military resistance would have made a 'more effective contribution to the Allied effort' if it had thrown all its resources into sabotage. He also claims that SOE's attempt to build a secret army gave way to the resistance's proposals for an underground force directed from Oslo. The author, however, does make the important point that constant sabotage undermined enemy morale and helped keep large enemy forces in Scandinavia. There are several British publications that contain chapters or sections on Norway, but these have not made use of the extensive SOE material in Oslo. They consist of either a short narrative of aspects of SOE activity, such as its use of the Shetlands Base, or an outline of some of its many operations, and therefore are not detailed and wide-ranging analyses.[7]

Studies of the Norwegian government in exile and the Home Front[8] – the collective term used during the occupation to describe all resistance to the German authorities and *Nasjonal Samling* (NS), the Norwegian Nazi party – have examined the impact of SOE's involvement in Norway upon Anglo-Norwegian relations and the development of resistance, but again are founded on the use of single archival material or were unable to use SOE files at Kew.[9] As with Denmark, however, a more multi-archival approach has emerged in recent years. Recent publications in Norway have begun to use SOE material in both Oslo and London, although they continue to consider only certain facets of special operations in occupied Norway. There are also many anecdotal accounts, memoirs or recollections written by ex-Norwegian SOE operatives that afford an insight into the human element of working underground in an occupied country and provide important background on some of SOE's actions. They do not, however, impart much information on the factors behind the operations.[10]

Consequently, there is a significant gap in the literature for an international, academic and multi-archival history of SOE in Norway, which rather than being a straightforward narrative will be an analysis of the many broader influences behind the organization's plans and consequent special operations. The many diverse issues surrounding SOE interest in this theatre will be explored within one publication. It will, therefore, unlike previous works, present a single and overarching interpretation, and through using a combination of British and Norwegian archives, re-appraise and offer new explanations of aspects of this organization's involvement in occupied Norway.

There were several factors that determined SOE's plan of action and ultimately the nature, mix and extent of its operations. The proposition here though is that the dominate factor was SOE's and particularly Norway's role and significance within the wider strategic context in the war against Germany in Europe, that was the principal influence behind its activity in this theatre between 1940 and 1945,[11] not political factors, defined in this case as relations with the Norwegian government in exile and the 'official' military resistance, *militærorganisasjonen* (henceforth *Milorg*). From the autumn of 1940, a clandestine organization began to develop in Norway with the aim of organizing an underground army that could contribute to the eventual liberation of the country through supporting a landing by Allied forces. In November 1941, *Milorg* was recognized by the Norwegian authorities in London and became part of not only its armed forces but also the 'official' military resistance in Norway. By May 1945, it constituted a force of apparently around 40,000.[12] In addition the nature of the occupation of Norway, along with collaborative factors, SOE's relationship with the other armed forces and organizations operating in this theatre, also had an impact. But in the case of Norway, although important, they remained secondary to strategic factors.

SOE was conceived in the summer of 1940 when Britain was militarily isolated and weak after the rapid collapse of France. Within this context, it became part of a British forward strategy that was built on the conviction that before major land operations against the German army in northwest Europe could recommence, its fighting strength had to be significantly reduced. The British believed this even after the entry of the United States into the war. SOE's contribution would be to carry out sabotage and subversion, which would undermine German fighting capacity and morale and help tie down its forces in peripheral theatres such as Norway away from the main battlefronts. In addition, but over the longer term, through the supply of arms, organization and training, it would harness the potential for resistance in the occupied countries and create secret armies that would support Allied landings as part of an eventual liberation of Europe. SOE's military contribution varied, however, across the different theatres of operations. Its role in Greece in 1943, which was close to the Allied campaigns in North Africa and Italy, was in many ways different from Norway, which at the time was marginal to the main course of events. Moreover, its significance changed as the war progressed. After the United States entered the conflict in December 1941, with its vast resources, the contribution of secret armies was finally demoted to a strategically and militarily far more subordinate and supportive role.[13]

By the end of 1940, SOE's plans for Norway reflected the military responsibilities that had been assigned to this new organization. In the short term, it would undertake *coup de main* operations, sabotage, assist raids and strategic bombing and carry out covert, 'black' propaganda. Over the longer term, it would prepare a secret underground army based on local resistance groups that would be organized and preserved in readiness to support a landing by regular forces at a time determined by Britain and its allies. At a local operational level these two objectives would be kept separate, although within the wider context they were inseparable. The aim of SOE's short-term activities in Norway and across Europe was to help create the conditions that would allow Allied forces supplemented by indigenous clandestine armies to undertake a final and decisive land offensive against Germany.

This combination of short- and long-term aims remained in place and was the template for SOE operations in Norway for the rest of the war. The military significance of these objectives altered, however, as SOE and Norway's position and role within the wider European context changed. The organization of a secret army, for example, was closely linked to British plans for a landing in Norway. These, however, never came to fruition and it was not until the final stages of the war, after the launch of Operation Overlord, the invasion of northwest Europe that preparations for Norway's liberation really got underway. Only then, after years of shortages, were significant resources made available to enable the establishment of an armed and trained underground army.

Political factors also influenced SOE's plans. By operating within the occupied countries across Europe, SOE inevitably became involved in internal issues and came into contact with their political representatives, primarily the governments in exile or other groups that were often based in London. In June 1942, in recognition of SOE's close links with the exile governments, the British Chiefs of Staff Committee appointed it as the official coordinating authority through which these governments were instructed to work on matters of sabotage and subversion.[14]

For SOE to operate effectively in Norway, it had to work with members of the Norwegian government in exile and the resistance organizations, which meant that it was regularly subject to external political pressure. Only Norwegian recruits had the required language skills and could cope effectively with the extreme climatic and topographic conditions found in Norway. To secure access to these potential operatives, it was necessary to make contact with the relevant figures within the Norwegian government and its military authorities in London. And to form a secret army that remained subservient to British strategic requirements, SOE also had to get in direct touch with and somehow bring under its direction resistance groups in Norway, particularly *Milorg*.

SOE was not, however, faced with a fragmented and unstable political background in Norway, something that distorted and complicated its efforts in other occupied countries. The nature of the German occupation ultimately gave rise to relatively organized and centralized resistance movements that had close links with their government in London. The Norwegian government in exile also had the authority, both domestically and internationally, to defend and pursue its country's national interests, which it eventually decided could best be done through collaboration with its allies.[15]

Finally, modern war has increasingly become a 'joint' effort,[16] and British and Allied strategy as it affected Norway was a combined military endeavour involving several organisations such as the RN, RAF, Combined Operations, SIS and the American Office of Strategic Services (OSS). Therefore, SOE did not act alone and its plans reflected an understanding that the organization would have to cooperate with these other agencies as part of a broad military front that set out to attack economic and military targets within the country. Consequently, its ability to collaborate was a further important factor in determining the nature, extent and success of its activities in this theatre.

Although SOE's policy and ultimately its operations in Norway were shaped by important strategic, political and collaborative influences, the eventual outcome of its activities was often decided by another set of more straightforward factors. These included the extreme weather conditions that regularly occurred in the North Sea, especially during the winter months, and the topography and demography of Norway, which meant that with the exception of the area around Oslo the arrival of a stranger in the small, isolated communities was quickly noticed by both the local population and eventually the local police. These elements all imposed a significant constraint on what SOE was ultimately able to achieve in this theatre. Having a set of aims and objectives was one thing, being able to carry them out in a heavily occupied country proved far more difficult.

A new and overarching perspective on SOE operations in Norway will follow. It will challenge some previous interpretations of the relationship between this organization and both the Norwegian authorities and *Milorg*. Moreover, it will bring together many of SOE's activities in this theatre and rather than explore them in isolation place them in the wider context. Some aspects of SOE's best known operations, such as the actions against the Norsk Hydro heavy water plant in southern Norway, will also be re-evaluated. It will not, however, be possible to examine all of the many SOE operations. Therefore, as an important addendum to the main text of this work, a series of appendices has been produced that for the first time attempt to synthesize all the available archival material on SOE into detailed chronologies and lists of its operations. This will provide an important database for future historians.

Chapter 1

THE FORMATION OF SOE AND ITS SCANDINAVIAN SECTION: A NEW STRATEGIC TOOL AND A NORDIC OPPORTUNITY

The formation and development of SOE, its Scandinavian section and the military units, such as the Shetlands Base, which were crucial to the implementation of its objectives in Norway, had a fundamental influence on the extent and nature of its operations. Importantly, however, they shared one common factor: all of them were ultimately a result of Britain's military circumstances after the fall of France and the forward strategy that this situation gave rise to.

SOE was created for strategic and military purposes at a time when Britain was weak, isolated and therefore inferior in both position and resources. It was a small but significant element of a strategy that at the time was seen as providing a means by which the nation could move towards the achievement of the ultimate objective of the war, victory over Germany. The origins of SOE have been covered extensively in the literature[1] but importantly for Norway it was created within a climate and context that fostered both a strong belief in and a call for a coordinated use of clandestine and subversive operations.

Norway was also a country where Britain could quickly take the offensive and target Axis power and resources. Factors such as its accessibility across the North Sea, long coastline, peripheral position, the specialist war materials it exported to Germany and its occupation by substantial enemy forces made it militarily very attractive. Consequently, SOE quickly formed a Scandinavian section that included Norway, which from the summer of 1940 was responsible for the implementation of its plans and operations in this theatre; it was also staffed by personnel who had a background in and enthusiasm for the implementation of indirect methods, particularly the application of economic pressure and the use of clandestine operations against the enemy.

In order to take effective action in Norway, it was necessary to have suitable operatives and transportation. These were provided through the Norwegian Independent Company No I (henceforward NIC (I)), the unit of the Royal Norwegian Army formed to carry out special operations on behalf of SOE and the Norwegian authorities, the Shetlands Naval Base and the RAF 'Special Duty' Air Squadrons that dropped SOE agents and equipment into Norway. All of these military units were crucial to the implementation of clandestine operations and will appear regularly. Furthermore, they embody the key elements that shaped SOE plans for this theatre. First, the importance of the strategic background, which although it led to an urgent and coordinated effort to create these facilities, also meant that there was a shortage of key resources for operations in Norway, particularly aircraft. Second, an early and clear understanding within SOE that it would not be able to operate effectively in Norway without both Norwegian cooperation and support from the regular armed forces, and that therefore these relationships were crucial to its future effectiveness.

The origins of SOE: The birth of a new weapon

SOE began its short five and half year life on 22 July 1940 when its charter, drawn up by Neville Chamberlain and which set out its future role, was approved by the War Cabinet.[2] Two factors were central in the creation of this new organization that was instructed 'to co-ordinate all action, by way of subversion and sabotage, against the enemy overseas'.[3] The first was a small but growing belief within political circles and especially within sections of SIS and War Office of the military value of this type of activity. The second and more important was Britain's military isolation and weakness after the fall of France, which led to the creation of a new forward strategy in the war against Germany.

By July 1940 a commitment to the potential of sabotage, subversion and guerrilla warfare had taken hold among many important political figures in Britain. The most significant of these was Winston Churchill, who when he became prime minister in May 1940, as a result of his previous experience as a soldier, journalist, amateur spy and politician, already had a strong faith in the potential of irregular and clandestine warfare. This meant that he placed his considerable weight behind the COS proposal of May 1940 for the creation of a new organization to coordinate sabotage and subversion in the occupied countries, and his support for SOE although not unquestioning was at times critical to its long-term survival.[4]

A belief in the potential of subversive warfare not only resided with the prime minister but also more widely. A fear of fifth columnists that developed in the country around the time of the defeat of France in May/June 1940 helped to foster this,[5] and it led to pressure for Britain to create its own fifth column. An early result of this was the establishment in the of summer 1940 of the so-called 'Auxiliary Units', perhaps better known as 'stay behind units', which would be used to operate behind enemy lines in the event of a German invasion.[6] In June 1940 a 'Guerrilla Committee' under Commander Stephen King-Hall, MP, was also formed. In July, it forwarded a memo to Sir Maurice Hankey, chancellor of the Duchy of Lancaster, whom the prime minister had given the task of coordinating the reorganization of subversive warfare. The memo describes winning the war 'by combining a disintegration of the Nazi regime from within and bombing and blockade from without' and points to the use of 'total guerrilla warfare', including raids by military forces, subversive action and sabotage and propaganda. It was eventually sent to many of the figures who were involved in the discussions with Hankey that led to the formation of SOE and highlights the considerable momentum that existed within the British political and military establishment for the use of irregular and subversive measures in the war against Germany.

The memo was sent to Sir Maurice Hankey on 4 July 1940. On 9 July, Hankey advised Stephen King-Hall that he had sent the paper to the 'leading hands in the organisation which is developing', by which he meant SOE. The paper was sent to Sir Stewart Menzies, head of SIS; General Bourne, head of Combined Operations; discussed with Lawrence Grand, head of Section D; and a copy probably reached Hugh Dalton, who a week later was given responsibility for SOE.[7] Furthermore, there was a belief, which had emerged before the outbreak of war, in Nazi economic and political vulnerability.[8] These factors created the fertile conditions that led to the germination of SOE and ultimately the implementation of special operations in Norway.

Alongside this, two small departments had been actively investigating the potential of subversive and clandestine warfare: Military Intelligence (Research) (MI [R]), a small section within the War Office under Lieutenant Colonel J. F. C. Holland that analysed the use of special or irregular forces, and Section D, a new section established within SIS under Major Lawrence Grand to examine attacking the enemy by means other than operations by military forces.[9] These developments were important for Norway and elsewhere as they indicate that even before the creation of SOE significant consideration had already been given within the military and intelligence establishment to both the potential of clandestine warfare and importantly the employment of fifth column or resistance groups within occupied Europe. Many of the personnel who were later employed by SOE's 'Scandinavian section came from within Section D and MI (R), and they provided not only the organizational but also more significantly the conceptual foundations upon which activities within this theatre were built. These departments were active before and after the outbreak of war in 1939 and were importantly 'seen as playing a part' within economic warfare.[10] They also took an early interest in Norway. Section D was active in Norway from as early as the summer of 1938 when H. H. Hartley was commissioned by Section D to survey Narvik harbour. He carried out the task and apparently brought back a 'full report'.[11]

Although there was a developing interest in irregular and subversive activities and a few small operations were undertaken within occupied Europe prior to spring 1940, they were largely uncoordinated and sporadic. With the rapid collapse of France in May and June, however, the context changed. Prior to this British strategy envisaged a three-stage process: warding off an attempted German knockout blow, followed by consolidation and a building of resources while German strength was undermined by economic pressure and propaganda and a final general offensive. It was a strategy based on a belief that 'the French army could hold out and the German economy was vulnerable'.[12] Rapid German success in France in May 1940, however, required the COS to reassess Britain's position, and on 19 May 1940 they met to consider a paper entitled 'British Strategy in a Certain Eventuality', the certain eventuality being the new conditions resulting from the collapse of France and the loss of a substantial part of the British Expeditionary Force (BEF) and its equipment. This document both marked a shift in strategy and led directly to the formation of SOE. It reaffirmed the British emphasis on economic pressure and air attack but more importantly placed them at the fulcrum of future strategy. An additional strand was, however, also added to the strategic mix, 'the stimulation of the seeds of revolt within the conquered territories'. The potential of widespread resistance to German occupation across Europe was seen as a valuable additional weapon, which could be used after conditions in these countries had begun to deteriorate due to economic pressure. As this activity was considered of the highest importance, it was decided that a 'special organisation' was required. On 27 May 1940, the War Cabinet accepted the recommendations of this paper and instigated the process that led to the War Cabinet's approval of SOE's charter on 22 July 1940.[13]

There was complex web of negotiations leading up to the formation of SOE in July 1940.[14] But since June 1939, it had been recognized that there was a need to harmonize 'paramilitary' activities. It was, however, only after the collapse of France that sabotage and subversion were considered 'of such importance' that it was decided that they had to be unified 'under one strong hand'. For example, in May 1940, the Inter-Services Project Board (ISPB) was set up to coordinate projects for attacking the enemy by sabotage or other irregular activities and met eight times during May 1940, but disappeared on the setting up of SOE in July 1940.[15] Consequently, on 16 July 1940, Hugh Dalton, the Minister of Economic Warfare, was invited by the prime minister to take charge of SOE. The new organization therefore had its own minister, and subversive activities were removed from their previous Foreign and War Office control. SOE was also, rather appropriately, placed under the minister whose remit included economic warfare against the enemy. Dalton, as a Labour minister, was given control of SOE to maintain the political balance between the parties within the coalition government. It was also considered appropriate that a Labour minister should be in charge of a subversive organization. SOE had to continue to 'consult' with the Foreign Office and other departments, and its relationship with the Foreign Office was often problematic.[16] Dalton's grandiose view of what SOE could achieve, a Europe in a state of 'permanent revolution', and his call for subversion to be an independent service, a 'Fourth Arm', were, however, ultimately rejected.[17] Therefore, although SOE represented a new element of Britain's forward strategy, it was very much a junior player.

The creation of a charter was an attempt to define SOE's function and its relationship with other organizations and government departments, such as SIS, MI5, the Foreign Office and the COS. And although the charter is vague in how these relationships would work, it does establish some important points of principle. Cooperation with the intelligence services and consultation with the Foreign Office are emphasized, as is the conviction 'that the general plan for irregular warfare offensive operations should be in step with the general strategical conduct of the war'.[18] Consequently, over the coming four years SOE was guided by a series of four separate directives that were approved by the COS. These set out in detail how subversive operations in the occupied countries of Europe including Norway would contribute to or support military operations. They also specified priorities and the role of SOE in the various theatres of war.[19]

In the autumn of 1943, by which time the planning and preparation of Operation Overlord, the invasion of north-west Europe, had become the Allies' strategic priority in the west, responsibility for SOE in Norway was placed under the operational command of the Chief of Staff to the Supreme Allied Commander Designate (COSSAC).[20] In line with this, SOE's London office was merged with the offices of its American counterpart, the Special Operations (SO) branch of OSS to form SOE/SO HQ. In January 1944, command of Allied operations in north-west Europe and Scandinavia was placed under the control of the Supreme Headquarters Allied Expeditionary Force (SHAEF), and in May SOE/SO HQ was renamed Special Forces HQ (SFHQ).[21] Therefore, from early 1944 through to the end of the war, it was directives issued by SHAEF that determined SOE activity in Norway.

The organizational realignment of special operations began during the summer and autumn of 1940 when Section D and MI (R) were merged into SOE. This new organization, which moved into its wartime residence in Baker Street in London at this time, was initially divided into three departments: SO1, which took over covert propaganda; SO2, which subsumed Section D and was responsible for operations; and SO3, which was responsible for intelligence and planning. In August 1941, however, after a year of interdepartmental wrangles, SO1 was abolished and its responsibilities taken over by the Political Warfare Executive (PWE). SO3 had already been wound up leaving only SO2, which took on the title of the Special Operations Executive.[22] From this point, the organization grew significantly in size and employed a total of almost 12,000 personnel by the spring of 1944. Altogether, 5,766 men and women were trained as organizers and instructors in the 41 training schools that were established during the war. At its peak, SOE had 500 clandestine wireless stations operating in Europe and the RAF flew over 15,000 sorties from the UK to France and the Mediterranean on behalf of SOE,[23] which reflected the increasing range and scale of its activities across occupied Europe. The organization remained politically responsible to the Minister for Economic Warfare, which from February 1942 was the Tory minister Lord Selborne. It was, however, its executive director (CD) who provided the 'leadership and strategic control'[24] of what was a hierarchical organization. The CD initially kept in touch with his senior officers through a series of senior committees, beginning with the 'D-Board' in August 1940, which became the 'SO2 Executive Committee' in December, was renamed the 'Board of Directors' in November 1941 and finally became SOE Council in February 1942. The Council was the executive body that 'prepared most of SOE's main policies and had a perceptible influence on resistance strategy'.[25] Under the Council came the country sections, often in regional groupings such as Scandinavia and which contained the staff officers responsible for operations in the occupied countries, followed by the technical departments such as finance, signals and operations. Importantly though occupied Norway was rapidly identified as a country where Britain could quickly employ clandestine operations, and where nascent resistance groups were beginning to develop.

SOE's Scandinavian and Norwegian sections: The continuation of a strategic and military tradition in Norway

It was the occupied countries that proved to be fruitful for SOE. After the withdrawal of Allied troops and the capitulation of Norwegian forces in June 1940, German control over Norway was confirmed and therefore the country became a potential sphere of operations for a range of clandestine and underground activities. It was deemed 'essential' that SOE was formed on a 'territorial' basis and as a result country and regional sections were created, including a Scandinavian section,[26] which contained the staff that would be responsible for administering and implementing SOE activity in this theatre. It has been argued that the attitude of the staff within this section, particularly toward the Norwegian authorities, was shaped by British experiences during the disastrous campaign in Norway in the spring of 1940.[27] The Scandinavian section, however, included personnel with a range of backgrounds often from much earlier. From the outbreak of the war in Europe, key figures in the eventual development and implementation of SOE plans for this theatre had contributed to efforts to apply economic pressure against Germany through Norway. Many of the Scandinavian section's staff also had experience of working within those organizations, Section D and MI (R), which were merged into SOE. They therefore brought with them many of the ideas and practices that these organizations had either conceived or advocated, such as the potential of sabotage and guerrilla warfare. Some of the staff also had direct involvement in irregular and subversive activities in Norway, both before, during and after the campaign of 1940, and therefore had developed an enthusiasm for the military potential of such actions.

For most of the war Norway, along with Sweden and Denmark, had its own subsection under the umbrella of a Scandinavian section, although for periods, such as in 1942, it was given its own independence. Two figures were central in the early formulation of policy toward Norway and the setting up of the Scandinavian section. Both moved onto senior positions within SOE but continued to have a major influence over its activities in Norway and its relations with the Norwegian authorities. These were Sir Charles Hambro and Harry Sporborg.[28]

Charles Hambro had been head of the Scandinavian section in the Ministry of Economic Warfare (MEW), but in August 1940, after a recommendation from Hugh Gaitskell, Dalton's private secretary, he was recruited by Hugh Dalton to set up and run the SOE's Scandinavian section.[29] He occupied this position until December 1940 when he took over responsibility for Europe, parts of Africa and propaganda in SO2 and began his rapid rise to CD in 1942.[30] Harry Sporborg, who was Hambro's deputy at the MEW, also joined SOE and continued to work under Hambro with responsibility for Norway until December 1940 when he took over the Scandinavian section, a position he retained until October 1941, when George Wiskeman replaced him. He, nevertheless, maintained a close involvement with Norway through 1942 despite his continued rise within SOE, eventually becoming its vice chief in September 1943.[31]

Hambro had family connections with Norway, he was related to C. J. Hambro, president of the Norwegian Parliament.[32] Prior to joining SOE he had also, along with Sporborg, made contact with the Norwegian government. While working for the MEW, both Sporborg and Hambro got in touch with Trygve Lie, the future Norwegian foreign minister, and requested that Britain be permitted to make use of the Norwegian ships in the United States and in Swedish harbours.[33] The British relationship with Lie would be critical for SOE through the war. Moreover, the MEW was created in 1939 'to advise the armed services on the measures that they should adopt in order to undermine the enemy's economy'.[34] Both Hambro and Sporborg's early war experience, therefore, came from their contribution to the application of economic pressure against Germany through attempting to deny it supplies of important materials from Scandinavia, particularly Norway. Between September 1939 and March 1940, Hambro was involved in negotiations with the Norwegian government on a War-Trade agreement, which set out to reduce the export to Germany of certain Norwegian products such as fish, fish products, non-ferrous metals and ferro-alloys. During a visit to Norway in February 1940, he also had discussions with directors of the Orkla Mining Company at Løkken south of Trondheim on how their exports of pyrite ore, an important source of sulphur and copper for the German munitions industry, could be reduced. This site was eventually attacked at least on four occasions by SOE teams between 1942 and 1944, more than any other industrial target in Norway.[35]

In August 1940, soon after his move to SOE, Hambro began to examine ways of interrupting supplies of fish oil to Germany, something the Scandinavian section continued to pursue until the end of 1941. During August 1940, several memos were exchanged between Lt. J. L. Chaworth-Musters in SOE's Norwegian subsection and CD (Sir Frank Nelson) on the Norwegian herring oil industry and the possibility of interfering with supplies to Germany. Hambro was behind these proposals and on 30 August presented a paper to the 'Board of Directors of D- Section' on possible attacks against the Norwegian herring oil industry. Interestingly, on 10 September the Board of Directors decided not to proceed without the tacit consent of the Norwegian authorities.[36] Sporborg had also advised Section D on an operation called the 'Norwegian Expedition', which it carried out in June 1940 against targets in the Bergen area, including the power plant for A/S Bjølvefossen at Ålvik in Hardanger, which produced ferrochromium. This was a joint Section D/MI (R) operation that targeted communications, factories, such as Høyanger aluminium smelting works, and power houses, such as at Ålvik, which were situated in the Voss, Sognefjord and Hardangerfjord region of western Norway.[37] The production of specialist metals and mining of ores became the most important strategic targets for SOE in Norway over the following years.[38] Strategic interest in Norway as a source of materials for the German war economy began well before SOE was formed, but significantly through the influence of Hambro and Sporborg it was continued.

SOE's small Norwegian subsection, which was formed during the summer and early autumn of 1940, also included personnel who had previous experience of subversive or irregular activities in Norway. It was British strategic interest in the export of Swedish iron ore through Narvik to Germany that led to Section D's involvement in Norway from the summer of 1938.[39] In 1939, it also established a Scandinavian section, followed later in the year by a small Norwegian subsection staffed by J. L. Chaworth-Musters. Musters, who had personal experience of Norway, worked under the cover of temporary vice consul in Bergen between January and May 1940, before escaping to Britain to work with the Norwegians recruited by Section D for the 'Norwegian Expedition'.[40] When Musters moved to SOE in the summer of 1940 to help set-up its Norwegian section, he therefore brought with him this experience as well as an understanding of the country, especially its language. This background made him ideally suited for the recruitment and preparation of Norwegian volunteers, and while carrying out this role he had an important influence on the development of early relations with the Norwegian authorities in London.

After Sporborg took over responsibility for the Scandinavian section, the Norwegian subsection was, from January 1941, placed under Lt. Commander Frank Stagg, Royal Navy (RN), who had been Sporborg's principal adviser. Stagg had worked for SIS and also had considerable experience of Scandinavia and its languages. It was, however, his naval experience and particular interest in northern Norway,[41] combined with Sporborg's background in economic warfare, which appears to have been another important contributory factor in the development of SOE's early plans for this theatre. In December 1940, Stagg had produced a series of proposals that recommended operations in the north of the country in order to interrupt the supplies of war materials to Germany.[42] This led to his instigation of or direct involvement in the planning of the series of amphibious operations that were undertaken against targets along the Norwegian seaboard during 1941.[43]

Last, MI (R) had a direct involvement in Norway during the British campaign in the spring of 1940 through special units such as the 'Independent Companies' and the 'No. 13 Military Mission', which attempted harassing operations against the enemy's flanks and lines of communication in support of regular forces.[44] Its ideas and experience were exported to SOE when it was subsumed into the organization at the end of October 1940. MI (R) influence percolated through to the Norwegian section primarily through Brigadier, later Major General, Colin McVean (McV.) Gubbins who joined the organization in November 1940 was made responsible for the supervision of training and the conduct of operations and raiding parties.[45] Gubbins had undertaken extensive research into guerrilla warfare behind enemy lines and had personal experience of Norway. He commanded the 'Independent Companies' in Norway during the spring campaign and rose quickly within SOE becoming its executive director in September 1943. He eventually had an important and direct influence over SOE's policy and activities in this theatre both while in charge of operations in the occupied countries and later as deputy executive director with responsibility for Western Europe and higher 'operational policy'.[46]

Gubbins had also been a mentor to John Skinner Wilson, who in January 1942 became head of an independent Norwegian section and in September 1943 regional head of the Directorate of Scandinavian and Baltic States. In 1908, Wilson had joined the Indian police eventually becoming senior deputy commissioner, Calcutta, and gaining considerable experience of dealing with civil unrest among other things. In 1923, he was appointed camp chief, Boy Scouts Association, thereby beginning a long career in the scout movement. In 1935, he toured Scandinavia including Norway as part of his scout work. He later claimed that his time in the scouts enabled him to deal with many nationalities.

Prior to joining the Norwegian section, Wilson had been an instructor in counter-espionage, anti-fifth column and offensive fifth column work, and had worked closely with Gubbins in the Training Section of SOE. In July 1940, he had joined MI (R) before transferring to the Training Section of SOE in December 1940. He was initially tasked with completing a training scheme for individuals who had fled their country and would be returned to set up radio links and carry out sabotage. In May 1941, he became lieutenant colonel and staff officer to the Director of Training (Gubbins) with responsibility for supervising training. His background was steeped in the concept and potential of using irregular operations behind enemy lines.[47]

The long frontier that separated Norway and neutral Sweden also made Stockholm an important location for the implementation of SOE operations in this theatre. For example, it was a major route for refugees and SOE and SIS agents who wished to move between the two countries. SOE involvement in Norway from its Stockholm Mission at the British Legation began with Malcolm Munthe. Munthe was another MI (R) officer who had been active in Scandinavia and Norway from 1939, often working from the Legation. Munthe's first trip to Stockholm was in December 1939, followed by a further trip at the end of February 1940. He was involved with Andrew Croft in moving military stores across Norway to Finland. At the end of March 1940, after arriving back in Stockholm, he was ordered to Oslo and then to Stavanger. In expectation of a German invasion and to act as liaison officers with the Norwegian army, four MI (R) men were established as 'assistant consuls' in Narvik (Captain Torrance), Trondheim (Major Palmer), Bergen (Captain Andrew Croft) and Stavanger (Captain Malcolm Munthe). Munthe, Torrance and Croft all went on to work for SOE. Munthe escaped to Stockholm during the German occupation and his employment as Assistant Military Attaché (AMA) at the Legation, his recruitment to SOE by Charles Hambro and his setting up of the 'Red Horse' organization to subsequently cover his courier operations, re-establishment of contacts and instigation of sabotage in Norway on behalf of SOE in 1940 and 1941 has been well documented.[48] The Swedish authorities were informed of Munthe's appointed as AMA on 9 June 1940, and he finally left Sweden on 19 July 1941.[49] His derring-do enthusiasm should be seen within the context of his military background, which was that he belonged to an organization whose *raison d'être* was to develop methods to harass the enemy.

His sponsoring of subversive activity, however, soon brought him to the attention of the Norwegian Legation in Stockholm and the Swedish government, which was keen to avoid any threat to its neutrality through the displeasure that Munthe's actions might cause Germany. The Swedish authorities originally called for his expulsion in January 1941[50] but were persuaded to back down by the British minister in Stockholm, Sir Victor Mallet. It appears though that Munthe's activities had the support of not only SOE but also, initially and more surprisingly, the British Foreign Office. At a time when the fear of a German invasion of Britain from Europe, including Norway, was still prevalent, Munthe's contact with groups in the country that could be organized to operate behind German lines was considered valuable. His relationship with Mallet, however, who grew to object to SOE using the Legation, undermined efforts to keep him in place and in the late spring of 1941 after the Swedish authorities again objected to his presence, SOE was forced to recall him to London.[51] This was an early example of how SOE had to balance its eagerness to become active in Norway with the local relationships that were ultimately crucial to its effectiveness.

Second Lieutenant Hugh Marks, who had fought in the Norwegian campaign before escaping to Stockholm, initially continued Munthe's work. His earlier association with Munthe's activities, however, also incurred the displeasure of both Victor Mallet and the Swedish government and he returned to Britain in early October 1941. The role of AMA was taken over by Andrew Croft, a former colleague of Munthe's in MI (R), who had also been in Norway when it was occupied. While Croft undertook more general work for SOE, it was Edgar (Tom) Nielsen who assumed responsibility for Norway at the British Legation, a role in which he continued until the end of the war. Nielsen, with Danish ancestry, had a diplomatic and an intelligence background in Norway and was working as assistant vice consul at Skien when the country was occupied. He was put forward by the Foreign Office and accepted by SOE as he was 'on the spot' and it meant agreement could then be reached over Marks' replacement. He was not, therefore, SOE's immediate choice and unlike many of his colleagues in London he did not have a background and therefore a particular understanding of the nature and requirements of special operations, which may have contributed to his difficult relationship with SOE's HQ in London.[52]

SOE military units for Norway: From Aviemore to the Shetlands

For SOE to be able to implement its plans, it required both suitable recruits to undertake operations on its behalf in the difficult conditions of occupied Norway and the transportation to get them there. Having a policy and a series of military aims and objectives would be fruitless without the means to achieve them, and in the autumn of 1940 SOE was a new organization with very few resources. Consequently, it began urgent attempts to recruit Norwegian volunteers. SOE also took part in a collaborative project to establish a small naval base on the Shetland Islands from where a handful of Norwegian fishing vessels and crew would eventually be used to provide an important link with Norway. With a severe limitation on the availability of aircraft for Special Duty operations, particularly for Norway, where SOE did not receive its first airdrop until early 1942, the North Sea route was critical.

The origins of NIC (1) and the Shetlands Base were the result of a resolve in the summer of 1940 to intensify and accelerate the implementation of clandestine and subversive operations in this theatre. Both were built on the experiences of SOE's predecessor organizations, Section D and MI (R). They also, however, reflect the joint nature of SOE activity in Norway, the collaboration that developed with both the Norwegian authorities and the other Allied agencies that took a similar military interest in this country.

SOE operations required Norwegian recruits and therefore, from the summer of 1940, building on a practice instigated by Section D, SOE began attempts to enlist and train Norwegians to undertake actions on its behalf. It started as an improvised small-scale effort, but during the summer and early autumn of 1940, under the auspices of the Scandinavian section, attempts were made through liaison with leading figures within the Norwegian government and military authorities to formalize and accelerate the process. There was an early realization that this process could not happen and would probably be jeopardized without Norwegian cooperation, although it would have to be on terms acceptable to SOE. This ultimately led to the establishment of what from March 1942 was officially known and jointly recognized as NIC (1), more colloquially called *Kompani Linge*, the 'Linge Company'.

It was from the trickle of refugees who began to arrive in Britain after the occupation of Norway that in August 1940 SOE recruited its first Norwegian volunteers. Two figures were central to this effort: Martin Linge, who had been a Norwegian liaison officer with the British forces at Åndalsnes in April 1940 and from whom the name of the unit came, and J. L. Chaworth-Musters.⁵³ It appears that Chaworth-Musters had meetings with Halvdan Koht, the Norwegian foreign minister at the time, and Colonel Birger Ljungberg, the Norwegian minister of defence, and from early August it was agreed, certainly on the British side, that Linge should act as the 'liaison officer' between the British and the Norwegian government. His role would be to deal with the recruitment of Norwegians from the Norwegian Armed Forces, to contact Norwegians who had recently arrived in Great Britain and to look after Norwegian agents in London. SOE, however, also wanted Linge officially seconded to them, and Ljungberg appeared to agree to arrange this, although there is no evidence that it ever happened, to the frustration of SOE.⁵⁴ Importantly, Linge symbolizes SOE's acceptance of the fact that it was dependent on Norwegian support and that it was necessary to have a systematic and ordered approach to recruitment.

Nevertheless, despite early contact with members of the Norwegian government and General Fleischer, the head of *Hærens Overkommando*, the Norwegian Army High Command (HOK) in Britain, along with the efforts of Linge, no more than six Norwegians were recruited by SOE during 1940, far less than the between twenty to thirty it was hoped would be employed. The six Norwegians had been trained at STS XVII, Brickendonbury Manor, near Hertford. These were Rubin Langmo, who had been recruited by Section D, Gunner Fougnar, Nils Nordland, Odd Starheim, Fridjof Pedersen Kviljo and Konrad Alf Lindberg.⁵⁵ From January 1941, however, despite some initial difficulties, an orderly process of recruiting Norwegian volunteers from the Norwegian army reception camp at Dumfries in Britain began. In January, Linge was at the camp from where through liaison with Fleischer he had by the end of the month selected the first party of twenty Norwegians to begin their training on 1 February at the SOE preliminary school at STS 1 Brock Hall in Northamptonshire. At the last minute, however, Fleischer interfered and held back eight of the party.⁵⁶ In March 1941, this process was placed on a more formal footing when an agreement, reaffirmed in June, was reached with General Fleischer that around twenty-five Norwegians could be recruited from the Norwegian army each month until this special unit reached a ceiling of 250 members, which it did in May 1943. Up to this point, regular cohorts of Norwegian recruits entered SOE's training pipeline and those who were deemed suitable ended up at a Holding School, initially at Grendon Hall in Buckinghamshire but from mid-June 1941 at Fawley Court near Henley on Thames, where they awaited assignment to an operation.⁵⁷ By the end of October 1941, a total of 143 Norwegian recruits were spread across SOE's training schools, including sixty-four at Fawley Court.[58]

However, because of the need to prepare for Scandinavian conditions, the Norwegian section was in November provided with its own Special Training School (STS 26) near Aviemore in Scotland. It was made up of three sites: STS 26a, Drumintoul Lodge; STS26b, Glenmore Lodge; and STS26c Forest Lodge.

In May 1943, these were taken away from SOE's Training Section and placed under the direct responsibility of Lt. Col. Wilson, where they remained until they were disbanded in July 1945. Altogether 654 Norwegians were trained by SOE during its lifetime.[59]

The recruitment and training of Norwegian volunteers were initially slow to get underway, although owing to certain important factors both eventually began to accelerate. First, the increase in the number of refugees who began to arrive in Britain during the early part of 1941. Almost 2,000 Norwegians crossed the North Sea and arrived in the Shetlands during the year, including 164 in March alone. Over 5,000 were also brought to Britain during the war as a result of Allied operations on Norwegian territory, beginning with the 285 that were brought back in spring 1941 after Operation Claymore.[60] Second, the nature of the relationship between SOE and the Norwegian authorities. The establishment in January 1941 of the *Forsvarsdepartementets etterretningskontor*, the Norwegian Ministry of Defence Intelligence Office (FD-E) under captain Finn Nagell, helped to improve the working relationship between SOE and the Norwegian military authorities in the matter of recruitment.[61] Linked to this was the involvement of both SOE and FD-E in the British amphibious raids that were carried out against economic targets in Norway during 1941. Through cooperation between SOE and FD-E, groups of Norwegians were enlisted and trained to take part in these operations, which helped to improve contact, liaison and accelerated the whole process of recruitment. Linge was actually based in the offices of FD-E, and both Linge and Nagell were jointly involved in recruiting Norwegians for service with the British.[62]

The employment of Norwegian volunteers by SOE, however, despite the close contact with FD-E, ran into difficulties at the end of 1941. Notwithstanding the involvement of a large number of its citizens, the Norwegian government was not advised beforehand of Operations Anklet and Archery, the British amphibious raids against targets on its territory in December. Disquiet also broke out among the Norwegian contingent on 'Anklet' after the naval and military forces were withdrawn prematurely. Consequently, the Norwegian authorities began intensive efforts to assert greater control over the use of their citizens on special operations. This led in March 1942 to the official recognition of NIC (1) and ultimately resulted in a more collaborative and integrated approach to the employment, organisation and preparation of Norwegian recruits on behalf of SOE. The claim that through the involvement of Harry Sporborg and Trygve Lie it was agreed that the Norwegian recruits at Fawley Court were given official recognition as NIC (1) in July 1941 is based on J. S. Wilson's history of the Norwegian Section. Wilson was responsible for SOE's training at this time, but there appears to be no available contemporaneous sources to confirm this. The minutes of the Anglo-Norwegian Collaboration Committee (ANCC) meeting of 4 March 1942 clearly state that 'it was agreed that the special unit should be referred to as "Norwegian Independent Co (1)" – "NIC (1)" and that the name "Linge Company" may be used unofficially'. It is only after this that the title NIC (1) is used in official documents. The British accepted that NIC (1) was a special unit of the Norwegian armed forces that was under the joint control of SOE and *Forsvarets Overkommando* (FO), the recently created Norwegian Defence High Command. It was made up of Norwegian personnel seconded from the regular army who were subject to Norwegian discipline administered by a Norwegian officer under the authority of the Norwegian commander in chief. The men were trained at STS 26 under the auspices of SOE but were sent to Norway on operations under the joint authority of both SOE and FO.[63] Subversive operations in Norway were therefore carried out on a partnership basis and reflected not simply British and Allied military interest in this theatre but also the level of cooperation and support that SOE received from the Norwegian authorities.

From spring 1942, when SOE activity in Norway began to take off, it was NIC (1) that provided the teams that were sent in to destroy key economic and industrial targets in the country, the organizers and radio operators who prepared and worked with local resistance organizations, and the groups that cooperated with *Milorg* in preparation for the eventual liberation. Between August 1940 and May 1945, 530 Norwegians were recruited to serve on behalf of SOE, although during the same period 160 never reached the required standard and were returned to the Norwegian army. At the end of hostilities in early May 1945, the unit's 'effective strength' was 245 men, close to its original target.[64] Altogether the company lost fifty-seven men, fifty-one on active service. It, therefore, had a survival rate that compares very favourably with a rate for SOE recruits across occupied Europe of between 60 and 70 per cent.[65]

SOE also had to find ways to transport its agents to Norway. Therefore, in the autumn of 1940, a small naval base was established on the Shetland Islands from where Norwegian fishing boats and later American submarine chasers were used to transport SOE teams, arms and equipment to the Norwegian coastline and to pick up agents or refugees who wished to return to Britain. There are a number of anecdotal and human-interest accounts of what has become known as the 'Shetlands Bus' service, but few scholarly accounts based on original sources.[66]

The base was extremely important for SOE. The concept of using Norwegian fishing boats to transport men and equipment to Norway was not new, but the organization and establishment of a permanent base was. Between late 1940 and mid-1944, the North Sea was the primary route for transporting SOE agents to Norway. As Special Duty flights were severely limited owing to both a lack of available aircraft and because Norway was both geographically and strategically peripheral, and therefore not a priority, it was the use of the fishing boats and later the submarine chasers out of the Shetlands Base that effectively allowed SOE to continue to operate in this theatre. Its long coastline and the relatively short 180-mile trip from the Shetlands also provided a large and important gateway in and out of occupied Norway. Moreover, the coastal waters off the Norwegian seaboard, which contained many small, uninhabited offshore islands (skerries), were an important locus for operations against enemy forces and shipping, often using vessels from the Shetlands Base.[67] The base was also another example of the largely positive working relationship that developed between SOE and the Norwegian authorities, who provided the fishing boats and crews, and a further indication of the collaboration that would develop between SOE and the other agencies operating in this theatre.

According to the Shetlands Base log, just over 200 trips to the Norwegian coast were attempted between November 1940 and May 1945 by Norwegian fishing vessels and the submarine chasers. Of these, close to 160 involved SOE and over 40 were on behalf of SIS; one was shared. Altogether close to 200 SOE agents and almost 300 tons of stores were delivered to the Norwegian coast and over sixty agents and several hundred refugees picked up.[68] Norwegian representatives were initially located at both Lerwick and Aberdeen to take part along with the British in the examination of any new arrivals to the country, although from the summer of 1941 this process was transferred to the Royal Victoria Patriotic School in London.[69] SOE also opened a second base at Burghead in Scotland from where five additional trips to Norway were attempted between November 1942 and January 1943, while SIS opened its own base at Peterhead from where it made twenty-seven trips to Norway between July 1941 and November 1943.[70]

The total number of trips across the North Sea was, however, restricted by certain factors. The vessels would not sail between the end of May and late August because of the long daylight hours found in this northerly region during these months, which made operating off the Norwegian coast too dangerous. The number of fishing boats available at any one time was also extremely small. In the three seasons between 1940 and 1943, at any one time there were usually only about six Norwegian fishing boats that were in a suitable condition to go to sea. These small wooden vessels were also not only vulnerable to the extreme conditions found in the North Sea but also to attacks from German aircraft. The worst single disaster was in November 1941 when the fishing boat, 'Blia', disappeared with seven crew and thirty-five refugees on board. Altogether at least eight fishing boats and forty-four crewmen were eventually lost. It was for this reason that in autumn 1943 the three faster and better protected American submarine chasers were acquired and manned by Norwegian crews until the end of the war, fortunately without further losses.[71] Nevertheless, the casualty rate of the men working on the fishing vessels was higher than for the NIC (1) teams that were sent to Norway.[72]

Between November 1940 and May 1943, there were only twenty Special Duty air sorties to Norway compared with at least eighty-five trips from the Shetlands Base.[73] Therefore, without the service that these fishing vessels provided, SOE activity in Norway would have been significantly curtailed. In August 1941, the British Joint Planning Staff (JPS) recognized that although Norway was only likely to be an area of 'subsidiary' operations, the process of organizing a secret army should continue as it was possible 'to introduce a large proportion of the arms and equipment by sea'.[74]

Nevertheless, the idea of using Norwegian fishing vessels manned by Norwegian crews was not new. It can be traced back at least to September 1939 when Section D, through its Scandinavian section, began exploring the possibilities of using trawlers or drifters for smuggling 'devices' into Norway. Frank Carr began efforts to organize smuggling between the Shetlands and Norway while Gerald Holdsworth travelled to Norway in an attempt to recruit Norwegian fishermen and made contact with Nielsen Moe, who owned a company called 'Olaf Preserving Co.'. The plan was to smuggle devices into Norway in tins.[75] This project never got off the ground but in the spring of 1940 Section D again considered linking England and Norway 'by means of Norwegian and Danish fishing boats, a number of which are in the hands of the Admiralty'.[76] Consequently, from May Section D and soon afterwards SIS began using fishing vessels to transport men and equipment to Norway. The 'Norwegian Expedition' used a Danish-fishing vessel, the 'Lady', obtained from the Admiralty's 'Small Boats Pool'. The boat was renamed V.2.S and towed another boat the *Snal*. V.2.S was later re-registered as the *Hospitz* while in Norway.

The first joint SIS/Norwegian intelligence operation left in a boat called the *Nordlys* on 14 August 1940. This Norwegian fishing boat had arrived from Bremnes in early July carrying, among others, the British consul from Stavanger.[77] And through the summer of 1940, a small 'ferry service' continued across the North Sea, in order to deliver agents, establish arms dumps and contact resistance groups.[78] When Section D was finally subsumed into SO2 in October 1940, the practice of using fishing vessels as a means of transport was therefore already established.[79]

Prior to the autumn of 1940, however, the use of fishing boats was ad hoc and improvised. The formation of SOE led to a coordinated effort to set up a permanent base on the Shetlands from where contact with Norway could be maintained, a fleet of fishing boats harboured, with residence for the Norwegian crews and SOE agents, and arms and equipment stored. A realization of the military potential of such a site also meant that there were joint discussions over its establishment involving SOE, SIS, Admiralty, MI 5 and indirectly the Norwegian government. The Norwegian fishing boats had been taken over by the Norwegian Department of Trade, which then hired them to the British, although it appears that the Norwegian government was not initially aware of what these vessels were being used for. They were then incorporated into the Admiralty's Small Vessels Pool from where they were allocated to NID (C), part of the Directorate of Naval Intelligence, for use by SOE and SIS.[80] Supplying the base and boats with stores and equipment was the responsibility of an army unit called Military Establishment No. 7 (M.E. 7), which was up and running by the end of 1940.[81]

The use of these fishing vessels, while remaining under local control and enjoying a high measure of independence, was therefore very much a collaborative project.[82] The flotilla of Norwegian fishing vessels was operated under the local supervision of the Admiral Commanding the Orkneys and Shetlands (ACOS).[83] The base was used jointly for most of the war by both SIS and SOE, and its first commander L. H. Mitchell was an SIS officer, even though the first trip from the base on behalf of SIS was not until 18 September 1941. This was 'Gamma' consisting of two agents, Billy Forthun and Ingebrigt Valderhaug.[84] SOE operations from the base were under the control of the Norwegian section, although the crews of the fishing vessels while trained by SOE eventually became the responsibility of the Norwegian authorities. From spring 1942, as with NIC (1) and as part of an effort to impose tighter control over the use of Norwegian volunteers for operations in Norway, the crews were placed under Norwegian discipline with a Norwegian officer stationed at the base. By the summer the crews constituted what was officially called the Norwegian Naval Independent Unit (NNIU), which was in the summer of 1944 placed under Norwegian naval command.[85] Close liaison with the Admiralty was maintained through the local naval officer on the Shetlands and the care and maintenance of the flotilla eventually became a naval commitment.[86] The submarine chasers were provided by the American navy.[87]

The North Sea was not, however, the only route for delivering SOE agents to Norway. Many crossed the border from Sweden by train, vehicle, or on foot, having been recruited in Sweden or transported to Stockholm using the small number of aircraft that provided an intermittent link between the Swedish capital and Scotland during the war. The first war-time flight between Sweden and Britain was in May 1940, and a civil air route was eventually set-up between Scotland and Stockholm. The Norwegians provided several planes and were anxious to ensure the route was kept open. By the end of the war, 3,309 passengers had been brought over from Stockholm using the Norwegian planes.[88]

Agents and equipment were also dropped into Norway by the Special Duty Squadrons from Bomber Command that operated on behalf of SOE and SIS. The first drop into Norway was for SIS on the night of 13/14 February 1941 when Sverre Midtskau, Operation Skylark, parachuted from a two-engined Whitley aeroplane. SOE's first airdrop was not until 2 January 1942, when 'Cheese' and 'Biscuit', Odd Starheim and Andreas Fasting, were dropped by parachute near Sirdalsvatn, north of Flekkefjord in southern Norway. After these, a further 1,310 sorties were attempted of which 747 were completed successfully. These dropped a total of 199 agents, similar to the total transported from the Shetlands Base, and a huge number of containers and packages, although 70 percent of this material was not delivered until the final nine months of the war.[89] There were two squadrons, 138 and 161, which Bomber Command allocated for special duty operations, but even by the spring of 1944 there was still only a minimum of thirty-six aircraft available for such operations in the whole of north-west Europe.[90] The prioritization of strategic bombing severely restricted SOE's capability,[91] and the low priority accorded to Norway, especially as the planning and preparations for Operation Overlord gained momentum, meant that special duty sorties on behalf of SOE to this theatre up until the final months of the war were extremely limited. In 1943, a total of over 600 sorties were flown to France as the build up to Overlord began, while only twenty-four were flown to Norway.[92]

The long flights to Norway across the North Sea during the dark winter months, when there was a high risk of bad weather, cloud, snow and icing, were also undoubtedly extremely hazardous. This did not, however, restrict the number of sorties flown during the final months of the war, by which time it had been accepted that the resistance would be required to play a significant role in the country's liberation. Local groups were in desperate need of training, arms and equipment and consequently after the assault phase of Overlord was complete and therefore more aircraft were available, there was a huge increase in special duty flights to Norway on behalf of SOE. From the beginning of November 1944 until early May 1945, close to 600 successful sorties were flown to this theatre compared to just 11 in 1942.[93] This massive but late increase is perhaps best highlighted by the night of 30–31 December 1944 when there were fifty-two aircraft in the air over eastern Norway and Nordmarka, the wooded area to the north of Oslo.[94]

There were also the Catalina flying boats from the Royal Norwegian 333 Squadron based at Woodhaven in Scotland that flew sorties to northern Norway, but these were primarily on behalf of SIS. Only three missions were flown for SOE and these were to coastal areas that were too distant for the Shetlands fishing boats to reach safely.[95] The priority accorded SIS also did not significantly affect Special Duty flights for SOE. A total of only fifty-two sorties were flown to Norway on behalf of SIS during the war, and in every year between 1942 and 1945 considerably more airdrops were made on behalf of SOE than SIS, even if the delivery of arms and equipment is excluded.[96]

The growth in airdrops to Norway during the final months of the occupation was made possible by an increase in the availability of the number of air squadrons, beginning with a special squadron of six B-24 Liberators loaned from the US 8th Air Force and led by the Norwegian-born American Air Force pilot Bernt Balchen. This flew a total of sixty-four sorties to the country during the summer of 1944. After the liberation of France, further British squadrons were freed up. These were 190, 196, 295, 296, 297, 298, 29, 570, 620 and 644 squadrons, all equipped with either Stirling or Halifax aircraft. In the new year, two squadrons from the 492nd Bombardment Group from the United States of America Air Force (USAAF) were added and flew 150 sorties to Norway up until the liberation.[97] Nevertheless, in the three years from the autumn of 1940 until the end of 1943, an average of less than one sortie per month was flown on behalf of SOE to Norway. Consequently, prior to 1944 SOE's activities, *coup de main* attacks or the organizing and equipping of resistance groups were very dependent on what could be transported using the Norwegian fishing boats based at the Shetlands Base. These were largely unprotected, slow and often unreliable vessels that could only operate for eight months of the year and when conditions in the North Sea permitted. This alone illustrates the huge difficulties that SOE faced in operating in this theatre.

The increased strategic and military significance that was placed on clandestine operations in the summer of 1940 meant that SOE urgently began to look for the means that would allow it to commence its work. It was this, and the opportunities that it was believed Norway would offer, that led to the establishment of the Shetlands Base and early attempts to recruit and train Norwegians. Both these small endeavours also symbolize the importance of cooperation and collaboration; it was clear that this new organization could not operate in this theatre without support. The next step was for SOE to articulate its aims and intentions for Norway.

Chapter 2

SOE POLICY IN NORWAY, 1940-5: THE COMBINATION OF SHORT- AND LONG-TERM OBJECTIVES

Special operations could not proceed with purpose in Norway without some guidance, and therefore through a series of directives SOE set out its policy – its intentions – for this theatre. Its plans have often been criticized by Norwegian historians and largely ignored by British historians, but importantly they demonstrate how the mix and nature of its operations were closely linked to Norway's peripheral place within wider strategic developments in Europe.[1] From December 1940, however, in line with the proposed role of sabotage, subversion and organized resistance in the occupied countries within Britain's forward strategy, they took on the essential structure of short- and long-term goals that would be retained for the rest of the war.

As the conflict in Europe progressed, however, and particularly after the entry into the war of the Soviet Union and the United States as allies with their vast resources in men and material, the strategic contribution of SOE and particularly Norway changed. This had a knock-on influence on policy and therefore operational priorities.

There were, however, additional factors that came into play. The first of these were in the early years of the war concerns over a possible German invasion of Britain from north-west Europe, including Norway. The second was Winston Churchill's 'obsession' with the country,[2] which began in 1939, was resurrected in the late summer of 1940 and was given added momentum during 1941 by Soviet and British calls for a Second Front.

During the summer of 1941, however, the British planning staff scaled back the role of secret armies within their strategic plans and decided that an eventual landing by Allied forces on the continent as part of a final and decisive military offensive would be concentrated in north-west France and the Low Countries. Therefore, by the end of 1941, notwithstanding continued pressure from the prime minister, the remote possibility of a British landing in Norway to liberate part or all of the country had effectively been sidelined, where it would remain until May 1945.

Between early 1942 and the end of 1943 with the entry of the United States into the war and with the strategic and operational focal point moving to the Mediterranean and in the longer term towards an invasion of north-west Europe, Norway remained a peripheral theatre. With the arrival, however, of a large part of the German surface fleet in Norway in early 1942 and its threat to the Arctic convoys, this increased the significance of Norwegian coastal waters.

By 1944, Norway was firmly under the dominant influence of Overlord. Consequently, the liberation of the country had to await the successful realization of the Allied campaign in north-west Europe, which meant that the forces required to enforce a reoccupation might not be available until well after military operations on the continent were complete. At the same time post-war political considerations, particularly the protection of Norwegian industries and infrastructure from German destruction, became increasingly significant.

SOE policy in Norway 1940–1: From rebellion to a secret army

After the fall of France, the British prime minister and the chiefs of staff (COS) began to build a strategic framework that reflected not only the desperate situation the nation found itself in but also within which it could move forward. British strategy fell to Churchill and the COS machinery; it was a corporate effort. Small nations, such as Norway, had very little access to or influence over this process even when it involved their interests.[3] In the spring of 1940, even as France collapsed, the COS had begun to review Britain's future strategy in the war against Germany. The assumption that Britain and France together would eventually be stronger than the Germans was self-evidently no longer applicable,[4] and by mid-June, with no major allies and facing a nation with a huge superiority in resources and position, Britain could no longer undertake large-scale land operations in Europe. Any forward strategy, therefore, had to overcome this imbalance and eventually create the conditions that would allow a final offensive on the continent leading to the ultimate objective, victory over Germany.[5] It was within this context that the concept of creating 'widespread revolt in the conquered territories' was seen as an important additional 'indirect method', along with economic pressure and strategic bombing, that could be used to undermine German military strength.[6] The British planning staff and MI (R) both produced several documents during the late spring and early summer of 1940 that examined the possibility of organized rebellions in the occupied territories. These papers reflected a belief that there was extensive anti-German feeling across Europe that if equipped and supported could be used to facilitate operations by British forces. The corollary of this was that subversive activities within the occupied countries should be undertaken with the eventual aim of promoting open armed resistance that would 'either be a forerunner to, or an auxiliary of direct military action'.[7]

In line with this between June and November 1940, a series of policy documents were produced initially within Section D and then SOE's Scandinavian section outlining the case for an uprising in Norway in early 1941.[8] In line with Hugh Dalton's views on subversion, the aim was to encourage local groups led by Norwegians trained in Britain, supplied with arms and ammunition from the Shetlands, to break into open revolt, attacking communications, small local garrisons and stores of arms and equipment. Britain would provide assistance and encouragement through raids but not a full-scale landing, and eventually the demoralized German forces in Norway would be overwhelmed. By November 1940, however, this ambitious concept had been reined back owing to a realization that the country was not yet ready for a general rising and in response to changes in British grand strategy during that autumn. Consequently, in December 1940, SOE's policy towards Norway took a new direction and the concept of rebellion was dropped.

At the heart of British military doctrine was this conviction that it was necessary to wear down and weaken Germany before Britain and her allies could once again undertake major land operations on the continent. At the time, this could be done only through a combination of indirect methods such as economic pressure, air action, propaganda, 'amphibious operations against the enemy's coastline' and small peripheral campaigns. Irregular and subversive activities would contribute in two ways. First, as part of a policy of attrition, the undermining of the enemy's fighting capability through sabotage and containing and extending his forces, and second, uprisings by secret armies that would coincide with and augment eventual land operations across Europe. The earlier concept of 'sowing the seeds of revolt' was therefore abandoned and subversive activity would be supplementary to 'regular operations' as part of a 'general policy'.[9]

It was within this context that on 25 November 1940 SOE's first directive was issued. A product of liaison between SOE, the Joint Planning Staff (JPS) and the COS, its objective was to provide guidance 'as to the direction in which subversive activities can best assist' strategy. In the short term, the priority was, alongside the elimination of Italy, to continue to 'wear down' Germany by 'amphibious and other operations within the limits of our resources', including the use of subversive operations, such as creating economic disorganization, to undermine enemy strength and morale. Over the longer term, SOE would prepare organizations in the occupied countries, Holland, Belgium, France and southern Norway, which could undertake coordinated revolts in cooperation with the eventual landing of British forces. These 'secret armies' would be preserved until the moment when their actions could augment 'decisive' operations against Germany.[10] It was an ambitious document but one that was in step with British policy at this time and the role it was believed that sabotage and subversion could ultimately play in the war against Germany.[11]

From an early stage, Britain had recognized the economic importance of Norway to Germany in any future military conflict. Even before the war, strategic targets in the country, such as the transportation of Swedish iron ore and the production of whale and fish oil, had been identified. In December 1938, the Industrial Intelligence Centre (IIC), in a survey of German economic vulnerability in war, identified Norway as supplying 69 per cent of Germany's whale and fish oil. The supply of Swedish iron ore had been intensively studied since the early 1930s and was seen as 'Germany's Achilles' heel. A significant amount of this product was supplied through Narvik.[12] During the spring of 1940, as the momentum to apply economic pressure against Germany gathered pace, the Ministry of Economic Warfare (MEW) and the Inter-Services Project Board (ISPB), the predecessor of SOE, highlighted the value of the specialist metals produced in Norway,[13] which directly led in the late spring of 1940 to the MI [R]/Section D operation against the production of ferro-chrome at A/S Bjølvefossen near Ålvik and which stopped production for four weeks.[14] There was also a growing belief, probably nourished by reports that Section D/SOE had received through its contacts in Norway, that the country was increasingly dissatisfied with German rule and therefore there was the potential for organized resistance. By early August 1940, it claimed that there were seemingly already 3,000 men in the Bergen district ready for action.[15]

It was within this background that in December 1940 SOE's Scandinavian section produced a paper entitled, 'Norwegian Policy'. This is a defining document because it lays down the core of SOE's policy, the combination of short- and long-term aims that would be the blueprint for its operations in Norway for the rest of the war. It has been criticized as unsuitable for Norwegian conditions, but at the time it was in step with the role envisaged for subversive operations within Britain's forward strategy, as expressed in SOE's first directive, and the possibilities that Norway appeared to offer for clandestine operations. The longer-term objective was to prepare and preserve the indigenous resistance, primarily across southern Norway, 'for simultaneous uprisings to assist either a landing by a British or Allied Expeditionary Force, or, an incipient German collapse'. The short-term aim was to carry out sabotage, both active and passive, and assist amphibious raids and air raids. Small-scale and unobtrusive sabotage would be undertaken by groups within Norway, while teams from the UK would attack 'special targets'. In both cases, these operations would not be allowed to threaten the longer-term process of preparing local resistance groups. The Norwegian authorities had no involvement in the development of this policy and therefore no influence over its make-up.[16]

At this time there was, however, another factor that also influenced SOE's plans for Norway. While a German invasion remained a possibility, the strategic importance of defending the UK remained a priority.[17] Therefore, SOE's December paper emphasizes preparing resistance groups not only to assist a landing in Norway but also to 'impede any German attempt to invade Great Britain'.[18] Norway was seen as a place where a 'workable machine' was being implemented that could hinder the activities of any German forces that took part in an invasion of Britain. The military importance placed on the development of local resistance groups that could operate behind enemy lines is reflected in SOE's defence and the Foreign Office's acceptance of Malcolm Munthe's work out of the British legation in Stockholm during the spring of 1941, notwithstanding the diplomatic risks.[19]

At the end of April 1941, SOE reaffirmed its short-term aim of carrying out sabotage while over the longer term making preparations for simultaneous rising across Norway that would support a landing by an 'Allied expeditionary force'. Moreover, and for the first time, it also stated that if the short-term policy resulted in the 'locking up' of German divisions in Norway, this would be 'desirable' from a 'strategic point of view'. Tying down large numbers of enemy forces in this theatre was, therefore, not simply a consequence but from a very early stage also an important and deliberate element of its policy. There was, however, a serious implication to this. Even though actions that forced the enemy to retain sizeable troops numbers in Norway were valuable, this also meant that a landing in a country ideally suited for defensive operations was made considerably more difficult and thereby less likely.

Over the next three years, therefore, there remained a tension at the heart of SOE's policy between its short- and long-term objectives.[20]

In the spring of 1941, British military fortunes reached a low point with the disasters in Greece, Crete, and North Africa, which reinforced the belief that British land forces were still not ready to take on the bulk of the German army.[21] A further complicating factor was the German invasion of the Soviet Union in June 1941. It was within this difficult and shifting context that during the spring and summer of 1941 SOE began to examine its future programme including an assessment of its requirements, in aircraft and equipment, for arming secret armies and sabotage groups across occupied Europe.[22] This was done in consultation with the British planning staff, who also reviewed the contribution of subversive and irregular operations to strategy.[23]

This led to important changes.[24] The defence of the UK remained the immediate priority, and there was no change in the conviction that German military strength had to be undermined through indirect means before Britain could again undertake a major land offensive on the continent. The priority was, however, to use Bomber Command to 'break the back of the Germans', although this would be supported by acts of sabotage.[25] Significantly, for SOE, this meant that in the immediate future it was recommended by the British planning staff that sabotage and subversive activities should be given preference over the longer-term aim of preparing and organizing secret armies, which by mid-August had been scaled back. There was a realization that arming resistance groups across Europe would require huge resources from Bomber Command, thereby threatening its contribution. This and the entry of the Soviet Union into the war, which meant that Eastern Europe became a Soviet sphere of influence, also led to a decision to concentrate SOE's long-term effort in north-west Europe, specifically Holland, Belgium and France, from where a final land offensive against Germany would probably commence. The first step for SOE would be to send organizers with wireless transmitters to these countries to establish 'patriot forces' prior to supplying arms and equipment.

Norway was not, however, immediately sidelined for three important reasons: it was seen as an area for possible future 'subsidiary' operations; considerable progress had been made in organizing a secret army and this should not be wasted; and, finally, because of the Shetlands Base it was believed that this clandestine army could be supplied by sea and was not dependent on airdrops.[26] Consequently, the long-term objective of organizing a secret army in Norway could continue despite the country's geographical and strategically marginal position. The reference to the suitability of Norway for 'subsidiary' operations was probably the result of the considerable attention that was paid to this theatre at the time within both military and political circles.

During the spring of 1941, certain senior SOE staff officers began to take a special interest in Norway and saw it as a possible location for operations by regular forces, which could be supported by local resistance groups. Col. A. M. Anstruther, SOE planning officer, believed Norway was the best area where SOE could assist an operation by a British Corp. On 29 May 1941, Harry Sporborg had a meeting with the Future Operations Planning Section (FOPS) to discuss 'a general assault to retake Norway'. He met, however, with significant scepticism.[27] Around this time though, even before the German invasion of the Soviet Union, the British planning staff also began to examine the possibilities of landings in both the south and north of the country. Operation Dynamite was a plan to land forces at Stavanger to establish a bridgehead in Norway.[28] One important influence behind this was probably the prime minister's preoccupation with Norway that had returned in September 1940, only five months after the failed Norwegian campaign began, when he commissioned a report on climatic conditions south of Bergen. General Sir Alan Brooke wrote that from October 1941 onwards 'we [COS] were to be continually in trouble riding him [Churchill] off mad plans to go back to Norway'.[29]

From the summer of 1941 there were, also, calls for a Second Front to support the Soviet Union, which Churchill used to sustain interest in the country. This initially culminated in October 1941 in Operation Ajax, a plan to establish a bridgehead in Norway through a landing at Trondheim. Hugh Dalton was directly involved in its preparation and it was also envisaged that SOE would take part in 'Dynamite' if undertaken. With 'Ajax' it was at one stage proposed that resistance groups should be used to support operations by regular forces. Therefore, the organization was fully aware of the considerable attention that was being given to this theatre at the time.[30] Nevertheless, despite pressure from the prime minister, a landing in central Norway was eventually resisted by the COS for both strong operational and strategic reasons. His trumpeting of action in the north was therefore silenced, at least temporarily, and the ambitious plans for the country were significantly scaled back leaving only a series of large combined operations against industrial and military targets close to the Norwegian coastline during December 1941. These were more in step with the British strategic aim of wearing down German fighting strength and little more than a sop to calls for a Second Front.[31] They are, however, symbolically important because they represent the absolute limit of what the COS were militarily prepared to undertake in Norway. From early 1942 and prior to its liberation in 1945, only small-scale amphibious raids, *coup de main* attacks, a small amount of strategic bombing and subversive operations were carried out in this theatre. Any possibility of a landing in the country by a British or Allied Expeditionary Force, although not completely forgotten, had therefore effectively been abandoned until the end of the war.

The attention paid to Norway was the result of the discourse within the British war management machinery,[32] between Churchill on one side, anxious to take the offensive at any opportunity, and the COS's more cautious step by step, measured and long-term approach to strategy, which won out in the end.[33] Importantly, however, this influenced SOE policy and operations in Norway in two ways during 1941. It created a temporary expectation that there could be a landing in the country before and independently of any final offensive across Europe. In April, in a document entitled 'Scandinavian Policy', the long-term objective was simply to prepare for a rising to support 'a landing by an Allied expeditionary force'.[34] But by July, it was envisaged that large-scale military operations could occur in Norway prior to and independent of a landing that was part of the 'opening of a British offensive on the Continent'.[35] By November 1941, however, after the rejection of Operation Ajax, and the concept of 'secret armies' exploding into action across Europe had been scaled back, the available SOE documents make no mention of a landing in Norway, either as part of a Europe-wide offensive or independently. The long-term policy was to prepare the indigenous resistance to support Allied military operations to reconquer Norway. In other words, to reassert legitimate control over the country and return it to lawful government – an exclusively political role. It was also not to be used prematurely to support 'insignificant' operations.[36] Therefore, by the beginning of 1942, SOE's long-term aim in this theatre had changed. It was no longer to create a secret army that would support a landing by regular forces, one of a series of such landings across Europe that were part of a final and decisive military offensive against Germany. Even before the entry of the United States into the war, the role of Norway within British strategy had altered. The country had been completely marginalized and SOE policy and ultimately operations quickly reflected this.

Prime ministerial interest in Norway during 1941 also had another immediate and disruptive impact on SOE plans. From late 1940 and during the first half of 1941, contrary to previous assertions,[37] Churchill attempted to block small raids and subversive actions in the country because he believed they threatened his wish for a landing by British forces.[38] This effectively undermined SOE, caused uncertainty and thereby made future planning problematic. In response and in order to make its case to be allowed to carry out its objectives unhindered, SOE began to make exaggerated claims about what it could achieve. For example, it asserted that both the Norwegian people and government were actively urging an intensification of operations against the Germans in their country. SOE's seemingly hyperbolic statements, which have been seized on by historians, were not a result of over enthusiasm after the success of operations such as 'Claymore' in March 1941, which Churchill had grudgingly agreed to, but part of an internal campaign to be allowed to follow its remit, which the prime minister appeared to be stifling. On 10 April, Hugh Dalton even drafted a letter to Churchill appealing for guidance on policy in Norway. Although never sent, it shows his frustration that SOE was not allowed to get on with its job.[39] By July, however, these difficulties had passed. Fortunately for SOE, the prime minister's opposition was only temporary, and in searching for ways to support the Soviet Union after the German invasion, his resistance to amphibious raids was abandoned. In early July 1941, Churchill requested that Admiral Keyes, the Director of Combined Operations, be asked to consider a raid in the north of Norway on the scale of 2–4,000 men. He also asked about a plan that the Commander-in-Chief Home Fleet had put forward for a small raid to destroy economic and military targets in Hammerfest.[40] Therefore, by the autumn of 1941, SOE was able to pursue its aim of attacking industrial and military targets in Norway without stifling interference.[41]

By early 1942, SOE's long-term aim was to prepare a clandestine army in readiness to support operations to liberate the country, something that became increasingly distant as the strategic and operational focal point moved to the Mediterranean and ultimately an invasion of northwest Europe. From this point, Norway and SOE's plans for this theatre became progressively subsidiary to Allied strategy as it was played out across Europe and North Africa.

SOE policy in Norway 1942–3: Subordinate to 'Torch' and 'Overlord'

The US entry into the war in December 1941 changed the strategic picture in Europe, with grand strategy no longer the sole responsibility of Britain but defined by the British and American coalition. Future American policy was based on the concepts of mass and decisive concentration and built on national optimism and a belief in its industrial might. Consequently, the Americans wanted to 'concentrate Allied forces as rapidly as possible and seek a decisive clash in the field'.[42] In contrast, the British wished to continue with the policy of reducing Axis military capability before undertaking a final offensive that would complete the defeat of Germany. It was the relationship between these two approaches that shaped the development of Allied strategy during 1942 and 1943. In the short term, it was the British view that prevailed and American calls for a cross-channel operation in 1942 were rejected. After agreeing to a 'Germany first' strategy, however,[43] it was politically unacceptable for American forces to remain idle in Europe and therefore Operation Torch, the landings in north-west Africa, was eventually agreed.

Allied strategy was hammered out during 1942 and 1943 at a series of conferences involving the British and American general staffs, political leadership and later Soviet representatives, at locations in North America, North Africa and the Soviet Union.[44] The first of these, the 'Arcadia' conference, was held in Washington from late December 1941. Although on the way to the United States, Churchill resurrected the concept of scattered landings across Europe supported by resistance forces,[45] at Washington this notion was finally discarded. With the entry of the United States into the war, it was no longer necessary to depend on secret armies; they could 'contribute to the execution of a plan but they were henceforward quite secondary to the making of it'.[46]

Although 'Arcadia' largely reaffirmed Britain's indirect, attritional approach, the Americans did not see it as definitive. Therefore, through the spring and early summer of 1942, they began to press for a landing in France. A series of protracted and complex negotiations followed that eventually led to the decision to go ahead with Operation Torch in November 1942, and to prepare for Operation Roundup, an invasion of north-west Europe in 1943. The British had rejected an early 'concentration of force' until German strength was visibly weakened. More significantly, the consequent decision to land in North Africa, although with American agreement, deflected Allied operations towards the Mediterranean during 1943, away from north-west Europe and Scandinavia.[47]

Nevertheless, in the search for an alternative to a cross-channel operation and owing to the threat to the Arctic convoys posed by the German surface fleet stationed in Norway from early 1942, Churchill's interest in Scandinavia resurfaced. In May 1942, this resulted in the refocusing on plans that had originated in the summer of 1941 for a landing in northern Norway, Operation Jupiter. This, however, despite further requests from the Soviet Union for a Second Front and notwithstanding its long life, was consistently opposed by the COS and ultimately rejected. Although protection of the Arctic convoys placed additional demands on the British Home Fleet, the requirements of home defence and the call for resources in the Mediterranean meant that a landing in Norway, even if it could be justified, remained unrealistic.[48]

Norway's real significance was evinced in the series of strategic deception operations that commenced with Operation Hardboiled in early 1942, a notional attack aimed at the coast south of Trondheim. Stavanger was eventually chosen for the main thrust of the operation, which was aimed for April, but to be postponed to May 1942 to extend the threat. The objective was to alarm the enemy, force him to divert his forces to this theatre away from the main battlefronts and deceive him as to Allied intentions.[49] It was followed soon afterwards by Operation Solo, which was authorized in July 1942 and included 'Solo I', which by simulating operations against Norway, specifically Narvik and Trondheim, was designed to cover preparations in the UK for Operation Torch.[50]

It was within this context that in May 1942, the COS issued their second directive to SOE, a document that was shaped by Allied proposals for a landing in Western Europe in 1943. Paramilitary organizations in the areas of projected operations would be built up and equipped in readiness to provide support during the initial assault. The only mention of Norway is as a potential theatre for raiding operations during the summer of 1942,[51] which is another indication that by this stage Norway was, despite Churchill's 'mad plans',[52] ancillary to the main strategic and operational momentum in Europe.

These contextual developments shaped SOE's policy for Norway during 1942. Significantly, the balance between and the importance of the long- and short-term objectives, began to change. As Norway became increasingly peripheral to the development of Allied strategy, the timing of operations to secure its eventual reoccupation became unpredictable. Consequently, the long-term objective became wrapped in uncertainty, especially as there was an 'absence of information concerning high policy'.[53] Internal SOE documents consistently refer only to an expected 're-conquest' of Norway,[54] and by June there is frustration and impatience within the Norwegian section over when if ever an invasion of Norway would happen, which made preparation very difficult.⁵⁵ The arming, equipping and organizing of a 'secret army' would continue so that it could be used at 'some future time' to be indicated by the 'Chiefs of Staff'.⁵⁶ Previous historians have suggested that Churchill's interest in and pressure to mount 'Jupiter' created an expectation within SOE and the operational teams it sent into Norway at this time that an invasion was coming, which then spilled over into the local population.⁵⁷ But the available SOE policy documents appear only to emphasize doubt over what might happen and make no specific mention of any plans to support an imminent landing by Allied forces.⁵⁸ Moreover, during the first half of 1942, the majority of its operations along with arms and equipment went into southern Norway with the objective of organizing and preparing guerrilla groups to attack appropriate targets, but only in the 'event of an Allied landing' or an invasion somewhere.⁵⁹ It is understandable, however, that the arrival of these teams, whose job was to prepare local groups to assist operations by regular forces, should have raised hopes that an invasion was impending. The long-term objective remained, as it had from the previous November, to organize and prepare a secret army that could assist an Allied landing that would lead to the 're-conquest of Norway' and the 're-establishment of the Government of H.M. King Haakon VII'.⁶⁰ In Norway, therefore, part of SOE's role would be purely political, although how and when it would be able to carry out this political task would increasingly depend on strategic and operational developments elsewhere in Europe.

In the meantime, the short-term objective of sabotage and subversion would be pressed on with. In August 1942, Brigadier Gubbins, recently appointed as the deputy executive director of SOE with responsibility for operations, approved a document outlining SOE's policy in Norway for the next six months. It called for *coup de main* operations to be undertaken as often as possible and an increase in 'incendiarism' and sabotage that 'could not be traced back'.⁶¹ By December it was Gubbins belief that SOE would be given a part in a future strategy, 'which will call for much greater sabotage activity in practically all territories', and therefore SOE 'may be directed to ease up' on 'efforts to organise secret armies'.⁶² Consequently, in the second half of 1942, there were indications from the senior hierarchy of SOE that the priority accorded to short-term objectives such as sabotage in north-west Europe would not only continue but also intensify, particularly in the case of Norway.

During 1943, the Allies focused on the Mediterranean, with operations moving from North Africa through Sicily and into Italy. According to Alan Brooke, the chairman of the COS, the intention was to wear out 'German forces, both land and air', and withdraw strength from Russia. Strategic bombing, economic pressure and subversive activities would also continue with the aim of 'softening up' Germany in preparation for a final campaign in north-west Europe.[63] In the meantime, important preparatory steps were taken towards the implementation of the 'decisive concentration of force' that would complete the defeat of Germany with the 'nature, timing, and priority of the cross-Channel attack', the landings in Normandy, eventually agreed.[64]

During 1943, Churchill also rather predictably returned his attention to Norway as a possible alternative to Overlord.[65] His views were again rejected, both by the COS and by Lt. General Frederick Morgan, who in the spring of 1943 was appointed Chief of Staff to the Supreme Allied Commander (designate) (COSSAC) in preparation for Operation Overlord. Although Morgan was directed to consider a landing in southern Norway, eventually given the title Operation Atlantis, he opposed the exercise for strategic, operational and administrative reasons and rather predictably it was never realized.[66]

Norway's value continued to be its contribution to the development of Allied operations elsewhere in Europe. The country was again selected as suitable for a strategic deception operation this time called 'Tindall', part of a larger plan Operation Cockade, to mislead the enemy as to Allied intentions during 1943 and pin down German forces in this theatre by once more creating the expectation of a landing in southern Norway.[67] Moreover, the damage inflicted on the *Tirpitz* by midget submarines in September, and the sinking of the *Scharnhorst* in December 1943, meant that from early 1944 the Allies were able to take the initiative in Arctic waters, bring the 'German forces based in Norway to battle' and sink U-boats, which would also help to exploit 'German fears' that the country would be invaded.[68]

In March 1943, the COS issued their third SOE directive, followed by a fourth in November 1944 that was largely a repeat of the previous directive, although it was stressed that the Supreme Commander Allied Expeditionary Force (SCAEF) would in future guide special operations in Norway. The emphasis for north-west Europe was on short-term sabotage operations and guerrilla warfare. In Norway, efforts would be concentrated on attacks against the transportation of materials through Norwegian waters and important industrial targets, while the value of increasing German security commitments in the country, a euphemism for tying down enemy forces, through local guerrilla activities, was also accentuated. No mention was made of preparing a clandestine army.[69]

At this time, there was even uncertainty within SOE's Norwegian section as to whether the building of 'secret army units in Norway was either advisable or necessary'. The decision was made, however, to carry on but without 'doing too much in the way of fresh organisation'. When Lt. Colonel J. S. Wilson read SOE's March directive it confirmed to him that no military operations were contemplated for Norway. This, he believed, would continue to handicap the long-term objective of organizing resistance groups, as it prolonged uncertainty over the future. Nevertheless, he largely supported an increase in sabotage although he thought that it should only be planned and executed from 'the UK'. He considered that the use of local guerrilla activities against the Norwegian railway network would, however, be more harmful to the local population than to the enemy and therefore unwelcome. And as the instruction was that such actions 'should be studiously avoided before the moment of strike has come', he felt that they should be held in abeyance until the time of an invasion.[70] Railway sabotage in Norway would, therefore, only be carried out in direct support of military operations either on the continent or possibly within the country.

It was within this background that in May 1943 SOE produced, for the first time, a separate 'Sabotage Directive' for Norway. This document, in step with SOE's March directive, places the main emphasis on attacks against coastal shipping and mines that supply raw materials to the enemy. Furthermore, it states that the 'organisations' that SOE had established, especially in the 'more populated' areas such as around Oslo, should begin to engage in sabotage activities, provided that this did not prejudice their ability to contribute to an eventual liberation. Therefore, in accordance with the strategic priority conferred on sabotage and in order to widen its impact, SOE's senior staff began to press for local involvement in attacks against enemy targets. The balance within SOE policy had by the spring of 1943 completed its shift in favour of short-term activities.[71]

Through 1943, the priority given to sabotage operations in the Norwegian theatre was directly linked to the process of intensifying the strain on Germany and thereby creating the conditions that would be conducive to a final and decisive Allied campaign in the West. From the middle of the year, however, the impact that this military offensive might eventually have on Norway also began to affect SOE's operational plans. For example, German units could be withdrawn from the country in order to bolster defensive operations elsewhere in Europe. Consequently, it was decided that a clandestine army should be prepared so that it could be used to support not only a landing in Norway but also to delay the withdrawal of enemy forces to 'meet any Continental Allied landing', if required, or carry out counter-scorch activities as these forces withdrew.[72] By June 1943, therefore, SOE's Norwegian section was cognizant of and beginning to plan for the impact that Norway's marginal position in relation to final Allied operations in Europe might have on the nature of the country's future liberation.

SOE policy in Norway 1944–5: The ascendancy of Overlord

After the completion of Operation Neptune, the assault phase of Overlord in June 1944, SOE policy changed and became directly linked to the progress of Allied operations on both the western and eastern fronts in Europe. Therefore, although as Supreme Headquarters Allied Expeditionary Force (SHAEF) recognized the liberation of Norway was a purely political issue,[73] it remained dependent on strategic and operational developments outside Scandinavia.

When the Allies, including the Soviet Union, met at the Tehran conference in November 1943, the date for the launch of Overlord was pinned down for 1 June 1944. It was later delayed to 6 June.[74] In autumn 1943, COSSAC took over operational command of SOE in north-west Europe, including Norway,[75] and from January 1944, in the final run up to 'Overlord', this control passed to SHAEF, which took over the final preparations for the landings in Normandy.[76] Therefore, in March 1944, it was SHAEF that issued an 'Operational Directive' to Special Forces HQ (SFHQ). According to this directive, a 'full-scale invasion of the Continent' was the supreme operation for 1944. Undermining German fighting capability through sabotage and subversion in the short term, to bring 'the conditions in Europe considered essential to the success of invasion operations' remained the immediate priority, although it should not to be allowed to put at risk the long-term aim of 'supporting' the invasion of Western Europe when it came. Preparations for activities that would be undertaken 'in conjunction with the allied forces under conditions of invasion or re-occupation' could therefore continue.[77]

Norway, however, remained marginal and subservient to the main course of Allied strategy. In the run up to the landings in Normandy, it was again allocated a role in 'inducing the enemy to make faulty strategic dispositions', as highlighted by the two strategic deception operations targeted at Scandinavia: 'Fortitude North' and 'Graffham'. Both of these were part of Operation Bodyguard, a plan to induce Germany to disperse its forces across Italy, the Balkans and Scandinavia, and to get the enemy to underestimate the Allied ability to undertake a cross-channel landing until late summer.[78] The nature and timing of a reoccupation of Norway, therefore, continued to be secondary to and dependent upon the success and progress of Allied operations on the European mainland. Norway, however, could not be militarily or politically ignored, especially while some eleven to twelve enemy divisions remained in the country. Consequently, from the summer of 1943, proposals for an eventual reoccupation based on the Rankin plans had begun to take shape. In addition to Overlord, COSSAC had also been instructed to prepare a plan for 'a return to the Continent in the event of German disintegration'. Out of this came the Rankin plans, which were submitted to the COS in August 1943. They consisted of Rankin A, a plan for an early invasion of Europe if the enemy became over stretched and significantly weakened; Rankin B, a plan to reoccupy a part of Europe from where the enemy had withdrawn; and Rankin C, a plan to deal with a complete collapse or surrender of Germany.[79]

It is outside the framework of this work to go into the tortuous and complex details of the run up to the liberation, especially as it has been extensively covered before.[80] It was predominately Rankin C and to a lesser degree B that became the templates for plans to reoccupy all or part of Norway; Rankin A was deemed extremely unlikely and quickly dropped,[81] which meant that the possibility of a landing in Norway, something that SOE had long prepared for, was initially viewed within COSSAC as extremely unlikely. Nonetheless, fears grew within the Norwegian government and eventually the Allies that German forces might attempt a last stand and create a *Festung Norwegen*, a fortress Norway. By early 1945, therefore, preparations had begun to deal with 'post-capitulation resistance' by an overland advance through Denmark and Sweden, although as the German forces in Norway capitulated unconditionally on 8 May 1945 it was fortunately never required.[82] Nevertheless, because of Norway's peripheral position, its eventual liberation remained shrouded in doubt and as a result plagued by a number of difficulties right up until the German surrender, which ultimately had an important impact on SOE plans and ultimately its operations in this theatre.

In August 1943, planning and preparation for the liberation was placed under Scottish Command (Scotco), commanded by Lieutenant-General Sir Andrew Thorne.[83] Although plans were made for a Rankin B scenario, a German withdrawal from all or part of Norway, it was the Rankin C plan, which 'dealt with the possibility of a complete collapse of Nazi power on the lines of the swift surrender of November 1918',[84] that became the basis for Operations Apostle and Doomsday, the final proposals for the reoccupation of the country.[85] These plans were, however, beset by two major problems from their inception until their implementation in the early days of May 1945. First, there was a lack of available forces and second an expectation that even after a German capitulation there would be a significant time delay before any Allied troops could arrive in Norway.[86]

Towards the end of 1943, there were intimations of a change in SOE's plans for Norway. There were signs of a growing reluctance to allow any intensification or widening of activities, particularly sabotage or *coup de main* attacks. In October although SOE received a directive to 'plan for the future interruption of railway communications' to slow down a German withdrawal, it was told not to take 'overt action' unless instructed.[87] SOE involvement in the strategic deception scheme 'Fortitude North' was also confined to incidental activities that would not result in a reaction from the occupying regime against the local population or resistance forces. Therefore, unlike Denmark, it was decided that sabotage should not be escalated.[88] SOE was not prepared to risk any damage to the resistance groups in Norway, particularly as the final stages of the war in Europe approached. There was a growing belief that they would probably be required to undertake an important role in the country's liberation, especially if regular forces would not be readily available.

It was, however, only after the successful completion of the landings in Normandy and the assault phase of Overlord that there was a fundamental and irrevocable shift in SOE policy. First, short-term objectives were modified to meet the needs of ongoing operations on the continent. From late June 1944, the emphasis on sabotage in Norway moved towards discarding all targets, 'the products from which are not of immediate value to the enemy',[89] and by July the general policy was to concentrate efforts on those industries that were of 'present value to the enemy'.[90] By the summer of 1944, therefore, SOE's short-term focus in Norway had shifted from strategic to tactical operations.[91]

After the successful landings in Normandy, *coup de main* and sabotage operations also no longer had precedence in Norway. From September 1944, until the liberation the following May, the first concern was the long-term objective of preparing and organizing a clandestine army. With a shortage of regular forces, SHAEF accepted that local resistance groups would be needed to play a significant part in the country's eventual liberation, and therefore their preservation, training, arming and equipment became a priority. In early August, when the

British 52nd Division, the proposed core of a future reoccupation force, was transferred to the continent, SOE saw this as confirmation that the possibility of military support for Norway's liberation was extremely remote, and therefore 'as a corollary' its responsibilities increased.[92] Moreover, there was a growing fear of the potential threat posed by the large number of German troops that remained in the country. And SOE and Scotco were agreed that the Norwegian resistance should be prepared to act as both a protective force and a force for law and order in the period immediately after an eventual German surrender or collapse and that this situation required a 'new directive'.[93] Post-war considerations therefore became an increasingly important factor in shaping future plans and operations.

At a crucial meeting on 17 August of the Anglo Norwegian Collaboration Committee (ANCC), the joint committee set up by SOE and Norwegian High Command in spring 1942, which was attended by leading figures from SFHQ, the Norwegian High Command and Jens Chr. Hauge, head of *Milorg*, the issue of the military contribution of clandestine forces in Norway to a future liberation was discussed. It was decided that an up-to-date set of instructions for the resistance was urgently required and therefore towards the end of the month a draft proposal was submitted to SHAEF.[94] This was eventually approved and at the beginning of September 1944 a new directive for the 'Employment and Development of Resistance in Norway' was issued under the authority of SFHQ.

This document set out SOE's intentions for Norway for the remainder of the war. It confirmed that 'no military offensive operations' were planned for the country, and that therefore there should be no 'overt' action that would require outside support. It was felt that the liberation would probably result from a German surrender, collapse or evacuation, and in these circumstances the primary role of the resistance would be to act as a protective force, preventing the execution of a German scorched earth policy, or as a force for law and order after a German collapse and 'pending the arrival of an Allied relieving force'. Current sabotage should continue and limited action to prevent or hinder an evacuation would also be permitted but only by 'specialist' groups. Consequently, the emphasis during the final months of Norway's occupation as expressed through this document was on preparing the resistance for the liberation, especially for the uncertain and potentially chaotic period immediately after the German authorities and troops in Norway had surrendered or withdrawn from the country. It also meant that with the full authority of the Allied High Command behind it, for the first time the objective of organizing, arming and training a clandestine army in Norway could really get underway.⁹⁵ It would, however, no longer be used to support operations by regular forces as part of an opposed landing. As a result of the very different conditions within which it had originated four years earlier, the contribution of a secret army had dramatically changed.

The directive also permitted limited action, such as railway sabotage, to prevent or hinder a German evacuation. Although only SOE teams sent into the country would undertake such activities in order that the resistance movement as a whole was not endangered. This element of policy did not, however, remain intact for long. By early October, SHAEF had decided to allow German forces to return to the continent, because the 'smaller number of Germans left in Norway' when they surrender, 'the less will be the commitment' that the Allies will have 'to free the country'.⁹⁶ Operations on the continent were, therefore, seen as the best way of reducing the difficulties of liberating a country that was occupied by several enemy divisions. Pressure from the Admiralty, however, which wished to intensify attacks against enemy shipping, and SFHQ, which argued that it would be difficult to sustain 'resistance groups in Norway in a state of discipline' if they could not contribute to the offensive against Germany, meant that on 26 October SHAEF partially backed down and agreed that 'a limited number of attacks' could be carried out by 'independent sabotage groups' against suitable targets on the main Norwegian railway routes'.⁹⁷

Despite this amendment to policy, however, the Admiralty, Scotco and SFHQ kept up the pressure on SHAEF to permit unlimited attacks on the rail network to hinder German troop withdrawals. They initially met with opposition, not only because it was feared that any action could result in harsh German countermeasures that would threaten the resistance's eventual ability to undertake its primary role of protection but also because SHAEF was concerned that if the Norwegian railways were brought to a standstill it might result in widespread famine in Norway, as it had in Holland.⁹⁸ This would require assistance from the Allies that in light of the commitment to Overlord would be extremely difficult if not impossible to meet.

What changed matters was Operation Nordlicht, the retreat of the German 20th Mountain Army – around 200,000 men – from Finland into northern Norway in October 1944, which eventually included an order to transfer six of its divisions out of the country. It was the withdrawal of these experienced and battle hardened forces and their potential threat to Allied operations on the continent that resulted in a change in policy.[99] In early December 1944, in response to a Joint Intelligence Committee (JIC) report that stated that if German movements south were not impeded up to seven divisions could arrive on the western front by January 1945, SHAEF agreed to allow unlimited attacks against the Norwegian rail network in order to impose 'the maximum delay and casualties' on the German divisions that were withdrawing through Norway and to force them to use sea routes where they were vulnerable to British air and naval forces. In line with this it was believed that the destruction of the *Tirpitz* in November 1944 would allow the navy to 'adopt a bolder policy'.[100]

Although it was realized that this change in policy could put *Milorg* at risk, it was decided that success must be ensured on the Continent 'even at the expense of Norway'.[101] The priority accorded to operations in north-west Europe therefore predominated and continued to cast a shadow over SOE's plans for Norway until well into 1945. Unlimited attacks on the Norwegian railway network were persisted with until 16 April 1945 when SHAEF decided that the arrival of enemy divisions from Norway could no longer influence the main battle and therefore were no longer a danger. The priority for the Norwegian resistance from that point was to build up 'in order that it may play an active part in the final liberation of Norway'. [102] All uncertainty ended when the German forces in Norway surrendered unconditionally on 8 May.

Norway was undoubtedly a 'strategic backwater'[103] during the war but it was exactly this and its relationship to the main strategic developments in Western Europe that fundamentally shaped SOE operations in this northern theatre. As Allied military plans evolved, SOE operational priorities in Norway changed between on the one hand sabotage and subversion and on the other creating a clandestine army. There were, however, other important factors that also contributed to the development of SOE's plans for this theatre. The first of these was the nature of its relationship with the Norwegian government in exile.

Chapter 3

SOE AND THE NORWEGIAN GOVERNMENT
AND MILITARY AUTHORITIES, 1940-5:
CONTROL THROUGH COLLABORATION

Through operating in the occupied countries of Europe, SOE inevitably made contact with or worked alongside various political representatives or groupings, such as the governments in exile based in Britain, or became drawn into the internal conflicts that broke out within some of these countries after 1940. Political factors therefore became an additional factor 'governing operations'.[1]

Norwegian interests were represented in London from June 1940 by the Norwegian government in exile. It was recognized as the constitutional representative of the Norwegian people, both at home and internationally, and although initially it had to face some unpopularity its legitimacy was never seriously challenged.[2] From the autumn of 1940, through its new foreign minister Trygve Lie, Norway pursued a policy of developing a close and positive affiliation with Britain and became a supportive and active ally. At the same time, SOE also set out to establish a pragmatic working relationship with the Norwegian authorities, in order to secure Allied strategic control over special operations in Norway and ensure that they remained in step with military requirements as laid down by the COS, and later SHAEF.

Furthermore, SOE set out to work with the Norwegian government and its military authorities in London in order to pursue its recruitment of the Norwegian volunteers that were required for operations in Norway. It was, however, initially a relationship built on individual contacts, subject to the prerequisites of security and based on a determination that all subversive activities should remain under SOE's complete control. It was not a relationship that was built on a unique scepticism or mistrust towards the Norwegian authorities: it was cooperation on SOE's terms. This rather one-sided association did not last.

In the autumn of 1941, the military resistance in Norway – *Milorg* – was placed under the direct authority of the Norwegian Army High

Command. From this point, SOE realized that if it wished to retain a measure of operational control, particularly over the development of a secret army in Norway, it had to take a more collaborative approach in its relations with the Norwegian authorities in London. At the same time, the Norwegian government, through its Ministry of Defence, began attempts to improve its contact and therefore influence with the British military authorities and SOE. It also accepted that the realization of its primary aim, the liberation of Norway, could only be achieved with the support of its allies. Towards the end of 1941, in order to help it accomplish these objectives, it therefore instigated a series of internal reforms to its military and defence set-up.

These developments led to a more structured and balanced relationship between SOE and the Norwegian military authorities, which allowed SOE to retain strategic direction over subversive activities and thereby ensure that they remained in line with policy. It also gave the Norwegian High Command authority over the use of its manpower and resources and some influence over clandestine operations in Norway, which meant that SOE had to accept some operational changes, especially in its approach to sabotage. Nevertheless, the Norwegian government fully accepted that the ultimate authority on special operations lay with the Allied High Command.

SOE and Norwegian government in exile, August 1940–August 1941: The attempt at control

A scepticism within SOE towards Norwegians, which remained in place until well into the war, has been cited by previous historians as the reason why the organization took an initially selective approach in its relations with the Norwegian authorities in London.[3] This was not the case. From the summer of 1940, there was a view within SOE that if it failed to communicate with the Norwegian government in exile it might put at risk any future intentions it had for Norway. At the same time, however, according to its charter it was obliged to keep its activities in step with strategic developments and therefore it needed to retain control over its policy towards and activities within the occupied countries. SOE was also a secret service, not answerable to Parliament, paid out of the 'secret vote', and part of a ministry where many of its employees did not even know of its existence. It was for these reasons that SOE initially confined its contacts with the Norwegian government to those individuals or departments that were expedient.[4]

Section D had already begun to enlist Norwegians before their government arrived in Britain. The 'Norwegian Expedition' undertaken in June 1940 was made up of Norwegians, a number of which had been recruited through J. Ingebrigtsen, secretary of the 'Norwegian Seaman's Association' in Britain, and from among the Norwegian whaling community which had fled to Britain.[5] But after the cruiser *Devonshire* reached Scotland on 10 June 1940, carrying with it the king, crown prince and most of the members of the Norwegian government, there was a recognized 'constitutional authority' in Britain to represent the interests of the Norwegian people. 'There was little doubt that the King and government, by virtue of the constitution, and constitutional necessity, and with the support of the authority given to it at Elverum on 9 April 1940, was Norway's only legal government whilst in exile, the country was at war, and the homeland occupied.'

The Norwegian government in exile was actually a coalition made up of ministers from parties other than the traditional Labour party. And not all the ministers arrived in Britain on 10 June. Two were in Stockholm and one in Paris, while Halvdan Koht, the foreign minister at this time did not arrive in London until 19 June.[6] British recognition was given at meetings on 27 June and 1 July between Lord Halifax, the British foreign minister, and Koht.[7] From this point, it became very difficult for initially Section D and later SOE, when recruiting Norwegians and undertaking operations in Norway, to ignore the concerns of their government.

Section D quickly recognized that the Norwegian government's help was required to obtain 'enough Norwegians' for its 'work' in Norway.[8] By late July, therefore, contact had been made with Halvdan Koht, both privately and through the War Office, which eventually led in August to the selection of Martin Linge to work as the liaison officer between the newly established SOE and the Norwegian authorities in London. On 23 July 1940, Koht met Anthony Eden, the British Minister of War and a 'general' from the War Office. This established relations with the War Office, and one of the topics considered was preparation for a 'rising against the Germans in Norway'. Following on from this, a British officer was appointed to liaise with Koht, probably J. L. Chaworth-Musters. Koht's meeting at the War Office arose out of his wish to establish an information service that could produce and distribute propaganda in Norway.[9] This was followed by contact with Birger Ljungberg, the Norwegian minister of defence, Major General Fleischer, the head of *Hærens Overkommando* (HOK), and Colonel Stenersen at the Norwegian army reception camp at Dumfries in Scotland where the

Norwegian forces in Britain were based.[10] SOE considered that these were the key members of the Norwegian government and military authorities.[11]

During the autumn of 1940, there were calls from within SOE for a more intimate relationship with the Norwegian government, as it was believed that it could 'wreck' everything if cooperation was withheld. There are indications that J. L. Chaworth-Musters strongly recommended closer collaboration with the Norwegian authorities. Nonetheless, Norwegian ministers were not kept fully informed of SOE activities and at this stage had no involvement in the development of policy.[12] This was not, however, down to any unique or particular British mistrust of Norwegians that emerged during the campaign in Norway the previous spring. Both Charles Hambro and Harry Sporborg, the dominant figures in the early development of SOE's Scandinavian section, had no involvement in the fighting in Norway and were quick to make contact with members of the Norwegian government. It was also only days after the inception of SOE that contact was made with Halvdan Koht, who had been responsible for Norway's pre-war policy of neutrality, a position that was unlikely to endear him to the British military authorities.[13] From the beginning, therefore, SOE's approach to the Norwegian government was not based on prejudice but rather on pragmatism.

Secrecy was also a major issue for SOE. It was the War Cabinet that decided that the activities of this new organization should not be disclosed in Parliament, that it was an 'official secret' and its 'affairs could not be debated'. It is rather ironic, therefore, that details of some of its operations were even withheld from the War Cabinet. As late as May 1945, the secretary to the Cabinet was still refusing to release details of SOE's raid on the heavy water plant in Vemork.[14] In these circumstances, it is perfectly consistent, particularly in the early stages, that this new organization restricted its contacts and limited the disclosure of information to those governments it worked with. It also seems harsh to describe SOE as 'playing on the requirement for security', especially when at the same time Halvdan Koht was withholding the details of his involvement with the British secret services from his own ministerial colleagues.[15]

Furthermore, SOE's disparaging view of Norwegians as defeatist, 'ill-disciplined' and 'great talkers' was an attitude that remained even after British-Norwegian collaboration had significantly improved. Lt. Col. J. S. Wilson's view that Norwegians were of a 'very simple nature', largely because they had not been engaged in military operations in the past hundred years, was expressed later in the war when relations were generally close.[16] It was an outlook not uniquely applied to Scandinavians either and therefore is not a satisfactory explanation for SOE's selective contact with the Norwegian government. It was typical of a 'certain condescension in foreigners' that was rife among British officers at the time. Within SOE there was also a 'presumed insecurity and indiscretion' among other nationalities, an attitude that was both 'universal' and persistent.[17]

SOE confined its contacts to those ministers who were most valuable and appeared most supportive, not only because of security considerations but also because it wanted to maintain a close and tight control over its activities in Norway. It had to ensure that when the time came to use any 'movement' within the country it could 'lay it on and lay it off' at its 'will' and not 'anybody else's'.[18] Sabotage and the organization of resistance groups had to be coordinated with broader strategic and operational requirements and therefore kept tightly under its wing. Nevertheless, by the early months of 1941, SOE felt that it had a close relationship with the Norwegian government although one forged on British terms. Hugh Dalton had even been in touch with Trygve Lie, who he rather patronisingly described as 'wholly in favour of the war'.[19]

This one-sided relationship also developed because at the time the Norwegian government, distracted by events at home, lacked coherence and direction and had no clear policy on clandestine operations in Norway. It also had no executive body to effectively represent its interests with its allies on military matters.[20] Although the Norwegian government was in a strong economic position when it arrived in Britain owing to its gold reserves[21] and its ownership of *Nortraship*, the fourth largest merchant fleet in the world consisting of over one thousand vessels, which was an important source of income during the war,[22] it faced many difficulties. Only twenty to thirty civil servants initially accompanied it into exile, whereas by the end of the war it had 2,500 employees working for it in London.[23] And it did not have the armed forces to allow it initially to make any more than a token contribution to the Allied war effort. In late June 1940, it only had 400 trained men at the camp in Dumfries.[24]

The government's position with the population at home was also weak, especially in light of the failure of its pre-war position of neutrality and a defence policy that meant that it was unprepared for the German invasion.[25] The negotiations in the summer of 1940 between the Presidential Board of the Norwegian Storting (Parliament) and the German *Reichskommissar* over the establishment of a State Council to take over the running of the country – the *Riksrådforhandlinge* – that resulted in the call from Oslo for King Haakon to abdicate and the government to stand down indicate both the weakness of the government's positon and the serious concerns it had to deal with back home.[26] It therefore became a priority to make contact, gain a foothold with and establish some influence over developments on the Home Front so that the government could ultimately be seen to 'represent one nation in the fight to regain its freedom'. This meant, however, that at this stage it was not a priority, even if suitable staff and institutions had been in place, to indulge in developing policy on such matters as subversive or clandestine operations.[27]

During the first six months of 1941, the relationship between SOE and the Norwegian government continued much as before, based on individual contacts and led by SOE. The interests or concerns of the Norwegian authorities therefore had little influence over the development or implementation of SOE operations. Nevertheless, a significant change in the Norwegian government led to closer political relations with Britain. This was the appointment of Trygve Lie as foreign minister in place of Halvdan Koht in November 1940,[28] which represented a major step towards an unequivocal pro-Allied Norwegian foreign policy. In May 1941, military cooperation was also formalized and placed on a more practical level when an agreement was signed with the British over the use of the Norwegian forces in Britain. In future, they would only be deployed either in the defence of the UK or the reconquest of Norway and were placed under British operational control.[29] Significantly, the view of Trygve Lie within SOE's Scandinavian section was that he was supportive of any activity that harmed the Germans or their war effort.[30] The new Norwegian foreign minister also maintained contact with both Charles Hambro and Harry Sporborg,[31] and his appointment was well received within the British Foreign Office.[32]

The establishment of FD-E also provided a more institutional avenue of contact between SOE and the Norwegian authorities. This small office, under Captain Finn Nagell, was directly subordinate to the Norwegian Ministry of Defence and officially responsible, among other things, for forming closer links between the Norwegian Foreign and Defence ministries and SOE.[33] SOE had already made contact with Nagell after interviewing him the previous November and thereafter it saw him and his staff, based in Norway House close to Trafalgar Square, as an important collaborator in recruitment.[34] The involvement of FD-E, members of the Norwegian naval staff and Trygve Lie in the preparation of British amphibious raids against herring and cod oil plants in northern Norway during March and April 1941 – operations Claymore and Hemisphere – also helped to cement the view within SOE that it was working closely with the Norwegian government. With their help the British were able to enlist Norwegians, obtain the use of a Royal Norwegian destroyer, gather intelligence and provide food and clothing for local inhabitants.[35]

At this early stage, therefore, relations with the Norwegian authorities assisted rather than forcibly reshaped SOE plans for Norway. The relationship was led by SOE and based on chosen contacts, although it is difficult to see how it could have been otherwise. A remarkable illustration of this is Operation Hemisphere, which alongside SOE and the British Admiralty also included a contribution from the Royal Norwegian Navy both in its planning and implementation through the provision of the destroyer 'Mansfield' with crew, along with ten Norwegian marines and one officer. According to Hugh Dalton the operation had the complete agreement of the Norwegian government, but despite the participation of Norwegian forces it was apparently carried out without the knowledge of the Norwegian defence minister, Birger Ljungberg.[36]

During 1941, SOE continued to pursue its objectives without undue external political interference. A further important example of this is provided by the arrival in London on 17 February 1941 of John Rognes, a leading member of *Milorg*. He was called over from Norway by the Norwegian minister of defence to deal with matters concerning *Milorg* and to work under the authority of FD-E.[37] It appears, however, that Rognes was quickly commandeered by SOE. It interviewed him a few days after his arrival in the country and the Norwegian authorities eventually gave permission for him to be used as a link, initially based on the Shetlands, between SOE and the headquarters of *Milorg* in Oslo. For SOE, he was seen as a means to bring the resistance under British 'control'.[38]

In June 1941, the central council of *Milorg* (*Rådet*) sent a report to Britain addressed to the Norwegian king. This report, outlining its views on issues concerning its role in occupied Norway, did not, however, go directly to the Norwegian government but instead via John Rognes was handed to SOE, which through Harry Sporborg quickly drafted a reply. SOE's response, which it rather suitably called a 'Directive' was, before being sent, placed before both Trygve Lie and General Fleischer. Lie, comforted by the presence of Rognes and Nagell at his meeting with SOE when the document was discussed, and under the apparent impression it would be placed before the Norwegian prime minister if that had not already been done, did not object to it being his government's answer. Fleischer' view was that the document gave 'precise and clear instructions'.[39] Consequently, SOE's 'Directive' to *Milorg* in July 1941, which as will be shown was an important statement of its policy, was placed before important figures within the Norwegian government and military authorities, although not the government as a whole. Its uncoordinated and rather haphazard response was symbolic of the relationship that the Norwegian government had with SOE during most of 1941; this situation, however, soon began to alter.

SOE and Norwegian authorities 1941–2: From control to collaboration

From the autumn of 1941, the relationship between SOE and the Norwegian government in London progressively changed and ultimately resulted in the government, through its newly appointed military authorities, having a greater involvement in the development, shaping, nature and implementation of SOE's operations in Norway. SOE also abandoned its previous ascendant position and accepted that collaboration, working together towards a common aim, was the best way to protect Allied interests. This, however, came at a price. Norwegian views and concerns would have to be considered, which led to the tempering of some undertakings, although not altering the principal objectives. The relationship that developed from early 1942 was positive and constructive, consistently although not always serving the interests of both sides.

The emergence and organization of military resistance in Norway and the creation of an underground army, represented by *Milorg*, will be examined in more detail in the next chapter.[40] Relations between *Milorg* and its government, however, were crucial to the development of the relationship between SOE and the Norwegian authorities in London. By the summer of 1941, *Milorg* had set up an administrative hierarchy centred on Oslo, based on a *Sentralledelse*, Central Leadership (SL), responsible for its day-to-day running, which was under the *Råd*, the central council (R), responsible for formulating policy.[41] In June 1941, *Milorg* in its communication to the king in London expressed concerns over SOE activities in Norway and began to look to the Norwegian government for authority and direction.[42] The arrival of Jacob Schive and Professor Johan Holst in London in October, two members of its central council, helped accelerate this process. Most significantly, by turning to its government for legitimacy, *Milorg* was outwardly rejecting SOE's attempts to directly control it.

On 28 October 1941, Schive and Holst met Charles Hambro and Malcolm Munthe, and on 12 November Schive wrote to Lt. Col. Harry Sporborg with his summary of the meeting. He called for a 'co-ordinating element' to bring together the British and Norwegian governments along with *Milorg*, which would be responsible to the Norwegian government and would only consult with the British through them.[43] Just over a week later on 20 November, *Milorg* was officially recognized by its government and placed under the control of HOK in London. That same day Charles Hambro met Trygve Lie and was told of the change, which according to Lie he fully supported.[44] Consequently, if SOE was to retain any future influence over the 'official' military resistance, the potential core of a clandestine army in Norway, it would be have to be through the Norwegian authorities not independently.

From this point, therefore, SOE changed its approach towards the Norwegian government and suggested a more equitable and structured relationship. On 25 November 1941, Charles Hambro sent a proposal, written by Sporborg, to the newly appointed Norwegian minister of defence, Oscar Torp, suggesting ways to ensure greater Anglo-Norwegian collaboration. This document was a watershed in SOE-Norwegian relations. In light of the 'official' incorporation of *Milorg*, Hambro realized that it was time to define more precisely the basis for subversive operations in Norway. While accepting the wishes of *Milorg* to be guided by its own government, the paper stresses that any mechanism put in place to enable collaboration must guarantee that the work in Norway is kept in step with 'general policy' as applied across occupied Europe. Behind Hambro's apparent magnanimity, therefore, was the British determination that all sabotage and subversive activity should ultimately remain under Allied direction. The mechanism put forward, an Anglo-Norwegian Committee, borrowed from Jacob Schive, to oversee special operations in Norway was accordingly a pragmatic means that aimed to ensure this objective. In return, the Norwegian authorities would have a say in the implementation of SOE policy in Norway, while retaining their authority over *Milorg* and regaining control over the employment of Norwegian recruits on operations on behalf of the British. It was a proposal that suited both parties.[45]

At the same time, through the relationship that developed between Charles Hambro and Oscar Torp, the Norwegian government began a determined effort to ensure greater involvement in and influence over Allied plans for Norway, especially those concerning an eventual reconquest of the country. Between late November 1941 and the end of January 1942, there was ongoing correspondence between Oscar Torp, Charles Hambro, Major General Sir H. L. Ismay, secretary to the COS and Anthony Eden regarding the setting up of an Anglo-Norwegian Planning Committee to cooperate on preparations for a future reconquest of Norway. This committee was eventually approved by the COS on 24 January but met only once. For the British at this stage of the war, it was nothing more than a 'façade to soothe Norwegian aspirations and susceptibilities'.[46] The Norwegian authorities were no longer prepared to stay outside the planning and decision-making processes when it concerned operations on Norwegian territory. This coincided with growing fears within SOE that it might lose the cooperation of the Norwegian authorities, something that was considered a 'very serious matter'.[47] Events at the end of 1941 threatened to lead to this scenario.

Despite the wishes of the British Foreign Office, the Norwegian government was not advised beforehand of the two British amphibious raids, Operations Anklet and Archery, which included large SOE-Norwegian contingents and in the case of 'Anklet' the assistance of the Norwegian navy. At a COS meeting on 24 November 1941, Commodore Mountbatten, Advisor on Combined Operations (ACO), mentioned that the foreign secretary had raised the question of informing the Norwegian authorities about certain operations planned for the Norwegian coast. The COS opposed this on operational grounds. The foreign secretary pressed the issue at a COS meeting of 28 November, but the COS argued that on 'military grounds it was unwise to give out information prior to an operation'. Trygve Lie could be advised, although it should be at the last possible moment. It was 25 December, after the forces had departed, that Lie was informed of the operations by the Foreign Office.[48] These raids also went against an agreement reached between Trygve Lie and Charles Hambro in October 1941. The agreement, which was sent to the COS, limited raids on the Norwegian coast to operations of half a dozen men. They also resulted in severe reprisals against the Norwegian civilian population. The 'Anklet' raid led to what was termed the *Jøssinglister* (*Jøssinger* was the term used by Norwegian Nazis to describe Norwegian patriots). This was a list of potential hostages, 1 per cent of the local population. Moreover, it led to sharp recriminations between the British and Norwegian contingents on the raids. J. W. Torrance, the officer in charge of SOE contingent, was extremely critical of the Norwegians, their lack of discipline and general behaviour.[49]

In light of this on 14 January 1942, at a meeting involving Harry Sporborg, Charles Hambro, Trygve Lie and Oscar Torp, SOE was made aware of Norwegian resentment. It realized it had little choice but to accept that its activities in Norway and the use of Norwegian recruits would have to have the approval of a joint committee, which would include Norwegian representatives who were responsible to the Norwegian minister of defence. Consequently, on the same day, Hambro wrote to Torp confirming the setting up of the Anglo Norwegian Collaboration Committee (ANCC) and agreed that SOE would not 'initiate any expeditions to or against Norway without the knowledge or consent of the Norwegian members of this Committee'. Within SOE there was an acceptance that failure to implement this new mechanism quickly could mean that 'the Norwegians would simply refuse to participate in future operations'.[50]

Alongside this there were also further changes within the Norwegian government, particularly the Ministry of Defence, which led to significant structural and policy developments. Although with the arrival of Trygve Lie as foreign secretary, Norway's pre-war neutrality policy was replaced by an alliance policy built on cooperation with Britain and America,[51] under the stewardship of Birger Ljungberg, defence policy drifted and lacked clarity.[52] This changed when in November 1941 Oscar Torp replaced Ljungberg. Johan Nygaardsvold, the Norwegian prime minister during the war, later described Ljungberg as 'not the right one to carry out a radical re-organisation'.[53] From this point onwards Torp initiated a series of reviews to examine the organization of the Norwegian armed forces, the making of policy and the primary issue of Norway's liberation.[54]

Out of this emerged important changes that would assist in the advent of closer relations with SOE. The first was the re-establishment of *Forsvarets Overkommando* (FO) on 6 February 1942 under Major-General Wilhelm Hansteen, the newly appointed Norwegian defence-chief, who became responsible to the minister of defence for all three Norwegian fighting services. FO was charged with coordinating and organizing 'everything on the Norwegian side as best possible for the liberation of Norway', including *Milorg*, and through preparation ensuring 'the greatest consideration of Norwegian interests and the best possible utilisation of the Norwegian contribution to the process of liberation'. In March 1942, FO consisted of five departments, which by August 1942 had been extended to six. FO 1 was responsible for administration; FO II, intelligence; FO III, land and air operations; FO IV, sea operations; FO V, information; and FO VI, signals. There was also a separate department FO-H responsible for relations with the Home Front.[55] Second, the policy reviews that were undertaken concluded that Norway's greatest direct military contribution to its liberation would be through the potential manpower reserves within *Milorg*.[56] Importantly, this was a view that fitted in well with SOE's aim of using a clandestine army to assist and support an eventual Allied landing in the country.

The first meeting of the ANCC was held on 16 February 1942 and included representatives from both SOE and FO. Hambro, Sporborg and later Brigadier Colin McV. Gubbins, all senior staff within SOE, were members of the committee at various times, which illustrates the importance that the British attached to this collaborative mechanism. From the Norwegian High Command, there was Leif Tronstad and Thore Boye. Captain John Rognes and Lt. Commander Marstrander joined the committee as representatives soon afterwards. Its membership would evolve over the next three years.[57] The ANCC has been described as the basis for trustful cooperation at the highest level,[58] and an important forum for the coordination of Norwegian and British policy on resistance, which ultimately bore rich fruit.[59] These are both correct and the regular meetings of the committee, initially once every two weeks, later once a month, through to the end of the war indicate the significance placed on this new machinery as a means to ensuring shared control of subversive operations in Norway.

It was through the forum of the ANCC that FO affirmed its responsibility for the Norwegian volunteers who were sent to Norway on behalf of SOE. From the spring of 1942, therefore, all the recruits in NIC (1) and NNIU were subject to Norwegian military discipline instigated under the authority of the Norwegian commander-in-chief. It was also decided that the military bases, such as STS26, although under British 'operational command' would be run with the cooperation of the Norwegian authorities.[60] It was the ANCC that became the collaborative mechanism that oversaw the administration of these military units and bases. Most significantly, it was also the body that over the next three years supervised sabotage and clandestine activities in Norway, including the organization of a secret army, with responsibility 'on the one hand to the Norwegian High Command and on the other to the COS'.[61]

Closer cooperation between SOE and the Norwegian authorities was not, however, only administratively based but also founded on a parity in policy, especially when it concerned long-term aims. Towards the end of 1941, the Norwegian government set up two committees to examine the issues surrounding a future 're-conquest' of Norway. The first committee examined Norway's economic and strategic significance in the ongoing war, while the second examined the Home Front and the Norwegian military forces in Britain.[62] In January 1942, the second committee produced its report.[63] An extract from this paper and other documents produced soon afterwards, which examined similar issues, were sent to Charles Hambro at the end of March.[64] They concluded that the cooperation of *Milorg* would be 'of such great importance for the re-conquest of Norway that every effort should be made to make its contribution as effective and extensive as possible'. Nevertheless, it was to take up arms 'only in conjunction with an invasion aiming at a permanent re-conquest of the whole country or a major part of it'.[65] This was remarkably close to SOE's view by this time that the future role of a clandestine army would be 'to assist Allied military operations designed to lead to the re-conquest of Norway from the Germans', although it 'must on no account be called out prematurely or for any insignificant military operation'.[66] In April, in a ten-page reply to the Norwegian surveys, SOE declared that part of its role in preparing for the reconquest of Norway would be assistance in long-term planning where it concerned 'the Military organisation in Norway'.[67] Therefore, although there were still issues to be resolved over the future contribution of *Milorg*, especially in the period prior to a liberation, SOE and the Norwegian military authorities in London had very similar long-term aims.

The Norwegian position on short-term activity in Norway, *coup de main* attacks and local sabotage was not, however, as compatible. Nevertheless, with the formation of FO and through the ANCC, the Norwegian military authorities became directly involved with SOE operations carried out by teams sent from the UK against sites that were of agreed economic or military value to the enemy. There was Norwegian involvement in the preparations for SOE's first *coup de main* operation in Norway – Operation Redshank – an attack against the transportation of pyrites from the Orkla pyrite mine near Trondheim. It was jointly sanctioned on 8 April.[68] From May 1942, when the first SOE *coup de main* attack against a major industrial target in Norway was undertaken, such operations were overseen by the ANCC, prepared jointly by SOE and FO, used NIC (1) teams consisting of recruits from the Norwegian army transported from the UK primarily on Norwegian fishing boats and had the authority of the Norwegian commander-in-chief behind them. According to Harry Sporborg, all operational orders were submitted to the Norwegians for countersignature and according to Lt. Col. Wilson, General Hansteen approved all suggestions put to him for *coup de main* operations.[69]

FO also had available Norwegian expertise through, as will be shown, very important figures such as Professor Leif Tronstad and Lt. Jan Reimers, who had significant technical and local knowledge. SOE chose many of its objectives in Norway from an industrial target list that was created with the help of FO and the MEW. The list contains forty-one targets in Norway, headed by the Knaben molybdenum mine in southern Norway. Next to each target in columns headed 'Norge FO', 'MEW' and 'SOE' is either a yes to confirm whether each party has agreed each target.[70] If it was believed, however, that these operations were more damaging to Norwegian interests than the German war effort the Norwegian authorities would not hesitate to object,[71] and as a result some of them were scaled back.[72] Nonetheless, over the following two and half years through its military authorities, the Norwegian government actively assisted and thereby indirectly gave approval to *coup de main* operations in Norway. This is not to say that all ministers were aware beforehand of each operation, for security reasons alone that would have been unacceptable and unnecessary. The government had specifically created FO to represent Norwegian interests with its allies on military matters, including subversive activities, and this it did both effectively and within an overall climate of cooperation.

There was, however, a twin-track approach to the implementation of sabotage in Norway. Although specialist teams from outside would undertake planned *coup de main* attacks against the most important economic targets, it was also intended that there would be an ongoing campaign of small-scale 'unobtrusive' sabotage undertaken by groups or individuals within Norway.[73] One of SOE's objectives was to set up within the occupied countries 'a system for the development of active sabotage', organized from and in touch with Britain, but using the local population to carry out attacks against identified targets.[74] Nevertheless, in autumn 1941, when relations with the Norwegian authorities were at a critical stage, and in recognition of the 'mixed feelings' and 'misgivings' within the Norwegian government owing to its concerns over reprisals against the local population and potential damage to *Milorg*, SOE decided to sideline 'immediate' and local sabotage. For the time being, only prepared and trained teams sent in from outside, under the authority of a joint committee, would undertake planned attacks against important strategic targets in Norway.[75] It is important to emphasize, therefore, that in contrast to previous assertions,[76] SOE put to one side its plans to organize a separate sabotage organization inside the country. Collaboration came at a cost and as a consequence policy was modified. But this was a relatively small price to pay in order to obtain the support and cooperation that was critical for the successful implementation of its plans for Norway.

SOE and Norwegian authorities, 1943–5: From collaboration to partnership

Between 1942 and 1945, the Norwegian Defence High Command (FO) became an increasingly multifaceted organization, which led to both advances in its policy on subversive activities and in its relationship to SOE. Moreover, its positive approach to collaboration helped to facilitate the significant increase in sabotage and subversion in Norway during the final year of its occupation and was critical in organizing the important role that was delegated to *Milorg* at the liberation.

Relations between SOE and Norwegian authorities were not only ongoing in London during the war but also in Stockholm, from where a significant proportion of special operations in Norway were instigated. Remoteness from London, which made control more difficult, and lacking a mechanism such as the ANCC through which collaboration could be formally conducted meant that contact generally operated at a personal level. It was therefore regularly subject to local difficulties between certain individuals. Nevertheless, while SOE and FO worked together closely and centrally made joint decisions on subversive activities in Norway, the problematic relationship in Stockholm had little, if any, impact on the development of policy, although it often made the implementation of operations more troublesome.

SOE Mission that was set up at the British Legation in Stockholm in the autumn of 1940 was important. It was only a train or car journey from the border, which made contact and communication with Norway easier. It therefore became an additional route through which SOE attempted to exercise direct control over resistance organizations in the country. Operations were often instigated or concluded in Stockholm, and it was a point from which couriers could be sent across the frontier to deliver materials and retrieve intelligence. The Norwegian authorities also opened a Military Office in the Norwegian Legation under their Military Attaché. It also used couriers to communicate with groups in Norway, made contact with *Milorg* and collected intelligence. It remained *in situ* until the spring of 1943 when it was reformed along the lines of FO in London. From then on, communication with *Milorg* and cooperation with SOE became the responsibility of a new department, *Militærkontoret IV* (MI IV). The first Military Attaché was Oscar Strugstad, followed in March 1941 by A. R. Roscher-Lund and in the autumn of 1941 by Ingvald Smith-Kielland. From spring 1941, Paal Frisvold became the contact with *Milorg*, while Ørnulf Dahl concentrated on intelligence. In the summer of 1942, Lasse Heyerdahl-Larsen replaced Frisvold. In the spring of 1943, Colonel Ole Berg became Military Attaché, and the Military Office was reorganized with MI IV placed under Lasse Heyerdahl-Larsen, and MI II under Ornulf Dahl. At the end of 1943, Axel Baumann replaced Heyerdahl-Larsen, until the spring of 1945 when Lieutenant-Colonel Arnold Rørholt replaced him.[77]

The relationship between SOE Mission and the Military Office at the Norwegian Legation never replicated the formal and organized collaboration that developed in London. During the period from the autumn of 1940 to the summer of 1941, Malcolm Munthe ran his own show and was extremely sceptical of the staff at the Norwegian Legation describing them as 'uninspired, nervous of reprisals and lacking in initiative'.[78] The Norwegian representatives also expressed their disquiet with the extent and nature of the subversive activities that were being carried out in Norway. Munthe was actually advised that the Legation had complained through the government in London that there were a large number of organizations working in Norway on sabotage. SOE was puzzled by this complaint, as they were not aware of any other organizations, other than themselves, carrying out sabotage.[79] There appears to be no evidence of an effort or even an inclination from either SOE or Norwegian authorities to cooperate or coordinate their work at this time. Furthermore, from the late spring of 1941, exactly as in London and using individual contacts, SOE set out to assert direct influence over resistance groups in Norway. When it was recommended to the Norwegian government that Paal Frisvold, the *Milorg* pioneer who fled to Stockholm in late March 1941, should be appointed to liaise with *Milorg's* leadership in Oslo, SOE attempted to bring him under its wing, very much as it had with John Rognes in London.[80]

Therefore, and despite cooperation between Frisvold and Hugh Marks in SOE Mission being described as 'splendid',[81] by December 1941 it was felt that the relations in Stockholm should be placed on a more structured footing. Consequently, Daniel Ring, yet another *Milorg* veteran, was sent to Sweden to liaise between the Norwegian Legation and SOE Mission in the recruitment of agents, establishment of contacts in Norway, choice of routes for agents, provision of equipment, necessary papers and money.[82] Although this was an attempt to improve matters, it was still built on individual contacts and appears to have had limited success. Consequently, despite the formation of the ANCC leading to formalized collaboration in London, relations in Stockholm remained difficult.[83]

Edgar Nielsen, Mark's successor, visited SOE HQ in the autumn of 1942 and returned to Stockholm apparently with a determination to achieve the same unity 'of purpose' as in London.[84] Attempts were also made to impose a more structured relationship when in November 1942 General Hansteen issued an instruction that agents arriving in Stockholm were the responsibility of SOE, should report to the British Legation before the Norwegian Legation and that there should be 'the best possible cooperation with the British'.[85] Nevertheless, by early March 1943, FO felt that there was an urgent need for a joint British-Norwegian organization, a branch of the ANCC, to oversee SOE and FO activities out of Stockholm, although unfortunately it appears nothing came of this suggestion.[86]

Despite the setting up of MI IV under Lasse Heyerdahl-Larsen, which was made responsible for working with SOE Mission, and a joint SOE and Norwegian decision to replace Daniel Ring with Sverre Ellingsen, who would liaise between the two parties in Stockholm, relations remained troubled.[87] During 1943 and into 1944, Edgar Nielsen continued to complain about the nature of cooperation in Stockholm. Perhaps more significantly, because it indicated a personal prejudice, he also expressed a distrust of Norwegians who he felt were not pulling their weight. Negative feelings were, however, not unique to the British. Jens Christian Hauge later described Nielsen 'as never really co-operative'.[88]

Although relations in Stockholm remained problematic, however, this does not appear to have had a direct impact at a policy level. Operations from Sweden into Norway either to carry out sabotage or organize local resistance groups continued and grew in number as the war progressed.[89] Sverre Ellingsen, based at the Norwegian Legation, and Edgar Nielsen often worked together in order to instigate some of these operations.[90] Both SOE and FO also recognized that there were difficulties and regularly attempted to find ways to overcome them, but while there was collaboration in London, where policy was formulated, the problems in Stockholm remained no more than a local complication. Nevertheless, this was not an ideal background for a coordinated implementation of clandestine activities into Norway from Sweden, especially during the final year of the war when the intensity and number of these operations increased significantly. Consequently, and perhaps reflecting a lack of confidence in conditions in Stockholm, SOE and FO staff officers were sent out from London in an attempt to ensure coordination and organization of effort. In mid-December 1944, Major H. A. Nyberg arrived in Stockholm to, among other matters, 'strengthen co-operation between SOE Mission, Westfield Mission [OSS], Major Baumann, and other Norwegian authorities'. In March 1945, Captain J. H. Reimers from FO was sent out to Stockholm to oversee the 'Antipodes' operations and work with Lt. Colonel F. W. Ram, who had by this stage taken on Nyberg's liaison duties.[91] In effect, the close collaboration between SOE and FO in London was eventually exported to Stockholm.

Meanwhile in the UK, cooperation between SOE and the Norwegian military authorities strengthened and between 1943 and 1945 it developed into what is probably best described as a partnership. This was symbolized by the growing synergy between the administrative infrastructures of both SOE's Norwegian section and FO.

In March 1942, soon after the establishment of FO, a small office entitled O II was set up to take care of issues concerning the Homefront. It consisted of three officers: Jacob Schive, responsible for charting *Milorg*; Leif Tronstad, with responsibility for the Linge personnel and the Shetlands Base; and John Rognes, who was responsible for obtaining equipment and instructors for *Milorg*.[92] It was also this department that initially worked directly with SOE. By the summer of 1942, however, SOE felt that with the number of issues that were being handled it would be valuable to have a Norwegian officer to work in its Norwegian section. This request was, nevertheless, turned down within SOE owing to the precedent it was feared it would set with other countries, where relations were not necessarily as close. Nonetheless, it was agreed that a liaison officer could be appointed to approve coordination between the two parties. Whether this happened on an 'official' basis is uncertain, but clearly SOE was prepared to work extremely closely with the Norwegian authorities.[93]

In December 1942, however, there was a major reorganization within FO. Department, FO IV, which had originally been responsible for naval operations, absorbed O II and, under the leadership of Lieutenant-Colonel Bjarne Øen, took on responsibility for operations of a purely military nature and also of a 'special' nature in Norway in the period prior to the liberation. Øen also became a member of the ANCC and over the next two and half years established a close working relationship with SOE's Lt. Colonel Wilson.[94] FO IV gradually expanded and by the summer of 1944 the office was divided into three sections that were responsible for administration, assistance with military plans especially those concerning *Milorg* and SOE and work on *coup de main* operations and preparations for the protection of Norwegian industry. Six district specialists were also employed to cover the various regions of Norway.[95]

In June 1944, a further collaborative step was taken. On the recommendation of SOE, a process began which led to the amalgamation of its Norwegian section staff with that of FO IV in offices at 17 Oxford Square in London. By this time, with the involvement of the American Office of Strategic Services (OSS), it was believed that the time was right to establish a 'joint Anglo-American-Norwegian staff'. As FO IV had been associated 'more and more in the intelligence, planning and carrying out' of joint activities in Norway, and with the level of understanding achieved it was believed best to form a joint organization 'to control resistance in Norway on behalf of SHAEF'.[96] Over the next two months therefore, with the support of the Norwegian authorities, plans were put together and approval sought for the creation of a single office. This was eventually given in principle on 28 August 1944.[97] By the final twelve months of the war, therefore, SOE and the Norwegian military authorities at an administrative level were as one. This was to be particularly valuable during 1944 and 1945 when there was a huge increase in both the number and complexity of sabotage and protective operations in Norway as well as a major effort to prepare *Milorg* in time for the liberation.

Relations between SOE and the Norwegian military authorities also flourished because they agreed over the nature of their relationship and continued to share the same broad objectives. Both parties persisted with their long-term goal of preparing a secret army that could assist with the liberation and the restoration of a free and independent Norway. SOE accepted that this would be done in the 'name of the Norwegian C-in-C',[98] even though 'the war against the enemy' had to be 'continued on the basis of the strategic considerations laid down by the Chiefs of Staff'. It was also still fully aware that it 'could not carry out any work against the enemy in Norway without the services of Norwegian army and navy personnel'.[99] Moreover, within FO IV it was acknowledged that the Allies had 'the supreme leadership of the war', the means to conduct the war and that to protect Norwegian interests it must 'co-operate as openly as possible'. It also agreed that SOE was responsible to the COS and that it would carry out operations in Norway on their instruction.[100]

While SOE and the Norwegian military authorities became close bedfellows, however, *Milorg* was slower to join the partnership. During most of 1942 communication and relations with its leadership in Oslo remained problematic, and the view of SOE was that 'the stage had not yet been reached' when it was 'under the direction and control of the Norwegian High Command in London'.[101] From the autumn of 1942, however, communication and contact began to improve and in May 1943, after a meeting at Köpmannabro in Värmland in Sweden with members of FO IV, *Milorg* accepted its subservience to the military authorities in London when it was agreed that only FO could decide if and to what degree it would go into action.[102] In these circumstances, it was imperative for SOE to continue its close association with FO.

The Norwegian military authorities also recognized that *Milorg* lacked weapons, equipment and officers, and that there was an urgent need for instructors from outside.[103] To achieve this, British support through SOE was vital. Moreover, from the summer of 1942, SOE had already come to accept that it should 'meet the requests of the Norwegian High Command and SNM [*Milorg*] for assistance in the provision of trained personnel, arms and transportation'.[104] There was also a shared commitment to the role that it was believed this force would eventually undertake. At a further conference in Sweden in March 1944, between representatives of *Milorg* and FO IV and including Bjarne Øen and Jens Chr. Hauge, it was agreed that the organization [*Milorg*] would be of most service by 'making preparations for a military state of readiness, which can be utilised as a link in larger plans, when the liberation draws near'.[105] In September 1944, in its directive to the resistance in Norway, SFHQ echoed this view when it prioritized the preparation of resistance groups in readiness to act as a protective force during the potentially chaotic period in the early hours or days after a final German surrender or collapse.[106]

Unlike the aim of organizing a clandestine army, however, the Norwegian government continued to face difficulties over sabotage. Strong opposition to such activities from the Norwegian Home Front, including *Milorg*, until well into 1943 meant that the government had to remain cautious in its approach to this issue. It was caught between its obligation to ensure that it was in touch with and represented the immediate interests of the Norwegian people, and its obligation to contribute as best possible to the Allied defeat of Germany and thereby the liberation of Norway. In the case of sabotage, it was difficult to satisfy both these requirements. This was illustrated during the summer of 1942 when owing to the action of a Communist group in Oslo, the civilian resistance leadership in Norway wrote to their government protesting strongly against acts that had severe consequences for the civilian population. In response, the Norwegian government set out its position on sabotage to the resistance leadership, the people back home and its British ally.[107] In August, Trygve Lie had a meeting with Laurence Collier, the British ambassador to Norway, during which he declared that Norway's policy was to support 'warlike action from outside' but not to encourage patriots in Norway 'to commit isolated acts of sabotage'.[108] This was confirmed soon after in a letter to the Soviet ambassador, in which Lie protested against radio broadcasts from Moscow that apparently encouraged random acts of violence. The letter, however, also confirmed that Norway 'was prepared to undertake certain acts of sabotage in so far that these would be of real military significance'.[109] In a BBC radio broadcast by the Norwegian prime minister in early September, he also emphasized his government's opposition to 'individual actions that did not serve any useful purpose'.[110] Soon after, a concerned British Foreign Office asked SOE to clarify its position on sabotage in Norway. In a terse reply, SOE confirmed that only teams from outside undertook such acts, and these would leave signs to indicate that it was personnel sent into the country that were behind the activities. Everything was done with the approval of the ANCC and General Hansteen. Significantly, the civilian population was not encouraged 'to indulge in acts of sabotage'.[111]

Nevertheless, in light of certain SOE/FO and Combined Operations actions in Norway that led, for example, in October 1942 to the German authorities declaring a state of emergency in the county of Trøndelag, around Trondheim, and eventually executing thirty-four Norwegians,[112] concerns continued within the Norwegian government and Home Front civilian leadership over the issue of active resistance. In early 1943, the civilian resistance leadership protested again to their government – the so-called Partisan letter – about requests from *Milorg* for arms and arms instructors. Members of staff from within FO were called to a government meeting and criticized for their involvement with such activities. And soon after the Norwegian prime minister described both SOE and FO as 'irresponsible'. Trygve Lie also wrote to the resistance leadership denying that the prime minister and himself had any knowledge of these actions beforehand and were therefore not responsible for them, even though FO had sanctioned them under the authority of the minister of defence. He also claimed that they shared the Home Front's view and agreed that people's lives should not be put in danger 'unnecessarily'.[113] In conversations with the British government, however, a different impression was presented. Lie, in a meeting with the British ambassador in October 1942, apparently described the British combined operation, Operation Musketoon, which along with SOE activity led to the tragedy in Trøndelag, as 'a very satisfactory achievement', and that executions 'were what might be expected from the Germans'.[114]

This seeming disparity is explained partly by the existence of different views on this issue within the government but more significantly by a requirement by the Norwegian authorities to take a different approach in its relations with the Home Front from those with its allies. In line with the wishes of the civilian resistance leadership and initially *Milorg* and until political conditions permitted, the government supported non-violent resistance in Norway. This, however, did not mean it opposed all sabotage. Provided attacks were undertaken against legitimate military targets by teams sent in from outside, they were acceptable. This was the line that SOE followed and which allowed it to continue to work closely with the Norwegian military authorities. In April 1943, it confirmed that it was 'SOE and Norwegian policy', not to encourage 'active internal resistance', but to 'carry out certain specific acts of sabotage from outside'.[115] By May 1943, even *Milorg* had accepted that 'in certain specific instances FO will operate actively during the time of waiting', in other words prior to the liberation.[116] In the summer of 1943, a copy of the 'Directive for Future Sabotage Policy for Norway' was sent by Lt. Colonel Wilson to Bjarne Øen with a note stating that he was 'glad to discuss it', exemplifying the commitment to ensuring that both parties worked together on this issue. In January 1944, Lt. Colonel Wilson also stoutly defended the Norwegian government's approach to sabotage, arguing it had never restricted SOE activity.[117] Although this is an exaggeration, it nevertheless reflects the determination to present a shared view on this difficult matter and a strong desire within SOE to defend its Norwegian partner.

During 1944, however, sabotage policy changed due to a transformation in the attitude of the resistance leadership. This will be examined in more depth in the next chapter, which deals with the impact of conditions and the development of resistance in occupied Norway on SOE activities. What is apparent, however, is that the positive approach to cooperation taken by the Norwegian authorities also meant that SOE did not have the difficult task of working with a troublesome ally. It eventually had a partner that took the view that the best way to protect Norwegian interests was by making an active and positive contribution to the war effort. Relations with resistance groups within occupied Norway were, however, far more problematic and difficult.

Chapter 4

SOE AND THE MILITARY RESISTANCE IN NORWAY, 1940-5: DIRECTION, SEPARATION AND FINALLY PARTNERSHIP

It was not only the SOE's relationship with the Norwegian government in exile that shaped the nature and intensity of its activities in Norway but also its interaction with the resistance movements that emerged in response to the country's occupation, particularly *Milorg*. SOE, Norwegian government and *Milorg* all shared the same long-term objective, which was to create a clandestine army that would eventually support British or Allied forces in the liberation of the country. *Milorg's* view on the nature and role of this underground army in the period prior to an expected Allied landing or German collapse was, however, at least until 1943, in several ways at odds with SOE.

Milorg was a centralized organization – for security reasons an anathema to SOE – covering a large part of southern Norway and with a leadership in Oslo. After its central council, *Rådet*, had made contact with the Norwegian authorities in London and been recognized as the 'official' military resistance it, however, had an important voice, which it used to articulate its views on its future role, and a leadership that began to resist attempts by SOE to control it.[1] Initially the resistance movements within the country, with the exception of Communist groups, were opposed to armed and violent action that could lead to severe reprisals from the occupying regime. The view within *Milorg* was that a clandestine army should remain underground, unarmed and not become involved in military actions before the arrival of Allied forces – not really an army at all. This quickly put it at variance with SOE and ultimately contributed to the British and Norwegian decision to restrict sabotage to *coup de main* operations carried out by teams sent in from the UK. Only in the final year of the war when the resistance leadership, owing to internal political pressures, changed policy did *Milorg* work in tandem with SOE in the implementation of sabotage. It also finally, after long wait, came to play a significant but sometimes overplayed role in Norway's largely peaceful and uneventful liberation.

SOE and military resistance in Norway 1940–1: Control over long-term policy

An understanding of the nature of the occupation of Norway in the summer of 1940 and the forms of resistance that this gave rise to helps explain the initial difficulties that arose in relations between SOE and *Milorg*. Not all facets of resistance to the German occupation are pertinent here, however, and have been extensively written about before.[2] Nevertheless, an understanding of the origins of *Milorg* will help to explain its initial attitude towards clandestine activities, which were so out of line with those of SOE.

Resistance in Norway after the German occupation in the spring of 1940 was stimulated and shaped by political events within the country, specifically those that occurred during the following summer. These were the negotiations (*Riksrådforhandlingene*) between the German *Reichskommisar*, Josef Terboven, and the Presidential Board of the Norwegian Storting to establish a new constitutional government in Norway, and which included a request to King Haakon and the government in London to step down. The king rejected this invitation and the negotiations were finally ended on 25 September when Terboven banned all political parties in Norway except the *Nasjonal Samling* (NS),[3] the Norwegian Nazi party led by Vidkun Quisling. Quisling formed NS in 1933, although it had little political significance until the arrival of the Germans. An extreme right-wing nationalist party, it aroused through Quisling hatred and resistance among the Norwegian people.[4] From this point, the German occupying regime through NS set out to form a 'national socialist state' in Norway.[5] Although there were many acts of individual and spontaneous protest in the country from the early months and throughout the occupation, including publically performing the king's song and the Norwegian national anthem, cutting the hair of someone who had had a relationship with a German and refusing to sit next to Germans and Norwegian Nazis on trams and buses,[6] by the summer of 1940 a small and central resistance leadership had appeared in response to these developments. This group, often referred to as the 'Organisation' or 'R-Group' located in Oslo close to political events, consisted of important figures such as Paal Berg, president of the Supreme Court, and Labour politician

Einar Gerhardsen. The aim at this point was to form a network around which future resistance could be built.[7] From an early stage, therefore, there were signs that resistance in Norway would be both organized and centralized. And by the spring of 1941, the two resistance movements that would dominate occupied Norway over the following years, the civilian-based resistance and the military-based resistance, eventually known as *Sivorg* and *Milorg*, respectively, had begun to take shape.[8]

In the broadest terms, the civilian resistance movement took the form of an unarmed but organized and active 'rejection of the Nazi ideology as it was expressed in Norway', and which is described by Norwegian historians as the *Holdningskamp*. It was fundamentally political and the 'dominant' form of resistance within the country. Two organizations were behind civilian resistance in Norway. First, the *Koordinasjonskomite* (KK), the Co-ordination Committee, that was formed in the autumn of 1941 and which directed the civilian resistance movement within Norway. Second, the *Kretsen* that was made up from a circle of leading figures in the country, such as Paal Berg and which gathered in Oslo from June 1941. This group became the body within Norway that communicated with the London government on political matters regarding the Home Front and immediate post-war constitutional issues.[9] Military resistance crystallized around *Milorg*, an illegal and underground organization that began to develop from late 1940, and which as seen set out to create a 'clandestine army' that would be preserved intact to assist in its country's eventual liberation.[10]

The relationship between these two movements, despite some difficulties in 1943, was never plagued by ongoing conflict. By late 1943, they were working together and the leadership of both had formed a close understanding. Nevertheless, it was the civilian resistance leadership that took the title *Hjemmefrontens Ledelse*, the Homefront Leadership (HL), and was recognized as the national leadership within Norway with the 'right to represent and speak on behalf of occupied society', while *Milorg* remained directly subservient to FO in London. During the winter of 1944/5, however, in the critical period running up to the liberation, a new structured and formalized HL was formed, which represented the various groups in Norway, including *Milorg*. It had a central committee that met weekly and an *arbeidsutvalg*, a working committee consisting of four members including Jens Chr. Hauge, head of *Milorg*, which met daily.[11] Resistance in Norway was therefore ordered, developed good working relations with the government in London and was not extensively driven by factions or internal feuding. Consequently, SOE did not have to confront a difficult political background, something that often complicated and degraded its activities in other occupied countries across Europe. Nevertheless, it did have to contend with resistance movements that had strong leaders who were prepared to articulate and defend their position on the role that they believed their organizations should play in occupied Norway and which had the ear of their legitimate government in London.

There were, however, several Communist resistance groups within occupied Norway that did not conform to the careful and predominately non-violent line followed by *Sivorg* and *Milorg*. Their activities also had an impact on the development of resistance policy, and therefore on SOE. The most prominent and influential faction was the 'Osvald Group', which was a continuation of a Norwegian offshoot of the Wollweber Organization, an anti-fascist group created in 1935 by the People's Commissariat for Internal Affairs (NKVD), the Soviet secret service. It aimed to continue the struggle against fascism through active measures, initially ship sabotage, and prepare the way for partisan or guerrilla warfare behind the frontline in a future world war. Consequently, after the German invasion of the Soviet Union, there was a Communist organization already in place within Norway that was prepared to take action against the occupying regime. It carried out its first operation on 21 July 1941 and over 100 further attacks in Norway, largely against the railways, before it was wound down in 1944. Although it was directly linked to the NKVD, the group also had contact with the Norwegian Communist Party (NKP) and from 1942 operated as its sabotage organization. Other Communist sabotage groups were also formed, such as the *Pelle Group* in Oslo and *Saborg* in Bergen, which had links to the NKP and continued the tradition of open and violent resistance to the German occupation. Unlike other countries in Europe, however, the Communist movement in Norway remained peripheral and was never represented within HL. Nevertheless, the Communist's 'active' approach to resistance was eventually to have consequences for *Milorg* and its relationship with SOE, although unlike other countries in occupied Europe it never had a major impact on SOE's plans for this theatre.[12]

In the autumn of 1940, members of the embryonic resistance leadership that had gathered in Oslo included army officers such as Major Olav Helset and Captain John Rognes, who had fought during the previous spring. They had been imprisoned but released after eventually pledging not to take up arms against the German occupiers. Norwegian officers were initially put in a prisoner-of-war camp at Grini outside Oslo. After signing a declaration not to take up arms against the German occupiers, most were allowed to leave. Helset and Rognes initially refused to sign the declaration, but after Otto Ruge, the commander-in-chief of Norwegian forces during the spring campaign, agreed to remain in captivity as a form of pledge on behalf of all officers, they backed down[13] During the winter of 1940-1 these men and other army officers, sometimes connected to the Norwegian General Staff from before the occupation, began to form an underground military organization within Norway by contacting and pulling together the many small informal groups of army veterans that had come together across the country after the fighting had concluded the previous June. The important *Milorg* pioneers included Lt. Col. Ole Berg, a divisional head in the Norwegian Army High Command during operations in southern Norway and later head of the 6th Brigade in northern Norway; Professor Johan Holst, head of the Army Medical Service in spring 1940; Lt-Colonel Johan Beichman, former member of the Norwegian General staff who in 1942 became head of the Norwegian Army High Command; Lieutenant Paal Frisvold, a former general staff officer; Captain Lasse Heyerdahl-Larsen who had led a Company; and Captain Jacob Schive who had also fought in the spring of 1940.[14] Legitimacy was given to this process when in October 1940 General Otto Ruge, while in prison,[15] passed on his authority to these *Milorg* pioneers. At the time, however, he spoke of only undertaking military appraisals, which was interpreted as a call for unarmed resistance and not action.[16] Consequently, *Milorg's* leadership was founded upon the experiences of the spring of 1940 and predominately influenced by men whose background was within the pre-war Norwegian military structure, which was set up to create a mobilization army that would only form in the event of an invasion.[17] At the beginning, therefore, *Milorg* was built on the conviction that it would only go into action to support major operations to reoccupy the country.[18]

Through the winter of 1940-1, small groups slowly came together in the provinces under local leadership and were organised into five *kampgrupper* (fighting groups) that corresponded to the country's old pre-war divisional borders, a process that has been described as an 'illegal re-forming of the Norwegian army'. Attempts were also made to link these groups to the central leadership that was gradually taking shape in Oslo, although at this early stage contact was tenuous.[19] This incipient organization eventually decided that it needed to formalize its leadership so that it could 'take a position on all the principal questions, appoint those that would occupy the leading positions within the organisation, and execute control over operations'.[20] Consequently, around Easter 1941 the military council (the *Råd*) was formed to act as the highest executive authority. Under this an administrative infrastructure was also gradually put in place to run the organization consisting of an organiser (O); a chief for fighting, signals and pioneer groups (I); and a chief of supplies and transport (II). Altogether this became known as the *Sentralledelse*, Central Leadership (SL).[21] By the late spring of 1941, therefore, *Milorg* was developing into a hierarchical organization based in Oslo, but with only weak links to regional groups in southern Norway. In October 1941, it was claimed that the organization could call on between 20 and 25,000 volunteers, although at this stage these numbers probably consisted of no more than lists of names. There were also only a few officers and with the exception of batches of rifles that had been hidden away after the campaign in 1940, the men were largely unarmed.[22] By the autumn of 1941, therefore, although *Milorg* was an organization with potentially considerable manpower reserves, it was a long way from constituting an underground army.

Between the autumns of 1940 and 1941, SOE attempted to make use of, develop and control 'anti-Nazi' groups within occupied Norway.[23] Its initial policy of instigating a rebellion meant that even while *Milorg* was in its embryonic state, SOE had attempted to make contact with and direct local resistance organizations. Through the Norwegian Expedition in the summer of 1940, Section D initially had made contact with groups in the Bergen area and established six arms dumps around Voss.[24] SOE planned to get in touch with individuals or groups that might be used to form military cadres, trained units that would stimulate and eventually lead an uprising by the civilian population across Norway. A lot of the early work was done through Malcolm Munthe in Stockholm, although at this stage of the German occupation resistance in the regions of Norway was still small-scale, local and improvised, and therefore his contacts, with the exception of those in Trondheim, do not appear to have led anywhere.[25] They do, however, illustrate that SOE was anxious to link up with any rudimentary group that it could eventually use for its own purposes.

In SOE's first directive one of the aims was to make the ground ready for offensive operations in southern Norway, and this included preparing an 'organisation' that could cooperate with British forces.[26] This was immediately reflected in SOE's plans for Norway. From December, the intention was that a separate 'anti-Nazi' organization, a euphemism for armed resistance groups, would be prepared in each region, from Bodø north of Trondheim and across the main strategic areas of Norway, including Oslo. SOE was aware that in the capital there was already the 'nucleus of an organisation' and this would be 'fostered', although on 'somewhat special lines'. This rather cryptic language probably refers to *Milorg*. The regional organizations would be formed from groups that SOE was either already in touch with, as in Trondheim, or where there was no organization, new ones would be established. Each organization would be kept in contact with SOE through Stockholm or across the North Sea and 'carefully picked members' from each group would be sent to the Shetlands for training.[27]

Consequently, from the autumn of 1940 and during the following eighteen months, attempts were made to send agents to western and southern Norway to contact or form local resistance groups.[28] Efforts were also made during 1941 to bring back parties to Britain from Norway, which after training would return home to help organize and lead the preparation of local networks. Moreover, contact was made with the *Milorg* leadership in Oslo, and as with other organizations it was also requested to send back officers for 'preparation'.[29] SOE's objective was to 'direct' the 'operations' of all these organizations in readiness for a 'simultaneous uprising all over Norway on the occasion of, but on no account in advance of, either a landing by an Allied expeditionary force, or an incipient German collapse'.[30]

From the spring of 1941, therefore, two organizations were taking the first small steps towards organizing a clandestine army in Norway. SOE wanted to create an armed and fully prepared military force, based on any suitable organization it was in contact with, and which could eventually be used to operate in tandem with regular units. Alongside this a group of pre-war officers in Oslo was in the early stages of preparing an illegal underground army, which would only be mobilized to assist the expected Allied reoccupation of Norway or after a possible German withdrawal. They did not, however, despite sharing a similar long-term objective, succeed at this stage in working together harmoniously. A number of issues including SOE's determination to assert control, whether or not a clandestine army should be armed and trained in readiness to support operations by regular forces and whether or not it should become active in the period prior to the country's reoccupation, all led to disagreement.

SOE's attitude towards resistance groups in Norway was that it would 'sponsor any responsible organisations of sufficient size to be useful'.[31] Therefore, until the autumn of 1941, its policy was, through employing ex-*Milorg* pioneers in London and Stockholm and using couriers from the Shetlands and across the Swedish border, to make contact with *Milorg*'s leadership in Oslo and thereby incorporate it into its vision of a secret army. SOE used its contact with the Norwegian authorities in

London in order to make use of John Rognes[32] and thus 'bring his whole organisation' under its 'control'.[33] Rognes was from March 1941 initially based on the Shetlands so as to establish a link with the headquarters of *Milorg*,[34] through which 'advice' could be sent to the organization on 'how to proceed' with its work and attempts made to bring back men to be trained as 'instructors' in SOE business'.[35] The original intention was that Rognes would have radio contact with Ålesund on Norway's west coast to help improve communications and thereby strengthen the link with the Shetlands Base. From mid-March, however, communication was established with Oslo through a courier, Arne Ekornes, who had been sent over to the Shetlands by *Milorg*. He arrived for the first time on 16 March on board the 'Sigurd' with a mission from Paal Frisvold. He returned to Norway on 22 March and met Frisvold the day before he fled to Stockholm. He returned from Oslo again on 11 April on a mission from Jacob Schive, Frisvold's replacement.[36]

SOE also hoped to improve contact with Norway and speed up its preparation of resistance groups through a plan to send fishing boats from the Shetlands at fortnightly intervals to predetermined locations on the Norwegian coast. Using the BBC's Norwegian broadcast, the aim was to send a signal five days prior to a boat's arrival in the country. This would have been a real, scheduled 'bus service' if it had ever been implemented.[37] Furthermore, SOE saw Paal Frisvold in Stockholm as someone belonging to an 'organisation' that it was 'working with', and although Frisvold proved less pliant than Rognes he became another route through which the organisation attempted to communicate with and direct *Milorg*.[38]

SOE's activities in Norway, however, soon led to expressions of concern. It became evident during the spring of 1941 that there were reservations in Oslo over what SOE was trying to do, although initially *Milorg* reluctantly continued to go along with British requests and agreed to send groups over to the UK for specialist training. Arne Ekornes reported that Frisvold, before he left for Sweden, had told him that future work must proceed 'very quietly and slowly' and that weapons must be left to later. He also claimed that Jacob Schive, Frisvold's replacement, had told him that weapons dumps were not welcome and that *Milorg* was not prepared to undertake hostile actions against the Germans. Nevertheless, when Ekornes was in Oslo in March he asked *Milorg*, on behalf of SOE, to send ten men to Britain to be trained as 'instructors' and an attempt was made to pick these men up from the Norwegian coast in early April, but was unsuccessful. Later Jacob Schive was instructed to send eight men to Britain, and these were successfully picked up at the end of May. In June, Munthe was also told to contact Schive and arrange for four wireless operators to travel to Britain for six weeks' training.[39]

With the formation of *Rådet*, its military council, however, *Milorg* not only began to take control of its own activities, but it also started to assert its own position on key matters. Importantly, it turned to its king and government in London for legitimacy. In June 1941, in its 'report' addressed to King Haakon in London, sent to the Shetlands sewn in the jacket of someone who was travelling to Britain to become a flyer, it stated that weapons should not be delivered until 'immediately' before they were required. It also expressed its strong opposition to sabotage, which it believed would put at risk both its organization and the local population. Its immediate purpose was to provide a military apparatus that would be available to any internal leadership that was recognized and responsible to the king. It was this civilian authority that would decide when it would be used.[40]

SOE's reply to *Milorg*, the revealingly entitled, 'Directive to the Military Organisation in Norway', was sent to Stockholm in August and deciphered and passed to Paal Frisvold. A courier then delivered to Oslo copies of the document, secreted using invisible ink on handkerchiefs. Despite an initial welcoming of *Milorg's* report, it largely rejects the views expressed within it. The directive outlines SOE's objectives in Norway to form a secret army and undermine German fighting capability through sabotage undertaken by teams from outside or by groups within Norway. A clandestine army, however, must receive arms and training 'in advance' so that it could 'play its part at a given signal and in accordance with a pre-arranged plan' for either a separate invasion of Norway or as part of a 'general offensive' and the calling out of secret armies all across Europe. It was also important to carry out sabotage to cause the Germans in Norway 'as much trouble as possible and to force them to keep large garrisons there'. Although SOE recognized that the work had to continue carefully and therefore not put at risk either the resistance groups or the local population, it rejected the unarmed, untrained and passive approach recommended by *Milorg*.[41]

A few weeks later, this divergence of views between SOE and *Milorg* continued when Jacob Schive in Oslo drafted a reply to SOE's directive. In this he states that only 'men living in Norway should be allowed to decide upon the uses to which the Military Organisation could be put', and that the organisation stood directly responsible to the 'King and Government in London'.[42] A conflict over the control and use of *Milorg* was underway.

SOE and Milorg, 1941-2: From control to separation

By the spring of 1941, *Milorg* was a hierarchical organization with a central leadership that began to formulate a position on principle issues such as the supply of weapons and sabotage. Some of its leaders had already been arrested or forced to flee the country, which appeared to justify its careful, go-slow approach to the organization of a secret army. Moreover, in a search for recognition, approval of its views and to strengthen its status with the British, it looked to its government in London for the authority to continue its work.[43] This ultimately resulted in an irrevocable change in its relationship with SOE.

In October 1941, after their arrival in Britain, Jacob Schive and Johan Holst reported on their organization direct to the Norwegian authorities.[44] From this point other members of the Norwegian government, not just its foreign minister, were fully aware of *Milorg's* existence, its work and its difficulties with SOE. Therefore, a decision had to be made about its future. The government concluded that it could not allow a military force to operate in Norway independently, and accordingly it was decided to bring *Milorg* under its control. Consequently, on 20 November 1941, at a meeting of the Norwegian Defence Committee, a resolution was agreed that formally recognized *Milorg* and placed it under the authority of HOK. From February 1942, it would come under FO. In the same resolution, it was also stated that 'all who are involved in military preparations for the fight to free Norway are loyally invited to subordinate themselves to this organisation. They shall be considered as standing under military command'.[45] From then on, *Milorg* was the fourth arm of the Norwegian armed forces and it was the only authorized military resistance movement in Norway. SOE could no longer influence *Milorg* directly or shape it as it wished. It would only be able to achieve its vision of a secret army in Norway through working with FO and using it as a means to bring military resistance in line with British thinking. This proved to be a difficult and problematic process and would ultimately only be successful when *Milorg*, in response to developments within Norway, decided to change.

On 28 October when Harry Sporborg and Malcolm Munthe met Jacob Schive and Johan Holst, Schive again raised *Milorg's* concerns over the issues of sabotage and the supply of arms.[46] In response, through Sir Charles Hambro's memo on Anglo-Norwegian collaboration that led to the formation of the ANCC, SOE acknowledged that it was important to have a system in place that considered the views of the official military resistance. And one of the tasks of a future, joint committee would be to prepare a secret army for action within Norway in conjunction with the heads of this clandestine organization. There were, therefore, signs that SOE was prepared to work with *Milorg*, give it a degree of parity and no longer saw it as simply another indigenous resistance group. Nevertheless, SOE still believed that a future underground army should be based on well-trained and equipped military cadres in each district of Norway, all with radio contact with the UK. It would therefore be a decentralized organization that could be controlled from London to ensure that 'the work in Norway' was kept in line with its 'policy in other parts of occupied Europe'. Hambro's memo also emphasizes that sabotage against key strategic targets would have to be continued but with the important concession that in the future it would be 'confined' to attacks against key targets undertaken by special sabotage teams sent in from the UK. These would be kept separate from the secret army, in order to preserve its integrity, and have the approval of a joint committee.[47] Passive resistance was still acceptable and the commitment to the eventual and 'appropriate' use of 'separate sabotage cells' was held onto within SOE's ranks, but while there was opposition from the Norwegian government and *Milorg*, they would not be developed. SOE, however, did not compromise its belief in a decentralized clandestine army controlled from the UK, which was significantly different from *Milorg*, which wanted a centralized organization that would wait passively for the day when Allied forces arrived and only then receive arms and go into action. The issue was how to accommodate these two different views.

From the late autumn of 1941 and especially after the establishment of the ANCC in February 1942 to 'control the Secret Organisation in Norway',[48] SOE worked closely with the Norwegian military authorities in order to achieve its idea of a guerrilla army. It did not set out to create its own organization separate from *Milorg* that could be 'active' in Norway through sabotage in the period prior to an eventual liberation[49] but decided that a clandestine army in Norway should be built on a combination of local SOE groups and *Milorg* district organizations. SOE objected to *Milorg*'s structure with a leadership based in Oslo that had links to the regions. The arrest of several members of its leadership during 1941[50] was in the eyes of SOE a symptom of the organization's over-centralization and vulnerability. It was considered by some that the *Råd* would be 'of very little use in the event of military operations directed from Britain', and therefore SOE decided it should 'entirely disassociate from the old central organisation in Oslo'. Work would be directed 'for the time being' through individual agents rather than through 'high military personages connected with the Norwegian army'.[51]

SOE wanted a secret army built on local 'guerrilla organisations' in the key strategic areas of the country. They would consist of trained and equipped military cadres, each the nucleus of a military force that could expand if required. These cadres would be made up of small ten-man guerrilla units recruited from local *Milorg* organizations or if necessary independent groups that SOE had set up, and which in support of regular forces could lead attacks against key tactical targets, such as communications and local garrisons.[52]

Consequently, SOE set out to persuade *Milorg* to revert to a more decentralized structure based on separate and independent districts.[53] Each local district would be made up of these cadres of armed and equipped men in contact with an organizer supplied by SOE, if it was believed safe. It would also have propaganda cells tasked with keeping up the morale of the local population, where appropriate separate sabotage cells, and be put in touch with the UK through the provision of radio operators from Britain. *Milorg's* central council would be discouraged from having contact with these districts. Alongside, this SOE also considered itself free to set up its own local groups that would have no contact with *Milorg* units, while specific acts of sabotage would be undertaken by teams sent in from the UK but without the knowledge of the local branch of *Milorg*.[54] In effect, a secret army would consist of both SOE groups and *Milorg* district organizations. They would be kept 'distinct', and there would be no 'crossing of lines', but the intention was that they would be two parts of one clandestine force in Norway.[55]

This vision of a composite and decentralized guerrilla army directed from London was formally and officially recognized in May 1942. At a meeting of the ANCC, attended by General Hansteen, it was agreed that *Milorg* groups, described as the 'Secret Army', and SOE groups, both under the authority of the Norwegian commander-in-chief, should be kept apart until it was decided to combine them. It was, however, also accepted that there could not to be complete separation. Local radio operators, through the use of a 'cut-out', could in exceptional circumstances still serve both organizations, and SOE would provide *Milorg* with arms and demolition instructors. It was also envisaged that small 'guerrilla bands' could be detached from *Milorg* to be trained by SOE to operate in advance of the main *Milorg* forces.[56]

SOE had lost all confidence in *Milorg's* leadership and in June 1942, Lt. Colonel Wilson launched a vitriolic attack against what he described as 'the military clique' of officers that 'demand to be informed of everything that is going' and 'resent outside interference'. To him they were 'amateurs'.⁵⁷ The Norwegian military authorities were also fully aware of the important contribution that *Milorg* could make to an eventual liberation but understood, however, that the organization lacked officers, arms and equipment, and it was nowhere near ready for action. It still needed a great deal of time and preparation to make it ready and it therefore had to be protected. Direct involvement with another organization could threaten its future.⁵⁸ Furthermore, SOE through collaboration was determined to put in place its vision of a secret army, which was based on the concept of using guerrilla units behind enemy lines in support of operations by regular forces. It was an idea that can be traced back at least to the work done within MI (R).⁵⁹

SOE and Milorg 1942-3: A move to integration

In June 1942, Lt. Colonel Wilson wrote, 'SOE's role [was] to endeavour to steer a safe passage amongst all these shoals and difficulties so as to create the maximum opposition and resistance to the enemy in event of an Allied landing.'⁶⁰ Attempts to steer a secret army in Norway composed of two 'distinct'⁶¹organizations, however, quickly proved unrealistic. The leadership of SOE's Norwegian section was also never totally convinced that this approach was viable. In a paper written in late June 1942, Lt. Col. Wilson expressed reservations about allowing two organizations to operate in a country with such a small population,⁶² and by the end of the month, after a series of local difficulties with *Milorg*, he felt that it was impossible 'to keep two or more separate secret organisations from becoming hopelessly entangled'.⁶³ It nevertheless remained essential for SOE to ensure that key military decisions were made in London, not Oslo. Consequently, Lt. Col. Wilson, in a paper produced at the end of June 1942, emphasized the importance of establishing a direct link between the *Milorg* leadership and the 'Norwegian C-in-C' in London through the provision of a radio operator. *Milorg* was a 'latent body' that would come into 'operation' only 'under the instructions' of the Norwegian military authorities in 'the event of an Allied landing'.⁶⁴ Copies of this paper went to Colonel Christophersen in the Norwegian General Staff and to Brigadier Colin Gubbins, SOE's Director of Operations and Training. Gubbins' reply is very revealing and indicative of SOE's attitude. He wrote that SOE was 'to assist Hansteen in every way possible to gain confidence and control of SMO [*Milorg*]', and by doing this SOE would 'eventually have Hansteen and SMO'.⁶⁵ At the heart of

SOE's relationship with both FO and *Milorg* was a resolve to dominate both, and during the first few months of 1942 it was believed that control over the military resistance could best be achieved through direct contact with its local branches and by avoiding the central leadership in Oslo. This policy was, however, abandoned in August 1942. There were two reasons for this. First, with the arrest or departure abroad of many of the leading members of *Milorg* in 1941 a new leadership began to emerge in Oslo that was not as closely linked to the pre-war army. This resulted during 1942 in a series of reforms that led *Milorg* to become what has since been described as a 'countrywide guerrilla organisation', which could support an Allied landing through guerrilla warfare.[66] The five *kampgrupper* were abandoned and *Milorg* was initially reorganized into fourteen districts, numbered eleven to twenty-four, later revised so that the districts were numbered eleven to twenty-seven in southern Norway and forty and forty-one in the north. Each district was made up of smaller administrative and operational units and had a district-chief and staff. The districts were divided into *Avsnitt* (Sections), and *Områder* (Areas), which included small local operational units *Grupper* (Groups) that were made up of two to four *Tropper* (Platoons), which were made up of two to four *Lag* (teams). The team was the smallest fighting unit of six to twelve men.[67] General guidance still emanated from *Milorg's* central leadership through a series of directives. It issued its first 'Directive' in the summer of 1942, which stated that the organization was to prepare 'itself for guerrilla and sabotage actions on an Allied invasion of Norway'. A total of twenty directives were released between the summer of 1942 and the spring of 1945. But importantly, this new structure was a move towards decentralization and therefore a break with the past. Alongside this, *Milorg* also announced that it was prepared to accept weapons and equipment from outside and to allow its men to be trained so that they would be able to support future Allied operations.[68] This reorganization meant that *Milorg* now had a structure and a view of its future role that was more in tune with SOE. Moreover, in spring 1942, in response to the difficulties that had occurred between SOE groups and *Milorg* in Norway, FO decided to send Jacob Schive to Oslo in attempt to improve relations.[69] He met leaders of the Home Front and on his return provided SOE at a meeting with Lt. Col. Wilson and Lt. Col. Sporborg on 13 August with a copy of *Milorg's* first 'General Directive', which set out the changes to the organization, and reported on his visit.[70] After meeting Schive, the attitude within the Norwegian section altered. The opinion was that there had been 'a considerable change for the better', 'safety' was the 'watchword' and importantly

Milorg was prepared to 'receive the orders of General Hansteen as C-in-C'.[71] For SOE, this meant the resistance leadership had become less of a security risk and there were indications that it was prepared to accept central direction. It was also accepted that the decision to allow two secret armies to develop in an occupied country with a small population, such as Norway, had proved unworkable.[72]

In August 1942, in response to these developments, Brigadier Colin Gubbins issued a 'Directive as to Future Policy' in Norway. In this document, *Milorg* is described as an organization of 25,000 members, divided into military districts, and with a leadership that is prepared to receive arms and instruction. It expresses the fear that if SOE agents arrived in the districts without proper accreditation they risked being treated as 'agent provocateurs', and that therefore contact with *Milorg* should be extended with the 'establishment of direct W/T communication, the provision of instructors, and the supply of arms'. Most significantly, in the future *Milorg* and the existing SOE organizations would 'be linked up as far as possible'.[73]

In September 1942, after 'cogitation' on Gubbins directive on Norway, Lt. Col. Wilson issued a paper entitled, 'SOE Long Term Policy in Norway'. This document sets out in more detail SOE's future approach to *Milorg*. With regard to the development of a clandestine army, SOE would endeavour to meet the requests of the Norwegian military authorities in London and *Milorg*, although initiative and planning would remain with SOE, with the agreement of FO. Most importantly, control should not be allowed to pass from 'London to Oslo' as the direction of 'final operations' had to remain 'with the Allied High Command'. Copies of this document were sent to Brigadier Gubbins; Charles Hambro, who by this time was the executive director of SOE; General Hansteen; and to the British and Norwegian Legations in Stockholm. Not everyone accepted its contents; Malcolm Munthe was very critical, arguing that too much power was being placed in the hands of the Norwegian authorities. Nevertheless, the policy on relations with *Milorg* as articulated in this document stayed in place for the remainder of the war.[74]

By late 1942, after a number of shifts in policy, SOE finally accepted that the creation of a clandestine army in Norway had to be a collaborative and joint effort. Its earlier attempts to assert direct control and operate outside the leadership in Oslo had proved unworkable. This collaboration still did not, however, at this stage, extend to sabotage. *Milorg* warned against actions that might lead to reprisals and even requested that 'instructors and other agents that came from Britain must be ordered not to shoot Germans, even in self-defence'.[75] Despite a request by Brigadier Gubbins for an increase in 'incendiarism' and for an attack against a target in the interior of the country to be carried out by an 'existing organisation',[76] SOE also realized that the ANCC had 'in part' to be guided 'by the views of those directing' activity in Norway in working out policy. This meant that at this stage, although 'passive' resistance, the adoption of 'go-slow' methods, was still acceptable, it continued to be only trained teams 'sent over to Norway to do the job' that would undertake sabotage in Norway.[77] Moreover, despite steps forward by the end of 1942, there was still not a unified and prepared underground army in place in Norway.

SOE and Milorg 1943-5: In the shadow of the liberation

Between early 1943 and May 1945, however, the relationship between SOE and *Milorg* developed into an effective and valuable working partnership. Owing to the significant role assigned to clandestine forces during Norway's liberation, this was important. Initially, however, difficulties remained as SOE continued to be concerned about the centralization of *Milorg*. But as contact and communication between FO and Milorg improved, and its leadership in Oslo formally accepted that it had to be subordinate to decisions made in London, relations improved. Moreover, a change in policy by the Home Front, which allowed *Milorg* groups to become active within Norway prior to the liberation, helped to extend cooperation between SOE and *Milorg* at a local level.

In the autumn of 1942, a set of instructions was drawn up jointly by SOE and FO for teams or agents going into Norway. This document, which went through several changes, was primarily the creation of Leif Tronstad but done in conjunction with Lt. Col. J. S. Wilson, who on 2 October 1942 wrote to Tronstad saying that he had signed each paper as a mark that they had 'been approved by SOE so far as general terms are concerned'. From this point the policy was that in districts where only *Milorg* existed, in the future NIC (1) teams would provide help, while in areas where only SOE groups operated, *Milorg* would when possible offer support. In areas where both organizations existed, however, SOE groups would come under the control of *Milorg*.[78] In future, *Milorg* would constitute the core of any clandestine army, although it would not necessarily be the only component. Nevertheless, despite this attempt to formalize relations, the problems associated with a policy of allowing separate groups to operate within Norway did not immediately disappear. During the autumn of 1942, local *Milorg* organizations continued to face difficulties due to the activities of SOE/FO teams. Three operations in particular, 'Bittern' around Oslo, 'Heron' in the county of Trøndelag and 'Swan' in the south resulted in difficulties for *Milorg*.[79] Frustration within the resistance was so strong that it was claimed after the war that the organization even considered 'giving up'.[80] At the centre of this was poor communication, especially between the UK and Oslo. An attempt in the autumn of 1942 to provide the *Milorg* leadership with radio contact – Operation Plover – failed after only a few weeks.[81] Importantly, these problems continued to fuel scepticism within SOE, which was quick to reaffirm 'the difficulties [that] one is up against when dealing with the Home Front'.[82]

From December 1942, however, SOE began working closely with FO in London in an attempt to resolve these issues. In early 1943, through the ANCC, both organizations reemphasized the importance of decentralization, and that contact with groups in Norway should be made not only through Oslo but also direct to the districts. The *Milorg* leadership would, however, in the future be advised when teams were sent to Norway.[83] This was not about SOE distrusting or deciding to work outside *Milorg*[84]; the policy of working with and through local groups when possible remained intact. By this stage, SOE was clear that large-scale subversive activity in Norway could only be carried out through 'the local military organisation'.[85] Nevertheless, it shows that there was still a residue of scepticism towards the *Milorg* leadership.

From the late spring of 1943, however, contact with the official military resistance undoubtedly began to improve, which ultimately and significantly led to greater level of accord. The first of a series of conferences involving representatives of *Milorg* and FO was held in Sweden in May – others followed in October 1943 and in March 1944[86] – evidenced this and marked the start of a close working relationship between Bjarne Øen, head of FO IV, and Jens Chr. Hauge, head of *Milorg*. They would also meet on several occasions in London, and in early 1945, Øen travelled to Stockholm and from there to Norway when he again met Hauge.[87] The meeting in May discussed the military resistance's role prior to an invasion, during an invasion and immediately after reoccupation. It was agreed that only FO would decide 'if, and to what degree, units of *Milorg*' would be used in the event of an invasion and that it would be trained in the use of arms in readiness to provide support 'from within'. It was accepted that FO had contacts in certain areas with other groups and that *Milorg* districts would have a direct radio link with FO, and most significantly *Milorg's* central leadership would in the future only 'co-ordinate and administer' the work across the country.

This agreement was a watershed in the relationship between *Milorg*, FO and ultimately SOE.[88] Although it did not take part, SOE was aware of the 'general agreement' reached in Sweden, which it saw as providing FO with the authority to issue 'directives', while *Milorg* was confined to 'general supervision'. Moreover, it was also accepted that as *Milorg* was more likely to accept instructors it could be better prepared for its contribution to the eventual reoccupation or liberation of its country.[89] Nevertheless, some residual concerns over *Milorg's* tendency to centralize refused to go away, and it was reiterated that SOE could not allow itself to be governed by 'the wishes' of the 'Military Organisation' in Norway.

At this time, the ranks of *Milorg* were increasing in number and by mid-1944 they totalled around 32,000 spread across the south of the country. Of this total, however, about 24,000 were in eastern Norway, the area around Oslo and along the Swedish border. In comparison, for example, Milorg had only about 1,100 members in the counties of Møre and Trøndelag, on the west coast around Ålesund and Trondheim. There were, therefore, still areas, particularly in the west, where SOE continued to build its own organizations and it persisted with a policy that at the time it described as a 'mid-way course between the Scylla of separation and the Charybdis of SMO [*Milorg*] centralisation'. Nevertheless, as relations with the leadership in Oslo improved, the relationship between SOE and *Milorg* groups across the districts strengthened and increasingly they worked together.[90] Eventually, they became indistinguishable and were no longer 'distinct'.

At this time, the uncertainty surrounding Norway's eventual liberation began to have an impact on the resistance movements in the country. Within SOE, there was a realization that the contribution of 'local organisations' and SOE groups might not only involve support for an Allied landing but also attempts to delay the withdrawal of German forces, prevention of enemy destruction or maintaining order before the arrival of Allied troops.[91] *Milorg* was equally aware that the country's future was unsure and in August 1943, the *Råd* sent a letter on this subject, written by Hauge, to FO. It examined the possible contribution of the organization during a future German evacuation, collapse or surrender. There was concern over what might happen in the transitional period before the arrival of Allied forces, and it was felt that in certain circumstances *Milorg* might act as either a protective force or a force for law and order in the potential chaotic conditions that could arise. It should, however, avoid becoming embroiled in military clashes with German forces.[92]

At the October 1943 meeting in Sweden between representatives from *Milorg* and FO, these issues were discussed in more detail and in November *Milorg* and the civilian resistance leadership sent a joint communication to the Norwegian prime minister on the matter. This states that a principal objective of the *Råd* would be to create a state of military readiness in Norway that could be used by the military authorities as part of their 'operational plans' to reoccupy the country.[93] A consensus was therefore also developing between the resistance movements in Norway that an indigenous military force would probably be required to play a central role at the time of the country's liberation. Moreover, with an improvement in communication between FO and *Milorg* through the establishment of reliable radio links during the latter months of 1943, it became easier to ensure that the eventual contribution of an underground army in Norway could be closely controlled and coordinated with wider strategic, political and military requirements.[94]

A final conference involving *Milorg* and FO was held between 14 and 28 March 1944 in Sweden to discuss yet again the contribution of clandestine forces after a German capitulation or during an evacuation or Allied invasion. By this time, the Norwegian authorities and Home Front together were anxious to create 'a state of readiness' within Norway with the aim of 'preventing chaos and relieving pressure on the civilian population'. Unlike the previous May, however, little time was spent considering an invasion. It was envisaged that *Milorg* would act as a force for law and order to defend Norwegian lives and property during the potentially unstable and chaotic period before the arrival of Allied forces or within newly conquered areas. It was no longer seen as a guerrilla force but more of a protective force.[95] SOE had no direct involvement in these negotiations as it was believed that it might commit it 'to a line of action which might not be approved' in the UK or by SHAEF.[96]

Significantly, it was in London in August 1944 that wide agreement was finally reached on *Milorg's* military contribution. With the trips made by Jens Chr. Hauge to Britain during the summer and autumn of 1944, along with the integration of the staffs of FO IV and SOE's Norwegian section, a tripartite coalition was formed. It was pressure from this coalition along with Scotco that persuaded SHAEF that the resistance groups in Norway should be prepared and preserved to act as a protective force or a force for law and order within Norway in the days immediately after the liberation. It was the role that the Norwegian resistance leadership had already envisaged for *Milorg*, but importantly the authority and the resources in arms and equipment needed to carry it out would come from SHAEF through Special Forces HQ in London.[97]

During his visit to London in the summer of 1944, Hauge also received approval for a draft paper that set out the contribution of the *Milorg* districts during the liberation.[98] This was the 'September Directive', which was issued by SL to the District Leaders after Hauge's return to Norway. It details the actions that *Hjemmestyrkene*, the Norwegian Home Forces (HS), as *Milorg* units were referred to by this time, would take in the case of a German surrender, disintegration, withdrawal or, most unlikely, an Allied landing. With the emphasis on protection and preserving law and order, the document closely resembles the directive on the employment of resistance issued by SFHQ earlier in September. After Hauge's second visit to London in November 1944, the section of the document dealing with the defence of Norwegian property against demolitions was updated and extended.[99]

By the autumn of 1944, a consensus had been reached between London and Oslo, backed by the authority of SHAEF and therefore under Allied control, on the contribution that resistance groups, especially *Milorg*, would make to the country's liberation. There was, therefore, at this crucial stage of the occupation, complete synergy over long-term policy for Norway.[100]

The decision to develop a secret army in Norway through collaboration, however, continued to have an impact on SOE's short-term policy. The request by SOE in May 1943 for its organizations in the Oslo area to take part in overt acts of sabotage did not lead to a change in *Milorg's* official policy on this subject. Attacks against industrial or military targets in Norway continued to be confined to NIC (1) teams sent in from Britain, although these began to remain in the country for longer periods and increasingly used local help.[101] The resistance leadership in Norway, both military and civilian, remained totally opposed to any form of violent armed action that could lead to severe reprisals against the civilian population and its organizations. During the latter months of 1943 and early 1944, however, in response to events both outside and inside Norway, it changed its view.

As the liberation drew nearer, it was accepted in Norway that an armed and trained military force would be required in the country during the potentially unstable period immediately after a possible

German surrender or withdrawal. Closely related to this, it was seen as important to ensure that all actions within the country were controlled and directed, and that the Communists' active policy, which could undermine preparations for the liberation, should not be allowed to prevail. Although the British saw the Communist groups in Norway as simply an 'aggressive minority' without Russian backing, they also believed that they should be brought under the influence of the Home Front leadership.[102] There was also the threat posed by German plans to mobilize the Norwegian workforce for military service on its eastern front, which the resistance leadership decided to actively resist. And there was a growing restlessness within *Milorg's* ranks arising out of a wish to make some immediate contribution to the Allied war effort combined with a natural hardening process within the resistance leadership in response to German threats and reprisals.[103]

In November 1943, the civilian and military resistance stated in a joint communication to London, the *Fellesbrev*, that *Milorg* could be used for the solution of 'operational tasks' prior to the liberation, if required. This letter was a response to a Communist attack against a German troop train in Mjøndalen, southwest of Oslo, on 7 October 1943.[104] This apparent change in policy was further crystallized in the conference held in Sweden in March 1944 between representatives of *Milorg* and FO, when it was agreed that 'it may become necessary for the organisations to co-operate with, or themselves put into effect, individual operations against objectives of military importance during the waiting period'.[105] Consequently, from May 1944, local *Milorg* units in cooperation with SOE teams resident in Norway, initially in attempts to disrupt the mobilization of Norwegian workers, began to undertake overt acts of sabotage.[106] From this point until the liberation, *Milorg* and SOE, where possible, worked together and undertook a large and widespread number of attacks against key tactical sites in Norway. Therefore, by spring 1944, three years later than hoped, SOE was able to achieve its objective of carrying out sabotage within Norway using local groups and organizations.

SOE could not fulfil its plans for Norway without the support of either the Norwegian government in London or resistance groups in the country, specifically the military resistance. The nature of the occupation of Norway and the consequential emergence of an organized and largely unified resistance movement that was recognized and supported by its government in London had a significant influence on the relationship between SOE and *Milorg*. Prior to 1943, SOE's uncompromising determination to impose and control its own notion of a decentralized guerrilla army undoubtedly disrupted and complicated its long-term plans. Ultimately, it had to wait for *Milorg* to reform itself, which fortunately never proved to be a major problem as it was only during the final stages of the occupation that a secret army began to have any military significance in Norway. SOE's relationship with the Norwegian government and resistance was also not the only collaborative factor that had an impact on its actions. It had to work alongside the other military organizations that operated in this theatre.

Chapter 5

SOE AND THE OTHER NEW ORGANIZATIONS OPERATING IN NORWAY, 1940-5: A MILITARY ALLIANCE

SOE activities in Norway were not only shaped by strategic factors and its relations with the Norwegian military authorities and resistance but on many occasions also by its ability to collaborate with the other new military organizations that were created during the war and which operated in this theatre. These were in effect joint operations and involved the Director of Combined Operations (DCO),[1] created in June 1940 and responsible for the planning and execution of raiding operations against the enemy coastline,[2] the Political Warfare Executive (PWE), which in August 1941 took over from SOE responsibility for covert 'black' propaganda in the occupied countries, and the American Office of Strategic Services (OSS), formed in June 1942 with a Special Operations (SO) department, the equivalent of SOE. They all shared the same strategic objective of using a range of amphibious, irregular or subversive activities to undermine German military capability and morale. Norway was also relatively easily accessible and ideally suited for these types of military operations, and therefore it was a theatre in which these organizations, often from an early stage, could take the offensive, albeit on a small scale.

The involvement and interests of the Norwegian authorities and *Milorg* also had an important influence on these joint operations. The Norwegian military authorities supplied the volunteers from their armed services, who had the necessary skills to operate in occupied Norway as well as important economic and industrial intelligence. The government in exile, however, also used its close association with SOE to ensure that proper consideration was given to the impact of joint operations on the local population and that damage to industrial sites and therefore the Norwegian economy was minimized and contained. Its involvement therefore came at a cost.

Military collaboration had an impact on SOE plans for Norway and ultimately on its operations in several ways. It meant that attacks against economic targets in Norway could commence from a very early stage, even before SOE was in a position to undertake its own, independent activities. It also resulted in a scale of sabotage and *coup de main* activity in Norway that SOE could not have undertaken alone. Many attacks against economic or military targets were the result of a pooling of skills. The coordination of operations also meant that they were largely not undermined by internal squabbles, clashes in the field or duplication of effort. Disagreements over priorities were regularly negotiated to a satisfactory conclusion. Discussions over the type of target, its location and the levels of security surrounding it invariably determined which organization would carry out the operation.

The nature of SOE's relationship with each of these organizations, however, had a somewhat different impact but perhaps the most significant in the early part of the war was that with Combined Operations (henceforth COHQ).[3]

SOE and Combined Operations in Norway: The ideal partnership

From the autumn of 1940 until the summer of 1943, the Scandinavian and Norwegian sections of SOE worked with COHQ in planning, preparing and carrying out amphibious raids and *coup de main* operations in Norway. Combined Operations, like SOE, had strategic origins. As part of Britain's 'future offensive strategy', it was created in the summer of 1940 to carry out raids against the coastline of occupied Europe. The objective was to 'harass the enemy', 'cause him to disperse his forces' and 'cause material damage' from an area from the north of Norway to the West Coast of France'.[4] In SOE's first directive, the COS affirmed the significance of raids and subversive activities as part of a 'strategy of attrition'.[5]

Consequently, from the beginning SOE and COHQ were natural allies. By September 1940, SOE's Scandinavian section had decided that it should establish close liaison with COHQ, as it feared uncontrolled raids could lead to a premature uprising in the country.[6] During that autumn, however, it also recognized the value of small raids against targets in northern Norway,[7] and by December 1940 'assistance with tip-and-run landings' had become part of its immediate objective of making Norway 'a thorn in the German side'.[8] At the same time, Hugh Dalton reached an agreement with Sir Roger Keyes, the DCO, over responsibility for raids. It was accepted that COHQ would have authority over attacks against coastal objectives on the western seaboard of Europe using parties of fifty or more British troops that would be withdrawn later, while SO2 operations would be carried out by parties of not more than thirty, usually foreigners.[9] It was also agreed that the two organizations, and the Secret Intelligence Service (SIS), should keep each other informed at an early date of projects under consideration and should examine coastal targets 'with a view to collaboration'.[10]

Accordingly, between September 1940 and January 1942 at least seven raids against targets close to the Norwegian coast were planned, attempted or completed, and SOE and COHQ collaborated on five of them.[11] They were the continuance of the economic interest in Norway that had begun during the First World War, when, for example, Britain had gone as far as to purchase 70 to 80 per cent of one year's catch of fish in the country.[12] As shown, this interest was resumed prior to the outbreak of conflict in 1939[13] and continued right through to the summer of 1940 when SOE highlighted herring oil production and the mining of specialist metals as important targets.[14] These raids also heightened the fear of a British invasion, which induced Germany to increase its military commitment in Norway, and led to the fortuitous capture of some important cipher equipment, which ultimately helped in the breaking of the German Enigma codes.

By October 1940, COHQ had begun to consider an operation against ilmenite production at Titania A/S near Sokndal just six kilometres from Jøssingfjord in southern Norway. It was believed that an attack against this target would, apart from denying Germany a significant although not vital war material, also give the organization some practical experience in raiding operations, raise Norwegian morale and generally annoy and create alarm among the Germans.[15] Preparations therefore began for Operation Mandible (formerly 'Castle'), a planned attack against the hydroelectric power station and loading appliances for ilmenite at the head of Jøssingfjord. It would be a joint operation, with SOE providing Norwegian guides, COHQ supplying Special Service troops to carry out the 'tip and run' raid and the Royal Navy (RN) making three destroyers and a submarine available. Malcolm Munthe had been asked to recruit local resistance groups to assist the operation, but after a change of heart it was decided to use Norwegians recruited locally in London.[16] On this occasion, however, although the COS and the commander-in-chief of the Home Fleet approved 'Mandible', they were overruled by Churchill, who at the time objected to disturbing the Norwegian coastline for objects he considered 'trivial'.[17]

Churchill's attitude caused frustration within SOE but it did not initially hinder preparations for further similar operations. The target changed, however, to the supply of Norwegian fish products to Germany. In the spring of 1941, three operations, against the Norwegian herring, cod oil and fish industry – 'Claymore', 'Hemisphere' and 'Almoner' – were proposed. There was an initial belief that fish oil was used in the manufacture of glycerine for explosives, but by early January 1941 this had been discarded although it was still believed to be an important source of vitamins 'A' and 'B' for Germany, and the country's 'most important deficiency foodstuff'.[18]

As seen, Churchill was against Claymore and his opposition was only overcome after the COS persuaded him that because it was against a target on the Lofoten Islands not the mainland it was less likely to stir up the Norwegian coastline.[19] There have also been claims that the operation's main objective, unknown to SOE, was to capture German cipher material.[20] It was, however, another offensive strategic operation with the intention of destroying an important economic target as well as German garrisons and bringing back Norwegian volunteers.[21] Its primary aim was to deny Germany what at the time was considered a significant war material,[22] and it was pressure from SOE that led to Claymore. Planning began under the direction of COHQ in consultation with SOE in late 1940, and this eventually ended in a combined operation involving SOE, Special Service troops, the RN and Norwegian men, officers, guides and naval pilots. It was carried out on 4 March 1941 and resulted in the destruction of factories, shipping and oil tanks, and according to participants in the raid, an important but largely fortuitous capture of German cipher material.[23]

Claymore shows how important collaboration with COHQ was to SOE at a time early in the war when it struggled to undertake its own, independent activities. Moreover, it was a small operation that ironically, despite the assurances of the COS, stirred up the Norwegian coast and led 'to reinforcements of German forces on the peninsula'.[24] Therefore, despite leading to reprisals against the local population,[25] it was a small but significant strategic success. On 26 March 1941, as a direct consequence of Claymore, Hitler issued a directive that led to a 'substantial flow of reinforcements' to the country, plans to construct 160 coastal batteries and instructions to build training camps in Norway so that a defence reserve could be built up. It also confirmed Hitler's view that the British would attempt a landing in the country.[26] As the operation included a significant Norwegian military contribution and, as far as SOE was concerned, it had the 'enthusiastic' support of Trygve Lie, it was also a truly joint operation.[27]

Despite the relative success of Claymore, no more similar raids were carried out in this theatre before December 1941. The reason was a combination of Churchill's opposition to small operations along the Norwegian coast[28] and the diversion of COHQ resources to Operation Pilgrim, the proposed seizure of the Canaries, which was the organization's main preoccupation during the first half of 1941.[29] After the German invasion of the Soviet Union in June 1941, however, which included an advance by Axis forces from the north of Norway into Finland, the strategic context changed. The prime minister's eagerness to support the Soviet Union through the creation of a Second Front in Western Europe intensified interest in Norway, but after the COS had successfully resisted Operation Ajax,[30] a myriad of smaller plans emerged. These set out to establish a temporary military presence in the north of Norway, to cut German land and sea communications with its forces in the north, and to attack economic and military targets.[31] They eventually crystallized into four operations, 'Anklet', 'Archery' and 'Kitbag' I & II, which were carried out in December 1941 and January 1942 with varying degrees of success. All were under the supreme command of the commander-in-chief Home Fleet and included contributions from SOE, the RN, RAF, the Norwegian armed forces and COHQ.[32] SOE, in consultation with COHQ, supplied Norwegian volunteers including local guides, naval pilots, and radio operators.[33] It also made a direct contribution through its own operation called 'Wallah', a plan conceived in the spring of 1941 to paralyze German sea-borne traffic along the Norwegian coast during the following winter and which was the original basis for and eventually became part of 'Anklet'.[34] It was also intended that another SOE operation called 'Archer', a plan to use a team of men to attack ferries, an aerodrome and a major bridge around Mosjøen in the north, would be part of 'Anklet' but after 'Anklet's' scaling back it was, however, never required.[35]

In January 1942, the COS pointed out that raids had a 'considerable moral effect and forced the Germans to keep more land and air forces in Norway than would otherwise have been the case'.[36] In response to 'Anklet' and 'Archery', the number of German troops stationed in the country was increased from 100,000 to 250,000, new fortifications built and a large part of the Germany surface fleet moved to Norwegian waters.[37] This was a large military commitment in a peripheral theatre and therefore there is considerable merit in the assertion that there 'was no need for Allied deception operations to persuade Hitler to reinforce his troops' in Norway.[38] More significantly, this meant that there was a sound strategic reason for continuing raids and *coup de main* operations, especially if they could be undertaken with only a small cost in men and equipment,[39] which is ultimately what happened. The German reinforcement of Norway, especially the expansion of its air cover and the arrival of the battleship *Tirpitz*, meant that large-scale British coastal raids involving hundreds of Special Service troops and the employment of capital ships from an overstretched RN were abandoned. After a gap of a few months, however, they were replaced by smaller sea-borne raids or by *coup de main* operations against inland targets.[40]

Despite the productive working relationship between SOE and COHQ during 1941, Lt. Col. Wilson stated at the end of the war that in 1942 Combined Operations was 'inclined to usurp SOE's function of *coup-de-main* activities in Norway'.[41] A total of five such operations were carried out during 1942, two organized by COHQ with SOE involvement and three by SOE.[42] Wilson's claim is therefore difficult to understand. Nonetheless, from early 1942, both organizations operated independently and this inevitably led to some rivalry. At a local operational and organizational level, however, cooperation continued, and many of the *coup de main* operations in Norway in 1942 and into 1943 were joint efforts.

From early 1942, through better relations with SOE and with the creation of FO, the Norwegian government also became more closely and formally involved in British operations against targets on its territory. Its participation was largely advantageous and supportive and was backed up by the good relationship that developed between Lord Mountbatten, Chief of Combined Operations (CCO) from March 1942, and General Hansteen, the Norwegian commander-in-chief. They met towards the end of February 1942 to discuss the issue of raids in Norway and Mountbatten 'took the most tremendous liking to' Hansteen. From this point, there are several occasions when both corresponded directly regarding operations in Norway.[43] Nevertheless, it also meant that the Norwegian government endeavoured to use its increasing involvement in order to minimize what it considered to be unnecessary long-term damage to the Norwegian economy and the risks to the local population. By early 1942, it had already ensured, despite objections from the MEW, that herring oil production in Norway was no longer an Allied target.[44]

SOE, assisted by the Norwegian military authorities, was involved in and contributed to three COHQ *coup de main* operations between the summer of 1942 and the end of the winter of 1943 against economic targets in Norway. The first in September 1942, Operation Musketoon, referred to as 'Knottgrass-Unicorn' in SOE files, was against the Glomfjord power station, which supplied energy to the aluminium smelting factory at Haugvik in north-west Norway. SOE provided Norwegian guides from NIC (1), training, intelligence and specialist equipment. Two officers and eight other ranks from No. 2 Commando undertook this operation, which initially was called 'Centaur'. The two Norwegians were Sergeant Magnus Erling Djupdræt and Corporal Sverre Granland. Seven of the Britains and Djupdrædt were captured, while four men escaped to Sweden.[45] The operation was successfully carried out and made a small but valuable contribution to the failure of Germany's ambitious plans for aluminium production in Norway.[46]

In January 1943, another operation, 'Cartoon', assembled by COHQ, but under the command of ACOS, was undertaken to disrupt the mining of pyrites at Lillebø on the island of Stord, south of Bergen. SOE initially suggested the operation and in cooperation with FO, which approved it, again provided intelligence and a Norwegian guide, Lieutenant Welle-Strand. The raid also included men from D troop of 12 Commando and Norwegians from No. 10 (Inter Allied) Commando. They were carried and escorted by Motor Torpedo boats (MTBs) from the 30th Royal Norwegian Navy (RNorN) MTB flotilla. The Norwegian authorities were, however, concerned about possible reprisals against the local population and therefore widened the role of their guide to include protection of Norwegian interests and forbade the Norwegian commandoes that took part from wearing the national flag on their uniform.[47] Significant damage was done to the mining and transportation equipment and even by summer 1945 production at the site had only reached a third of its original level of about 150,000 tons per year.[48]

In February 1943, SOE and COHQ also attempted to link operations against economic and military targets in southern Norway. Early in January, SOE and Norwegian naval operation 'Carhampton' sailed with the aim of capturing a transport convoy off the coast of southern Norway, thereby disrupting the transportation of important war materials to Germany. At the time, it was estimated that 800,000 tons of important war material was transported annually by sea along the Norwegian coast on its way to Germany. This ambitious project eventually failed in its objective, and the party sent in to undertake it withdrew to the mountains.[49] In early February, it was decided to combine this operation with the COHQ operation 'Yorker', a planned attack against the titanium mines at Sandbekk also in southern Norway, which were of major significance to German armament production. Yorker was never carried out due to continual severe weather in the North Sea and the Carhampton team was eventually forced to make its own way back from Norway, which ended in tragedy for a large part of the expedition.[50]

These operations were still only 'pin-pricks' but altogether they had a significant strategic payback, disrupting the production and supply of important war materials and more importantly continuing to foster German fears over British intentions towards Norway. As a result of 'Cartoon', coastal artillery in Norway was reinforced and Hitler himself intervened. It was eventually decided that a mobile reserve should be built up, additional troops sent and more artillery and small vessels allotted to the Norwegian Command.[51]

Collaboration between SOE and COHQ was also directed against what at the time was considered as one of the most important military targets of the war. This was Operation Freshman, the attempt to halt the production and destroy stocks of heavy water at the Norsk Hydro plant at Vemork in southern Norway. This substance, a by-product of the electrolysis of water, a process undertaken to produce hydrogen and oxygen for use in the local production of nitrate fertilizers, was potentially an important constituent in German attempts to develop an atomic bomb. Its technical name is deuterium oxide and is 10 per cent heavier than normal water. It could be used to moderate the speed of neutrons set free in a nuclear reactor, allowing them to split uranium atoms in a controlled chain reaction, thereby producing plutonium, a fissionable element that could be used in a bomb.[52] A great deal has been written about this operation and will not be repeated,[53] but importantly it highlights a number of important issues concerning SOE interest and involvement in Norway.

From early August 1940, SOE was aware of heavy water when the Ministry of Supply asked it for details of its electrolytic production at Vemork.[54] It initially targeted it in 1941 as part of Operation Clairvoyant, its ambitious plan to 'immobilise' important industries in Norway through attacking local hydroelectric power stations. It was, however, decided that the plant that supplied the power for production at Vemork, which consisted of ten double generators and one reserve, was too big for an SOE team and therefore bombing was recommended. Ongoing Norwegian concerns, especially concerning possible collateral damage, however, at this point eventually resulted in the abandonment of any air attack.[55]

In the spring of 1942, in response to intelligence coming out of Norway and other sources, the Department of Scientific and Industrial Research (DSIR), which was part of the Directorate of Tube Alloys, the organization responsible for Britain's atomic bomb project, became concerned over production levels of heavy water at Vemork and contacted SOE.[56] The involvement of DSIR meant that from this point disquiet over heavy water production in Norway circulated within much higher levels in government and was no longer confined to SOE.[57] It was, however, again made clear that the best way to interrupt production long term was to target the power station. Owing to its size this would, however, in the absence of bombing, require a 'combined operation'.[58] Out of this came Operation Freshman, a joint effort to interrupt heavy water production at Vemork by putting the local power plant out of action and destroying ancillary equipment and stocks. The COS finally approved 'Freshman' in principle in October and 'invited the Chief of Combined Operations' in consultation with the Air Staff, the GOC Airborne Division and the Ministry of Aircraft Production to make recommendations. So it was coordinated by COHQ, and as after extensive discussion it was decided to use gliders towed close to the target it included contributions from the 1st Airborne Division and No 38 Wing of the RAF, as well as SOE and FO.[59]

SOE provided training in demolition and survival for the Royal Engineers who were chosen to undertake the destruction of the power station,[60] and FO supplied important intelligence on the site. Leif Tronstad, who had helped set up the heavy water plant in the 1930s was in contact with Jomar Brun, its chief engineer, who up to the autumn of 1942, when he fled to Britain, sent back a flow of information, including building plans, details on production levels and samples of heavy water.[61] The hydroelectric plant at Vemork, however, was part of a network of power stations in the area that supplied 60 per cent of the electricity requirements for eastern Norway.[62] It therefore had huge economic significance for the local population and the involvement of the Norwegian military authorities provided them with an opportunity to voice their concerns. Consequently, it was eventually agreed that of the ten main generators at the power plant only eight would be put out of action, leaving two intact to provide at least enough energy for the production of fertilizers at the Norsk Hydro plant at Rjukan further down the valley. This would mean that phosphate supplies to local farmers could continue.[63]

SOE and FO also made available an NIC (1) team, 'Grouse II', which was given the task of receiving the party of engineers and guiding them to the target. On 28 March 1942, Einar Skinnarland – 'Grouse I' – had been parachuted into Norway to prepare the way for 'Grouse II', which would follow at the end of April and begin to organize small local guerrilla groups around the strategically important Vestfjord valley where Vemork is located. It was later claimed that he was also given the task of gathering information on developments on heavy water production, although this does not appear in his operational instructions at the time.[64] Air transport, however, was not available before the lighter nights set in during May and therefore 'Grouse II' was delayed. It appears that in an appreciation produced on 15 September 1942, SOE formally suggested using 'Grouse II' as a forward party for 'Freshman' after planning was underway.[65] The men were eventually dropped into Norway in mid-October. On the night of 19/20 November, two gliders, towed by British aircraft, attempted to deliver thirty Royal Engineers to a rendezvous point on *Hardangervidda* in southern Norway. Both gliders and one of the aircrafts crashed and all the Royal Engineers were eventually killed either as a result of the crash or at the hands of the Germans. One of the aircrafts returned home. The support of a forward party was, therefore, never required and on 23 November for security reasons, the 'Grouse' party was renamed 'Swallow'.[66]

Cooperation at a local operational level during 1942 and 1943 was also assisted by organizational collaboration between SOE and COHQ through the exchange of target lists, discussions over target priority and by a general effort to coordinate activities in Norway. Both organizations, however, increasingly planned their own independent operations and therefore a degree of competition inevitably broke out. All of this is illustrated by the conflict that ensued over whether the combined operation 'Musketoon' or Operation Seagull, SOE's proposal to attack the Sulitjelma mines in northern Norway around the same time and which were only seventy miles from Glomfjord, should have priority. In the end, however, after lengthy discussions it was decided that both operations would go ahead, although 'Seagull' was eventually and rather ironically cancelled due to the increase in security in the area that was a result of the attack against the Glomfjord power plant.[67]

Furthermore, after the prime minister's call in October 1942 for an intensification of 'small-scale raids' by COHQ,[68] Norway became an increasingly popular choice for small sea-borne operations. With several Allied organizations operating along the Norwegian coast, it therefore became increasingly necessary to coordinate and prioritize their activities. Consequently, in November 1942, the Admiralty appointed ACOS, Vice Admiral L. V. Wells as the 'co-ordinating authority for small operations on the Norwegian coast'.[69] In January 1943, the COS stamped their seal of authority on this decision when they confirmed that all planning of clandestine sea-borne operations, whether originated by SOE, SIS or COHQ, would be overseen by the 'Admiralty or a Flag Officer delegated by them'.[70] These activities, with the agreement of SOE, were also prioritized, with intelligence on the German fleet at the top, followed by interference with the enemy's communications along the coast, operations that extended the enemy's defensive efforts and last the building of resistance.[71]

It was within this framework that during the winter and spring of 1943 COHQ continued to consult with SOE on its proposals for Norway, even though Operation Cartoon was the last operation on which they directly cooperated.[72] SOE was not reluctant to raise objections if it was felt that they directly interfered with its own operations. It opposed Operation Pullover, a plan to destroy the Nordals Viaduct near Narvik in an attempt to interdict the transportation of Swedish iron ore. It argued that the loss of supplies to Germany would be relatively small; as it involved a landing in Norway it would undermine its efforts in the area, and because Special Duty aircraft would be used other SOE missions could be delayed. The operation was, however, eventually cancelled due to 'lack of suitable weather'.[73] SOE also objected to Operation Cobblestones, a plan to leave parties of No. 14 Commando on islands off the Norwegian coast from where, by using kayaks or canoes to attach limpet mines, they could attack enemy shipping. Again SOE felt that this would disturb the local conditions and therefore refused the loan of fishing vessels to carry out the operation.[74] The Norwegian military authorities also protested against 'Cobblestones' because it was believed that such operations could put the local population at unnecessary risk.[75] The Admiralty was, however, the final arbiter in these matters and if an operation did not directly clash with SIS or naval activity, it was invariably allowed to go ahead.[76] It was the severe weather conditions that regularly occurred in the North Sea, not organizational differences, that was the most disruptive factor in this theatre.[77] And despite these differences, SOE's view of COHQ was that it had sought consultation from the beginning, was prepared to modify aspects of its proposals as a result of SOE's recommendations and that 'co-operation was more likely to intensify than otherwise'.[78]

As COHQ became increasingly involved in preparations for the invasion of north-west Europe in 1944, the Commando groups operating out of the Shetlands were gradually moved south or disbanded during the summer of 1943. Consequently, cooperation between SOE and

COHQ in Norway came to an end.[79] The two organizations had been natural partners and by working together they had from an early stage been able to take the offensive against German interests in this theatre. Their close relationship also illustrates how beneficial collaboration was for SOE in carrying out its plans in Norway, although by 1943 it was more than capable of operating independently.[80]

SOE and the political warfare executive: Subversion through propaganda

According to its charter, one of SOE's responsibilities was also to coordinate subversion against the enemy overseas, and an important element of subversion was propaganda.[81] In the years prior to the outbreak of the Second World War, two new organizations, Electra House (EH) and Section D, had begun to examine the possible contribution of covert propaganda in the war against Germany.[82] But with the creation of SOE in July 1940, a reorganization occurred and SO1 took over this responsibility.[83]

In 1940, subversive propaganda was another small element of Britain's forward strategy, which set out to undermine the spirit of the German armed forces, 'especially in the occupied countries'.[84] The establishment of SO1 did not, however, end the fragmentation and overlapping that characterized the dissemination of and responsibility for propaganda, and it was a further attempt to coordinate activity and agree responsibility within this field that led in August 1941 to the creation of PWE. This new organization, initially run by an Executive Committee responsible to a ministerial team with representatives from the Foreign Office, Ministry of Information (MOI) and SOE, was according to its charter set up to 'co-ordinate and direct' all 'propaganda to enemy occupied countries'.[85] This cumbersome structure lasted until the following spring when day-to-day responsibility passed to Bruce Lockhart, its director general.[86]

PWE was responsible for creating and laying down policy on political warfare, including both overt and covert propaganda, and with its creation the short life of SO1 was ended. It was divided into regions, including Scandinavia, under regional directors, who were responsible for administering and controlling the work in their respective theatres.[87] As part of the agreement that led to its formation, it was accepted, however, that 'all activities of the Political Warfare Executive outside Great Britain' would be 'conducted through the medium of the Special

Operations Executive'.[88] This was reaffirmed in a new agreement signed in September 1942, which stated that all work in the field will 'continue to be done by SOE as agents for PWE'.[89] To enable it to undertake subversive propaganda activities in Norway, PWE therefore required the assistance of SOE, which was the source of its Norwegian agents as well as equipment and transportation. Moreover, it was part of SOE's remit to ensure that the German forces in Norway remained 'generally as uncomfortable as possible'.[90]

There was, however, also a political dimension to the use of propaganda that made the implementation of this type of subversive activity in Norway extremely problematic. The Norwegian government considered that the dissemination of all information at home was both its constitutional responsibility and an important element in rebuilding its relationship with the Norwegian people after it had been severely damaged by the German occupation.[91] This determination to retain control over all forms of communication with its people would both delay and complicate PWE's and SOE's efforts to undertake their own subversive propaganda operations.

'Operational propaganda', the production and distribution of leaflets, posters and clandestine newspapers, through agents working in Norway, was something particularly dependent on SOE involvement. Propaganda disseminated to Norway through the BBC, 'Freedom Stations' (clandestine broadcasting), the dropping of leaflets or by the spreading of subversive rumours or 'Sibs' as they were referred to, was something that SOE was much less involved in.[92]

In the COS directives to SOE, studies by the British Planning Staff and in SHAEF directives, there was from as early as the autumn of 1940 regular reference to the use of propaganda as a means to subvert the morale of German troops.[93] From even earlier, SO1 had begun to consider the use of subversive propaganda in Norway, and in July the Norwegian-born journalist Thomas Barman produced the first of a series of lengthy papers on the subject. Until SOE's ideas had 'further matured', however, Barman was largely interested in disseminating information through leaflets or radio broadcasts, which he believed should be done in collaboration with the Norwegian authorities. Although Barman did not always practice what he preached, often upsetting his Norwegian colleagues, he did develop a close working association with a fellow journalist, H. K. Lehmkuhl at the *Informasjonskontor*, Information Office (IK), which was set up in London in February 1941 to coordinate propaganda on behalf of the Norwegian government.[94]

From the summer of 1941, PWE continued the interest in Norway, which by this stage, however, had gone beyond simply using radio broadcasts or dropping leaflets, and included sending specially trained propaganda agents into the country. Consequently, from the autumn of 1941, PWE and SOE began to work together with the objective of disseminating propaganda within Norway in order to make the German occupation 'a drain on enemy resources' and to maintain Norwegian morale at a time when 'no Allied initiative of any importance' was expected in the country.[95] The agents, transportation, security and communications would be supplied through SOE; training and directives in propaganda would come from PWE.[96] At this time, Captain Hackett (later major), head of PWE's training school, visited STS 26 at Aviemore and eventually with the backing of Charles Hambro began to recruit Norwegian volunteers. Between 1941 and the spring of 1943, at least fifteen Norwegian SOE agents eventually received propaganda training.[97] Hackett's initiative was the beginning of a joint SOE/PWE project that aimed to get 'field-workers' into Norway to undertake subversive propaganda work. The initial steps would be low key with agents sent in to survey and collect information on local conditions, although activities such as staging passive 'go-slow' resistance and setting up 'patriotic black markets' to undermine German rationing were also envisaged.[98] In February 1942, however, in a 'Plan of Political Warfare against Scandinavia', it was concluded that the cooperation of the Norwegian government was necessary if this type of activity was ever to be carried out successfully.[99]

After arriving in Britain it was important for the Norwegian government, at a time when many blamed it for Norway's lack of readiness in April 1940, to make contact and strengthen its position with the Norwegian people. It also believed it was vitally important for it to retain control over all forms of communication with the Home Front, whether through BBC broadcasts, the dropping of leaflets or the sending of propaganda agents into the field. It therefore instituted a series of measures, including the setting up of IK in early 1941, to maintain and strengthen links with occupied Norway and to represent the country's interests with her allies and neutral countries.[100]

Although there were difficulties between the British and Norwegian authorities on issues such as BBC broadcasts and the dropping of leaflets,[101] the practical view that Norwegian support would be beneficial when undertaking propaganda activities that aimed to help the 'Allied cause' prevailed.[102] It was, however, the close collaboration between SOE and FO, exercised through the ANCC that ultimately proved decisive in creating a framework within which the planning and implementation of subversive propaganda operations in Norway could be carried out. Consequently, from this point the sending in of 'field-workers' to undertake propaganda activities, directed by PWE but using SOE agents and facilities, could only be achieved in collaboration with the Norwegian authorities. Therefore, between April and July 1942, through the medium of the ANCC, a series of discussions was carried out with the aim of setting up an organizational structure for conducting propaganda operations.[103] This eventually led to an agreement in the summer of 1942 that gave the Norwegian government a significant measure of control over the production and distribution of subversive material. The IK was made responsible for propaganda and the directives that were passed to the Norwegian agents, FO and SOE were together to manage the agents, while a subcommittee ensured collaboration with PWE. A Propaganda Office under Bård Krogvig was also set up to represent FO.[104]

This collaborative framework, despite its bureaucratic complexity, led in the summer of 1942 to a joint British/Norwegian plan called the 'Operational Propaganda Field-Work Scheme', which was the culmination of the work that SOE and PWE had begun the previous autumn with the training of specialist propaganda agents. This divided southern Norway into ten districts, each with its own separate team including a radio operator that would undertake propaganda activities in the local area.[105] The hope was that propaganda agents would begin to operate in Norway from mid-September 1942, but despite its involvement the Norwegian government was slow to accept the scheme and it was November before it was approved. Moreover, it was also agreed by both SOE and the Norwegian authorities that the plan should be laid before the Norwegian Home Front before implementation and on 27 November 1942 Gunnar Fougner, with the code name 'Petrel', travelled to Norway to meet resistance leaders. He eventually returned to London via Stockholm, indicating that the scheme had been well received. In late February 1943, however, a letter arrived in London rejecting the plan because it was believed that the further infiltration of agents from outside was unwise and because such activity could be done better from Oslo. Consequently, at a time when the Norwegian government's relationship with the resistance leadership was at a delicate and difficult stage, the project was abandoned.[106]

The dissemination of underground propaganda was delayed, complicated and ultimately obstructed by the concerns of both the Norwegian government and the resistance leadership in Oslo. Because it was also targeted at the civilian population in occupied Norway, it played a role in the development of the relationship between the Home Front and the Norwegian government and resistance leadership, which was a sensitive political issue. It was this that ultimately set back and restricted its overall use in this theatre.

Despite these difficulties, however, SOE and PWE did not give up and continued with their efforts to instigate operational propaganda in Norway. The Norwegian Home Front was contacted again in June 1943, but once more rejected Allied advances, arguing that with a large underground press and many people still listening to the BBC's London radio the population was already fully aware of and largely supported the British view.[107] Attempts were also made to have an officer with responsibility for 'black' propaganda attached to the Press Office at the Norwegian Legation in Stockholm, but this was rebuffed.[108] Nevertheless, during the second half of 1943 and early 1944, SOE and PWE began to make some headway. In response to Norwegian concerns, they changed their approach to propaganda operations in Norway in two important ways. First, the plan to use separate propaganda teams was abandoned; teams already assigned to Norway on other tasks would carry out propaganda as an additional role.[109] This allowed PWE to hide behind SOE respectability in the eyes of the Norwegian military authorities and therefore avoid the suspicions of its government towards propaganda operations.[110] Second, the Norwegian authorities were advised that future propaganda undertaken by SOE teams would only be directed against the morale of the German occupying forces.[111] In the future, therefore, it would be a purely military exercise and the Norwegian population would not be involved, thereby excising the political element. Compared to what had originally been planned, this compromise curtailed the extent of operational propaganda operations in Norway during the final stages of the war but meant that they could at last be carried out. This was at a time, in the run up to the liberation and while several enemy divisions remained in the country, when it was especially important to undertake any activity that might undermine German morale and thereby help to achieve the objective of a peaceful capitulation rather than a violent last stand.

Prior to these changes, little in the way of subversive propaganda was carried out in Norway. In March 1943, however, Operation Mardonius, consisting of Gregers Gram and Max Manus, which had the task of attacking shipping in Oslo harbour, also undertook work that had propaganda implications.[112] Both agents had received propaganda training,[113] and while in Oslo they conducted a Gallup Poll, which was used as the basis of a report on conditions at home. Although Gram and Manus admitted that the report could not give a 'reliable picture of the situation as a whole', they nevertheless concluded that the population in Norway tended 'towards passivity and the onlooker attitude'. It was eventually passed to PWE.[114]

Furthermore, by this stage, a PWE/SOE Co-ordination Committee had been established to discuss issues of policy and which included members from both SOE's Norwegian section and the Northern Region of PWE.[115] Nevertheless, little was happening at a local operational level and in June 1943, Lt. Col. Wilson made the self-evident observation that Anti-Axis propaganda required 'development'. In an attempt to accelerate efforts, a decision was therefore made to give 'basic propaganda training' to all the members of NIC (1) 'so that those who go out into the field can deal with this requirement in addition to their other duties'.[116] This was the first sign that SOE was abandoning the idea of sending independent propaganda 'field-workers' into Norway. A few months later Operation Bundle, which also included Manus and Gram, was initiated. It was another operation against shipping in the Oslo fjord but at the request of PWE the operation would also examine a number of propaganda issues, including ways to demoralize the Wehrmacht.[117] Due to the strict security measures implemented by the German authorities around Oslo, especially the harbour areas, 'Bundle' was initially a failure. The large amount of information on conditions in Norway accumulated by Gram and Manus while in Oslo, which the following February was passed on to PWE, and their establishment of an underground newspaper called *Aftonbladet*, indicates, however, that their propaganda activities were more fruitful.[118]

This led in January 1944 to the implementation of Operation Derby, a plan for Gram and Manus to undertake activities that were designed to undermine the morale of the German forces in the Oslo area. It was instigated from Stockholm and given priority over 'Bundle'. It resulted in the establishment of a propaganda organization that produced illegal newspapers and distributed posters, stickers and leaflets across eastern Norway.[119] It was carried out with the acceptance of the Norwegian authorities in London, and knowledge but non-involvement of the resistance leadership in Oslo.[120] It eventual employed almost 500 people, divided into nine districts stretching from Drammen in the south-west to Sarpsborg in the east, and produced two German papers *Beobachter* and *Im Westen nichts Neues*.[121] Through Operation Durham, a similar endeavour was undertaken in Trondheim between March 1944 and April 1945. Minor propaganda activities had been carried out in this area before, but 'Durham', supplied with material primarily out of Stockholm, operated on a large scale. It had over 100 men producing posters, pamphlets and brochures with the aim of irritating the Germans, undermining their morale and even encouraging them to desert to Sweden.[122]

These operations mark the late but eventual initiation of SOE's plan to undertake subversive propaganda in Norway. They were built on the back of SOE teams or agents that were already in the field and they denoted the opening of a propaganda offensive that targeted the morale of the German forces in Norway in the period running up to the country's liberation.

PWE initially felt, however, that the attitude of the Norwegian government had limited the scope of propaganda activities in Norway, and even at the end of 1943 it still hoped to recruit independent Norwegian 'political warfare agents', to go into Norway to support SOE tasks that aimed to undermine German morale and prepare the population for an Allied invasion.[123] By the following spring, however, it acknowledged that in respect of operations against the Germans, the 'Norwegian authorities had accepted that this was a British province', and that through SOE 'practical progress had been made'.[124] From spring 1944, therefore, PWE began to shift its attention away from operational propaganda and towards preparing the Norwegian people for the country's liberation and began to work closely with Scotco and the Norwegian government. A Political Warfare Branch was set up within Scotco under Lt. Col. Petch,[125] and in July Mr Brinley Thomas from PWE was appointed liaison officer between the Political Warfare Division (PWD) of SHAEF and the Norwegian authorities.[126] The focal point of their work over the following months was the distribution of leaflets to Norway. SOE involvement was limited, although after initial reluctance it agreed to allow the use of Special Duty aircraft to drop these leaflets.[127]

SOE and OSS in Norway: American subjugation

The use of subversive propaganda in Norway was another strand of SOE activity that depended on collaboration. The ability to cooperate was also important in shaping its relationship with a new American clandestine organization that was created in June 1942. After the United States joined the war against the Axis powers, it entered into a close military partnership with Britain. This alliance was quickly extended into the area of special operations and in the summer of 1942 the American OSS under the leadership of William Donovan entered into discussions with SOE over their future relationship. The close organizational and operational relationship between the two organizations in north-west Europe was symbolized by the setting up in May 1944 of the Special Forces HQ (SFHQ). This collaboration was also extended to Norway. In the spring of 1943, it was agreed that this country would be an SOE sphere of operations and that the SO section of OSS, which was responsible for sabotage and subversion, would have to work with SOE and FO through the forum of the ANCC. A triumvirate was therefore formed, although in Norway, SO was always a junior partner.

SOE operations benefited from SO support in two ways. Most importantly through OSS, and the direct contact it had to the American Joint Chiefs of Staff (JCS), SO provided additional resources, especially equipment and transportation, which often helped to advance special operations at a local level within Norway. The SO was, however, also anxious to carry out its own sabotage and subversion, while SOE was keen to make use of OSS American/Norwegians recruits as a source of additional manpower. Consequently, there was a good reason for them to combine their efforts and several attempts were made to make use of American volunteers, although ultimately with limited success. American involvement in special operations in Norway was therefore primarily supportive.

The relationship between SOE and SO in Europe and Norway was eventually based on negotiated agreements. After OSS was formed in June 1942, it was decided that both organizations should coordinate their activities in the various theatres of operations across the globe. Discussions began almost immediately and an agreement was reached and confirmed by both countries the following September. Norway was perhaps surprisingly defined as an 'Invasion' country where there would be 'one integrated Field Force controlled jointly by SOE and the London Office of OSS'.[128] This arrangement, however, did not prove to be enough to ensure 'joint' control over special operations in this theatre. In the autumn of 1942, OSS made contact with Lt. Stromholtz, who had been sent to the United States on a lecture tour by the Norwegian authorities, with a view to recruiting him and sending him to Norway as its own agent.[129]

This provoked concern both within SOE and FO. Therefore, after an American proposal to carry out psychological warfare in Norway from a base in Iceland, again using its own agents, discussions were instigated in early January 1943 involving SOE, SO and FO in order to clarify their relationship.[130] An accord was quickly reached at a meeting involving Sir Charles Hambro (SOE), General W. Hansteen (Norwegian commander-in-chief), Colonel Huntingdon (SO) and Sir James Marshall-Cornwall (SOE). It was accepted that SO would set up a Norwegian desk in London and that all its personnel would be under the control of and be administered by the ANCC, which would have an American representative. All supplies and training facilities would also be pooled, although SO would normally service operations north of parallel 65°N (around Namsos, north of Trondheim).[131]

This provisional agreement and OSS proposal for operations in Norway using a base in Iceland was from 15 March 1943 repeatedly placed before the COS before being accepted by them with additions at a meeting on 24 March. With the Admiralty anxious to protect SIS from the potential risk of another organization operating in this theatre, the proviso that was eventually added was that although all OSS operations would be subject to the control of SOE and the Norwegian High Command, sea-borne operations would come under the authority of the Admiralty and would be subject to agreement with SIS.[132]

The SO section of OSS had therefore accepted that the whole of Norway was a SOE sphere of operation and that it had to work with both SOE and Norwegian military authorities. As a result in May 1943, Sir Frederic Cromwell from SO was attached to SOE and joined the ANCC until April 1944 when Lt. Commander F. W. G. Unger Vetlesen replaced him.[133] In the future SO would not act independently anywhere in Norway, even in the north where it eventually made its largest contribution. And any possibility of a 'crossing of lines' or duplication of effort was at least theoretically ruled out.

This arrangement was quickly replicated in Stockholm where it was agreed in June 1943 that an American special operations base could be established. In August Major (later Lt. Col.) George Brewer visited the city to commence preparations,[134] and in October 1943 a covenant was drawn up for the operation of this base, named 'Westfield', which was eventually located at the American Legation. The 'Westfield Mission' eventually had five officers, including its head Major George Brewer (Apollo) and Hans Ericksen (Vaudeville), who was responsible for Norwegian affairs. It was also accepted that all OSS missions out of Stockholm would be considered joint SOE/SO operations, that consultations would be held in advance and that there would be a full exchange of personnel and equipment when possible.[135]

By mid-1943, therefore, SO had not only subordinated itself to SOE and FO partnership but also become part of the network of organizations that played such a significant role in shaping SOE operations in Norway. American power soon came into play through the provision of additional equipment and resources. OSS helped in obtaining the three American submarine chasers – the 110-foot diesel-engined boats that from the autumn of 1943 were used to transport men and equipment across the North Sea to Norway's west coast. The loss of several of the fishing boats from the Shetlands Base, during the winter of 1942–3, resulted in SOE's decision to replace them, but unfortunately the Admiralty was unable to help. Eventually, it was General William Donovan that persuaded the JCS to agree to allow three American fast craft to join the Norwegian flotilla, under OSS command, provided the American 'Theatre Commander' agreed. Through the help of Admiral Stark, US naval representative in London since 1941, agreement was obtained and over the next eighteen months SOE was able to use these vessels to safely and significantly increase the volume of men and equipment it delivered to Norway.[136]

William Donovan and Colonel David Bruce, head of SO in Europe, were also directly involved in establishing Operation Sonnie. This set out to create an air transportation service adequate to bring initially 2,000 Norwegian refugees from Stockholm to Britain. The project began in early 1944, when five B-24 Liberators from the American 492nd Bomber Group were assigned to the US Army Air Force officer Bernt Balchen. The first flight to Stockholm was at the end of March 1944, and over the next seven months 1,547 Norwegians were flown back to Britain to become another pool of potential recruits for the Norwegian armed forces and merchant navy during the final stages of the war. By the end of the war, Operation Sonnie had flown over 5,000 refugees out of occupied Europe. As an offshoot of this, however, Balchen also managed to obtain the use of the six Liberators that carried out sixty-four sorties to Norway between June and September 1944 to drop supplies to *Milorg* groups. OSS personnel were attached to this unit and organized the provision of supplies, including food, medicine and sabotage materials, from their packaging station near Birmingham.[137]

It was also OSS that asked that SHAEF back a request for the provision of Arctic equipment from the United States in order to supply a series of reception camps for members of *Milorg* that SFHQ planned to set up in the Norwegian mountains during the final months of the war.[138] In early February, the JCS gave approval for OSS to ship 450 tons of equipment, sufficient for 30,000 to 40,000 Norwegian resistance fighters, to the UK. By mid-March, this material was ready for transportation to

Scandinavia, although by this time it was too late for it to be distributed and thereby be of any significant benefit to *Milorg*.[139]

It was also hoped that the Americans could provide additional manpower in order to help escalate special operations in Norway. In discussions in October 1942 over how to put the Knaben molybdenum mines in southern Norway out of action, the use of Americans was at one stage proposed.[140] After herring and cod oil were rejected as economic targets in Norway, both SOE and Norwegian authorities turned their attention towards the frostfilet factories. In February 1943, OSS was offered the opportunity to contribute to Operation Midhurst, a plan to attack the frostfilet factories at Hammerfest and Melba in northern Norway. The Norwegians approved the operation and although OSS initially received its invitation to take part with 'alacrity' there were bureaucratic difficulties. The mission was, however, eventually cancelled due to local operational difficulties, primarily the 'unhealthy state' of the north-west coast of Norway[141]

After the inception of OSS, William Donovan also began to examine the possibility of preparing groups of uniformed guerrilla soldiers recruited from ethnic Americans or foreign nationals, which could be used to operate behind enemy lines in areas specific to their language skills. This led in May 1943 to the setting up of OSS Operational Groups (OGs) Branch.[142] In July 1942 the American War Department had also constituted the 99th Infantry Battalion (Separate), with an authorized strength of 1,000 men, which would be made up of either Norwegian citizens or Norwegian-speaking American citizens. It was earmarked from an early stage for Norway's liberation. From the summer of 1943, this unit became the source of recruits for a Norwegian uniformed guerrilla unit called OSS Norwegian Operational Group (NORSO).[143]

Liaison between the Norwegian military authorities and OSS in the United States was established from early 1943 and with the NORSO group from that summer.[144] In December 1943, however, this unit, composed of eighty-four men and twelve officers, sailed for the UK. After its arrival, it was temporarily housed, equipped and trained at Forest Lodge, part of STS 26 near Aviemore. By April, it had been divided into two groups and a Field Service HQ and totalled eleven officers and eighty men.[145] While it was accepted that NORSO was technically a 'Commando' group for use behind enemy lines and therefore primarily designed for 'D-Day' operations in Europe,[146] SOE's Norwegian section wanted to make use of this additional manpower in Norway. After some deliberation, therefore, it was decided to use the

Americans for Operation Barter, a proposed attack against the pyrite mines on the island of Stord south of Bergen. SOE, FO and SO jointly prepared plans, but after some acrimony with William Donovan over the use of the American subchasers, it was eventually accepted that there was a lack of suitable transport and the operation was cancelled.[147]

In May 1944, however, NORSO was allocated to post D-Day activities in France, although they were not actually committed until 19 August. Consequently, despite protests from Scotco, who wanted them for 'Rankin B' preparations, the case of a sudden German withdrawal from Norway, the unit was at least temporarily not available for operations in Norway.[148] This did not, however, end OSS support for SOE and Norwegian activities, particularly in northern Norway. In the spring of 1944, in an effort to obtain much needed equipment for *Milorg* groups in the northern counties of Troms and Nordland, contact was made between Håkon Kyllingmark at the MI IV office at the Norwegian Legation and the Westfield Mission in Stockholm, which was seen as a potential source for these supplies.[149] It was, therefore, another attempt to tap American resources that led to the 'Sepals/Perianth' plan to establish bases along the Swedish border that under the cover of an intelligence operation and with the support of C-Bureau, the Swedish Intelligence Service, would act as a supply point. By mid-September 1944, two bases, 'Sepals' and 'Sepals I', and three field parties, 'Perianth' and 'Perianth I and II', were established in northern Sweden close to the Norwegian border in the area of Narvik.[150] OSS paid for most of the cost of setting up and running these bases as well as supplying the initial two and half tons of arms and equipment.[151]

After German forces had withdrawn from Finland into northern Norway in November 1944, however, the military importance of these bases increased and they were no longer simply involved in supporting local resistance groups or collecting intelligence. Their role was widened to include the sabotage of enemy fuel, ammunition dumps and its communications in the area.[152] It was also agreed that three new bases should be set up on Swedish territory.[153] Nevertheless, it was difficult to supply these bases and by the end of the year only a few handguns had been delivered and no sabotage material.[154] The only effective way to equip these remote locations, which were 300 kilometres from the nearest Swedish railhead, was by airdrop. Consequently, in early November, SFHQ contacted the American 492nd Bombardment Group (H) but was told that at that point there were no suitable aircraft. After this OSS became involved and in December wrote to the 'Commanding General, United States Strategic Air Forces' in Britain, and asked for long-range aircraft to be made available, but apparently with no success.[155] Despite the involvement of the Swedish Intelligence Services, the Swedish government had also not been informed of these operations and it was 10 March 1945 before permission was received to transport military material from Britain to Bromma airfield outside Stockholm.[156] Prior to this, supplies, arms and equipment were flown from the UK in Norwegian diplomatic bags, and although some of it eventually got through to the bases, it was a trickle and not the significant flow of material that was required.

Eventually six bases were established in Sweden close to the county of Nordland: 'Sepals' I, II and III; 'Sepals Gorgon'; 'Freethorpe'; and 'Coton'. Altogether about eighty men worked from these camps carrying out a range of activities including sabotage, gathering intelligence and supporting local *Milorg* forces in preparation for the liberation. Nevertheless, even after the flow of supplies to the area increased, by the time of the German capitulation many of the *Milorg* groups in the region were still largely unarmed.[157]

SOE also looked to American assistance for its operations elsewhere in Norway. After completing its work in France, NORSO returned to England, although eventually more than half of the unit was shipped back to the United States.[158] As early as September 1944, however, Scotco, SOE and SO had attempted to have the group assigned for railway sabotage. The original plan was to use two units of NORSO in northern Norway around Bodø to disrupt rail and highway transport, harass the enemy, destroy supplies and transmit intelligence.[159] But this came to nothing and the decision was taken to place them under the 'operational control' of Scotco in preparation for Operation Apostle, the plan to take control of Norway after a final German surrender.[160] In December 1944, however, after SHAEF authorized unrestricted operations against the Norwegian rail network, it was decided to make use of the remainder of the NORSO unit on operations in northern Norway, where it was felt the use of uniformed troops would not provoke a widespread German reaction. On 8 December 1944, Col. J. H. Alms from SHAEF had discussions with HRH the Crown Prince of Norway and it was decided that the use of uniformed troops south of Trondheim was undesirable because *Milorg* wanted to strike a blow on its own and it was feared that the presence of uniformed troops might provoke a major German reaction.[161] By mid-January, the decision had been taken to 'despatch an OG of thirty men by air to attack the railway north of Trondheim'.[162] Consequently, a party of thirty-six men under the command of Major William E. Colby, a future director of the Central

Intelligence Agency (CIA), was prepared for Operation Rype, an attack against the Norwegian rail network in the county of Nord Trøndelag. Unfortunately, only sixteen Americans were successfully dropped in March 1945, but they remained in the field until the liberation carrying out a small amount of sabotage as part of the widespread effort to delay German troop movement southwards. This was ultimately the only example where OSS forces were used in active operations within Norway.[163]

At a local operational level, therefore, the Americans made only a very small and largely ineffectual contribution to clandestine activities in Norway. American involvement was largely confined to the provision of equipment and transportation, and its overall influence on SOE's activities, although supportive, was therefore minimal. Even American power and resources could not overcome the many difficulties of operating in this peripheral theatre. Along with COHQ, PWE and the Norwegian military authorities, however, OSS became part of the wide collaborative effort that was behind special operations in Norway and which altogether had a largely favourable and expansive impact on SOE's activities in this theatre.

SOE never set out to work in isolation and was fully aware that it was part of a joint military effort. It was, however, not only relations with the new organizations that shaped SOE operations in Norway but also relations with the established and traditional armed forces. The RAF, USAAF and RN took a relatively small but significant interest in Norway, but despite their often-cited reservations over this new organization, from late 1940 they worked closely with SOE on a number of undertakings and were therefore also an important influence on its actions in this theatre.

Chapter 6

SOE AND THE MILITARY AND INTELLIGENCE ESTABLISHMENT OPERATING IN NORWAY, 1940–5: AN UNEXPECTED PARTNERSHIP

The professional military and intelligence establishment including the Royal Navy (RN), the Royal Air Force (RAF), the United States Army Air Force (USAAF) and the Special Intelligence Service (SIS), for a combination of operational and strategic reasons, along with SOE and the other new clandestine organizations, also took an active interest in Norway. There is, however, a dominate narrative that the 'professional military' and SIS at the highest level were particularly sceptical towards SOE and had little appreciation of what it was attempting to achieve.[1] Therefore, there was the potential for a conflict of interest within this theatre of operations, which could have had a detrimental impact on SOE actions. In Norway, however, SOE often worked closely with both the RN and RAF and even SIS when carrying out attacks against important strategic targets, and therefore rather than being undermined by difficult relations it was often able again to broaden its effort through collaboration.

Although strategic bombing in this theatre was very limited, it was often carried out either in partnership with SOE, which provided intelligence on targets, or independently after agreement had been reached that a particular site was deemed to be more suitable for an air attack than a local sabotage operation. Throughout the war in Europe, the Admiralty also had powerful reasons for taking an interest in Norwegian coastal waters. It was an important route for transporting both war materials and enemy forces, and from early 1942 was the location of the bulk of Germany's surface fleet, including the 52,600 ton battleship, the *Tirpitz*, which exceeded the most modern British capital ships in her combination of speed, size and power.[2] Consequently, the RN carried out a series of operations against economic and military targets in Norwegian waters, particularly enemy shipping, often in close partnership with SOE.

SOE's plans, contrary to previous assertions,[3] were also not significantly hindered by the interests of SIS, which was also very active in Norway from the summer of 1940. SIS was responsible through its agents for collecting military intelligence from the occupied countries and had a particularly close relationship to the Admiralty when it concerned Norway with its long coastline. It was given strategic priority over SOE in north-west Europe, but this never seriously curtailed SOE operations in this theatre. The two organizations often cooperated, both organizationally and at a local level.

The Norwegian government also had an involvement in and an impact upon many of these collaborative activities. It endeavoured to have some operations curtailed or at least restricted to targets that had been approved by all parties. This was particularly the case with air attacks, which could have a disproportionate and dreadful impact on the local population and therefore significant political ramifications. Overall, however, its contribution was again largely supportive and its provision of men, materials and local intelligence was often vital for the successful completion of many of the joint Allied operations within this theatre.

SOE and SIS in Norway: Ship watching and sabotage manage to coexist

SIS, established in 1909 as the foreign section of the Secret Service Bureau and responsible for espionage and counter-intelligence,[4] was very active in Norway between 1940 and 1945. It recruited over 200 agents and sent 190 operations to the country to obtain and through wireless telegraphy (W/T) send back military intelligence to Britain.[5] The total number of SIS agents described as those it 'called its own' plus those that were openly a telegraphist or the head of a station was 206, some of which were recruited but never used. Altogether, 187 agents can be identified through their operational name, place and time. The 190 operations include delivery of agents, courier operations and provision of supplies, although not the evacuation of agents. The chief duty of SIS in Norway 'was to provide shipping intelligence',[6] and most of its radio stations were situated along the coast, particularly around Trondheim. Many radio stations were, however, also established in Oslo, inland and even across the Swedish border, and sent a range of intelligence including details of German troop movements and of railway traffic between Oslo and Trondheim.[7] Nevertheless, Trondheim was the main German naval base in Norway and close to where the *Tirpitz* was berthed during approximately eleven of the first fourteen months of its stay in Norwegian waters.⁸

From the summer of 1940, SIS agents were sent to Norway. The first SIS operation in June 1940 was 'Hardware'. This was a hurried and improvised effort and although the station had radio contact between 10 June and 7 August 1940, it was quickly broken up and the eighteen people who were eventually behind the operation were arrested.⁹ Along with SOE, this interest and activity in the country continued over the following years within a context that included a battle for influence and control between the two organizations at a higher level that at times threatened the very existence of SOE.¹⁰ Nevertheless, despite the natural conflict between intelligence gathering and special operations,¹¹ and the strategic priority accorded to SIS,¹² the two organizations operated in Norway with relatively little conflict and both at an organizational and local operational level there is significant evidence of cooperation.

From the autumn of 1940, SOE's Scandinavian section gradually began to communicate and eventually share intelligence with its counterpart within SIS. The initial impetus behind this was the contact that both organizations made with the Norwegian authorities in London during summer 1940 in an effort to enlist new recruits. When on 23 July 1940, the Norwegian foreign minister met Anthony Eden, British minister of war, this led to meetings with Major Foley and Colonel Ramsden from SIS and an agreement to work together. Initially, SIS worked with a small department within the Norwegian Foreign Office called the *Utenriksdepartementets E-kontor*, the Foreign Office Intelligence Office (UD/E), which in January was incorporated into FD-E, under the Norwegian minister of defence.¹³ This eventually led both of them to work with FD-E, which in January 1941 under Captain Finn Nagell had been made responsible for contact with the 'English Secret Services'.¹⁴ Both SIS and SOE had interviewed Nagell shortly after his arrival in Britain,¹⁵ and therefore from an early stage and through that year he was in contact with and worked with both organizations. It was probably this tripartite relationship that created a closeness between the organizations that in January 1941 enabled J. B. Newill, section head for Norway in SIS,¹⁶ to send to SOE a report entitled 'Military Organisation in Norway', which had been produced by one of his operatives recently in the country. It included details of the agent Sverre Midtskau's contact with John Rognes from the emerging military resistance movement¹⁷ and was not the last time during 1941 that SOE received important intelligence on *Milorg* from SIS. By the following summer, after it feared that the Germans had penetrated the leadership of Milorg, SOE readily turned to SIS for help.[18]

A second factor that helped to increase contact between these two organizations was their shared use of the Shetlands Base. It was SIS officer, Captain L. H. Mitchell, who had worked in Oslo during the winter of 1939–40,[19] who initially commanded the base, and in the beginning he kept an eye on where SOE and SIS trips were heading, 'thus avoiding a clash'.[20] This process was undermined, however, when in July 1941, SIS opened its own naval base at Peterhead in Scotland. It did not apparently supply SOE details of the operations that it despatched from this base, unless requested. Therefore, from the summer of 1941, there was the possibility that both organizations could send agents to the same location at a similar time,[21] and in the spring of 1942 this lack of coordination was seen to have been the cause of the major tragedy that occurred in the small west coast settlement of Telavåg near Bergen. An SIS operation from Peterhead and an SOE operation – Penguin – from the Shetlands in quick succession sailed to similar points on the island of Sotra, where Telavåg is situated. Information obtained soon afterwards indicated that SIS operation had attracted local attention and therefore when SOE team arrived the suspicions of the local security police were already aroused. This ultimately led to a clash between two SOE agents and the Gestapo, with horrifying consequences for the local population. One of the SOE agents Arne Værum was killed and one captured and later executed. Two Gestapo officers were killed, which resulted in the execution of eighteen Norwegians, all the men in Telavåg between sixteen and sixty-five being deported to Sachsenhausen in Germany and all the houses in the town, over 300, being burnt to the ground.[22] This terrible incident, however, had one positive result in that it induced SIS in future to 'exchange lists of projected trips in advance',[23] and in September 1942 SOE reaffirmed this liaison to avoid any future 'crossing of lines' as far as transport and reception were concerned.[24]

A further indication of a growing working relationship between SOE and SIS was their willingness to exchange both experienced staff officers and more significantly agents who had already worked in the field. For example, in August 1943, Lieutenant Chaworth-Musters, who had worked for Section D and helped establish the Norwegian section of SOE, moved to SIS with the support of the organization's senior hierarchy. The movement of staff officers between the two organizations was not completely unusual, as is shown by the example of P. L. Johns and Chaworth-Muster's move had the full approval of Brigadier Colin

McV. Gubbins.[25] There are also several examples of men who began their career working for SIS in Norway, either as agents sent from England or as agents recruited within the country, who eventually moved on to work for SOE. Bjørn Rørholt began working for SIS in Norway as part of the 'Skylark B' team. He eventually returned to England but at the beginning of 1942 went back to Norway to set up SIS station 'Lerken'. He eventually fell out with SIS and joined SOE, working initially at SOE's STS 52, at Thame Park in Oxfordshire. Bernhard Haavardsholm also began working for SIS and Norwegian government in 1940. He eventually returned to Norway in October 1941 as the organizer for SOE operation 'Arquebus'.[26] Perhaps the best example is Knut Haukelid, who through his friendship with SIS agent Sverre Midtskau began his wartime career working for British intelligence in Norway. On arriving in England in 1941, however, Haukelid, anxious for more active work and with the recommendation of SIS, joined SOE and became a member of its 'Gunnerside' team that attacked the heavy water plant in Vemork in southern Norway in February 1943. Midtskau was originally sent into Norway on behalf of SIS and the Norwegian authorities in the summer of 1940, returning to Britain the following January. He was dropped back into Norway in February 1941. Haukelid knew Midtskau and began working for him at the Trondheim submarine base collecting intelligence that appears to have been sent to England via the 'Skylark B' station set up outside Trondheim.[27]

Even in the early stages of the war, SIS's intolerance of SOE at a senior level does not appear to have had a detrimental effect at an operational level. Moreover, it is possible to argue that the relationship between the two organizations ultimately had a positive impact, because the willingness of both to share intelligence led to closer contact and a growing coordination of activities. Lt. Col. Wilson, in his internal history of SOE's Norwegian section, claims that there was 'frequent intercommunication between the two sections', and that although weekly meetings eventually failed, 'information of any interest was passed immediately to SIS'. He does, however, criticize SIS for not being as helpful. This appears to be unjustified.[28] In January 1941, SOE's agent, Odd Starheim (Operation Cheese), was landed by submarine off the coast of southern Norway. He soon established wireless contact and sent back a stream of intelligence that contained details of potential sabotage targets, German troop dispositions and importantly for SIS shipping movements including information on the location of the German battleship *Bismarck*. Although at this time all wireless traffic was sent using SIS equipment and intelligence had to be passed to it before general circulation, SOE still made an effort to contact SIS and urged it to make immediate use of the material provided by Starheim.[29]

SOE and SIS also both took an active interest in the production of heavy water at the Norsk Hydro plant at Vemork, which led them to communicate regularly and work together. In the spring of 1941, SIS station, 'Skylark B', which operated in and around Trondheim, was used to request up-to-date information on the site,[30] and from this point SIS continued to make a concerted effort to obtain intelligence on Vemork, often with the help of SOE. Professor Leif Tronstad and Jomar Brun, who were key figures in the supply of intelligence and planning of operations against the plant, worked closely with both Eric Welsh, Newill's successor as head of SIS's Norwegian section but also owing to his chemistry background and knowledge of heavy water its scientific liaison officer with DSIR, and Lt. Col. Wilson of SOE. They effectively served as a bridge between the two organizations.[31] Moreover, in April 1943, Lt. Col. Wilson wrote that with regard to Operation Gunnerside, SIS was 'fully cognisant of this operation beforehand, as a result of information personally conveyed to them by me'.[32] From this point, SOE, using the intelligence supplied by its 'Swallow' W/T station, also regularly sent information to SIS on heavy water along with details of the final operations carried out against its production and transportation.[33]

This stream of intelligence was not, however, one way but also flowed from the offices of SIS to SOE. The furnishing of information about *Milorg* was only the beginning. Over the next four years, there were several examples of SIS forwarding intelligence provided through its radio stations in Norway, on to SOE. SIS station 'Theta' supplied details on the fate of the two SOE agents 'Anchor' and 'Penguin', who had clashed with the Gestapo outside Telavåg.[34] SOE was informed of the arrest of its 'Archer' W/T operator and of the fate of Operation Martin by SIS.[35] SIS was fully aware of 'Martin' because several months previously both organizations had agreed to keep each other informed of their operations.[36] By June 1943, therefore, Lt. Col. Wilson was able to write that liaison with SIS was 'better' and that 'advance notice of operations is exchanged monthly, and weekly meetings are held'.[37]

Both organizations had clandestine wireless operators working in Norway, often in close proximity, communicating with the Home Station back in Britain. But instead of working in isolation they often supported each other. In October 1942, SOE's W/T operator 'Plover', Per Solnørdal, took over SIS station 'Beta' and using its equipment and signals plan operated it for several weeks on behalf of both SIS and SOE.[38] At the beginning of 1943, SOE station 'Swan' sent a message on behalf of SIS station 'Orion', which had trouble with its set, and SIS replied to 'Orion' via 'Swan'.[39] In 1945, when SOE station 'Snowflake' had problems with its set, the nearby SIS station 'Roska' helped by sending telegrams.[40]

This sharing of stations was not just a consequence of expediency but also the result of direct requests from SIS. In November 1943, SIS asked if it could send a ship watcher to link up with SOE wireless station 'Arquebus'. In September 1943, while preparations were being made to send SOE's 'Redwing' team to the Bergen area, SIS asked if it could be made available to them.[41] Conditions in Norway, the small, isolated communities, meant that SOE and SIS teams often worked in the same locality, shared the same contacts and on occasion crossed lines. SOE operation 'Martin' and SIS station 'Upsilon' shared the same contacts in the Troms region of northern Norway, initially unbeknown to each other, which caused a crossing of lines between the two. SOE team 'Antrum' established its radio station literally next door to SIS station 'Koppa' in the Ålesund district.[42] Although SIS's policy was initially to set up wireless stations in isolation from the local community, so-called 'hermit' stations, this proved impossible. It has been estimated that as many as 2,000 Norwegians assisted SIS in Norway,[43] and its agents not only cooperated with SOE agents but also with indigenous resistance and intelligence groups across the country. As early as 1941, SIS station 'Skylark B' had made contact with *Milorg* and sent messages on its behalf. SIS also eventually worked closely with the indigenous intelligence organization in Norway called 'XU', which collected static intelligence on German troop dispositions, numbers and fortifications. In November 1942, SIS sent two agents who were to make themselves available for XU. One of SIS's best known agents, Oluf Reed-Olsen, was sent to Norway in June 1943 to set up the radio station 'Aquarius', and the local XU groups in Stavanger, Egersund and Flekkefjord helped to get him established and supplied him with intelligence.[44]

As SIS was given strategic priority over SOE in north-west Europe, including Norway, it has been suggested that this limited certain of its activities in this theatre.[45] This does not appear to have been the case in Norway and SOE was able to implement all aspects of its policy, even attacks against economic and military targets through *coup de main* operations, without significant hindrance and despite the concerns of SIS. When on 4 January 1943, COS confirmed that ACOS would be 'the coordinating authority for small operations on the Norwegian coast',[46] it was also agreed that 'where the proposed activities of SOE and SIS and minor raids' clashed, SIS would 'ordinarily be given priority'. In the future it would be the Admiralty, through ACOS, who would decide whether the activities of either COHQ or SOE prejudiced the security of SIS operations in Norway.[47] At a meeting held at Admiralty House in London on 28 May 1943 to discuss operations along the Norwegian coast, and which included representatives from the Admiralty, SIS, SOE and COHQ, it was agreed by all parties that 'intelligence affecting movements of the German fleet' had top priority.[48] Notwithstanding this, however, and despite the many occasions that SIS objected to SOE operations along or near the Norwegian coast, it rarely got its own way. Therefore, the precedence conferred on SIS never resulted in a so-called 'ban' on SOE activities in this theatre.[49]

In August 1943, SIS objected to Operation Feather, a planned SOE operation against the Orkla pyrite mines,[50] but the operation eventually went ahead on the understanding that the party did not approach anywhere near the Trondheim fjord area. In December 1943, SIS objected to Operation Osprey, a plan to send an SOE party to the Stavanger area,[51] but without success. SIS also opposed some of SOE's plans to attack enemy shipping in Norwegian coastal waters using kayaks and submersible vessels. In February 1944 it objected to Operation Vestige V, a plan to use kayaks to get close to and attach limpet mines to shipping in Sagvåg harbour, the transportation point for pyrites from the Willebø mines on the island of Stord.[52] The operation, however, after its details had been passed to SIS[53] and it had been referred to ACOS, was allowed to go ahead. It was ultimately a failure, but in a spirit of cooperation, the intelligence obtained during the operation was passed to SIS.[54] In August 1944, SOE decided that it would reattempt the 'Vestige V' operation and SIS again protested. As it was about to land an agent in the vicinity at the same time its objection was upheld and the operation cancelled.[55] In 1944, SIS also opposed three of SOE's 'Salamander' operations – the attacks using the 'Sleeping Beauty' mini-submersible canoe against enemy shipping along the Norwegian coast. Five operations were proposed and two appear to have been cancelled due to SIS objections; two, however, went ahead and one was cancelled for local operational reasons.[56]

There appears to be no evidence in either SOE archives in London or Oslo that any major SOE *coup de main* operation against an industrial target in Norway was called off because of an SIS objection.[57] The activities of both these organizations occasionally led to the arrest of each other's agents and therefore the break up of operations, and in this theatre SIS was equally if not more culpable. The Abwehr agent Otto Robsahm, who was disastrously recruited by SIS in Stockholm, caused immense damage to SOE. He contributed to the failure of Operation Performance, an attempt to sail Norwegian ships out of Swedish harbours and over to the UK, and which ultimately led to the death of 16 men and imprisonment of a further 233.[58] Close examination of correspondence between the two organizations reveals that both made an effort to coordinate their activities and generally to cooperate, therefore their relationship was largely constructive.

SOE and the Admiralty: New and old combine in Norwegian waters

Norway is 1,752 kilometres (approx. 1,100 miles) long, but the total length of its coastline is 21,111 kilometres (approx. 13,000 miles). The coastal waters consist of the inner leads, the channel of water that runs between the many offshore islands (skerries) and the coastline, where vessels can escape from the worst ravages of the North Sea.[59] This was not only an important artery for the transportation of war materials to Germany but also for the movement of German forces, especially after the invasion of the Soviet Union in 1941. In peacetime, Germany had taken 14 per cent of Norway's exports, of which 97 per cent, by value, were sea-borne,[60] and therefore attacking this artery was yet another way to subvert the enemy's war effort.

By early 1942, Norwegian waters had also become the location for both units of the German surface fleet and some of its U-boats. By May 1942, the German navy had one battleship, the *Tirpitz*; three heavy cruisers (Admiral Scheer, Admiral Hipper and Lutzow); eight destroyers; four torpedo boats; and twenty U-boats located in the area between Trondheim and Kirkenes. These were seen as a potential threat to maritime routes across the Atlantic and an immediate danger to the Allied convoys transporting important materials around the North Cape to the Soviet Union.[61] Consequently, between late January 1942, when the first air attack was carried out against it, and November 1944 when it was finally put out of action, the *Tirpitz* became a major target for the RN. A total of fifteen direct attacks were carried out against the German battleship: of these seven were by the RAF, seven by the Fleet Air Arm and one under the authority of the Flag Officer Submarines (FOS) using midget submarines (X-craft).[62] The protection of the Arctic convoys from the German fleet was, however, an additional unwelcome burden on Britain's overstretched Home Fleet and added 'enormously to the Admiralty's global strategic problems'.[63]

Norwegian coastal waters were not, however, only important to the RN. As seen, they were a gateway through which SOE sent many of its teams into Norway to carry out *coup de main* attacks or to organize local resistance groups. Moreover, these coastal waters were the location of a series of SOE attacks against enemy shipping, and these sea-borne operations required naval support, either through the provision of transportation or technical aid. Several of SOE's activities in or close to Norwegian waters were also a direct consequence of its assistance to the RN in operations against units of the German surface fleet, particularly the *Tirpitz*. After conventional methods failed, the RN was fully prepared to make use of more unorthodox means, including the employment of a selection of submersible vessels. SOE was then able to contribute by supplying intelligence, Norwegian volunteers and special equipment.

Furthermore, cooperation between SOE and the RN was assisted by an important contribution from the Norwegian military authorities. The Royal Norwegian Navy and, from 1942, the Defence High Command (FO) became actively involved in SOE's operations against economic and military targets along the Norwegian seaboard through both the provision of vessels and the supply of expertise and local intelligence. The Norwegian authorities were also less likely to oppose Allied operations in coastal waters, as unlike attacks on the mainland they were not liable to lead to severe consequences for the local population or resistance.

Only with the support and consent of ACOS, who had overall responsibility for many of the minor operations carried out from the Shetlands against targets close to the Norwegian seaboard or in its coastal waters, was SOE able to expedite the bulk of its sea-borne activities. From the autumn of 1940, with the setting up of the Shetlands Base, SOE had a good local working relationship with ACOS,[64] and when an independent Norwegian section was established in early 1942, Major F. W. Ram was given responsibility for liaison between the two parties.[65] Moreover, it does not appear that the Admiralty, through the commander-in-chief Home Fleet, ever objected to or interfered with this relationship and often contributed to it by directly assisting many of SOE's sea-borne operations.

Towards the close of 1940, both the RN and SOE began to show an interest in applying economic pressure against Germany through interdicting the transportation of war materials through Norwegian coastal waters. Churchill's interest in hindering the movement of Swedish iron ore through Narvik and along the Norwegian coastline, which had begun in 1939, resurfaced in late 1940. On 22 and 26 December 1940, the prime minister wrote to the First Sea Lord pressing for the sowing of magnetic mines in the leads in an effort to stop the export of this important war material to Germany. The reply from the First Sea Lord was that the German ore traffic was 'watched continuously'.[66] In early 1941, SOE also began to consider the possibility of interrupting supplies of sulphur and ferrochrome from Norway, which led to two provisional plans, called 'Gertrude' and 'Landlubber'.[67] Furthermore, it began to instigate Operation Maundy, a plan to use Norwegian fishing boats from the Shetlands to lay mines in the leads, thereby forcing enemy shipping into the open seas where it was vulnerable to naval attack. The first 'Maundy' operation left on 29 April 1941, and laid eleven of eighteen 'R-Type' mines provided by the Admiralty, which also loaned a chief petty officer from Rosyth to assist preparations. A second operation left the Shetlands on 19 October 1941 with forty-two mines, which were laid on 21 October. A proposal in 1942 to use members of SOE team 'Lark', based in the Trondheim area, to mine the local fjords using a rowing boat was never carried out, and four further attempts to lay mines in 1944 using a submarine chaser failed due to bad weather.[68]

In the spirit of 'Maundy', the more ambitious project called Operation Wallah was also put together.[69] The objective was to paralyse 'as far as possible the German sea-borne traffic along the coast of Norway'.[70] In July 1941, the Admiralty approved the plan and with the assistance of the Norwegian Naval Staff and *Nortraship* (the Norwegian Shipping and Trade Mission), the SS *Anderson* was provided as the base for the operation. The RN supplied two 'Q-ships', heavily armed merchant vessels, which would be used to intercept German shipping along the coast. It was also proposed that local Norwegian fishing boats should be purchased and used to sail into harbours and affix explosives to enemy ships. To assist collaboration, a planning committee was set up and included representatives from the 'Q- ships', SOE and Norwegian naval officers. In October 1941, the operation was placed under ACOS and in November under the C-in-C Home Fleet before it became part of Operation Anklet, which was eventually no more than a larger-scale but less ambitious version of 'Wallah'.[71] An element of 'Wallah' was, however, resurrected in January 1942 when the two 'Q-ships' sailed from the Shetlands with the aim of attacking enemy shipping using Norwegian coastal waters. SOE supplied intelligence, an officer, army and navy personnel, arms and explosives, but the ships were spotted by enemy aircraft and forced to return.[72]

Collaboration between SOE and the RN also extended to joint operations against economic targets along or close to the Norwegian seaboard, especially the Norwegian fish industry. An early indication of this was Operation Almoner, a plan to seize the Norwegian herring fleet and German escorting trawlers working between Haugesund and Egersund off the south-west coast of Norway. The original request for the operation came from the Admiralty, but it was believed that SOE would play a role through providing the Norwegian seaman who would act as special armed guards. Although the COS approved the operation in 'principle', by 18 March it had been abandoned at the request of the Norwegian government;[73] the potential damage to an important industry was apparently too much for it to sanction.

Operation Hemisphere, however, the attack against a herring oil plant at Øksfjord in northern Norway, went ahead a few weeks later. The party, consisting of ten Norwegian marines and one SOE agent, sailed on 8 April 1942 on the 'Mansfield', an ex-American destroyer belonging to the Norwegian navy, and returned on 15 April having completely destroyed the plant. Commander Frank Stagg from SOE conceived the plan, and SOE provided arms and explosives. Rear Admiral T. S. V. Phillips, deputy chief of the naval staff, and Captain E. C. Danielsen, the Norwegian naval chief of staff, both approved the operation.[74]

From an early stage, the Admiralty understood the military contribution that SOE could make in this theatre. Nevertheless, during 1941 cooperation achieved very little, and in the first half of 1942, as with the larger amphibious raids, small sea-borne operations along the Norwegian seaboard tailed off.[75] From November 1942, however, the RN was able to expand small-scale operations against enemy shipping in Norwegian coastal waters through the creation, under the command of ACOS, of the Royal Norwegian 30th Motor Torpedo Boat (MTB) Flotilla (RNorN MTB Flotilla). This consisted of eight 'Fairmile type D' MTBs with Norwegian crews, which were used in a series of anti-shipping operations, code-named 'VP'. The Special Service Brigade and Norwegian authorities also provided the troops for Combined Operations North Force (CONF), which carried out boarding actions, provided shore guards and undertook small raids.[76]

Furthermore, from March 1943, SOE's primary concern in north-west Europe was with 'current activities', a euphemism for sabotage, and the priority for Norway was 'direct or indirect interference with coastal shipping', which meant that SOE increasingly concentrated its efforts in Norwegian waters.[77] By necessity, these had to be based on close cooperation between SOE and ACOS, and consequently in the spring of 1943 Sir George Montagu Pollock RN, who had been specifically engaged by SOE's Norwegian section to take on responsibility for sea operations, was chosen to act as liaison officer between the two parties.[78] The result of this collaboration was two series of operations called 'Vestige' and 'Barbara', respectively, which were prepared under the command of ACOS but received the full support of SOE. The 'general intention' was to 'supplement' strikes by surface craft through attacking enemy shipping 'anchored' in Norway's coastal waters.[79]

Altogether, between September 1943 and April 1944, eight 'Vestige' operations were sent to Norway. They consisted of teams of Norwegian personnel from NIC (1), who had been trained to use a Norwegian-designed kayak or the Folbot (a folding canoe) to get close to and then attach limpet mines to enemy shipping anchored within the inner leads. ACOS would assist either by making available MTBs to transport SOE teams across the North Sea or by using these vessels to force enemy shipping into safe anchorage where it could be attacked. The operations, however, achieved little with just two teams having some success. The terrible weather conditions that often occurred along Norway's west coast during the autumn months made the use of kayaks particularly hazardous and the delivery and pick-up of the SOE teams extremely problematic. It took five attempts to pick up the 'Vestige I' team, and some of the operations eventually stayed in the field for several months carrying out other activities. The 'Vestige IV' operation, which arrived in southern Norway in March 1944, remained in the country until the end of the war.[80]

Alongside 'Vestige' were the 'Barbara' operations, another plan to attack enemy shipping but this time using the Welman one-man midget submarine. SOE had begun to develop this vessel in the spring of 1942 in response to an Admiralty request for it to consider methods for attacking large capital ships – in particular, the *Tirpitz*. Professor Newitt and Lt. Col. Dolphin of SOE's Technical Section conceived the 'Welman' at the research station (Station IX) in Welwyn. It was originally for Operation Frodesley, a plan to attack the *Tirpitz* in spring 1942. The operation never took place but the first 'Welman' was tested in July 1942. It was a 20-foot submersible craft, electrically driven with a range of approximately thirty miles, able to carry one person and with a warhead containing 560 lbs of explosives.[81] It turned out, however, to be a drawn out and lengthy process but interest in the potential of the Welman continued with COHQ, the Admiral (Submarines) and SOE. At a meeting in early 1943, it was decided to place an initial order for 150 of these vessels, of which 80 would be required by SOE. It was agreed that the Admiral (Submarines) should be responsible for their sea training and handling, while SOE would appoint a liaison officer to assist.[82] By April 1943, however, ACOS had also began to take an interest in the Welman and wrote to the Admiralty requesting an allocation of twenty-five vessels, which it planned to use against enemy shipping in Norwegian waters.[83] In July, SOE made Lt. D. A. Howarth responsible for examining the possibilities of the Welman, and this eventually led him to work with ACOS on the planning and preparation of operations using these craft.[84] Moreover, seven Norwegians from NIC (1) were selected to undergo training in their use and a special base was established at Lunna Voe on the Shetlands.[85]

The perceived potential of the Welman as another unorthodox means to attack enemy shipping, therefore, led to further collaboration between SOE and the RN. Typically, however, conditions in the North Sea again proved insurmountable and of the four proposed Welman operations only the first, 'Barbara I', was attempted on the night of 20 November 1943 against the Laksevaag floating dock used for submarine repairs and shipping in Bergen harbour. Nevertheless, in order to assist further proposed attacks, SOE provided forward parties at strategically important locations along the Norwegian coastline in readiness to collect intelligence on the movement of enemy shipping. But owing to a range of local difficulties, the three remaining 'Barbara' operations were never carried out.[86]

There were also plans to attack enemy shipping by employing Chariots, self-driven torpedoes for two, which would be carried on MTBs to be used at an opportune moment. In September 1943, four 'Chariots' arrived in the Shetlands and one or two MTBs were fitted with davits to carry these craft. The 'Chariot' was an electrically driven, torpedo-shaped vessel with a range of twenty-four miles. The crew sat astride the vessel, which had a detachable warhead containing 600 lbs of explosives that could be fixed to a ship by magnets. In October 1943, Karl Vilnes was landed on Atløy, a small island off Norway's West Coast near Florø, to report shipping movements to an MTB that lay in wait with Chariots on-board, but no suitable targets arrived. Owing to the continually bad weather, it appears that after this no further such operations were ever attempted, and as with the Welmans, the idea was dropped and never resurrected.[87]

Notwithstanding the failure of the 'Vestige' and 'Barbara' operations, the use of midget submarines and submersible vessels was not, however, completely abandoned. Norwegian coastal waters continued to be strategically important to the Allies during 1944. In August, Sweden placed a ban on the use of its merchant fleet for trade with Germany and more importantly in September it closed its Baltic ports to Axis shipping. The Germans were therefore compelled to make greater use of Norwegian ports, especially Narvik in the north, and with the withdrawal of German troops into Norway from Finland in the autumn of 1944, the inner leads became an important route for moving or supplying these forces.[88] Furthermore, as the Allies advanced across France, German U-boats were moved from the Biscay ports to Norway to supplement units that were already there. With new technical developments and patterns of deployment, this was seen as a matter for 'concern' within the Admiralty.[89]

Within this context and with support from within the Admiralty, SOE prepared the 'Salamander' operations, which targeted U-boat depot ships, U-boats and enemy shipping in Norwegian harbours. Along with sabotage, this was SOE's contribution to the Allied offensive against the German U-boat presence in Norway that began in 1944.[90] Altogether five operations to attach limpet mines to ships at anchor, using the 'Sleeping Beauty' motor submersible canoe developed by SOE during 1943, were proposed. As seen owing to SIS's objections and local operational difficulties, however, only two were attempted, and these were unsuccessful.[91]

In addition, SOE worked with the RN's FOS on X-craft (midget submarine) operations against the German U-boat presence in Norway. The 'X-craft' was a fully equipped miniature submarine with a range of 150 miles. The craft had a crew of three and could carry six commandos on a short passage. It also carried two two-ton charges that could be laid on the seabed beneath the target. It assisted in the preparation of Operations Guidance and Heckle, attacks carried out in April and September 1944, respectively, against the Laaksevaag floating dock in Bergen, by suggesting lurking places and escape routes for the crews. On this occasion, the operations had some success. In April a coal ship, the *Bärenfels*, was sunk, and in September four sections of the dock were destroyed along with two merchant ships.[92]

Unlike the actions of Coastal Command and the MTBs,[93] SOE operations against enemy shipping in Norwegian waters, using an array of improvised or submersible vessels, were largely failures. Out of the at least nineteen planned attacks against enemy shipping using the inner leads in 1943 and 1944, two were cancelled as a direct result of SIS objections and two operations achieved some success. The remaining fifteen were either hindered by bad weather or were unable to identify a suitable target at a time when the operation had any chance of success. This compares unfavourably with the efforts of the 30th and 54th Norwegian MTB Flotillas, which between the end of 1942 and the spring of 1945 sank at least twenty-one merchant vessels, one destroyer and twelve or thirteen patrol vessels.[94] These operations should not, however, be seen in isolation but as a small part of the wider offensive that was carried out against enemy shipping in Norwegian waters, and which helped to divert enemy manpower and resources to this peripheral theatre particularly in 1943 and 1944 in the run up to Overlord.[95]

This offensive was also given added urgency by the arrival of the *Tirpitz* off Trondheim in January 1942. The *Tirpitz* was sent to Norway to protect the German position and to tie down British naval forces in the Atlantic away from other theatres,[96] and the many operations launched against this battleship indicate that at the time it was considered a serious threat to British interests. Furthermore, its presence in Norwegian waters became an additional encouragement for the RN, especially after air attack had failed, to work with SOE and make use of its unorthodox methods to help sink or at least severely disable this powerful vessel.

SIS supplied extensive intelligence on the position and movements of the *Tirpitz*. It was SIS station 'Theta' that reported the arrival of the *Tirpitz* in Trondheim. From this point, a major effort was put underway by the intelligence services to establish a number of its agents in the vicinity of Trondheim to watch over the German battleship. During 1942, five SIS clandestine radio stations were established in this area and made contact with the Home Station: 'Lerken I', 'Lerken II', 'Leporis', 'Scorpion' and 'Virgo'.[97] SOE organization, 'Antrum', however, which had been established in the Ålesund district from December 1941, also transmitted telegrams in February and March 1942 that contained details on the location of the battleship.[98] From February 1942, the first steps were also taken to establish the 'Lark' team in the Trondheim area. The objective of this SOE operation was typically to organize, train and arm local guerrilla groups in readiness to assist a still anticipated landing in Norway, but its location made it an important asset for gathering intelligence on and assisting operations against the *Tirpitz*. It has also been claimed that until the end of May the 'Lark' W/T set was probably used by an SIS operative to send intelligence and that SOE HQ was not made aware of this.[99]

In March 1942, the Admiralty requested that SOE consider ways of placing explosives close to the *Tirpitz* using a one-man submarine and as seen it was the resultant project called 'Frodesley' that ultimately led to the development of the Welman. It was originally proffered that SOE recruits would be used to carry out the attack, but SOE saw it as a job for naval personnel and its role was therefore confined to supplying intelligence and possibly transportation.[100] At the time, however, it appears that there was considerable urgency within the Admiralty to undertake some form of operation against the German battleship, and as the development of the Welman was a long-term project 'Frodesley' was dropped.[101] Within this context in May 1942, SOE began to examine ways of carrying out sabotage against the *Tirpitz*, and these included attacking the submarine nets or smuggling explosives and incendiaries onboard the ship through using the 'Lark' organization.[102] It also continued to provide intelligence on the battleship's position and defences, and in April/May 1942, SOE agent, Johnny Pevik, returned to Britain bringing with him important local intelligence.[103]

In June 1942, however, SOE was approached by the Admiral (Submarines) and asked if it would cooperate in a plan to attack the *Tirpitz* in Åsenfjord, a branch of Trondheimsfjord. This was Operation Title, a proposal to use Chariots to place explosives under the battleship. By June 1942, this new craft was ready for its initial trials and therefore, despite an awareness that the German battleship was temporarily in northern Norway, preparations for 'Title' were pressed on with. The 'Lark' organization was initially asked to persuade a local man to lend his fishing boat so that the Chariots could be towed through the local security controls. But when this failed, it obtaining the paperwork that enabled SOE to produce the false documents that would allow a boat from the Shetlands to gain close proximity to the German battleship. Preparations were also made by the 'Lark' organization to assist the escape of the fishing vessel and Chariot crews to Sweden after the operation had been completed.[104] On 26 October 1942, two days after the *Tirpitz* had arrived back in Trondheim to be overhauled, the Norwegian fishing vessel, *Arthur*, crewed by four Norwegians from the Shetlands Base and with two Chariots and six naval personnel onboard, left the Shetlands.[105] The operation was, however, never completed as the Chariots were lost while being towed in heavy seas.

The resolve to sink or disable the *Tirpitz*, however, remained and led to further collaboration. As early as October 1942, SOE was asked to provide a Norwegian fishing vessel for towing trials of a new and fully equipped miniature submarine, the X-craft.[106] These would eventually be used in Operation Source, a successful attempt against the *Tirpitz* in September 1943. The initial plan was to tow them to an island off Trondheim from where they would proceed independently to attack the German battleship. As with 'Title', the 'Lark' organization would help the submarine crews to escape to Sweden if they were forced to swim ashore.[107] By February 1943, however, it had become clear that the craft would not be ready for an attack that spring and the operation was postponed to the following season. In March 1943, the *Tirpitz* joined the *Scharnhorst* in Narvik and then Altafjord in northern Norway. As SOE had no presence in this area, its involvement in Operation Source ended. Nevertheless, on 11 September 1943, six submarines left British waters towing the six 'X-craft' that would attack the *Tirpitz* and *Scharnhorst* in Altafjord in northern Norway. Two craft were lost on the way, but eventually on 22 September two vessels managed to place charges below the *Tirpitz*, and considerable damage was done to the battleship. Repairs took five months. The *Scharnhorst*, however, escaped undamaged.[108]

A significant number of sea-borne operations were carried out by SOE in Norwegian waters between 1940 and 1944. They were a result of both the strategic importance placed on attacks against enemy shipping in this theatre and the level of collaboration that developed between SOE, the RN and ultimately the Norwegian military authorities. It was also a similar story for air-borne operations.

SOE and the British and American air forces in Norway: Bombing, sabotage or a combination?

SOE not only collaborated on sea-borne operations but also with attacks from the air, although in comparison to the scale of the strategic air campaign against Germany, Norway received very little attention. Nevertheless, both the RAF and the United States of America Army Air Force (USAAF) eventually carried out a small number of actions against selective targets in this theatre. The official histories of the RAF and USAAF, respectively, only refer to a total of four bombing operations in Norway: an attack on Stavanger aerodrome on 11 April 1940, an attack on the Knaben molybdenum factory in March 1943, an attack against *Nordisk Lettmetal* at Herøya in July 1943 and the air attack against Rjukan and Knaben in November 1943.[109] In addition, however, there was also the string of operations undertaken by the RAF and Fleet Air Arm against the *Tirpitz*, the dropping of thousands of mines in Norwegian coastal waters and the Skagerrak, and Coastal Command's campaign against enemy shipping.[110]

Previous histories of SOE have tended to focus on its struggle with Bomber Command over the availability of aircraft.[111] There was, however, another aspect to the relationship between these two parties that in the case of Norway was far more constructive. From the autumn of 1940, one of SOE's objectives in this theatre was to make sure that it was in a position to render 'active assistance' to attacks from the air on the few occasions that they were undertaken.[112] When in the summer of 1941 strategic bombing was upgraded to the 'main campaign aimed at the "wearing down" of German power' and it was decided that sabotage should be directed 'in accordance with the bombing policy aim', this link between SOE activities and air operations was confirmed.[113]

The use of this powerful and devastating strategic instrument, however, also had potentially major implications for the civilian population, which often suffered as a direct result of the RAF's recurring inability to hit the intended target.[114] Therefore, it became an important political issue. The Norwegian government could not ignore collateral damage and a large number of civilian deaths and consequently attempted to ensure through cooperation with its allies that strategic bombing was used sparingly in Norway and only against what were considered targets of legitimate military value. Here it had some but certainly not complete success. Rather paradoxically, however, the Norwegian authorities through SOE were not averse to calling on the RAF to assist in attacking targets in Norway if it was believed an operation could have an important internal political value, such as bolstering morale or encouraging resistance.

Because of its political ramifications, the role of strategic bombing in Norway has attracted significant interest among Norwegian historians.[115] Notably, however, with the bulk of Bomber Command's resources focused on Germany, along with the small number of strategic targets and the large distances involved, sabotage and *coup de main* operations were usually more suited to attacks against economic and military targets in Norway. Consequently, unlike on the continent, they constituted the predominant means used to attack German power in this theatre. Nevertheless, certain important sites could only be assaulted from the air and therefore when required SOE would not hesitate to turn to and collaborate with the RAF or USAAF, and if ultimately necessary ignore the concerns of the Norwegian authorities. Decisions over whether to bomb or sabotage a target were based on what was most suitable at the time, not a predetermined policy. The aim was ultimately the same: to deny Germany supplies of key war materials.

SOE and RAF collaboration in Norway began as early as the autumn of 1940. Representatives of SOE, including Charles Hambro, attended a meeting at the Air Ministry in November, which led to Operations Youth and Beauty, three attacks by Coastal Command's No 18 Group against the railway line and a hotel at Finse, which accommodated German troops, north-east of Bergen. The three attacks were carried out on the nights of 17/18 December, 19/20 December and 21/22 December 1940 and targeted the snow sheds along twenty-five miles of railway between Myrdal and Haugastøl and the hotel at Finse. It was claimed that both the railway and snow sheds were hit, as was the hotel, but with little apparent damage.[116] SOE had already identified the Oslo-Bergen railway as a potential objective and provided the Air Ministry with maps and cine-films of the targets. According to Coastal Command, the aim of the operations was to encourage local resistance,[117] and as SOE had already built up contacts with groups in this area, there is good reason to believe this is correct. SOE papers from the autumn of 1940 refer to possible attacks against the Oslo-Bergen railway and the snow sheds as part of cutting communications within the country in support of an eventual rebellion. As seen this policy was dropped in December 1940, but there was a belief at the time that there was a significant resistance movement in the area and this operation was probably designed to encourage and support its development. Others have argued that the attacks were a defensive measure aimed at hampering any proposed invasion of Britain from Norway but the 'Claribel' schemes, which were designed exactly for this purpose, were not put together until after these operations were carried out.[118] Regular meetings between SOE and Coastal Command were suggested and further targets considered, but at a time of restricted resources nothing appears to have come of this.

As shown, during 1941, raids were the predominate form of operation against economic and military targets in the Norwegian theatre.[119] There were a small number of attacks carried out by the Fleet Air Arm and Coastal Command against economic targets along or close to the Norwegian coastline during the autumn and winter of 1941–2. In September 1941, planes from HMS Victorious, part of 'Force M' that had sailed with the first convoy to the Soviet Union, attacked the quay to the A/S Frostfilet factory near Bodø, while planes from 823 squadron attacked the power station at Glomfjord and the aluminium works in Haugvik. In December 1941 and January 1942, planes from Coastal Command attacked herring oil factories along the Norwegian coast.[120] But at a time when Bomber Command lacked the resources to undertake anything close to a sustained and widespread air campaign against Germany, Norway was largely ignored. It began the war with just thirty-three squadrons, half of which were only light bombers, and even the heavy bombers lacked the range-payload combination to be really effective over Germany. In the second half of 1940 although numbers had increased to thirty-eight squadrons, no more than twenty bombers were usually available for a single night's operations.[121] Nevertheless, SOE began to prepare its own operations against major sites, and while putting these together it became clear that certain targets, because of size or location, were more suited to attacks from the air.

From the spring of 1941, SOE's Norwegian section began to prepare Operation Clairvoyant, the proposed action against crucial hydroelectric power plants across southern Norway, including the one at Vemork that was deemed more suitable for an air attack than sabotage. The plan was that support would be provided by SOE on the ground through a party of three under Jens Poulsson, the future leader of the 'Grouse' operation, which would light flares to lead the aircraft to the target.[122] Bombing was, however, initially abandoned because of the objections of the Norwegian military authorities,[123] but the idea of using an air attack against Vemork never completely went away. During preparations for Operation Freshman, COHQ saw a daylight raid by the American air force as the 'best alternative' should their plans prove impracticable. SOE apparently raised no objections to this, although they felt 'in the best interests of future co-operation', General Hansteen should be informed beforehand.[124] The Americans also approached the Norwegian authorities at this time suggesting a daylight-bombing raid by USAAF but were turned down.[125] After the failure of 'Freshman', the idea of bombing was resurrected through Operation Gerd, a plan to attack either the intake dam for the water for the Vemork and Såheim power station in Rjukan or the ventilator plant that regulated the supply of water. Norwegian concerns over civilian casualties, however, meant an air attack was again at least temporarily sidelined.[126]

By the summer of 1943, however, intelligence provided by the 'Swallow' team made it clear that 'Gunnerside', SOE/FO's sabotage operation against the Vemork plant the previous February, had not achieved the interruption in heavy water production that was expected.[127] Therefore, FO began to reconsider ways of halting supplies, including an attack on the intake dam, stopping its transportation or internal sabotage. Leif Tronstad was, however, convinced that the bombing of the heavy water plant, which was structurally well protected, would fail. He argued that bombing would not penetrate the several floors of concrete that lay above the heavy water plant, which was in the basement of a seven-storey building.[128] Nevertheless, SOE believed that every option should be considered, including an air attack.[129] Moreover, there was still a great deal of uncertainty amongst the British and American authorities as to Germany's progress towards the development of an atomic bomb. Although through SIS and Norwegian authorities information and intelligence was over time obtained from several scientific sources including Leif Tronstad and Jomar Brun, Brynjulf Ottar and Professor Harald Wergeland in Norway, Njål Hole in Sweden, Paul Rosbaud in Germany and Professor Nils Bohr in Denmark, it was 'extremely difficult to form a definite opinion as to the urgency and purpose' of Germany's atomic research.[130] Therefore, the opinion within DSIR was that production at Vemork should be stopped, and that 'only a daylight bombing attack would be really successful'.[131] On 5 October 1943, Sir John Anderson, who had ministerial responsibility for Britain's atomic bomb project, asked SOE to produce an appreciation on the matter. Based on a report by staff officer J. C. Adamson, SOE recommended that sabotage had little chance of success and that a daylight-bombing raid was the only effective way to end the production of heavy water in Norway.[132] Furthermore, by this time the American authorities also placed 'great importance on the thorough destruction of the plant'.[133]

Later in October, Sir Charles Portal, chief of the air staff, contacted General Eaker commanding the American 8th Air Force in Britain, who thought that 'his forces would be able to attack the objective' [Vemork], as a 'convenient alternative to targets in Germany when attacks on the latter were prevented by weather'.[134] Consequently, on 16 November 1943, as part of Operation 131, 160 B-17 and B-24 American aircraft from bases in Britain attacked the electrolytic hydrogen works at Vemork, where heavy water was produced, and sixteen aircraft attacked the Norsk Hydro nitrate plant at Rjukan, a few miles down the same valley. Operation 131 included three missions in Norway. The first was against the Oslo-Kjeller aerodrome, with the Electrolytic Hydrogen plant at Vemork as a secondary target and the nitrate plant at Rjukan as a target of 'opportunity'. The second mission was against Knaben, with the nitrate plant at Rjukan as a target of 'last resort'. The third mission had the Electrolytic Hydrogen works at Vemork as the primary target, with the nitrate works at Rjukan as a target of 'opportunity'. For Mission no 3, 169 B-17s took off but only 143 attacked the primary target and 4 the target of opportunity. For Mission no 1, seventeen B-24s attacked the secondary target and twelve the target of opportunity.[135] Although the operation did not substantially damage the heavy water plant and only fifty kilograms of the liquid were destroyed, the bombing led to a decision by the local authorities to dismantle the site and transport the equipment and its contents to Germany.[136] These attacks, which resulted in twenty-one civilian deaths, produced a sharp response from the Norwegian government, which had not been informed beforehand. The Norwegian government sent a protest note to the British and Americans on 1 December and the British replied on 4 January after instructions from Anthony Eden.

There was anger and frustration within the Norwegian authorities that they had not been consulted on the decision to bomb the plant, especially as since the summer of 1942 the Norwegian authorities had worked closely with the Air Ministry in producing a 'target list' for Norway. On the list, Vemork was marked as a site better suited for attack by other means. Nevertheless, as with other air operations in Norway, such as the one against the *Nordisk Lettmetall* (light metal) and *Eidanger Salpeter* (Saltpetre) plants on Herøya in southern Norway in July 1943, the Norwegian authorities often had little influence over the final choice of target, which was often decided by other factors such as economic and military priorities, opportunity, availability of resources and even weather conditions.[137]

Production of heavy water was considered potentially so important that a series of methods to halt production, including air attack, were considered and ultimately used. The political concerns of the Norwegian authorities did, however, have an impact and meant that an air operation was a last resort, although when sabotage failed to achieve the expected results these concerns were put to one side and SOE, as it had from the beginning, was fully prepared to support the use of air power. Previous assertions that SOE did not participate in the decision to bomb Vemork are incorrect; it was directly involved.[138]

Vemork was not the only strategic target in Norway that SOE viewed as more suitable for air attack than a *coup de main* or sabotage operation. The Knaben molybdenum mine near Fjotland in southern Norway was considered by the MEW as the 'most outstanding objective in Norway from the economic point of view'.[139] Molybdenum was used in the production and hardening of specialist steel for German armaments production and once war broke out Germany obtained 80 per cent of its supplies from this mine. Consequently, by the early autumn of 1941, SOE had begun to consider an operation against this site.[140] It was, however, eventually decided that it was a target more suitable for an air attack, probably because of its position sixty miles from the coast in remote and difficult countryside. Therefore, in March 1942, negotiations commenced with the Air Ministry to 'secure the bombing of the Knaben mines', and arrangements were made with Operation Cheese II, Odd Starheim and Andreas Fasting, who had been dropped into southern Norway in January, to lay out guiding lights. By mid-April, Bomber Command had accepted the target but a few weeks later it advised SOE that there were not the 'machines' available and consequently it was unable to undertake the operation.[141]

SOE project to put the Knaben mines out of action, which was given the code name 'Alfriston', was, nevertheless, not abandoned and during 1942 there were negotiations involving SOE, COHQ and OSS as to what were the most suitable means to attack the plant. SOE targeted the local power supplies but believed a really effective operation would require a parachute attack against the mine installations, which fell under the remit of COHQ. The position of the mine, however, made a successful withdrawal impossible and it was therefore offered as a 'suicide' operation to OSS. All these proposals were, however, ultimately rejected because the 'tactical difficulties were too great', and therefore it eventually came back to using air power.[142]

By early 1943, after the small supply of molybdenum that Germany had obtained from French Morocco was cut off, Knaben became almost the sole source of this material and as a result by mid-February 1943, Bomber Command had it 'under review'.[143] Eventually, with assistance from FO, which provided important intelligence through Lt. J. H. Reimers from the Norwegian High Command, and Lt. Tycho Moe from the Norwegian Air Force, who knew the area around Knaben and provided information on the topography and local weather, and SOE, which attempted to retain agents in the area of the mine, it agreed to undertake an air attack against the plant. On 3 March 1943, therefore, ten Mosquito aircraft from No 2 Group Bomber Command attacked Knaben, with the result that full production could not recommence until August. In total, however, sixteen Norwegian civilians were killed. Nevertheless, this was followed by further attacks in November 1943, when 132 B-17s of the American 8th Air Force dropped 282 tons of high explosive on the site, and again in December 1943.[144]

Cooperation between SOE and the RAF was not, however, confined to attacks against military or economic sites. The Norwegian resistance, both civilian (*Sivorg*) and military (*Milorg*) through their government in London, and for political reasons, twice called on SOE to obtain the assistance of the RAF in attacks against targets in Norway. In the summer of 1942, *Sivorg* requested the bombing of the headquarters of the German security police in Oslo, which included the offices of the Gestapo, and the RAF after the intervention of SOE attacked the site in September. In this operation by four British Mosquitoes, most of the bombs missed their target and six civilians were killed. The request for the air raid was in response to a gathering of Quisling's *Nasjonal Samling* party in Oslo at the same time. It was considered so important that on 3 September General Hansteen had taken the request to Lord Selborne, Hugh Dalton's successor. In December 1944, RAF undertook a further attack against the same target after a request from the leadership of *Milorg* was received through SOE. Twelve Mosquitoes carried out the second raid on 31 December 1944. Houses around the target were hit along with a nearby tram, resulting in seventy-seven Norwegian deaths. The request for this operation appears to have originated with SL and was supported by J. Chr. Hauge when he visited London in November 1944. Both operations achieved little, apart from the death of many civilians and the destruction of surrounding buildings, but these political gestures were considered legitimate by the Norwegian authorities and they were fully prepared to use their close relationship with SOE to gain the assistance of the RAF.[145]

As the final stages of the war in Europe arrived, especially after the assault phase of Overlord was complete, air attacks against military targets in Norway, such as the U-boat bases in Bergen and Trondheim, oil and petrol stores and enemy shipping, increased and were part of the final campaign against Germany.[146] Calls for air support for SOE operations also continued, especially as part of the effort to slow down the movement of German forces southward through Norway in the winter of 1944–5. On 16 January 1945, it was decided at SFHQ that the issue of the bombing of key points on the main railway lines should be taken up with the air authorities. By the end of January, however, SHAEF had indicated that it did not approve of the diversion of the strategic bombing effort to an attack against Norwegian rail centres. It was believed that in this case the bombing effort was better targeted against shipping.[147]

In the spring of 1942, soon after taking over from Hugh Dalton and in response to the many earlier criticisms that had been directed towards the organization, Lord Selborne produced an examination of the current state of SOE. In this report, he described relations with 'the Services' as 'cordial'.[148] At a local operational level within Norway, however, the relationship was also functional and often effective. Norway was a country where other new organizations, such as Combined Operations, PWE and OSS, along with the British and American armed services, were able at little cost to undertake a small number of offensive operations against German interests. SOE's objective from an early stage was not only to contribute to these operations but also to use collaboration as a means to achieving its own aims. Nevertheless, SOE undertook most of its activities in this country without the direct or central assistance of the other British and American military agencies.

Chapter 7

SOE OPERATIONS IN NORWAY, 1940-4: THE COMBINATION OF SABOTAGE AND THE ORGANIZATION OF A CLANDESTINE ARMY

Most of SOE's activities within Norway were prepared under its direct guidance, although with the important proviso that they were ultimately carried out in cooperation with the Norwegian authorities through the Norwegian Defence High Command (FO), and later *Milorg*. Operations that fall within the period from the autumn of 1940 until the spring of 1944 will initially be explored as contextually it was a significantly different phase from the final twelve months of the war in Europe during the run up to the country's eventual liberation.

SOE's activities in Norway reflected the composite nature of its policy. The immediate objective was to contribute to a British 'strategy of attrition'[1], through a series of attacks against major economic and military sites that commenced in earnest from 1942 and which intensified during 1943 in order to help prepare the way for an invasion of north-west Europe in 1944.[2] Alongside this, although completely separately, SOE was to prepare the ground for future 'offensive operations' in southern Norway[3] through organizing a secret guerrilla army that would come into action and operate behind enemy lines in support of a landing by regular forces. Norway's geographically marginal position, however, ultimately meant that a landing by a British or Allied Expeditionary force to liberate part or the whole of the country never had strategic validity or was militarily viable. Consequently, SOE and *Milorg* groups had to be kept in *situ* in an occupied country for an indeterminate time period and in conditions of uncertainty about the future. They were subject to regular infiltration and break up as a result of the activities of the German and Norwegian Nazi police organizations and plagued by a shortage of arms, equipment and transportation.

By mid-1943, however, it was clear Norway's subordinate position meant that the nature and timing of its liberation would be dependent on the eventual progress and success of Allied operations elsewhere in Europe. Consequently, a secret army had to be prepared to deal with a number of possible scenarios such as a German collapse or withdrawal, and not just an invasion, and with Allied manpower concentrated elsewhere it also became apparent that clandestine forces would probably undertake a significant role in the country's liberation. Accordingly, it became progressively important to protect them from infiltration and break up by informers.

As these were joint operations, Norwegian interests also played a part in determining their eventual shape and outcome. Protection of *Milorg* and the Norwegian population from German reprisals meant that before 1944 almost all sabotage in Norway was undertaken by NIC (1) teams sent in from outside and confined to *coup de main* operations against targets of agreed military or economic value. Every effort was made to give the appearance that these were British operations. Although, as the pressure to intensify sabotage increased during 1943, SOE/FO teams began to stay in the country longer and they increasingly made use of local help. Nonetheless, using only teams sent in from outside these operations were subject to the limitations imposed by the difficult weather conditions and long summer days found so far north. The initial attempts to organize a secret army without the full and equal involvement of *Milorg* also made the whole process problematic.

Short-term activities in Norway prior to 1944: coup de main *operations*

Between early 1941 and September 1944, SOE considered, planned, attempted or completed at least twenty-seven *coup de main* or sabotage operations in Norway. Only thirteen of these, however, had some success, less than 50 per cent, and therefore the overall scale of SOE sabotage in Norway prior to 1944 was relatively small. Seventeen operations, the majority, targeted specialist ores or the production of specialist metals, four targeted shipping, two the production and transportation of heavy water, one a frostfilet factory, one the quays at Narvik, one the rail network and one Sola aerodrome outside Stavanger. The majority of the actions were therefore against economic targets. Preparation and planning began in the spring of 1941 and the work of classifying and studying Norwegian targets was carried out methodically and assisted by the MEW, which supplied a list of priorities.[4] The first attempted operation against a military target in Norway by a small team sent in from Britain was undertaken in April of that year. The first major operation,

'Redshank', against the Orkla pyrite mines close to Trondheim was not, however, successfully carried out until May 1942 and only one further action was completed in that year. *Coup de main* attacks in Norway were therefore slow to get going and confined to a comparatively small time period of two years. Nevertheless, fifteen operations were considered, proposed or completed between the beginning of 1943 and summer 1944, which is when SOE attacks against strategic targets in Norway reached their peak.[5]

Initially, in the autumn of 1940, SOE decided that using small, specially trained teams sent in from outside was the best method of sabotaging major strategic targets in Norway. These teams would not be 'brought in touch' with local resistance groups and would remain 'quite distinct' from them. They would also have 'intensive training and rehearsals for attacks on a particular objective' and only remain in the country for a short period of time before retreating across the border into Sweden.[6] As seen to be able to undertake these operations successfully, however, SOE was dependent on Norwegian volunteers who had to be adequately prepared. It took twelve months from the autumn of 1940 for it to increase its total of fully trained Norwegian recruits from six to sixty-four.[7] Therefore, during 1941 it was only able to carry out one planned sabotage action in Norway, Operation Barbara, which was a largely an unsuccessful attack against the rail network around Trondheim. To obtain the required manpower, this operation used a team of eight Scandinavians recruited in Sweden. Nevertheless, it was necessary to send these men to Britain for their training, which was carried out on the Shetlands in over just three weeks by an SOE captain sent up from London. They were then returned to Norway by fishing boat, although it took three attempts before they were successfully landed on the Norwegian coast.[8] 'Barbara' symbolizes the improvised and amateurish approach that SOE was forced to adopt at a time when as a new organization it was still building up and developing its infrastructure. SOE inherited very little in terms of training establishments from its predecessors. It took over the paramilitary training schools in Scotland from MI (R) and Station VII in Hertfordshire from Section D.[9] To send teams into Norway from outside, whether across the North Sea or via Stockholm, required transportation, and in the first half of 1941 only six sorties were flown to north-west Europe on behalf of SOE, and none to Norway. Transport was therefore confined to the handful of small fishing vessels operating out of the Shetlands Base, which were subject to the dreadful weather conditions that regularly occur off the Norwegian coastline, sidelined by the long hours of daylight in the summer and had a regular propensity to break down.[10] On top of all these logistical problems there was the prime minister's opposition to operations of a 'trivial' nature in Norway, which not only meant that SOE did not have backing at the highest level for its policy but which also created a certain degree of uncertainty over its immediate direction.[11]

Moreover, SOE activities were also circumscribed after the plans to set up local sabotage groups to organize attacks against selected targets had by the autumn of 1941 been postponed in deference to the sensitivity of the Norwegian government to the involvement of the civilian population in such actions.[12] Prior to this, some ad hoc sabotage initiated in Sweden had been attempted or undertaken inside Norway, but without large-scale local support it was small and ineffectual. Malcolm Munthe's presence at the British Legation in Stockholm had provided an early opportunity to instigate operations from Swedish soil. A Norwegian volunteer recruited in Sweden and contacts that Munthe had in Oslo were behind an attack on the Oslo-Bergen railway in the winter of 1940/1, which resulted in the blowing up of an engine in a tunnel near Voss. In July 1941, Munthe also arranged the placing of 'delayed action bomb' on a goods train that was on its way to Norway. Unfortunately, the bomb went off prematurely while the train was at Krylbo in central Sweden. It appears that the aim was to disrupt the transportation of armaments from Germany through Sweden to Norway, but it just exacerbated relations with the Swedish authorities.[13]

These activities achieved very little but were an early attempt to do something, move forward and at least begin the process of making Norway a burden on Germany's war effort. At this early stage, however, SOE was not capable of launching a widespread sabotage campaign and therefore its efforts were little more than tokenism. More significant at this time were the preparations that SOE began for operations against the mining and production of specialist ores and metals in Norway. Early indications of intent were operations 'Gertrude' and 'Landlubber', the plans to disrupt the supplies of sulphur and ferrochrome to Germany. These were followed, probably as a result of the prime minister's renewed interest in interdicting the transportation of Swedish iron ore through Norway, by a plan to revise Operation Arctic, the old MI (R) plan to sink vessels alongside the quays at Narvik.[14] Alongside this SOE began to prepare Operation Clairvoyant, its most ambitious plan for Norway,[15] which apart from its scale was typical of SOE *coup de main* operations in this theatre.

The objective of 'Clairvoyant' was,[16] through attacking the hydroelectric plants and ferries in southern Norway, to 'immobilise part of the industries in Norway' that were 'of vital importance to the enemy'. The primary target was the aluminium industry, and it was hoped that the production of aluminium oxide and metal could be stopped for at least six months.[17] Norwegian aluminium production had originally been built up with significant British support. Normal production was around 30,000 tonn (metric ton), but Göring planned that by 1943 this would increase to 180,000 tonn per year. The plans proved a fiasco and in 1943 Germany received only 17,256 tonn. But at the outbreak of war Norway was the sixth largest producer of this metal in the world, and after the occupation Germany decided that it would base its future expansion of the Luftwaffe on Norwegian supplies.[18]

Preparations for 'Clairvoyant' were protracted; they began in the spring of 1941, continued through the summer and autumn and were ready by early 1942. It had been planned to undertake the operation in autumn 1941 but training did not begin until late September under the guidance of Captain Rudolpho and J. L. Chaworth-Musters.[19] The initial plan was to attack seven different sites in southern Norway using six parties, of which five would be dropped on the same night using up to three Halifax aircraft and one transported by fishing vessel. Special explosive devices were also developed to blow-up the intake pipelines to the power stations. But by the third week of January 1942, however, probably due to the difficulties of obtaining transportation, the number of targets had been reduced to four.[20] The implementation of the operation was far more difficult than the preparation. It proved to be impossible to obtain the necessary aircraft, either directly through the Air Ministry or by means of the COS, and as the Norwegian authorities objected to most of the targets 'Clairvoyant' was eventually scaled back even further to just one attack against the important Høyanger aluminium works north of Bergen. Høyanger was particularly important because it was the only smelting site to have an alumina plant – alumina is processed ore, the intermediate stage in the manufacture of aluminium – which otherwise was largely imported from France and Germany. One attempt was made to drop a sabotage team on the night of 25/26 February but owing to the poor weather conditions the aircraft was forced return to the UK. The operation was eventually postponed after members of this team were involved in a fatal car crash. It was revived the following autumn, with plans to use SOE's 'Pheasant' party to reconnoitre the site, but by the beginning of 1943 it appears to have been dropped and this time it was never resurrected.[21]

During 1941, SOE planned and prepared operations against several other important economic targets in Norway, such as the Knaben molybdenum mine, although this was eventually as seen deemed more suitable for an attack by other means.[22] The target that received most attention between 1941 and 1944 was the mining and export of iron pyrites from the Orkla mines at Løkken just south-west of Trondheim. About half a million tons per annum of this raw material was exported to Germany in the years running up to the outbreak of war, which provided about 25 per cent of its requirements of sulphur and copper. After the outbreak of war, however, as ammunition production expanded, Germany's own pyrite mines quickly reached full capacity and therefore Norway became an increasingly important source of supply.[23] Probably owing to Charles Hambro's influence and previous contacts, the British quickly recognized the strategic importance of Orkla and by June 1941 an SOE operation called 'Burnous', a plan to attack the mine and refining process, had been put together. But the MEW argued that the site was not worth attacking unless it could be put out of action for several months, which SOE believed was an impossible task. At the end of August, therefore, it was accepted that the mine was too large for SOE to be able to interdict production for a significant length of time, and therefore it was decided to concentrate on the transportation of the ore.[24]

This was typical of many sabotage operations in Norway in that a direct assault against the target was often ruled out and it was the local transport system or power supplies that were deemed a weak point and more suitable for an attack by a small team inserted from outside. Consequently, between May 1942 and the spring of 1944, a total of four joint SOE and FO operations using NICI (1) personnel were carried out against Orkla; a final operation 'Dodworth' was commenced in the summer of 1944 but abandoned due to 'strong defences' and an 'altered general situation' before it could be completed. These consisted of one attack against the transformer station that helped regulate the supply of power to the thirty-kilometre railway line between the mine and local port at Thamshavn, an attack against shipping at the port and two attacks against the electric locomotives that transported the ore.[25]

The regularity of these assaults illustrates the significance placed on Norwegian pyrite exports to Germany up to the summer of 1944, especially after Italy, the other major source of sulphur, was closed off in 1943.[26] As these attacks were directed against the transportation of the materials and not the plant, they were fully supported by the Norwegian authorities. The initial operation 'Redshank' was discussed at the first meeting of the ANCC in February 1942 when Leif Tronstad spoke up for it and recommended two men, one of which was Peter Deinboll, son of the chief engineer at the mine. From this point, through the ANCC, the Norwegian authorities were directly involved in the planning and preparation of all attacks against this target.[27] The location of Orkla, close to the Norwegian coast and the Swedish border, also made it accessible by sea, land or air, and despite some objections by SIS the operations went ahead and had some limited success.[28] It appears that 'Redshank', in May 1942, reduced the transport capacity of the railway line by 50 per cent for six months. And by the summer of 1944, only one locomotive was left operating on the Thamshavn railway. In desperation, the German authorities decided to widen the tracks so that standard Norwegian steam locomotives could be used, but the work was not finished until early May 1945, too late to be of use. Consequently, exports during the final months of the war were significantly disrupted. According to German sources, only just over 56,000 tons of pyrites were delivered to Germany from Norway in the first two months of 1945.[29] Nevertheless, the actions of the plant management probably had a greater overall impact on production and deliveries to Germany. They ensured that only the poorest quality ore was exported and that production levels at the mine were 40 per cent lower than they could have been if the German authorities had taken over its running.[30]

Between 1942 and summer 1944, a further six operations were planned or undertaken against the mining and production of specialist ores in Norway. Only two, however, were successfully completed. These were Operation Kestrel against the Fosdalen iron ore mines north of Trondheim in October 1942 and Operation Company against the Arendal *Smelteverk* (furnace) at Eydehavn in southern Norway in November 1943. Production was reduced by 25 per cent for two months at Fosdalen and at Arendal *Smelteverk*, which produced 4,000 tons of ferro-silicum annually for Germany; production was stopped for six months.[31] These attacks also had the full support of the Norwegian authorities, which through NIC (1) supplied the men, provided local intelligence and cooperated in their planning. Nevertheless, the outcome of many other operations was less satisfactory.

Industrial targets were often in remote locations, especially in northern Norway, which with the huge distances involved made access from the UK extremely difficult. On these occasions both the fishing boats and air transport were not viable, and therefore SOE was often reliant on the availability of submarines. After their arrival in occupied

Norway, they also had to avoid detection by the German and Norwegian security police and then overcome the extensive security measures that were put in place to protect these important industrial and military sites. It is therefore not surprising that many operations were either abandoned or ended in tragedy.

The team sent on Operation Marshfield in November 1942, an attack on the Rødsand iron ore mines south of Trondheim, disappeared without trace.[32] A second attempt to carry out Operation Seagull in February 1943, a planned attack against the mines at Sulitjelma in northern Norway, which had the capacity to produce up to 140,000 tons of pyrites per annum, ended in disaster when the submarine carrying the party vanished. A final attempt against this site in the summer of 1944, Operation Docklow, was recalled at the last moment when it was discovered that transportation of materials to Germany had ceased.[33] The Sulitjelma mines, although strategically important, proved too distant and inaccessible for SOE ever to carry out a successful operation against them. Operation Midhurst, the plan to attack the *frostfilet* factories in Hammerfest and Melbu in northern Norway in early 1943, was also abandoned because of security fears in the area.[34]

SOE operations were not, however, confined to attacks against the mining or transportation of specialist ores or metals. There were other sites of strategic importance. In early 1942, the Air Ministry approached SOE to assist in an operation against the Focke-Wulf Kondor reconnaissance bombers that used Sola airfield outside Stavanger. These bombers had proved a significant threat to British merchant shipping crossing the Atlantic and therefore SOE made strenuous efforts, in cooperation with the Norwegian authorities, to sabotage the aircraft, but again the difficulties of inserting a team into the Stavanger area from outside proved insurmountable. By the spring of 1942 a party of three men was standing by ready to go and one effort to deliver them was made in the second half of May, but due to complete cloud cover the attempt was cancelled and the aircraft returned to the UK. After this, owing to the longer daylight hours, the operation was postponed and it appears that it was never resurrected.[35]

Perhaps the best known *coup de main* operation undertaken in Norway during the war is 'Gunnerside', the attack against the concentration plant for heavy water at Vemork in February 1943. The details of this operation have been recounted so often that they will not be repeated here.[36] Nevertheless, there are some important aspects to this operation. 'Gunnerside' was one of the series of attacks planned or undertaken against heavy water production in Norway between 1941 and 1944.³⁷ SOE was involved in all of these, although 'Gunnerside' was significantly a prime example of a jointly led SOE/FO operation.³⁸ The interests and involvement of the Norwegian authorities were important factors in all these attacks, but in the case of 'Gunnerside', they were crucial. The Norsk Hydro factory at Rjukan manufactured 200,000 tons of fertilizer per annum using the hydrogen and oxygen produced at its electrolysis plant at Vemork further up the *Vestfjord* valley.³⁹ Both sites were therefore two parts of a major concern that employed a large section of the local population and made a significant contribution to the Norwegian economy. Consequently, FO and specifically Leif Tronstad enthusiastically worked for 'Gunnerside', not simply because it was his idea but also because it was a precision operation directed at the heavy water equipment and stocks and therefore would restrict both the economic and structural damage to the remainder of the plant.⁴⁰ The intelligence supplied by Jomar Brun, Leif Tronstad and other SIS sources was vital and meant, for example, that a wooden mock-up of the high concentration plant had been built at STS 17, SOE'S Industrial Sabotage Training School, and used to prepare for the operation. This was an important contributory factor in ensuring that the attack was exact and ultimately brilliantly executed.⁴¹ Therefore, although 'Gunnerside' was typical of SOE's *coup de main* operations in Norway in that it set out to deny Germany what was believed at the time possibly to be a critical war material, it was also a product of Norwegian concerns and the desire for a more measured and precise approach that would result in less long-term damage to the country's immediate and possibly post-war industrial and commercial interests.

On the night of 27/28 February 1943, the 'Gunnerside' team along with members of the 'Swallow' party, which had been in the area since the failed 'Freshman' operation, successfully destroyed the bulk of the heavy water high concentration plant at Vemork.⁴² This led to the loss of 400 kilograms of production and 500 kilograms of heavy water *in situ*.⁴³ It did not, however, lead to the eighteen-month interruption in production that was SOE's original objective⁴⁴ and sensational and exaggerated claims that it halted Hitler's 'advance' towards an atomic bomb are difficult to substantiate.⁴⁵ In June 1943, the plant produced the highest monthly quantity of heavy water of the war and transportation to Germany was quickly recommenced, which was why it was decided to bomb the site. The Germans re-established production by moving concentration cells intended for another new plant at Såheim, a few kilometres away, to Vemork, and by bringing back 100 kilograms of 97.5

per cent partially diluted heavy water from Germany.[46] The operation, therefore, shows that the effect of *coup de main* attacks in Norway, although often successfully executed, was largely only disruptive and temporary, and therefore sites, such as Orkla and Vemork, had to be regularly revisited.

'Gunnerside', and other operations against economic and military targets in Norway, however, did have another perhaps more valuable strategic outcome. They created local security scares that forced the German authorities to position significant troop numbers in remote areas. In March 1943, Lt. Col. Wilson expressed the view that recent operations such as 'Gunnerside' had kept 'the German occupying forces on the move and on tenterhooks'.[47] And after the operation 2,800 enemy soldiers were employed to search for the sabotage party on *Hardangervidda*, the mountain plateau in southern Norway. Around 5,000 men were also stationed in German military barracks in the area around Orkdal close to the Orkla pyrite mine.[48]

Although the origins of *coup de main* attacks were strategic, not only their form but also the nature of their implementation was influenced by Norwegian concerns. Despite being SOE/FO collaborations, local *Milorg* groups had no direct involvement in carrying out these operations.[49] The aim was to give the appearance that they were purely British and thereby avoid possible reprisals against the local population and resistance groups. During the first SOE *coup de main* attack in Norway in May 1942 – Operation Redshank – the party took a parachute badge with them, which it was planned would be left behind to indicate that the British had carried out the attack. The 'Gunnerside' team wore British uniforms and even brought uniforms with them for the 'Swallow' party.[50]

By making these operations appear British, SOE *coup de main* operations did not on the whole result in widespread reprisals against the local population, so politically they did not present SOE with any significant problems. After 'Redshank', the Germans took six hostages, who were held responsible for any further actions. But despite the later attacks, it does not appear that any major retribution was inflicted on the area. After 'Gunnerside', the Germans eventually arrested around 250 Norwegians, burnt down mountain huts and forced members of the local resistance to go under cover or flee, but there were no extensive loss of life. The exception was Operation Kestrel, which along with 'Musketoon', and the killing of two German soldiers by members of SOE's 'Heron' team all in September 1942, led to the series of arrests in the counties of Trøndelag, Nordland and Troms and the eventual execution of thirty-four Norwegians. In this case, however, it was the unique occurrence of all three events within a few weeks of each other and in close proximity, which gave the Germans an excuse to institute a wave of terror in the region. Furthermore, although these activities undoubtedly made conditions extremely difficult for local resistance groups, which were often broken up or forced to go into hiding, they had generally been approved of by the Norwegian military authorities through the ANCC and involved men from a unit of the Royal Norwegian army. According to Lt. Col. Wilson, Oscar Torp, the Norwegian minister of defence, consistently withstood every attempt to make reprisals 'a political instead of a military question'.[51]

As the strategic priority in north-west Europe during 1943 was to help prepare the way for an invasion in 1944, it became increasingly important to maintain the pressure on Germany, deny it important resources and to ensure its forces remained stretched across the European mainland and Scandinavia. SOE was, therefore, instructed to prioritize and prepare attacks not only against 'industrial targets' but also coastal shipping and German communications.[52] In the Oslo area this led, through operations 'Chaffinch', 'Mardonius', 'Bundle' and 'Goldfinch', to a number of attacks against enemy vessels. Notwithstanding this in the two years between the spring of 1943 and the spring of 1945, only six ships were significantly damaged by these teams, and therefore it appears that SOE's efforts had only a relatively limited impact.[53] Moreover, the reservations within SOE regarding attacks against the Norwegian rail network because of the 'political issues' involved, and the instructions from the COS that such operations should be avoided until the 'moment to strike' came, had an important impact on the nature and timing of this category of operation.

In October 1943, COSSAC instructed SOE to plan for the 'possible future interruption of railway communications', although no overt action was permitted without authority.[54] Consequently, the three teams, 'Grebe', 'Lapwing' and 'Fieldfare', and the leader of a fourth operation, 'Woodpecker', which between the autumn of 1943 and the spring of 1944 were parachuted into Norway with variable success, were only instructed to reconnoitre the railways with a view to future action. They would only disrupt enemy troop movements in the case of either an Allied invasion or a German withdrawal from Norway.[55] These teams therefore had a long wait often in difficult conditions, because as seen it was not until the end of 1944, when it was agreed that the transfer of German divisions from Norway could be a potential threat to the Allied advance into Germany, that they were called into action.

Despite the increased importance placed on sabotage during 1943, it was also still only NIC (1) teams that undertook *coup de main* operations in Norway on behalf of SOE and Norwegian authorities. Nevertheless, there were the first signs of a change in the nature of these operations – a change that became widespread during 1944. The increased emphasis placed on attacks against targets of direct value to Germany led to the instruction from SOE for its 'organisations' in the 'more populated' areas of Norway to engage in 'open' sabotage,[56] and this ultimately had a significant impact at a local operational level. NIC (1) teams began to stay in the country, especially around Oslo and Bergen, for longer periods, sometimes several months, and often undertook a number of tasks, including weapons instruction and sabotage. In September 1943, Operation Redwing was sent to Bergen to form a sabotage and liquidation group. Operation Chaffinch, which was dropped in Norway in January 1943, was instructed to train local groups and carry out shipping sabotage. It also developed close links with SL.[57] They also began to make use of local recruits, sometimes from *Milorg*, to directly assist them in carrying out an operation. 'Mardonius', the operation to sink enemy shipping in Oslo harbour during the spring of 1943, stayed in Norway for several weeks. There was particularly stringent security around the Oslo port area and therefore it took a great deal of preparation before any attacks could be undertaken. The team of two, Max Manus and Gregers Gram, was also instructed to train local volunteers and eventually received considerable help from employees at the workshops where enemy ships were repaired. Sigurd Jacobsen, who had 'quite a high position' within *Milorg*, provided considerable assistance by placing limpet mines on three vessels, although none of these exploded.[58]

SOE's final operation against the heavy water produced at Vemork was carried out in early 1944.[59] On 20 February, a team of Norwegian saboteurs including Knut Haukelid, who had arrived in Norway as part of the 'Gunnerside' team, sank the train ferry that linked the railheads at either end of Lake Tinnsjø, east of Rjukan. On board the ferry were most of the remaining stocks of diluted heavy water, which the Germans were transporting back home after deciding the previous December to end production. Operationally, it was largely a successful operation, although fourteen civilians lost their lives. At the end of March 1944, after Knut Haukelid's report on the sinking of the Tinnsjø ferry arrived at HQ, SOE's security section (BSS) raised doubts over its accuracy. These were eventually dismissed by Rear Admiral A. H. Taylor, SOE's naval director (D/Navy). The writer, David Irving, has questioned the success of the operation. He quotes Doctor Kurt Diebner, a leading figure in Germany's atomic research project, who claimed that the Germans had 'got wind' of the planned sabotage operation, and that the drums on the ferry had been filled with water and the heavy water had been transported by road. SOE had important contacts within Norsk Hydro, including Gunnar Syverstad, a laboratory assistant, and Alf Larsen, an engineer at Vemork, who confirmed that over ninety barrels containing over 600 kilograms were destroyed by the operation, although four barrels were retrieved. A small amount of heavy water was later sent out of the country via Oslo. The heavy water apparatus at Vemork was dismantled in August 1944 and taken back to Germany. After the war, the barrels of heavy water were recovered from the bottom of Lake Tinnsjø and all contained diluted heavy water.[60] The objective was once again to interdict the supply of a major war material to Germany and despite a clear risk to the local population the operation was approved by the Norwegian minister of defence, seemingly with little hesitation.[61] It was, however, particularly significant because it was organized and undertaken by an SOE operative who had been in the country for a long period, in direct collaboration with Knut Lier Hansen from *Milorg* and Rolf Sørli, the leader of *B-org* (the industrial resistance organization) in Rjukan. It was, therefore, a joint operation involving SOE and local resistance members and indicative of how sabotage would be carried out in Norway during the final months of the occupation.[62]

Prior to 1944, *Milorg*'s official policy on the ground continued as before – to keep their organization intact and not to become active prior to the liberation, especially if operations could be carried out by groups sent in from outside in British uniform.[63] Therefore, widespread collaboration between *Milorg* and SOE on sabotage operations was still several months away. There were signs, however, that the political context within Norway was beginning to change. For example, there was a growing willingness and eagerness within the ranks of *Milorg* to become active, and this along with other events would have a significant impact upon the nature of sabotage operations in Norway during the final months of the occupation.

Long-term local operations in Norway: The creation of a clandestine army under British control

While SOE pursued its objective of attacking economic and military targets, it also implemented its long-term aim of organizing and preparing a clandestine guerrilla army in Norway. Therefore, between autumn 1940 and late spring 1944, at least sixty SOE operations were sent into Norway by sea, air or across the Swedish border, with the aim of organizing local groups into fighting units that through cutting lines of communication and carrying out acts of sabotage behind enemy lines could support operations by regular forces.[64]

After Section D's first operation in Norway in June 1940 and through Malcolm Munthe in Stockholm, contact was continued and developed during the summer and autumn of 1940 with resistance groups in western Norway, Trondheim and around Oslo. While working for MI (R) in Bergen with Andrew Croft in December 1939, Munthe had made contact with Ivar Borge, whose father owned 'Interspeds', a shipping firm. Munthe also made contact with an organization called 'Delphin' in Oslo, run by a jeweller called Prytz, and from Trondheim he was contacted by Johnny and Arthur Pevik, and Odd Sørli, who became the basis of the 'Lark' operation in 1942.[65] SOE's early policy was also to recruit Norwegians in Britain, who would then be made ready to return home in order to organize local 'cells' that would together form a general movement leading to a rebellion against the German occupation.[66] SOE's first operation from the newly established Shetlands Base in November 1940 was an attempt to build on previous contact with groups in the Bergen area and to begin the groundwork for the development of a resistance network in southern Norway. Unfortunately the *Abwehr*, the German military intelligence organization, had infiltrated the boat crew and all three SOE agents were arrested soon after landing in Norway and later executed. This was a very early example and a warning of how dangerous enemy agents would be to SOE activities in Norway.[67]

After the policy of rebellion had been replaced by plans to organize an armed and trained secret guerrilla army based in the key strategic areas of Norway,[68] two new important operations were put together. 'Claribel' was a scheme to use resistance organizations across northwest Europe, including Norway, to attack lines of communications or cause general disruption behind enemy lines and thereby spoil any attempt by Germany to invade Britain. The scheme for Norway was called 'Claribel A'. It was believed that conditions in the country, the emergence of resistance groups under SOE control, made it an ideal location to undertake guerrilla operations against enemy shipping and aircraft if the need ever arose. Fortunately, the plan never had to be used and in March 1942 was abandoned.[69]

From the spring of 1941, SOE also began to implement Operation Cockfight, its generic plan for developing a decentralized clandestine army in Norway consisting of armed and trained local resistance groups all under its control.[70] It initially consisted of three strands. First, the attempts made during 1941 to bring back members of resistance groups, including *Milorg*, to Britain for training before sending them back to Norway to continue the preparation of their own organizations. This had some success but was restricted by the availability of transport, the handful of fishing boats at the Shetlands Base and the difficult conditions that these boats had to operate under. Nevertheless, the contact that was established with *Milorg*'s leadership and with the Sørlie group in Trondheim meant that eventually a handful of men were brought back to the UK. By the autumn of 1941, however, by which time the *Milorg* leadership had not only been hit by a series of arrests but had also turned to its government in London for authority, this aspect of 'Cockfight' was no longer viable.[71]

The second part of the plan was to set up a series of arms dumps in key locations across Norway, but by the end of 1941 according to SOE only one had been established at Hammersett, south-west of Trondheim, and some arms and equipment delivered with the 'Archer' team to Selvær off the coast of Nordland.[72]

Last, SOE set out to send its own teams, made up of recruits trained in Britain, to the key strategic areas of Norway to make contact with and prepare local resistance groups, or to establish new organizations. The objective was that they would all be armed, organized and trained in guerrilla warfare, and through W/T put in direct contact with and therefore placed under the supervision of SOE headquarters.[73] In the first half of 1941, however, only one operation, 'Cheese', was sent to southern Norway for the purpose of working with and developing local resistance groups.[74] As with *coup de main* operations, a shortage of trained recruits, insufficient transportation and terrible weather conditions, particularly during the autumn of 1941, slowed the implementation of 'Cockfight'. On 17 December, six SOE agents were ready to be dropped into Norway. Owing to the severity of the weather, two of them had been waiting for seven weeks.[75]

During the 1941–2 season, however, by which time SOE had a significant pool of prepared volunteers to call on, a total of fifteen operations were eventually sent to the pivotal areas of Norway from Mosjøen in the north, along the west coast from Trondheim to Stavanger, on the east and west side of Oslo fjord, and in the valleys running north and west from the Oslo region. The bulk were, therefore, located in southern Norway where it was initially believed 'offensive operations' might occur.[76] Beginning with Operation Letterbox in September 1941, and finishing with Operation Raven the following April, these consisted of teams usually made up of an organizer, W/T operator and possibly an arms instructor. In addition, over eighty tons of arms and equipment were delivered to a range of locations along the coastline and inland in order that the preparation of local groups could begin.[77]

By the summer of 1942, however, due to an array of difficulties, Operation Cockfight had achieved relatively little. The shortage of available transport continued especially airdrops. The Shetlands boats made thirty-three journeys during the 1941/2 season to land or pick up SOE agents or deliver arms. There were, however, only four airdrops made to Norway on behalf of SOE at the same time.[78] Operations were regularly held up by the severe conditions found in the North Sea and there were frequent problems with radio equipment. Operation Arquebus was typical of the difficulties that SOE faced in undertaking such activities. Landed on the west coast in mid-October 1941, it was the following April before it made radio contact and then only by using SIS station Theta.[79] The nature of the occupation and the conditions within Norway were also a major barrier to progress. In the small isolated communities that are characteristic of Norway, the arrival of strangers was quickly noted and regularly brought to the attention of the local German security police or Norwegian informers. By the summer, SOE had recognized that there was 'still a tendency to overrate the loyalty of relatives and former friends' and 'to underrate the enemy's contre-espionage [sic] service'. Five of the thirteen arms dumps that were eventually established during the 1941/2 season had been captured,[80] and during 1942, six of the fifteen long-term operations that had been sent to Norway were broken up by the German security and Norwegian Nazi police organizations through the use of local agents and informers.[81] This had severe and tragic consequences for the civilian population as well as important repercussions for SOE. Both the tragedy at Telavåg near Bergen and the arrests and executions undertaken after the break-up of Operation Heron in the autumn of 1942, which have previously been blamed on the activities of SOE and SIS, were at least partially the result of the work of Norwegian agents. A Norwegian employed by the Abwehr had initially led the German authorities to take an interest in SOE's contact near Telavåg, and a Norwegian agent Rolf Hammer had infiltrated the 'Heron' operation.[82] Altogether this meant that efforts to organize a secret army proved to be extremely problematic and instead of building for the future, the organization was continually on the defensive.

After the capture of the 'Crow' W/T operator Ernst Kirkeby Jacobsen in July 1942, he agreed to work for the Germans and transmit messages back to Britain under Gestapo supervision. Fortunately, due to intelligence from a source in Stockholm, SOE was quickly informed about Jacobsen and therefore aware that the messages he sent during the summer of 1942 were under outside control.[83] In May 1942, however, Torbjørn Gulbrandsen, the organizer for Operation Anchor, a plan to establish guerrilla groups along the west side of Oslo fjord, was arrested by the Gestapo. After agreeing to work for the Germans, he was in September 1942 allowed to escape and he eventually returned to Britain via Sweden, from where he was instructed to supply information on SOE and its agents using either letters sent to cover addresses in Oslo or through a locally obtained radio set. The initial interrogations of Gulbrandsen by SOE and MI5 failed to pick up that he was effectively working for the Germans, even though it doesn't appear that he ever provided any intelligence. It was only in late January 1943, owing to information supplied by Jacobsen, that SOE learnt that the Germans had recruited Gulbrandsen. A plan was then put together to use him to send misinformation back to Norway, so as to deceive the Germans as to SOE's intentions, but it seems that Operation Omelette, as this was called, was never carried out.[84] Nevertheless, both operations illustrate how effectively and quickly the German authorities infiltrated SOE operations, broke them up and attempted to use them for their own purpose.

By the summer of 1942, therefore, there was little semblance of a clandestine army in Norway. In the highly unlikely event of a landing by a British Expeditionary force in Norway at this time it seems improbable that it would have had any support from guerrilla groups operating behind enemy lines. Therefore, strategic ambition was alone not enough. Organizing local resistance groups into a viable military force was dependent on local conditions, not least the occupying regime in Norway.

From early 1942, the development of a secret army in Norway had also become a joint effort by SOE and FO using the forum of the ANCC, and involving *Milorg*. The relationship between these parties also had an important impact on operations at a local level. Owing to its distrust and dislike of *Milorg's* centralized structure, SOE sponsored organizations and local *Milorg* groups were largely developed separately up until the autumn of 1942. This was the result of the decision to create two 'distinct' organizations across the regions of in Norway, a policy that ultimately held back attempts to organize a clandestine army. SOE teams arrived from Britain unannounced and attempted to work independently in areas where local *Milorg* groups retained links with SL, which created a series of difficulties. Operation 'Anvil' was to establish W/T contact and organize guerrilla groups in the Lillehammer area. The unannounced arrival of the 'Anvil' organizer, Jon Gunleiksrud, meant that local *Milorg* groups initially treated him as an *agent provocateur*. Several messages were transmitted to London by 'Anvil' saying that Oslo insisted on asserting its authority in the district. The reply from London was that this contact must be broken. Nevertheless, instructions kept arriving from Oslo, which continued to cause tension.[85]

SOE, eventually supported by FO, was not, however, instigating a deliberate policy of complete non-cooperation with *Milorg* as an organization. It was attempting to operate in a manner that ensured that its teams did not become entangled with the leadership in Oslo.[86] The instructions issued to SOE teams were that the groups that they worked with should be 'isolated' as 'far as possible' from other groups within their area in an 'urgent need for security' and to avoid the break-up of local organizations that had previously occurred because of a 'common link to the central organisation'.[87] It was, however, an approach that within the conditions of occupied Norway proved to be unrealistic and contact with Oslo was unavoidable. Tor Stenersen, the organizer for Operation Crow, was asked to make his radio available for *Milorg's* central leadership (SL) so that it could communicate directly with the Norwegian authorities in London. He met Einar Skinnarland, the 'Grouse' organizer, who was also in touch with the leadership in Oslo, as were several of the other NIC (1) teams that had arrived in Norway during the spring. In June 1942, Lt. Col. Wilson expressed his frustration that SOE teams had become 'mixed up with Oslo HQ', something that SOE 'wanted to avoid'.[88] Relations were particularly difficult in the area around Kristiansand and Flekkefjord on the southern tip of Norway, where the NIC (1) team and the *Milorg* district organization coexisted in a state of hostility from summer 1942. It appears that the local resistance had built up an impression, possibly from SOE, that there would be an Allied invasion in that year. This, it has been claimed, led them to organize too fast, resulting in lax security and ultimately penetration by local police forces. Although SOE accepted that it might have created the expectation of a landing in Norway,[89] the real significance of this local difficulty was that it represented the inevitable problems and dangers that resulted from a political decision that allowed two underground organizations with different views over their role to operate often in close proximity. Regular intervention from SL, which was attempting to both assert its authority across southern Norway and obtain access to the W/T contact that SOE groups had with the UK, also exacerbated the situation. All of this severely disrupted the progress of several SOE operations and had serious repercussions for *Milorg*.[90]

The development of relations and contact between SOE/FO in London and SL in Oslo had an impact on operations in Norway in one other important way. *Milorg* was directly under the authority of its government in London, but if it was to have day-to-day involvement in decisions regarding the organization and use of a clandestine army in Norway it had to have a direct wireless link with Britain. Moreover, if *Milorg* was to be brought under effective control by FO, communication also had to be improved with its leadership in Oslo. Einar Skinnarland had originally been sent to Britain in March 1942 by *Milorg* to obtain consent for a radio connection with the UK.[91] In early 1942, FO had also expressed a desire to have a W/T operator sent to Oslo, and consequently in May an agreement was finally reached with Rolf Palmstrøm, *Milorg's* signals-chief. This led in September 1942 to Operation Plover, Per Solnørdal, who was sent to Norway to establish the first W/T link between SL and FO and SOE in London. Solnordal was, however, owing to the activities of a Norwegian agent employed by the *Abwehr*, arrested at the end of 1942. It was only after the arrival of Operation Thrush, Norman Gabrielsen and Operation Curlew, Knut Haugland and Gunnar Sønsteby, in the autumn of 1943, that communication between London and Oslo was finally placed on a sound and reliable long-term footing.[92]

In the meantime, in response to changes within *Milorg* in the summer of 1942, it was decided where possible to base the future development of a clandestine army in Norway on an amalgam of SOE and *Milorg* groups.[93] In recognition of this the name 'Cockfight', which symbolized SOE's vision of a guerrilla army under its direct control, was dropped and replaced by the broad term 'secret army' to cover the underground organization that would be formed in Norway by SOE and FO jointly.[94] From the autumn of 1942 until the late spring of 1944, close to forty NIC (1) teams or individuals were sent into Norway in order to continue the process of organizing and preparing this army. Conditions within Norway, the infiltration of informers and the work of the local police organizations meant, however, that during 1943 many of these activities, such as the 'Lark' operations in Trondheim, the 'Falcon' operations in Nordland and the 'Sandpiper' operation in the south were often no more than attempts to rebuild local networks in areas where previous resistance groups had been broken up.[95] It was also felt that it was 'difficult to organise for "The Day" in secrecy without even a vague idea of the interval of time that may elapse'.[96] This uncertainty over Norway's future owing to its peripheral position meant that SOE accepted that not only could no indication be given by its teams that an invasion was pending but also that although the organization of a secret army during 1943 should continue, it would not have the same degree of urgency.[97] Moreover, with operational priorities elsewhere, material for Norway continued to be extremely limited and therefore this embryonic clandestine army remained largely unarmed and unprepared. During 1943, only 192 containers with arms and equipment were dropped into Norway compared with 5,299 containers delivered to France during the same period.[98]

Nevertheless, despite nervousness over its centralization, SOE/FO teams began to work with the *Milorg* leadership and its local organizations, especially in eastern Norway where it was strongest. Operations such as 'Chaffinch', 'Puffin' and 'Goldfinch' all worked closely with SL during 1943.[99] In the other districts of Norway, however, around Stavanger for example with Operation Osprey, and north of Trondheim with Operation Martin, where it was often weak or non-existent, NIC (1) teams either took much longer to strike up a working relationship with *Milorg* or continued with attempts to organize their own local groups.[100]

By June 1943, however, the possible impact on Norway of Allied plans for north-west Europe began to reshape the preparation of a secret army. The possibility of a German withdrawal from the country and the implementation of a scorched-earth policy meant that SOE and FO agreed that long-term operations in Norway should incorporate both 'defensive and preservative' measures, which was confirmed at the ANCC meeting in November.[101] Therefore, from the end of 1943 and through 1944, NIC (1) teams were also instructed to prepare protective measures against important local industries and communications networks should German forces adopt such a policy. It appears that the first NIC (1) team that went into Norway with orders to undertake such measures was 'Sandpiper' on 10 December 1943, followed in January 1944 by 'Antrum Green' and in February by the 'Merlin' team that was sent to the Bergen area.[102] These were small beginnings, but during the second half of 1944, in cooperation with *Milorg*, they would become part of a massive and widespread increase in protective activities across the country.

By early 1944, therefore operations to organize a secret army in Norway had been adapted in response to the wider strategic context in Europe. Political changes, the improvement in relations with *Milo*rg, also meant that the basis of this clandestine army had begun to change. At the same time, however, conditions within Norway, the nature of the occupying regime and its attempts to break up any form of resistance, meant that SOE was forced to adopt measures to ensure that a secret army was protected, especially as it became increasingly likely that it would be required to make a significant contribution to the country's liberation.

Rat work in Norway: Internal preservation

During the first half of 1942, as seen, several of SOE's operations in Norway were broken up through the efforts of informers or police agents with major consequences for the local population and *Milorg* groups. This threat had to be curtailed; otherwise, any effort to organize and prepare a secret army would ultimately fail. Consequently, from the summer of 1942 several SOE teams were instructed to assassinate or prepare the way for the execution of informers and German and Norwegian Nazi police officials.[103] These began as defensive measure and a response to conditions in Norway. But during the final two years of the occupation, in order to ensure that resistance groups would be in a position to make a direct military contribute to the liberation, these became offensive operations and part of a coordinated 'campaign' that was instigated across Europe. Owing to its position on the strategic and geographical margins, the contribution of a secret army to Norway's liberation was, however, particularly significant, and therefore as the final stages of the occupation approached its preservation became increasingly important. Assassinations were, therefore, not just a response to the brutality of the regime in occupied Norway.

Liquidations during the occupation, the authorized killing of Norwegian citizens, are naturally a very sensitive moral, legal and constitutional issue. This meant that although relatively small in number, these actions to have legitimacy had to be and were in Norway a major collaborative effort involving SOE, Norwegian government, its military authorities and *Milorg*.

The threat to SOE/FO and *Milorg* activities came from the German and Norwegian Nazi police and military organizations that were set up in the country from the summer of 1940. In 1939 the criminal police (*Kripo*), uniformed police (*Orpo*) and the *Geheime Staatspolizei* (Gestapo), which together made up the German security police and the *Sicherheitsdienst*, the Nazi intelligence organization (SD), were merged into one office in Germany under the leadership of Reinhard Heydrich, *Chef der Sicherheitspolizei und des SD* (Sipo u. SD). Moves to transfer this structure to Norway began almost immediately after its occupation. In June 1940, all the German police in the country were placed under the authority of Frederick Wilhelm Rediess, while Sipo u. SD (henceforth *Sipo*), housed at Victoria Terrase in Oslo, was under Lieutenant-Colonel Heinrich Fehlis. *Sipo* was made up of six departments, including *Abteilung IV*, the Gestapo, which led the offensive against the resistance organizations and SOE in Norway. It was also divided into several sections; the most significant of which was *Referat IVN*. This was responsible for the department's intelligence network in Norway, which consisted of employed Norwegian agents, usually those that had Nazi sympathies such as members of NS, or criminals who saw this as an easy way to get hold of money, cigarettes or alcohol.[104] Over 4,000 Norwegians were eventually sentenced for being denouncers or spies, and at the liberation the Gestapo had 312 registered Norwegian agents each with their own cover name. Among these numbers were notorious individuals such as Marino Nilsen, Finn Kaas, Astrid Dollis, Ivar Grande and most famously Henry Rinnan, who created a huge network of informers in Trøndelag and western Norway that was a constant threat to both SOE and *Milorg*.[105] It was not, however, just the Gestapo that posed a danger to SOE and resistance groups. There was also the *Abwehr*, Germany's military intelligence organization, which up until the summer of 1944 also had a permanent establishment in Norway. It was responsible for operational intelligence against enemy forces, sabotage behind enemy lines, the prevention of enemy espionage and the protection of German military forces.[106]

Prior to 25 September 1940, however, while negotiations continued between the German Reichskommissar and the Presidential Board of the Norwegian Storting over future constitutional government in Norway, the German police were 'deliberately and openly' held back. The change in the political climate after 25 September, however, the ending of negotiations and the move to Nazify the country and all its institutions, combined with increasing resistance to this move, meant that from this point the German security police were given a free rein.[107] In July 1941 the Norwegian *Statspoliti* (Stapo), state police, was also established. All of its employees, with the exception of four, consisted of NS members,[108] and under the leadership of General Karl A. Marthinsen, it worked closely with *Sipo* in order to protect the occupying regime in Norway. The invasion of the Soviet Union and Allied raids against Norway during 1941 also made the German and Norwegian police and security forces increasingly sensitive to any form of resistance. The Germans were not prepared to tolerate unrest in the occupied countries, including Norway, particularly as their military situation worsened. Perhaps the best illustration of this is the 'Commando Order' signed by Hitler on 18 October 1942, which stated that any commandos, agents or saboteurs that were captured should be handed over to the *Sipo* and shot.[109] The imprisonment of 40,000 Norwegians and the execution of 369 during the occupation are an indication of the lengths that the German and NS authorities were prepared to go to stifle any opposition.[110]

With the exception of Malcolm Munthe's last-minute and improvised attempt to organize the assassination of Heinrich Himmler in Oslo in early 1941,[111] SOE interest in liquidations does not appear to have re-emerged again until the spring of 1942, by which time Operation Cockfight was fully underway. In May, a local resistance group established by SOE in southern Norway through its agent Odd Starheim ('Cheese') was badly hit by the Gestapo.[112] Accordingly, it was decided that 'instructions' should be issued 'to the effect that Norwegian informants and traitors may be put out of the way by our bands'. At the same time, the Norwegian commander-in-chief, Major General Hansteen requested that this directive be sent to the 'secret army' (*Milorg*).[113] Therefore, by the summer of 1942, both SOE and FO had decided that they must actively protect the Home Front from the threat posed by 'denouncers and traitors'.[114] Assassinations did not start out as predetermined offensive against the German security police but a defensive response to the difficult conditions in Norway. Moreover, as both SOE and FO shared and were committed to the same long-term objective of creating and preserving a clandestine army in Norway, collaboration on this issue, although potentially controversial and risky, was never as problematic as other matters such as sabotage.

Whether 'instructions' were ever sent in the spring of 1942 is unclear but probably in response to these local difficulties, SOE decided to take appropriate action. Operation Swan, a team of two, was sent to the area around Kristiansand in southern Norway in August primarily to establish a W/T link and to provide arms instruction for guerrilla groups in the area. It was, however, also required to train small teams in the 'best means of disposing of dangerous denouncers by assassination', although no acts would be undertaken until approval had been obtained from Allied HQ in London.[115] This operation plagued by local difficulties achieved very little, and soon afterwards and rather ironically the activities of the Gestapo broke up clandestine activity in the area and resulted in the arrest and brutal execution of several leading local figures from *Milorg*.[116] Nevertheless, between the summers of 1942 and 1943, a further five of the eighteen SOE operations that were sent to Norway to help organize guerrilla units were also instructed to train local groups to carry out assassinations or were given authority to undertake such acts themselves.[117] This was the beginning of a joint effort led by SOE and FO together, and eventually including *Milorg*.

The first of these operations in October 1942, 'Bittern', proved to be contentious. The party, supplemented by thirty grams of cocaine, included the ex-criminal Johannes Andersen better known as *Gulosten* (yellow cheese), who had assassinated an *Abwehr* agent before fleeing to Britain. Moreover, due to confusion over its role, the behaviour of members of the party and because the Home Front was not informed of the operation beforehand, it turned out to be a fiasco.[118] This caused difficulty for the Norwegian government, both internally and in its relations with the civilian resistance leadership, and for these reasons it has received considerable attention from previous historians.[119] 'Bittern' was, however, primarily a Norwegian operation and the use of such potentially controversial means indicates that not only SOE but also FO were prepared to make every military effort to ensure that the development of a secret army in Norway could continue.[120]

The difficulties with 'Bittern' also did not deter SOE and FO in their future efforts to deal with 'denouncers' or undermine future collaboration with SL. In the Gudbrandsdal and Østerdal, the two valleys running north-west from Oslo, the 'Gannet' team continued to carry out its instructions to make ready 'Saccharine Squads', small teams especially trained in silent killing.[121] The 'Chaffinch' team, which parachuted into southern Norway in early January 1943, was also ordered to prepare a local team of three men to use the 'special devices' intended for use on Quislings. Furthermore, the view within *Milorg*, which had taken up the issue of informers as early as the summer of 1941,[122] was according to Tor Stenersen, the leader of 'Chaffinch', that 'something effective should be done' although 'preferably by men from the UK'. Consequently, SL was anxious to deal with denouncers, although they wanted them to be taken silently and their bodies to disappear without trace, as this would reduce the risk of reprisals. And it was eventually willing to contribute to these operations. The result was the so-called 'X-Groups', teams of six men trained especially for the purpose of disposing of informers. They were organized by SL, instructed by the 'Chaffinch' team and before they were used the necessary permission had to be obtained from the UK, but through *Milorg*.[123] Initially, this joint effort appears to have had little impact; five assassinations were carried out during the first half of 1943 in Norway, but none involved SOE or groups trained by it. They were carried out by the Communist 'Osvald' group and unknown individuals. The commitment to prepare and undertake assassinations was by 1943 based on a shared view both in London and Oslo that the threat posed by informers and the Nazi police forces had to be counteracted.[124]

Liquidations were on the whole part of a coordinated and planned military effort and therefore were not random, uncontrolled and indiscriminate acts of revenge, which perhaps explains why there were relatively few in comparison to other occupied countries. For example, there were around 350 assassinations in Denmark compared with less than 100 in Norway.[125] As the final stages of the war in Europe approached, however, assassinations became an offensive weapon that was used to help ensure the integrity of resistance organizations in the important period in the run up to liberation. In June 1943, SOE's Norwegian section announced it would take part in a 'general plan of campaign', a series of coordinated operations against Gestapo officers and informers. The initial failure of 'local means', however, meant that for Norway 'specially trained agents' would be 'sent in from the UK to carry out the actual work of execution'.[126] The result was Operation Rat Week, which was launched in November and marked the commencement of a synchronized offensive against informers across parts of occupied Europe. At least three NIC (1) teams, 'Goldfinch' in Oslo, 'Goshawk' in the Gudbrandsdal and 'Redwing' in Bergen, were assigned to take part in this joint action. They were instructed to wait for a message, *Dei som skulle vekia – mot de som skulle siga* (those that shall give way – against those that shall win), which would signal that 'Ratweek' should begin. It was eventually broadcast over the BBC on 6 December 1943 at 18:00 hrs. Although owing to local concerns 'Goshawke' and 'Redwing' did not take part in this 'campaign', on 8 December 'Goldfinch' undertook the first assassination by an SOE group in Norway. It was the first of four executions carried out by this team in the Oslo area over the next four months.[127]

Although 'Rat Week' was an SOE offensive, *Milorg* was, nevertheless, still involved. The 'Goldfinch' party was instructed to 'proceed to contact SL in Oslo to arrange for Rat Week', and it was *Milorg* that would provide the names of those to be liquidated. The training of the 'X-Groups' in collaboration with Milorg was also not abandoned, and during the autumn of 1943 three 'killing-squads' and four 'shadow-squads' were prepared. These eventually attempted to liquidate six named informers, although without success.[128] At the conference held in Stockholm in March 1944 between members of FO and *Milorg*, it was also agreed that 'certain military actions against the occupying power and its tools', a euphemism for attacks against the Gestapo, should be instituted.[129] As a result a request was sent to London asking for support, which in April resulted in the arrival of Operation Buzzard in Norway to 'provide help' in 'executing denouncers'.[130]

In September 1944, SHAEF accepted that *Milorg* had to be safeguarded so that it could act as a protective force during the early stages of the country's liberation, and therefore it was agreed that action against Gestapo agents should continue.[131] By December, the execution of collaborators was at the top of a list of targets given to Gunnar Sønsteby, leader of the NIC (1) teams and link with *Milorg* in the Oslo area.[132] Consequently, the number of assassinations of informers and senior Nazi police officials, carried out by both SOE and *Milorg* groups, grew during 1944 and 1945. The 'Buzzard' team supported by members from other SOE groups working in the Oslo area undertook several executions during this period.[133] In Trondheim, SOE made several attempts with little success during 1943 and 1944 to liquidate Henry Rinnan, whose network of informers had done so much damage to resistance groups in the area. Rinnan had created an organization called *Sonderabteilung 'Lola'*, which employed between sixty and seventy Norwegians and which by the end of the war was responsible for around eighty deaths.[134] In Bergen, the SOE's 'Razorbill' team linked up with a local Communist group that in November 1944 assassinated two local police officials.[135] In Ålesund on the west coast, a local *Milorg* group assassinated Ivar Grande, Henry Rinnan's second-in command, after orders had been received from London via a W/T link provided by the SOE's 'Antrum' operation.[136]

From the beginning of 1944 and up until the German capitulation in May 1945, SOE undertook or were in some way involved in at least eighteen assassinations in Norway, while *Milorg* carried out even more.[137] There was, therefore, a determined and joint effort to protect Norwegian resistance as the liberation approached. This is perhaps best exemplified by the assassination of Major General Karl Marthinsen, head of the Norwegian *Stapo*, in February 1945. He had been listed as a legitimate target in London, the 'Buzzard' team carried out the action and although the attack resulted in the execution of twenty-eight people, it received the unequivocal support of the Norwegian government.[138]

Unlike sabotage, which remained a difficult issue through to 1944, assassinations on the whole had the support of the Norwegian military authorities and *Milorg* and were therefore largely controlled, planned and considered a legitimate military tool to be used in defence of Norwegian interests, in this case the preservation of the Home Forces.

By the end of 1943, however, it was the impending Allied invasion of north-west Europe and its potential impact on Norway that increasingly began to impose its influence on all SOE activity in this theatre.

Chapter 8

SOE AND THE LIBERATION OF NORWAY, 1944-5: OPERATIONS IN THE SHADOW OF OVERLORD

The nature and scale of the SOE's operations in Norway changed significantly in the months leading up to the German capitulation in May 1945. By the summer of 1944, Norway was firmly entrenched in the shadow of events on the mainland of Europe, which meant it remained sidelined and isolated. Consequently, uncertainty continued over its eventual liberation, especially while over 300,000 German military and civilian personnel remained in the country. Alongside this, with the end of the war in Europe in sight, post-war considerations also became significant. Norway's future economic prosperity and the transition to lawful, constitutional government, therefore, became additional factors that had an important impact on the make-up of special operations in the country during the final year of its occupation.

From the summer of 1944, the contribution of sabotage changed and instead of preparing the way for Overlord it became directly supportive to Allied operations on the continent. Anything considered of immediate importance in sustaining German resistance or a potential threat to the Allied campaign became a target, including the units of the 20th Mountain army that began to withdraw from Norway in the autumn of 1944.

Moreover, from September 1944, SHAEF decided that precedence should be given to arming, equipping, preparing and preserving resistance groups as a local force for protection and law and order during the potentially uncertain period after a collapse of German authority either centrally or in Norway, and before the arrival of regular troops from the continent. Consequently, through SFHQ, in collaboration with the Norwegian High Command (FO) and *Milorg*, a major effort was made to prepare the resistance, put in place a huge array of operations designed to protect industrial and economic sites from destruction and help facilitate a peaceful transfer of power back to the Norwegian authorities.

Political factors also had a particular significance during the final months of the occupation. Relations between SOE and the Norwegian authorities had by this stage become extremely close and the leadership of *Milorg* looked to FO for direction. All parties were committed to the shared aim of assisting Norway's liberation and therefore SOE operations in 1944 and 1945 were built on a solid collaborative basis. Furthermore, events within Norway, the emergence and growing authority of *Hjemmefrontens ledelse*, the Home Front leadership, preparations for the approaching liberation, German backdoor efforts to conscript young Norwegians and the actions of Communist groups, all contributed to a decision to allow the direct involvement of *Milorg* units in sabotage. This resulted in a major intensification in attacks against military targets during the final months of the occupation. Nevertheless, the outcome of all these activities, especially preparations for the liberation, continued to be plagued by local and logistical difficulties and therefore despite a huge increase in the flow of resources to this theatre from the autumn of 1944, a fully armed, trained and prepared secret army was never fully created in Norway. The country's marginal position ultimately meant that the whole process was left too late.

In May 1945, however, Germany capitulated and over the following months there was a gradual return to legitimate government in Norway. And despite some difficulties, SOE alongside FO helped *Milorg* to play a significant, although largely symbolic, role in ensuring that this was a peaceful and largely uneventful process.

SOE sabotage operations in Norway 1944–5: A tactical and collaborative offensive

After the successful launch of Overlord, sabotage in Norway changed from being strategic *coup de main* strikes against economic and military sites to tactical operations in support of the Allied campaign on the continent. This meant that attacks against targets, such as the Orkla pyrite mines near Trondheim, were eventually replaced by actions against objectives such as fuel, armaments and the German divisions that began to retreat through Norway, all of which were considered of 'immediate' and 'present value to the enemy'.[1] The amount of sabotage also increased significantly due to the decision by the resistance leadership in Norway to allow units of *Milorg* to participate in operations against targets of military importance. Attacks undertaken by teams sent in from Britain were replaced by attacks carried out by local teams, either NIC (1) or *Milorg* units alone or in collaboration.

During the first half of 1944, in the run up to Overlord, SOE sabotage activity in Norway was sparse. At least four *coup de main* operations using teams from Britain were planned, but only one, 'Feather II' against the locomotives at the Orkla pyrite mines, was eventually undertaken. By the end of September 1944, when operations 'Dodworth' and 'Docklow' against the Orkla and Sulitjelma mines, respectively, were terminated, SOE attacks prepared and instigated from outside Norway were brought to an end.[2] The view within the Allied High Command was that a 'premature sabotage campaign in Norway' was 'more likely to hinder than help their general D-Day plans'.[3] Consequently, SOE's support for 'Fortitude North' was restricted to minor activities such as maintaining the frequency of journeys to the Norwegian coast and increasing W/T traffic, and because of a fear of reprisals and potential damage to *Milorg* it was decided not to escalate sabotage.[4] There was seemingly a growing realization that the resistance in Norway had to be kept intact and not prematurely sacrificed in a sabotage campaign that might achieve very little. It was appreciated that conditions in Norway, especially the 'extent of enemy control', meant that a major increase in activity could be extremely hazardous.[5]

From early May 1944, however, as part of the Home Front struggle against plans to conscript young Norwegians for military service on the eastern front, *Milorg* units carried out attacks against the registration offices of the *Arbeidstjeneste* (Labour Services) in Oslo, Skien, Ulefoss, Hønefoss and Sarpsborg, and abortive attacks took place at Holmestrand and Stavanger.[6] Events within Norway and the resultant stepping up of resistance to the actions of the occupying regime were the trigger that ultimately led to an increase in sabotage. The resistance leadership at last believed that the Norwegian people wished 'to play a part in the fight against the enemy' and would 'endure the sacrifices entailed by military actions on the part of the Home organisations'.[7] This was the end of a policy of largely non-violent resistance in Norway and the beginning of widespread collaboration between the Central Leadership of *Milorg* (SL) and SOE groups on sabotage operations, especially around Oslo. Gunnar Sønsteby had been SOE's pre-eminent agent in the capital since the spring of 1942. He had also developed links with SL and built up a network of contacts, including the many NIC (1) teams that were by that time working in the locality.[8] In mid-May 1944, Jens Chr. Hauge asked for Sønsteby's assistance in the fight against conscription,[9] which led to direct SOE involvement in the attacks against the Labour Services. It was this that also gave rise to the formation of what was referred to as the 'Oslo Detachment' – a group made up from SOE agents operating in the area. Before May 1944, although the various NIC (1) teams around Oslo knew of each other's presence, there was no special contact or cooperation. From 18 and 19 May and during the summer, members from these teams worked together under Sønsteby, carrying out sabotage actions aimed at scuppering efforts to mobilize young Norwegians. The 'Oslo Detachment' eventually included members of the 'Curlew', 'Company', 'Puffin', 'Buzzard', 'Bundle', 'Goldfinch' and 'Turkey' teams.[10] This unit became officially attached to SL with Sønsteby as its sabotage leader[11] and over the following months it carried out at least thirty-five successful attacks against major industrial and military targets around Oslo,[12] sometimes assisted by members of *Milorg*. From this point, therefore, sabotage in Norway, particularly in the south, was a joint effort involving NIC (1) teams and *Milorg* units.[13]

The direct involvement of the Home Forces meant that during the final year of Norway's occupation, even though SHAEF gave it a lower priority than preparations for the liberation,[14] sabotage increased significantly. The number of attacks carried out against industrial and military targets in Norway by NIC (1) teams and *Milorg* units between the early summer of 1944 and May 1945 was considerably greater than the total number of *coup de main* operations carried out during the previous four years. One official Norwegian report cites at least seventy cases of sabotage against industrial plant in Norway during 1944 alone,[15] while another report, the result of an insurance investigation of war damage between July 1944 and spring 1945 that excludes railways and actions by the 'Oslo Detachment', lists at least 140 cases of possible sabotage.[16] Another estimate based on the traces that can be found in original documents, and which includes railway and shipping sabotage alongside attacks against economic and military targets, puts the total at between 350 and 400 acts of sabotage during the final months of the occupation.[17]

It is somewhat ironic that in the summer 1944, when *Milorg* was for the first time prepared to become directly involved in military operations, SHAEF was reluctant to allow the resistance in Norway to be active.[18] Nevertheless, it meant that from the summer of 1944 *Milorg* groups carried out a series of operations against targets across southern Norway where many important industrial sites and military stores were concentrated. In *Milorg's* District 13, in and around Oslo, a separate action group called *Aks 13000* was set up under the district leader. It had a military structure, with a staff, a 'Head of Actions' and sabotage teams that were responsible for reconnaissance of the objective through to the actual operation. During the final eight months of the occupation, between 300 and 400 men from D13 were involved in operations against identified targets around the capital.[19]

There was not just an increase in the amount of sabotage in Norway from the spring of 1944; the nature of the targets also changed. From early July after the successful completion of Operation Neptune, the assault phase of Overlord, NIC (1) personnel, assisted by *Milorg* and with permission from London, attacked chemical factories in Oslo that produced sulphuric acid, a key component in the production of both explosives and more significantly U-boat batteries.[20] Also in July, SFHQ decided that 'petrol and oil' were 'targets of greatest importance and should be attacked whenever possible'.[21] Consequently, over the following months, at least twenty-eight operations were undertaken against oil and petrol stores and several hundred thousand litres were destroyed through actions by *Milorg* groups and NIC (1) teams either alone or in collaboration.[22] Operations against U-boat fuel and the power supply to the shipyards in Bergen, including yet again the Laksevaag floating dock, were another part of the Allied effort to end the potential threat posed by the U-boats stationed in Norway.[23] Further important targets attacked by NIC (1) teams, particularly the 'Oslo Detachment' under Sønsteby and local *Milorg* groups, included aircraft parts, arms and ammunition production, mechanical workshops, the remaining stocks of ball bearings in Norway[24] and finally shipping. SHAEF continued to place a high priority on attacks against enemy vessels and Operation Bundle, local *Milorg* units and Communist groups taken together had some success, eventually sinking or badly damaging several ships in the Oslo harbour area as well as undertaking attacks in Bergen, Horten, Porsgrunn and Moss harbours during the final months of the occupation.[25]

It is very difficult to assess their overall military contribution of these sabotage actions within the broader context. They undoubtedly led to a significant amount of destruction of vital materials, as exemplified by oil and petrol, at a time when Germany could least afford it, and at little cost to the Allies. They were also symbolically significant, as this was the first time that SOE and *Milorg* had worked together on operations that made an immediate and direct military contribution to the war in Europe. It has also been claimed that they were a further complicating factor for the German occupation of Norway and had a positive impact on the morale of both the civilian population and *Milorg*.[26]

It was important, however, that as the objective of these sabotage operations was to support the Allied offensive across Europe, they were coordinated and directed against appropriate military targets by SFHQ and FO IV in close liaison with SHAEF. The improvement in W/T contact with *Milorg* from the autumn of 1943, which was extended during the spring of 1944 when several new clandestine radio stations began operating in the Oslo area, was crucial to this. When Knut Haugland, a member of the original 'Grouse' team, returned to Norway in November 1943, one of his tasks was to improve communication between SL and the UK. By spring 1944, SL had two stations, 'Barbette Red' and 'Corncrake', in contact with the UK and from this point communication continued unhindered. For example, by March 1945, SL had three W/T stations working for them in the Oslo area: 'Chiffchaff', 'Crossbill Red' and 'Coppersmith Blue'.[27]

Milorg also contributed to this joint effort by separating out those industries that were of immediate importance to the German war effort and suitable for sabotage from those that were less significant but important to post-war Norway and therefore should remain untouched. This information was passed to London via Stockholm and resulted in a paper that was sent back to the Norwegian capital in June, and which became the basis for industrial sabotage over the coming months. Targets were, however, only attacked after they had been released or authority had been obtained through FO in London, either directly by the *Milorg* districts or more often by its leadership.[28] Even if an objective of high priority was selected, if an operation could lead to reprisals against *Milorg* or the local population, prior approval had to be sought from London.[29] The excellent working relationship between SOE, FO and *Milorg* was therefore a crucial factor in ensuring that sabotage in Norway was used as an extensive and effective tactical weapon in the final offensive against Germany, without resulting in political difficulties with the Norwegian government and unnecessary damage to the country's post-war economy.

Finally, there was one other category of sabotage that became widespread during the final months of Norway's occupation. This was railway sabotage. As shown, during 1943 and early 1944, SOE sent four operations to Norway in readiness to sabotage the main railway routes in the event of a German withdrawal or to support a possible Allied invasion.[30] In the run-up to Overlord, however, and during the summer and early autumn of 1944, these teams remained idle as SHAEF continued to fear that unrestricted attacks against the railway network would threaten the long-term integrity of *Milorg* and could lead to widespread famine among the civilian population. After the success of the preliminary stage of Overlord, it also preferred to allow German forces to leave Norway.[31] Nevertheless, SOE believed that it could and would eventually be called on to make a contribution to slowing down German withdrawals by attacking the railway network in Norway. Therefore, it continued with its preparations and in September and October 1944, operations 'Woodlark' and the main 'Woodpecker' party were also sent to the country to prepare attacks against the railways both north and south of Trondheim.

By late October 1944, when a 'limited' number of attacks against the railways was permitted,[32] there were therefore five NIC (1) teams resident in Norway or just across the border in Sweden in various states of readiness. It was, however, only from early December 1944 and owing to concerns over the arrival of units of the 20th Mountain army on the continent that these teams were given permission to undertake unlimited action and a widespread offensive began.[33] From this point until April 1945, a sabotage campaign that included NIC (1) teams, *Milorg* units, a team from the Norwegian Parachute Company (Operation Waxwing), an OSS team (Operation Rype) and plans to use the Special Air Services (SAS), was launched against the Norwegian rail network in an attempt to delay and disrupt the withdrawal of German forces from Norway.[34]

This offensive resulted in probably at least 100 actions against the railway routes that were used to transport German troops southwards. The Norwegian State Railway's (NSB) war history records over seventy different attacks against the Norwegian railway between October 1944 and May 1945. The central management's security office, however, recorded eighty-nine cases of sabotage in 1945 alone. This probably includes actions by Communist groups but is nevertheless a much higher and probably more reliable total than in SOE archives.[35] These included the destruction of small sections of rail line, the demolition of bridges and larger-scale attacks such as Operation *Betongblanding* (Concrete Mixer) on 14 March 1945, which was the largest coordinated sabotage action in Norway and involved 1,000 men from *Milorg* attacking the railway lines on both sides of Oslo fjord.[36] Despite some initial reluctance within SHAEF to use *Milorg*, this was therefore a major collaborative tactical effort.[37]

Notwithstanding the scale of railway sabotage in Norway during 1945, there is, however, doubt over its effectiveness. In July 1945, in response to a request from the COS, G-3 Division of SHAEF produced a 'Report on the Value of SOE Operations in the Supreme Commander's Sphere'.

This rather self-congratulatory paper made the claim that the impact of railway sabotage in Norway was 'striking' and led to a reduction in the rate of withdrawal from Norway from 'four divisions to less than one division per month'. It is a claim that was repeated after the war in British publications but has justifiably been treated with some scepticism in more recent Norwegian histories.[38] From the summer of 1942 until April 1944, there was relatively little change in the number of enemy forces in Norway, which despite the rotation of troops in and out of the country remained fairly static at around eleven to thirteen divisions.[39] The Germans, however, withdrew at least nine complete divisions from Norway between July 1944 and May 1945. In July, the 196th Infantry Division was pulled out followed in the autumn by the 269th Infantry Division, the 560th Volks-Grenadier Division and the 710th Infantry Division. The 6th SS-Berg Division was withdrawn during late December 1944 and early January 1945, the first 'Nordlicht' division to leave the country, followed by the 2nd Berg Division, the 163rd Infantry Division, the 169th Infantry Division, 199th Infantry Division and last the 7th Berg Division, which was not transported out of the country before the war ended. Other manpower, such as 11,000 men from the Luftwaffe, also left. It is also important to point out that several thousand troops were also sent to Norway during the final months of its occupation.[40] There was, therefore, an uninterrupted flow of enemy forces out of the country after the launch of Overlord, which actually accelerated despite the instigation of extensive railway sabotage. The destruction of rail line and the demolition of bridges in the area north of Trondheim had little impact on the movement of German forces as new routes were found, motorized transportation used or temporary bridges quickly erected. Even most of the damage caused by Operation *Betongblanding* in March was repaired within a few hours. The most serious single action against the Norwegian railways was the blowing up of Jørstad Bridge on 13 January 1945, which resulted in the death of seventy-seven German soldiers. Nevertheless, despite the destruction of the bridge it only delayed troop transport for a few days. Initially troops went on foot, but after just six days a temporary bridge was completed, which railway traffic used until a new and permanent bridge was built.[41]

This sabotage was nevertheless an additional major security and logistical problem for the occupying regime in Norway during the final months of the war. At the time, it was estimated that at least 2,000 German troops were used as 'line guards' in an attempt to protect the rail network.[42] German withdrawals did begin to slow down in the spring of 1945, but other factors such as the mining of Norwegian waters, lack of shipping and coal and Allied air superiority were probably the major causes behind this.[43]

SOE and the liberation: The preparation of a protective force

From the summer of 1944, SFHQ, in collaboration with FO and under the authority of SHAEF, also began a major effort to prepare both *Milorg* and SOE-sponsored groups to act as a protective force that could be utilized within Norway during the early stages of its liberation. Preparations were predominately built on an expectation that the most likely scenario was that the German forces would eventually capitulate, despite some fears that there might be an enemy withdrawal or even a last stand in the country. Consequently, after four frustrating years, and within the particular strategic conditions of 1944, SOE's plans to prepare a secret army in Norway came to fruition. This underground army would not, however, be used as a guerrilla force to support an opposed landing by Allied troops, as originally intended, but to assist in the peaceful transition to lawful government in Norway. Scotco espoused the contribution of resistance forces, particularly in light of the shortage of regular troops for operations in Norway, and therefore liaised closely with SFHQ. SOE's Norwegian Section and FO IV jointly oversaw and helped to prepare this underground army. By this stage, *Milorg* had over 30,000 men under its control, a military staff structure spread across the regions of Norway, an internal communications network and a leadership that looked to London and ultimately the Allied High Command for direction and authority.[44]

All this ultimately led to a huge array of operations in Norway during 1944 and 1945 that were designed to ensure that a clandestine army was in a position to make an effective contribution to the liberation of the country from German occupation. There was an acceleration and increase in the supply of arms, equipment and training. Teams of officers were sent in from Britain in an effort to improve local leadership and measures were taken to ensure that resistance groups remained intact and undiminished. *Milorg* in collaboration with SFHQ and FO initiated a huge array of counter-scorch measures. Arrangements were put in place to ensure close liaison between SFHQ/FO, Scotco, *Milorg* and the Norwegian police battalions in Sweden, along with measures to facilitate the rapid deployment of forward parties to the key areas of Norway immediately after a German surrender. The objectives were to ensure protection of key industrial sites and communications, maintain law and order and prepare the way for the arrival of the main contingent of Allied forces that would ultimately enforce the armistice conditions. In addition, in response to the retreat of German forces into northern Norway in October 1944 and the implementation of a brutal scorched-earth policy, SFHQ responded to requests for help from the Norwegian government and agreed to prepare local resistance groups in this remote region, although with little success.

From the autumn of 1944, the supply of materials to Norway increased and nearly three-quarters of all arms and equipment delivered by air were dropped during the final nine months of the occupation.[45] Between September 1944 and May 1945, the RAF and USAAF undertook a notable but costly effort to distribute these supplies and twenty-three British and six American planes were lost on dropping operations over Norway.[46] There clearly was a determination within SHAEF to ensure that the Home Forces in Norway were adequately prepared. At the same time, however, the number of recruits in *Milorg* also increased, especially during the final months of the occupation when it grew from a little over 30,000 to around 40,000,[47] and therefore, by May 1945, despite Allied efforts, it was still not fully armed. In *Milorg's* District 21, in the county of Møre and Romsdal on the west coast south of Trondheim, of the 1,500 men mobilized in May 1945 only between 700 and 800 had weapons. In District 17, in the county of Telemark west of Oslo, only 1,764 men out of a total of 3,151 mobilized in May 1945 were armed, despite receiving fourteen successful drops during the final months of the occupation. The leadership of District 25, close to Lillehammer north of Oslo, also complained after the war of a general shortage of arms and equipment; nevertheless, the important Sunshine protective operation around Rjukan and Notodden appeared to have a plentiful supply of arms during the winter of 1944–5. During 1944 and 1945, there was also an increase in the number of NIC (1) teams that went into Norway to help prepare local resistance groups, mostly from *Milorg*. Nevertheless, the proportion of those that eventually received instruction was patchy. In eastern Norway, where *Milorg* was at its strongest, only 75 per cent received military training despite the arrival of fifty instructors from Britain. And in the area around Trondheim, only 50 per cent of *Milorg* recruits were trained.[48]

In late April and early May 1945, however, there were several clashes between German patrols and armed groups from two of the reception camps, 'Bjørn West' near Bergen and 'Elg' north-west of Oslo, which had been set up in the mountains to receive and train members of the Home Forces in preparation for the liberation. Unlike the local groups, the Germans suffered heavy casualties during these encounters,[49] which appears to indicate that the training and preparation of the resistance was having some effect and that in small and isolated confrontations with occupying troops they were capable of acting as an effective military force. Nevertheless, while visiting Norway at the end of the occupation, Lt. Col. Wilson wrote in his diary that it was fortunate for 'Bjørn West' that 'the end came so soon after the action'.[50] In other words, he felt it was unlikely that the resistance could have withstood the full force of German power for very long if it had ever been brought to bear against them. Although a last-minute but significant effort was made by the Allies to prepare a secret army in Norway, at the time of the German surrender the '40,000 *Milorg* personnel' were certainly not fully equipped and trained. It is, therefore, difficult to see how this clandestine army, without prompt support from regular forces, could have ever defended the country from a determined German effort to instigate a widespread scorched-earth campaign, let alone a last stand, if either had ever been carried out.[51]

A huge effort was also put in to ensuring that this underground army would be able to communicate both internally and externally so that its contribution could be effectively coordinated and closely managed. As with any army, command and control is essential and this requires not only having the necessary equipment but also a sufficient quantity in the right place at the right time. By 8 May, there were sixty-nine clandestine wireless stations operating in the country, compared with only two in 1941, and during 1945 over 4,000 messages were sent from Norway, over 50 per cent of the total sent during the war. From early 1944, attempts were also made to set up an internal radio network so that local *Milorg* organizations could communicate within their area, across districts and with SL in Oslo. By May 1945, through using radio sets assembled in Norway under the code name 'Olga', as well as equipment brought into the country, twelve districts were able to intercommunicate. In addition about 100 SCR/195 'walkie-talkie' sets were also sent to the country to aid communication in 'battlefield conditions'.[52]

An army, secret or otherwise, also has to have a competent leadership. By the early summer of 1944, both SFHQ and FO had recognized that there was a shortage of trained officers within Norway, something that was confirmed by *Milorg* soon afterwards. In July, the concept of reinforcing the district leaders in Norway was approved by the ANCC, and at its August meeting J. Chr. Hauge stated that there was a definite shortage of suitable leaders in Norway.[53] Consequently, it was decided to send in specialist teams to link up with and where possible reinforce the *Milorg* district leadership. This eventually happened in two ways. First, through Operation Farnborough, which set out to send specialist teams largely made up of recruits from *Den norske krigsskolen*, the Norwegian War School in London, to eastern Norway, especially in and around Oslo where *Milorg* was at its strongest. The objective was to increase 'the preparedness of the district' through supplying teams of officers and NCOs. And between the end of December 1944 and mid-February 1945, nine out of a total of ten such operations were sent to Norway. The 'Farnborough' operations commenced with 'Farnborough I' when second lieutenant Johan Møller Neerland was dropped into eastern Norway on 28/29 December 1944. Farnborough IV was never sent and Operation Chacewater eventually replaced it. Fourteen men were recruited from *Den norske krigsskolen* in London and especially trained for the 'Farnborough' operations.[54]

Second, in the outlying *Milorg* districts, NIC (1) teams were progressively authorized, when possible, to link up with and provide support for the local resistance leadership. For example, in early November 1944, Operation Auk arrived in the Haugesund area between Bergen and Stavanger. The leader of the team was instructed to take over responsibility for SOE groups already there, reorganize the district and become military adviser to the *Milorg* district leader. In mid-February 1945, Operation Diver was sent to the *Milorg* District 21, around Ålesund on the West Coast, also to act as military adviser to the district leader.[55]

During the final months of the occupation, therefore, *Milorg* became the unequivocal basis for a clandestine army in southern Norway, and a major effort was put in to ensuring it was an effectively led military force. Nevertheless, there were areas where the organization remained weak and ineffectual, such as around Sogne north of Bergen, where SOE and FO retained responsibility for organizing local groups. By this stage, however, SOE, owing to a number of 'favourable' reports from the field, appears to have lost any reservations it had about the reliability of *Milorg*.[56]

Preparing, arming and equipping a clandestine army in Norway in readiness for the liberation was on its own not enough. This underground force had to be kept intact and its numbers preserved and if possible increased if it was ever to make a viable military contribution. Conditions within Norway during the final twelve months of the occupation made this increasingly difficult. As shown, the threat to *Milorg* from the German and Norwegian security police using informers and provocateurs continued and even intensified as the liberation approached and therefore the number of liquidations undertaken by SOE and *Milorg* groups increased.[57] A further hazard to this clandestine army was also the attempt, using the cover of the Labour Services, to conscript young Norwegians for German military service, thereby denying the resistance to both new and current recruits and thus weakening its ranks. In response to this, both SL and FO in collaboration with SFHQ decided to set up reception camps or cells in the woods and mountains where young men could hide and receive training and weapons instruction.

Although the series of cells that *Milorg* set up in the woods across eastern Norway during the summer of 1944 were a refuge for a significant number, almost 3,000 around Oslo, they nonetheless proved difficult to maintain. Owing to a lack of provisions many of the men, over 1,500, were forced to flee to Sweden, while others found local jobs or returned home. Some cells, however, particularly those close to and even across the Swedish border, were kept going through the winter of 1944–5. *Milorg* District 11 set up four cells in the woods, and one of them called 'Fritjof' was located across the Swedish border. Supplies of clothes and food, along with a few weapons, were brought over from Sweden during the autumn of 1944 by so-called 'Planet Groups' established by the Norwegian authorities in Stockholm. Arms and equipment were also dropped by air and NIC (1) officers carried out instruction, but the total effort in men and materials was relatively small.[58]

From as early as March 1943, SOE had also contemplated setting up a small number of secret bases in Norway.[59] And during the winter of 1943–4, FO also began to consider the idea of establishing a series of camps in the mountains where young men could be trained. Consequently, in May 1944, instructions were given to plan several large 'bases' or 'reception centres' in isolated locations where *Milorg* recruits could not only escape the threat of mobilization but also be formed into armed and trained guerrilla units that could be used during the liberation, if required. The project was provisionally approved by SHAEF in July 1944[60] and at the end of August preparations commenced for the first base called 'Elg' situated in the lower Valdres valley about 100 kilometres north-west of Oslo.[61] The intention was to establish five camps across southern Norway but despite the efforts through OSS to obtain supplies of Arctic equipment from the United States, only three of these bases, 'Bjørn West' north of Bergen, 'Varg' east of Stavanger and 'Elg', received enough material to be able to grow their numbers. The other two bases were 'Orm' in Hedmark, 180 kilometres north-east of Oslo, and 'Hjort' north-east of Trondheim. Because of its size, 'Bjørn

West' was divided in two, 'Bjørn West' and 'East', and in December 1944 a party was dispatched to establish the second base on the eastern side of the area. Very little was, however, achieved with few supplies received and only a small force put together. Even 'Bjørn West', the largest of these reception centres, was only able to send 250 fully armed men into Bergen on the evening of 9 May 1945 to help maintain order after the German surrender.[62]

The manpower in *Milorg* symbolized the Norwegian government's main military contribution to the liberation and therefore its preparation and utilization was politically very important. Moreover, as the final stages of the war in Europe approached post-war considerations, the safeguarding of the Norwegian economy and industrial infrastructure from long-term and costly damage became increasingly important. Therefore, from December 1943 and during the following spring, NIC (1) teams began to go into occupied Norway with instructions to prepare local groups to protect key industrial sites.[63] In the spring of 1944, the Norwegian military authorities and *Milorg* leadership also affirmed that 'preventive' measures needed to be prepared in advance,[64] a view that was reinforced in July when intelligence was received from MI IV in Stockholm that indicated that the Germans might attempt to destroy industrial sites, communications, harbours and ship-works at the end of their occupation. From the spring of 1944, Leif Tronstad and Peter Deinboll Snr in FO IV, who both had valuable local experience, began preparations for the protection of Norwegian industries and communications, and during his visit to London in July/August 1944, J. Chr. Hauge attended the meeting of the ANCC where all parties agreed to the importance of protective operations.[65] From the beginning of September, after instruction from SFHQ, it became the primary task for the Home Forces. FO provided expertise; SOE and FO jointly supplied specialist teams, arms, equipment and training; whilst *Milorg* provided the bulk of the men who would undertake these preventative measures.[66] Most importantly, this tripartite relationship, backed by the authority of the Allied High Command, meant that the number and scale of these operations could increase dramatically over the following months.

From September 1944, built on help provided by OSS in Paris, and drawing on Allied and resistance experience of German demolitions in France, preparations began for a whole raft of counter-scorch operations in Norway. From July 1944, J. H. Reimers from FO IV was given responsibility for counter-scorch preparations and in September 1944 he was sent to France where Colonel Temple from OSS office in

Paris assisted him. He was introduced to leaders in the French resistance who took him to see examples of German demolition.[67]

The first major collaborative counter-scorch operation was 'Sunshine'. The party, under the command of Major Leif Tronstad, was parachuted into Norway in October 1944. Its objective was to protect the power stations in the counties of Telemark and Buskerud, as well as the Norsk Hydro industrial plants in Rjukan and Notodden. Divided into three sections, 'Moonlight', 'Starlight' and 'Lamplight', it included many of the men from operations 'Grouse' and 'Gunnerside' who would eventually work closely on the project with both the local *Milorg* organization and SL in Oslo. The hydroelectric plants in Norway and the production of heavy water had been major strategic targets for SOE. From the early autumn of 1944, the priority, because of their economic importance, was to ensure their protection. Consequently, 'Sunshine' was in many ways a watershed that marked the point at which post-war factors became the determining factor in shaping operations against major industrial targets in Norway.[68] The aim was no longer to damage these sites but to stop them from being damaged.

During October and November 1944, FO, *Milorg*, represented by Jens Chr. Hauge, SFHQ, Scotco and MEW put together and agreed three major protective plans. The first of these was the 'Foscott Plan', which set out to protect the priority targets in Norway, the power supply and telecommunications network. Altogether 118 sites, including thirty-four power stations and twenty-seven transformer stations, were identified. In addition, local *Milorg* groups would protect sixty-one secondary targets that were identified as part of the 'Carmarthen' plan, while the *Bedriftsorganisasjon* (B.org), the industrial organization, a resistance group based on factory workers under the control of SL, would protect many smaller targets under the 'Catterick' plan. The 'Foscott' plans were presented to Hauge on his arrival in London in November 1944. The 'Carmarthen' plans, including targets in Districts 18 and 22, were also worked out before Hauge's arrival.[69]

To implement the 'Foscott' plan, the 'Farnborough' teams provided expertise and worked with local *Milorg* organizations to protect key sites in eastern Norway. In addition, as with Operation Sunshine, other sites across the country were allocated to teams either sent from Britain, such as 'Clothall' and 'Crowfield', or to NIC (1) teams that were already resident in Norway, such as 'Arquebus' or 'Razorbill'. Many of these teams also worked in collaboration with local *Milorg* groups. Finally, there were operations such as 'Barming' that for various reasons never reached Norway and in these cases it was *Milorg* or other local groups that stepped in to help. SOE and FO, in cooperation with *Milorg*, put together at least forty operations in the final nine months of the war that set out to help protect Norway's power stations, industries and telecommunications network. It was a major collaborative effort;[70] the improvised and sporadic nature of SOE's earlier activity had been left far behind. These operations were sophisticated, well planned and organized.

There is one other protective plan that because of its scale and military importance to the liberation should also be mentioned. This was 'Polar Bear', an operation that set out to safeguard the main Norwegian harbours from German demolition, something that had happened to the French ports and as a result slowed the Allied advance in the autumn of 1944. It involved FO IV, SOE and on this occasion it also included help from the Norwegian navy, which supplied the manpower, and the Royal Navy, which organized a trip to Dieppe so that the Norwegian personnel could study the German destruction at first hand. The planning for 'Polar Bear' was a joint effort between J. H. Reimers (FO IV), Commander Thore Horve (Norwegian Naval High Command) and Lt. Col. J. S. Wilson from SOE. Horve established a 'Polar Bear' office and began by recruiting sixteen Norwegian naval personnel to be trained to carry out the operations. Between mid-January and May 1945, a total of ten 'Polar Bear' teams were eventually sent to Norway to cover a total of ultimately thirteen Norwegian harbours from Narvik in the north to Fredrikstad in the east.[71]

Despite the explicit priority given to protective operations, however, while uncertainty remained over the intention of the German forces in Norway, the idea of using local guerrilla forces in support of Allied military operations to reoccupy the country was not completely abandoned. It seems that SOE still believed it needed to continue to prepare for all possibilities, no matter how unlikely. Therefore, some of the NIC (1) teams that went into the country during the final months of the occupation, such as 'Snowflake', 'Avocet' and 'Diver', still received instructions to prepare local groups to undertake guerrilla operations in support of Allied forces, if this proved to be necessary. For example, Operation Diver, which arrived in Norway as late as mid-February 1945 to work in the Ålesund area, was instructed to plan actions to assist the 'Allies in the event of an invasion'.[72] Such instructions, however, were by this stage not widespread and seem to have been confined to teams operating in areas where *Milorg* was traditionally weaker, especially along the west coast. There also appears to be no evidence that they were directly linked to a last-minute expectation or fear that the German forces in Norway might make a last stand and probably represented no more than a continuation of earlier work.

During the final months of the occupation, the bulk of SOE's operations reflected the view that Allied military success in Europe would ultimately lead to a collapse or surrender of German authority in Norway. It was, however, important for post-war political stability if the return to legitimate, civilian government could happen in a peaceful and orderly environment. In September 1944, therefore, SFHQ had directed that the Home Forces should work closely with the civilian resistance in Norway to help establish and maintain law and order prior to the arrival of a relief force,[73] a point reinforced in the 'September Directive' that was issued to the *Milorg* district leadership soon afterwards.[74] In step with this, the Norwegian government in London accorded the Home Front Leadership an important executive role in the transitional period prior to the reinstatement of legal authority in Norway. On 5 May 1945, the Norwegian prime minister issued the following message: 'in the case of a German capitulation the Home Front Leadership is herewith authorised on the Government's behalf, until Government representatives arrive in Oslo, to undertake what is necessary to ensure the establishment and maintenance of Norwegian civil administration on the basis of Norwegian law and agreed resolutions.'[75]

Ultimately, it was the Home Forces in collaboration with newly appointed local government officials, local police and the district commanders (DKs), the Norwegian government representatives responsible for resistance forces once the liberation had commenced, that would help to ensure that this transition was controlled and uneventful.[76] Alongside this, the Norwegian police battalions in Sweden, made up from some of the thousands of Norwegian refugees that had fled the country since 1940, would be made ready by the Allied and Swedish authorities to act as an additional local force that could also be quickly deployed in Norway.

By May 1945, a total of nearly 11,000 men in units of the *Rikspoliti* (state police) and *Reservepolitikorps* (police reserve corps) were awaiting a call to return to their homeland. From early 1942 the Norwegian authorities began to consider military training for the Norwegian refugees in Sweden, but due to difficult relations with the Swedish authorities nothing happened before 1943. During 1943, however, a *Rikspoliti* including uniformed and criminal police under the Department of Justice and a *Reservepolitikorps* under the Norwegian military authorities were formed, which would lead to 10,000 Norwegian refugees in Sweden receiving military training. By

December 1943, the Swedish authorities had given permission for the development of the *Reservepoliti* and in January 1944 training began. By the end of the war, a total of 14,300, including camp and administrative personnel, had served in either the *Riks* or *Reservepoliti*. From the autumn of 1944, after the Soviet occupation of part of northern Norway, 2,400 men from both these police units were transferred to northern Sweden and eventually 1,300 were transferred to Finnmark to assist in the liberation of the area.[77]

Considerable effort was also made to institute close liaison between SFHQ and Scotco and to ensure that when the time came there would be close operational liaison between the Allied land forces in Norway, *Milorg* and the police battalions. Contact between SOE's Norwegian section and Scotco was formalized in April 1944 when Lt. Col. C. S. Hampton was appointed as a liaison officer between the two. A further step was taken when in the summer of 1944 authority was given for the formation of a 'Special Force Detachment' (referred to as M.E. 12), under Hampton, to ensure direct and close collaboration between SFHQ and Scotco in the planning for the liberation. This led to the formation of an HQ Detachment and five Special Force sections, one for each of the main regions of Norway, which were given the task of working with the Allied forces that would oversee and enforce the liberation. Three Special Force subsections were also created to accompany the police battalions as they crossed from Sweden into Norway en route for Narvik, Trondheim and Oslo, respectively. The objective of these special force units was once in Norway to provide liaison between the Allied forces and local *Milorg* groups, including SL in Oslo, the DKs once they arrived and with the police battalions as they moved into Norway.[78] At the same time, although *Milorg* would remain under the executive command of its own leaders and the relevant DK, local military commanders would be able to issue orders for their employment through the DK or a representative of SFHQ.[79]

Further evidence of the military significance placed on *Milorg* and the police battalions is the proposals, which originated in early September 1944, to send Allied representatives of SHAEF, through SFHQ, to both Norway and Sweden. There was a belief within Scotco that there was a need to 'advise and assist the Home Front in organising all available forces', to 'co-ordinate action taken within Norway with that undertaken by Allied forces outside', to 'hinder German attempts at wrecking' and to make 'preparations for the speedy arrival of supplies'.[80] This was given added impetus by fears within SOE's Norwegian section that the impending armistice between Finland and the Soviet Union could result in an early German withdrawal, instigation of a national scorched-earth policy or maybe even a capitulation, leading to conditions of unrest and disorganization across Norway. With no military action possible within this theatre at this time, it was felt that a great degree of responsibility could therefore fall on the Home Front and SFHQ. This led to the 'Scale' operations, which were plans to send Allied representatives to Norway to liaise with local resistance leaders, provide SHAEF with intelligence and, if necessary, receive the surrender of local garrisons and gain German recognition of the role of the Home Front.[81]

Initially, several missions were planned in order to cover *Milorg* HQ in Oslo, the region around Trondheim, the county of Nordland centred on Mosjøen, the Stavanger/Kristiansand area and Bergen, as well as one to work with SOE and OSS missions in Stockholm. The leading operation, called 'Octave', set out to send an Allied team to link up and cooperate with SL to assist it to prepare the Home Forces in Norway, undertake counter scorch operations, hinder German withdrawals if required and receive the capitulation of German forces if necessary. Although 'Octave' was kept alive at least until the end of 1944, only three 'Scale' operations were eventually sent into the field: 'Quaver' and 'Semi-Quaver' in Nordland and 'Minim' to Stockholm. The reason for the eventual abandonment of 'Octave' and the missions to Stavanger/Kristiansand and Bergen is unclear. Contact between SFHQ and *Milorg* HQ in Oslo during the autumn of 1944 was very close, especially after J. Chr. Hauge's visits to London, and with the improved W/T links it was probably felt that the mission was no longer necessary. The withdrawal of German forces from Finland also did not have the widespread impact that was feared.[82]

The first 'Scale' operation to go ahead was 'Quaver', in October 1944. It has attracted previous attention because it was the only SOE operation sent to Norway that primarily used British recruits,[83] including SOE staff officer, J. C. Adamson. Owing to the strategic geography of the area, which made it a potential transportation bottleneck, it was an important locus for gathering intelligence on and for the initiation of operations against the German forces moving southwards. Previous attempts by NIC (1) teams to build up resistance groups further south – Operations Heron and Falcon – had been broken up by the work of the German security police and local informers and *Milorg* had also failed to build up a significant organization in the area. Consequently, operations 'Quaver' and 'Semi-Quaver' were a final and, after Adamson's early capture, a failed Allied attempt to establish armed and trained resistance groups in this strategically important region.[84]

The other 'Scale' operation that went ahead was 'Minim', the proposal to send a representative of SFHQ to Stockholm to act as a liaison officer between SHAEF and SOE office, OSS mission and MI IV. This was more successful. The most important issue for 'Minim', who was Major H. A. Nyberg from SOE's Norwegian section, was Operation Beefeater, the training and preparation of the Norwegian police battalions. From December 1944, Nyberg, under the cover of 'Honoury Assistant Military Attaché' at the British Legation provided SFHQ and Scotco with regular and up-to-date information on 'Beefeater'.[85] The police battalions were eventually incorporated into Operation Doomsday, the plan to establish forces in southern Norway as soon as the German commander had accepted the Allied terms of surrender.

As part of this there was also Operation Antipodes, which was approved in February 1945. This was a plan, put together in Stockholm by SOE, FO IV and *Milorg*, to use teams from Britain, Sweden and within Norway to protect the bridges along the vital routes into the country. The objective was to ensure that the advance of the Norwegian police units was not delayed. Altogether twenty-two Norwegian officers were trained in Britain and forty-five in Sweden for this operation, which was planned in Sweden in March 1945 by Lt. Reimers (FO IV), Colonel Ram (SOE), Captain Rolf Eriksen (MI IV) and Ole Berg from *Milorg*. It, however, only proved possible in the short time scale available to get eight of the original planned fourteen 'Antipodes' operations in place on the ground, although local *Milorg* groups in eastern Norway were also used to help secure the numerous bridges that straddle the River Glomma on the routes into Oslo.[86]

Finally, there was one other major event that had an impact on the development of SOE operations in Norway during the final months of the occupation. This was the retreat of the German 20th Mountain Army followed by the advance of Soviet forces into northern Norway in autumn 1944, which led to the forced evacuation by the German authorities of 40,000–45,000 Norwegian citizens from the northern counties of Finnmark and Nord-Troms and the instigation of a brutal scorched-earth policy.[87] As a result the Norwegian government turned to its allies, including SOE, for assistance in its effort to make a contribution to what it saw as the liberation of a part of its country and to protect Norwegian interests and citizens in the region.

This resulted in two failed attempts to instigate actions against German forces in the north of Norway through arming and preparing local resistance groups. The first operation was called 'Husky', a plan to establish an SFHQ base in Finnmark using Norwegian and British personnel and where selected local recruits could be trained and equipped to carry out actions behind the German lines. The second operation called 'Scapula' was an attempt, in response to appeals from SIS station 'Gudrun', to supply weapons to local groups, who would then lead efforts to resist the forced evacuation of the civilian population. SOE strongly opposed both operations, primarily as it was felt they had no military value and that there were better ways of using scarce resources, but eventually it bowed to political pressure from the Norwegian authorities and agreed to implement them. The remoteness of the area, which made contact extremely difficult, the threat posed by small enemy vessels and the rejection by the SIS operator of the British and Norwegian proposals meant, however, that both projects were eventually abandoned.[88]

The collapse of German authority and the liberation of Norway, May–June 1945

At 2:41 am on 7 May 1945, Germany surrendered unconditionally on all fronts. This was confirmed in a BBC broadcast to Norway at 18:30 pm and during the same evening people began to appear on the streets of Oslo to celebrate the end of the war. On the afternoon of 8 May an Allied 'Herald Party', a forward party from Scotco, flew into Oslo with the capitulation dictate, which was presented to the German High Command at Lillehammer later that evening. On 9 May, General Böhme, in command of the German forces in Norway, confirmed that he would work loyally to ensure that its terms were carried out.[89]

When the German High Command accepted the Allied terms and conditions of surrender in Norway on 8 May 1945, uncertainty over the route to liberation was at an end. Over the coming weeks and months, there was an orderly and largely uneventful German capitulation. There were some small and sporadic disturbances, particularly in northern Norway, and there was considerable tension in Bergen, but these were isolated incidents.[90] According to General Thorne, C-in-C Allied Land Forces Norway, the smoothness of the early stages of the liberation was the result of 'the good discipline of *Milorg* and of the German Command'.[91] While the view of Jens Chr. Hauge was that it was primarily because of the 'brilliant German staff work' and the 'unbelievable discipline of the Germans' rather than Allied efforts.[92] On 8 May, however, there was still the potential for chaos and disruption within the country, especially in the period before the arrival of an Allied force to oversee the surrender.

Close to 350,000 Germans remained in the country, including many of the war-weary divisions that had fought in Finland before retreating into Norway in the autumn of 1944.

In this potentially unstable situation, it was important that all the plans that SFHQ, FO IV and *Milorg* had put together over the previous months to protect Norwegian industry and communications, ensure law and order and to assist a prompt return to civil authority in Norway were rapidly set in motion. Alongside this, the framework that had been created to ensure that once the Allied forces arrived in Norway they could effectively coordinate their work with the local resistance leadership across the country had to be put in place.

In the days prior to 8 May, everything was done to avoid any clashes between the Home Forces and German units that might threaten an orderly capitulation. To assist this objective on 7 May the Home Front leadership, using contacts that had been developed earlier, began discussions with the German High Command in order to prevent any possible misunderstanding or disagreements. From the autumn of 1944, SL was in touch with two officers, Frithjof Hammersen and Joachim Von Moltke, in the Wehrmacht High Command. When Jens Chr. Hauge visited London in November 1944, he made SOE fully aware of this contact, which eventually provided the Allies with a great deal of important intelligence on the German authorities during the final months and weeks of the occupation. For example, Hauge was told that 'responsible German military circles in Norway' proposed 'to finish the occupation' after 'the collapse of Germany' and that three weeks before the capitulation there were still 350,000 enemy soldiers and civilian personnel in the country. On 7 May, it was Hammersen who became the official liaison officer between the Wehrmacht and *Milorg*.[93]

On 8 May, the general order for the mobilization of the Home Forces across the country was issued and from this point it was no longer an underground army. In line with the directives issued by SL in September and December 1944, key sites, such as harbours, communications and important public buildings were quickly taken over by *Milorg* units in order to ensure the protection of the country's industrial and communications infrastructure. Of the estimated 40,000 members of the Home Forces in Norway, 19,000 were eventually mobilized for protection duties and although preparations had been made to destroy some key sites, 'not a single bridge' was blown or 'a single quay or power station' destroyed. For example, in Bergen, the Germans made preparations to blow up the quays by placing explosives in containers resembling gas cylinders 1.60-metre long suspended in shafts in two rows 5 metres apart.[94]

In accordance with lists that had been drawn up earlier, *Milorg* units arrested members of NS, Norwegians who had fought for the Wehrmacht and informers as well as some members of the German security apparatus.[95] All these tasks were undertaken by recruits from a clandestine army that had been given leadership, largely trained and at least in part lightly armed and equipped through the efforts of SOE in close collaboration with the Norwegian High Command.

According to General Sir Andrew Thorne when the Allied troops arrived in Norway, 'peace and order prevailed everywhere', which meant that the whole of the forces under his command were 'available for the control of the German forces' and this allowed him to 'impose disarmament terms' from the very beginning without distraction. Nevertheless, as Jens Chr. Hauge wrote later, it was the Germans who still 'held real power', and it needed an Allied operation to liberate Norway. In other words, the Home Forces were only ever able to undertake a supportive role alongside regular forces.[96] Many of the recruits were unarmed, some were untrained and most only had light weapons: a 'very special army' according to Hauge. Members of the Home Forces had white armbands with Norwegian colours while the police had black armbands with *Politi* written in red.[97] The view of General Thorne was that they were a match for any force that was not 'well supplied with support weapons', by which he presumably meant artillery, tanks and aircraft, which the German units in Norway still had.[98] Nevertheless, the Home Forces played an important symbolic role in the early hours and days after the German surrender in Europe. Their presence on the streets and at key sites across Norway represented an immediate return of some form of legitimate national authority in the country in the period prior to the arrival of Allied forces.

From 9 May, through the implementation of operations 'Doomsday' and then 'Apostle', Allied forces moved into Norway and by the middle of June 'Force 134', as it was called, totalled around 30,000.[99] Included in this were the Special Force Detachments that accompanied the police battalions from Sweden and Allied troops as they arrived in the country. These provided an important link between the local *Milorg* leadership and the DKs, the Allied 'Zone Commanders' that had military responsibility for the regions of Norway, and the HQ of 'Force 134'. They also worked closely with local *Milorg* units in helping to enforce law and order in the more remote areas, such as in the north and west.[100]

Under the terms of surrender, the German forces were moved to reserves, disarmed and ultimately returned to their homeland. The arrival of King Haakon on 7 June saw the end of the military phase of the liberation and the return of constitutional government in Norway. On 9 June, 15,000 men from *Milorg* filed past the king in Oslo, followed on 28 June by 205 men from the Linge Company and 60 men from the Shetlands Base in their last official duty. On 15 July, the Home Forces were disbanded followed by the Special Force Detachments. During June and July, the formation of eighteen light infantry battalions had also begun and these would provide the core of a provisional Norwegian army that when the German forces were no longer considered a risk would take over from Allied forces in Norway. SOE's Norwegian section was closed on 7 September 1945, and the last British troops left Norway on 27 December 1945.[101]

During 1944 and 1945, SOE operations in Norway in close collaboration with FO and *Milorg*, reached a scale and intensity that had not been seen over the previous four years. The nature of these operations also changed with a move from *coup de main* attacks against strategic targets to tactical sabotage, and a shift from preparing a guerrilla army in Norway to support an eventual Allied landing, to preparing an indigenous clandestine army that could act as a protective force within the country in the days after the expected German surrender or collapse and the arrival of significant Allied forces from the continent.

The difficult post-war issues that plagued SOE activities in other theatres also did not hamper collaboration in Norway. The constitutional authority of the government-in-exile was recognized both at home and abroad and agreement had been reached with the Home Front as to how the democratic process would be restored in Norway after the liberation. Although conditions within the country, the nature of the occupation, still hampered the efforts of SOE, FO and *Milorg*, cooperation and organization had reached such a level that the major effort to prepare the Home Forces for the liberation was pushed forward with, notwithstanding many local difficulties. Consequently, even though there was never a fully equipped or prepared secret army in Norway, local forces eventually made a valuable contribution to the liberation, although it was not the contribution that had originally been envisaged in the difficult months following the collapse of France in 1940.

CONCLUSION

SOE carried out an assortment of activities in Norway between the summer of 1940 and the liberation in May 1945, ranging from sabotage and subversion to attempts to organize a clandestine guerrilla army. In the case of Norway, the initial proposition was that it was strategic factors, SOE and particularly the country's contribution within the wider strategic context in Europe that remained the fundamental influence behind the evolution of its plans and therefore ultimately operations at a local level. Political issues, represented by the interests of the Norwegian government in exile, and the resistance organizations that emerged in response to Norway's occupation were also important, but although they moulded policy and tempered it in some ways, they did not dictate its essential structure. This was the same for collaborative factors, defined as the relationship between SOE and the other agencies such as the Royal Navy and Royal Air Force and even SIS, all of which took an interest and were active in this theatre.

SOE operations in Norway were, however, ultimately the result of a successful coming together of all these influences. The first and most significant of these was strategic. The combination of short- and long-term aims, which remained at the heart of SOE's plans for Norway from the autumn of 1940, originated within a British strategy that was formulated during the difficult conditions of the summer of 1940. More significantly, however, the military worth of the short- and long-term strands of policy and their interrelationship between 1940 and 1945 was ultimately determined by Norway's peripheral position and subservience to the main thrust of British and later Allied strategy and operations in Europe.

Nevertheless, SOE's plans for Norway could not be divorced from political matters. The crucial point about these influences, however, was that they were on the whole beneficial. This meant that SOE was able to implement its aims in Norway largely on its terms and without the disruption or complication that was often caused by the major political difficulties it experienced when operating within other occupied countries. Through and as a result of its successful collaboration with the Norwegian authorities and ultimately *Milorg*, SOE ensured that its plans for Norway remained predominately intact, under the control of the Allied High Command, and therefore in step with wider strategic requirements.

The benefits of successful collaboration were also not confined to relations with the Norwegian government. A significant proportion of SOE's activity in Norway, such as the series of amphibious raids carried out in association with COHQ or the sea-borne operations that were coordinated under the authority of ACOS, was the result of its ability to successfully work with or alongside the other organizations that also took a military interest in this theatre. Relations at a local operational level in Norway were predominately cordial and often close.

The strategic factors that were pertinent to Norway were all ultimately linked to its marginal position in relation to the rest of Europe. Initially, this meant that SOE's early plans for the country originated within a policy that was not specifically designed for Norwegian conditions and were part of a strategy that meant that clandestine activity, particularly the organization of secret armies, had to be coordinated across the occupied countries. Nonetheless, Norway was from a very early point also considered to be a theatre where sabotage and subversion could be quickly and effectively implemented. It had a long and accessible coastline and produced a number of what were considered important war materials. This seemed to make it ideal for small offensive operations such as amphibious raids or *coup de main* attacks, which required relatively little resource in terms of men and materials.

As a result of the German occupation, which from the beginning had been opposed, it was also believed that there were the seeds of organized resistance that could be cultivated over the longer term into a guerrilla army that would be able to support a possible future landing by regular forces. Moreover, there was a significant body of experience of both applying economic pressure against Germany through Norway and of carrying out clandestine operations within the country, which was brought to SOE by many of the figures that helped to establish its Scandinavian section in the summer of 1940. This gave added impetus to the development and implementation of its policy. Therefore, the various actions carried out by SOE in Norway during 1940 and 1941 were not opportunistic or a case of the organization 'justifying its existence'[1] but were strategic.

Nevertheless, Norway's position in relation to the rest of Europe, both geographically and strategically, soon led to tensions within SOE policy. As the defeat of Germany was never going to be achieved through Norway, the description of the country as a strategic backwater is apt.² It was, however, exactly this that ultimately defined its contribution to the war in Europe. Despite early indications of an interest in a landing in the country, from at least the spring of 1941 there were also signs that Norway's strategic value lay elsewhere. From April, SOE was fully aware that its activities could help to lock-up German divisions in this so-called backwater and thereby make it a constant drain on enemy resources.

This effort would, however, at the same time undermine SOE's own long-term plans for Norway as an increase in the number of German divisions in a country that was ideally suited for defensive operations made an Allied landing extremely implausible, especially during 1941 and 1942 when militarily resources were scarce and there were other priorities, such as the defence of the UK and the protection of Britain's position in North Africa. Consequently, Norway was ultimately seen only as a theatre for possible subsidiary operations, and notwithstanding repeated calls for a Second Front and Churchill's enthusiasm prior to late 1941 the country had been deemed suitable for carrying out just two relatively small combined operations against economic and military targets along the Norwegian seaboard. From this point until May 1945, only minor sea-borne operations, *coup de main* attacks, a limited amount of strategic bombing and local sabotage would be undertaken in the country.

Norway was ideal for the extensive use of small offensive operations against economic and military targets, which it was believed would contribute to the undermining of German fighting strength. Not simply or primarily through disrupting supplies of important war materials, or through provoking a spirit of unease and apprehension among the occupying forces thereby adding to their security commitments, but also by helping to encourage enemy fears of an invasion. All of this helped to mislead Germany as to Allied intentions and led it to make an unnecessarily high military investment in a country that was marginal to the outcome of the war in Europe. In this sense, SOE operations can be seen as a strategic success.

Norway's main strategic value therefore was as part of the process of weakening and undermining the enemy and thereby helping to prepare the ground for the implementation of a final Allied offensive in north-west Europe that would complete Germany's defeat. In that sense, the country was from even as early as 1941 in the shadow of what would eventually be Operation Overlord. Unfortunately, however, its marginal position also ensured that its liberation would have to await the successful completion of the war in Europe.

This is perhaps at odds with the view that Norway's strategic significance was represented by the threat posed by the presence from early 1942 of the bulk of the German surface fleet and a significant number of U-boats in the country, which along with the German air force posed a real threat to the Arctic convoys and a perceived threat to the Atlantic trade routes. This undoubtedly placed an extra burden on the Home Fleet and created a great deal of concern within the Admiralty. The threat to the Arctic convoys was largely confined to the period between the winter and autumn of 1942, after which it began to decline, and ultimately major German warships only sank forty-seven Allied ships – about the same number as were lost to mines during any three-month period. By the end of May 1943, the Battle of the Atlantic had been won, and after the disabling of the *Tirpitz* and the sinking of the *Scharnhorst* at the end of the year, the balance within northern waters had turned clearly in the Allies favour. It is also doubtful, as has been argued, that the Atlantic war was ever 'within Germany's power to win' and that it had any 'appreciable influence on the outcome of the war'.[3] Consequently, the importance placed on the threat posed by the German fleet stationed in Norway, although of significance to the British Admiralty, was short-lived and has probably been overplayed.

Norway's marginal position in relation to the development of Allied strategy and operations in Western Europe had an important impact on SOE operations in two ways. First, it meant that from the end of 1941 and up to the summer of 1944, the immediate objective of attacking war materials in Norway became the priority. The importance of this element of policy reached its peak in 1943, as the pressure grew to intensify the burden on Germany and prepare the way for Overlord the following year. Second, it meant that the preparation of a secret army was not only given a lower priority, but that it was hampered by a lack of resources and had to continue in conditions of uncertainty over when and how the country would be liberated. From the summer of 1944, however, the relationship between these two strands of policy changed. With Allied manpower deployed elsewhere and therefore not immediately available to enforce the liberation, the preparation of a secret army became the priority. Sabotage was considered to be of lesser importance, although it continued in support of and therefore directly linked to operations on the continent.

SOE's plans for Norway were also inevitably somewhat shaped by political considerations. Through successful collaboration, however,

SOE was predominately able to accommodate Norwegian concerns and retain the use of Norwegian expertise and resources, which it was so dependent on, without having to significantly distort its aims. This contradicts previous accounts of the contact between SOE and Norwegian authorities, which argue that it was founded on scepticism and distrust towards Norwegians and built on British terms. And it was only from early 1942, in response to the concerns of the Norwegian government, that relations began to improve.[4]

There were two factors that defined SOE's attitude towards the Norwegian authorities. The first was its complete dependence on recruiting Norwegian volunteers to undertake its activities in this theatre – something that from the beginning it believed should and could only be done through and in association with their political representatives based in London. The Norwegian government in exile was the lawful representative of its nation's interests, something that was quickly recognized in the summer of 1940, and to disregard its authority would have been very risky. Consequently, from early August, SOE made contact with the relevant figures within the government and military authorities in order to allow it to begin the process of recruitment. Scepticism towards Norwegians, as with many other nationalities, was undoubtedly expressed, but pragmatism outweighed this. Contact was not therefore developed just on a dogmatic 'need to know' basis but also on a practical basis – with those individuals who would ensure SOE received the manpower and support it required to become operational in this theatre. Restricting its contacts and the amount of information it passed on about its activities was also not unnatural for a new secret organization and not uniquely applied to the Norwegian government. Moreover, SOE was required through its charter to ensure that clandestine and subversive activities across the whole of Europe were kept in step with strategical requirements, which meant that it had to remain in control. And it was the need to strike a balance between retaining the use of Norwegian volunteers while safeguarding its dominant position that underlay its approach to and association with the government in exile throughout the war. It was not a relationship founded on negative, ethnocentric views. From the beginning, SOE believed it was working closely with the Norwegian authorities, and it is difficult to see what other approach it could have taken during 1940 and 1941other than working through individual contacts. At the time, however, it meant that SOE had a free reign in Norway and its plans for this theatre were not in the beginning reshaped or undermined by Norwegian interests.

It was the fear of losing influence and control, primarily not only over the use and development of *Milorg* but also over Norwegian manpower, that forced SOE to change tack and work with and through their military authorities in London in a more equitable and open way. At the same time, the Norwegian government initiated important reforms to its military command and staff structure in exile. This led in early 1942 to the creation of *Forsvarets Overkommando* (FO), its Defence High Command, which enabled it to work in a far more coordinated and effective way with the British, develop clear policies in the sphere of clandestine operations and ensured that it retrieved some control and influence over the use of its citizens on operations carried out on its soil. There was a clear understanding within FO that SOE was answerable to the COS, that its allies had the leadership of the war and the means to conduct it and therefore its objectives could only be achieved and interests served through cooperation.

From this point until the end of the war, relations with SOE were built on a collaborative basis that ultimately served the purpose of all parties. For SOE, it meant that through NIC (1) it secured the use of a unit of the Royal Norwegian army to carry out special operations in Norway, under the military authority of the Norwegian High Command but ultimately under the strategic direction of the COS. Collaboration, however, also meant that plans for this theatre had to be developed and implemented on a joint basis. Consequently, SOE had to accept that to cement its relationship with the Norwegian authorities and to guarantee its control over special operations in Norway, it had to adapt aspects of its policy to meet Norwegian concerns. This led to the abandonment or scaling back of some of SOE's *coup de main* operations and the original aim of developing a sabotage organization within Norway was reluctantly sidelined. The longer-term aim of creating a clandestine army was, however, strengthened by collaboration as both parties shared the view that the resistance in Norway would ultimately play a significant role in the reoccupation of the country.

The other factor that had a significant impact on the evolution of SOE's plans for this theatre was the response within Norway to the nature and form of its occupation. From the summer of 1940, this gradually resulted in organized and coordinated resistance to the German authorities and NS, which crystallized around two movements, *Sivorg* and *Milorg*. Both had a strong and influential central leadership based in Oslo that eventually worked closely with the government in London, with each other and with the Norwegian people. *Milorg*, which became a section of the Norwegian armed services, quickly developed its own stance, based on local conditions and past experience, on what its military contribution should be both prior to and at the liberation. The resistance in occupied Norway therefore had an authority both at home and in London that SOE was eventually forced to recognize and accept, although it took some time.

From the autumn of 1940, the relationship between SOE and *Milorg* was shaped by Britain's determination to make sure that an underground army in Norway conformed to British views over its structure and its role, prior to and during the country's liberation. There was never an intention to avoid or ignore *Milorg*; the objective was to incorporate it and make use of the potential manpower resources that it could call on. It was, however, this effort by SOE to take on the ownership of all armed resistance in Norway that was at the heart of the difficulties between the two organizations. As *Milorg*'s early leadership was a product of local circumstances and recent experience, its vision of a clandestine army did not readily conform to British ideas. This led to ongoing difficulties and distrust. Within this context, SOE's attempts to impose itself on *Milorg* and then to work around its leadership both failed. It was only after events within Norway led to changes in the resistance leadership, structure and ultimately its policy, combined with a realization that Norwegian conditions would not allow two clandestine organizations to operate alongside each other, that SOE accepted that it would have to collaborate fully with the military resistance.

The issues surrounding sabotage and assassination perhaps best exemplify how crucial local factors were in shaping attitudes within *Milorg* and ultimately its relationship with SOE. Both are violent acts that when carried out risked major reprisals from the occupying authorities against the local population and resistance groups. Prior to 1944, however, after which local circumstances made it both necessary and acceptable, *Milorg* refused to support the use of indigenous groups or civilians to undertake sabotage. The risk of carrying out such acts in the view of its leadership far outweighed the potential benefits. The destruction of an important industrial site might have a strategic or military value but did nothing within the setting of occupied Norway to help in the development of a clandestine army, which was *Milorg*'s single objective. Paradoxically, however, it was fully prepared to collaborate in carrying out assassinations, which were also extremely hazardous and violent acts, and from the beginning of 1943 it was working closely with SOE in training execution teams. In this case, local factors, specifically the actions of informers and the Nazi police organizations, were a direct and serious threat to its objective of organizing an underground army, and therefore something had to be done, whatever the danger.

It was during 1943, as communication and contact improved and after *Milorg* had fully accepted its subservience to FO and that decisions over its deployment would be made in London not Oslo, that relations with SOE improved. By the summer of 1944, these three parties had formed a close partnership under the authority of the Allied High Command. It once more came back to the country's position on the periphery of Europe, which meant that relations with *Milorg* only became particularly significant during the final months of the occupation, when the preparation of clandestine forces in this theatre became a priority. It had, however, been left too late, and at the time of the German capitulation, despite a huge last-minute effort, there was still not a fully armed or trained secret army in Norway.

The importance of successful collaboration on SOE operations in Norway was also reflected in its readiness to work with the other British and American military organizations that took an interest in this theatre. From the autumn of 1940, SOE recognized that it would be required to assist with operations such as raids and air attacks, and that through working with COHQ or the Air Ministry it would be part of a wider strategic effort. It was, however, not only SOE that was aware of the potential benefits of cooperation. Even the 'professional military' had an appreciation of the value of SOE's more unconventional methods. The RN was fully prepared to make use of the organization's skills in order to develop and employ various submersible vessels in its attempt to sink the *Tirpitz*. Bomber Command was also prepared, when resources allowed, to attack targets that SOE had flagged up as unsuitable for sabotage. There was an understanding within the regular services that this country, its terrain, long coastline and the location of many of its important targets often made it particularly suited for more unorthodox methods. Ultimately, SOE's success in working with and alongside the regular armed services and other new military organizations was again advantageous to its plans for this theatre. It enabled it to extend and intensify its activities, especially at times when it neither had the resources nor the ability to undertake such actions alone.

The culmination of SOE's policy was its operations, and it is these that exemplify how the strategic and collaborative factors eventually came together and affected its actions at a local level. It is important to reach a conclusion as to whether or not its actions had any militarily value or significance, especially as this is an issue that has so preoccupied previous historians.[5]

From the spring of 1942, NIC (1) teams, made up of Norwegian volunteers often transported in Norwegian fishing boats, carried out attacks instigated by SOE but planned and prepared in cooperation with the Norwegian authorities. Therefore, even though *Milorg* had no involvement in these operations, there was a direct and crucial Norwegian contribution. Many attacks were also undertaken in cooperation with or had an important input from the armed services or other military organizations such as COHQ. All SOE operations against economic and military targets in Norway were therefore joint operations, and the participation of other agencies was crucial to both their implementation and eventual shape. The attacks against the production of heavy water in Norway, operations 'Freshman' and 'Gunnerside', exemplify this.

'Freshman', in the autumn of 1942, was a collaborative project that involved SOE, COHQ, the RAF, the 1st Airborne Division and the Norwegian authorities, and which following SOE's recommendation targeted the hydroelectric plant at Vemork. As an air attack had initially been ruled out, owing to Norwegian concerns, it was believed that an operation to disable such a large site required a team of at least thirty, and therefore it was placed under the remit of COHQ. 'Gunnerside', the follow-up attack in February 1943, was predominately Norwegian. It was a Norwegian idea that was actively promoted because it was a precision operation that would avoid widespread damage to the Norsk Hydro plant and power station and reduce the possibility of reprisals against the local population. It was based on Norwegian intelligence and used NIC (1) teams, many of whom were locals. SOE instigated and authorized the operation, provided training and arranged transportation to the target. It was brilliantly executed, although it did not achieve its objective of a lengthy interruption in production of heavy water.

Ultimately, *coup de main* operations and raids against strategic targets in Norway had a limited impact. Delays and disruption were often caused, but unless a target was regularly revisited, such as the Orkla pyrite mines, the influence was temporary and overall production levels were not always seriously diminished. Everything was, however, done to make these operations appear British and on the whole, unless leading to German fatalities, they did not result in widespread reprisals against the local population. They were also significant in other ways. They required little resource: just small teams of Norwegian volunteers, with a relatively small amount of equipment, and for the most part using only a handful of fishing vessels. Notwithstanding this, they often created security scares out of all proportion to their size.

From the summer of 1944, the nature of sabotage in Norway not only changed but with the support of *Milorg* and the Norwegian authorities it also intensified and became widespread across the south of the country. This intensification did not mean, however, that all objectives were achieved. While a considerable amount of material that was directly and immediately important to the German war effort was destroyed, as with oil and petrol, the effort to stem the flow of German divisions out of Norway through railway sabotage had little impact. The results were therefore patchy. Nevertheless, the involvement of *Milorg* was symbolically important, as this was its first direct and major contribution to the Allied war effort and a reflection of the growing confidence and maturity of the resistance movements in Norway. It also illustrates how far *Milorg*'s policy on the use of clandestine forces in Norway had moved from the original aim that it should never be more than a mobilization force employed and armed only after the arrival of Allied forces in the country. It was an evolution that continued even after the war when plans were put together by the Norwegian authorities to organize 'stay-behind' units that would mobilize and go into action in the event of a Soviet occupation.[6]

The other category of SOE activity consisted of operations that set out to organize and prepare a secret guerrilla army. Although these also had strategic origins, they were particularly affected by Norway's position as a strategic backwater. With little prospect of a landing in the country, the training and equipping of clandestine forces was until the autumn of 1944, plagued by a lack of resources. The lower priority accorded to these operations and the uncertainty surrounding the future role of a clandestine army also complicated matters. Teams sent into Norway eventually had to prepare local groups for a series of possible scenarios, not just an Allied landing. The failure to work with *Milorg* in the early years also slowed the whole process and made it more problematic. And the attempts to keep resistance groups *in situ* over a long time period also proved extremely difficult in the face of the efforts of Norwegian informers and the German security police, who caused considerable harm to not only SOE but also *Milorg* and the local population. All this meant that prior to 1944, SOE was largely on the defensive and made only sporadic and limited progress towards organizing an armed and prepared clandestine army.

The outcome of SOE activities was also governed by another set of factors. They were all beset by the many local difficulties of working in occupied Norway. These included the extremes of climate, topography, hours of daylight and surviving in an occupied country with small isolated communities. The decision and determination to carry out an operation was therefore alone no guarantee of success. Nevertheless, SOE in cooperation with its partners carried out a range of operations that, for example, meant that at the end of the war there was an underground army in place that, although certainly not fully prepared or equipped, was able to make a significant contribution in ensuring that the liberation of Norway and the transition from occupation to lawful government ran particularly smoothly. In many ways, Norway was an ideal country where irregular and clandestine methods of warfare could make a very small but cost-effective strategic contribution to the Allied victory in Europe.

Appendix A

SOE *COUP DE MAIN* OPERATIONS IN NORWAY, 1940-4
(Planned, attempted and completed)[1]

Date	Operation	Objectives	Details
March 1941	Arctic	The resurrection of an old MI (R) plan to sink a vessel alongside the quay at Narvik.	In December 1941, Churchill once again turned his attention to the export of Swedish iron ore through Narvik. Consequently, Operation Arctic was reconsidered although ultimately never undertaken.
March 1941	Gertrude	A proposal to interdict the supply of sulphur from Norway to Germany.	During spring 1941, both this and 'Landlubber' led to Operation Maundy, the plan to use fishing vessels to lay mines in the Norwegian leads (see Appendix B), and Operation Clairvoyant (see below).
March 1941	Landlubber	A proposal to interdict the supply of ferrochrome from Norway to Germany.	
March 1941	Barbara	A plan to use a team recruited in Sweden by Malcolm Munthe to sabotage the railways around Trondheim.	A team of eight men was recruited in Sweden and in early March 1941 picked up from the Norwegian coast by fishing vessel. They were trained in the UK and returned to Norway. Two groups of three eventually remained in Norway to carry out the sabotage; the other two men returned to the UK. On the night of 17/18 April, one group managed to attack the Trondheim-Storlien railway line and the carriage of one train was damaged as it went through a tunnel. All six men fled to Sweden where eventually they were arrested.

Date	Operation	Objectives	Details
Preparations commenced in April 1941. Last reference in the ANCC minutes at end of 1942	Clairvoyant	Initially: Tyssedal, Vemork (including nitrate factories), Bjølvefoss, Høyanger, Saude and Stangfjord hydroelectric power stations and the Tinnsjø ferries.	An ambitious plan to attack the major hydroelectric sites and ferries in southern Norway in order to disrupt the manufacture of specialist metals, predominately aluminium. Also included a plan to bomb Vemork to stop the production of heavy water. After it failed to obtain the required aircraft and because of objections from the Norwegian authorities, the plan was scaled down to a projected attack against Høyanger. One sortie was made but failed due to bad weather, and then members of the party were badly injured in a car crash. Nevertheless, it continued to be resurrected at least until the end of 1942.
June 1941	Burnous	The first of many plans to attack the Orkla pyrite mines at Løkken near Trondheim.	Stores and personnel were available in the area and intelligence collected but at the end of August 1941, the MEW told SOE that the plant needed to be put out of action for several months if an attack was to be worthwhile. This led SOE to concentrate on disrupting the transportation of pyrites from the mine to Germany.

Date	Operation	Objectives	Details
By Autumn 1941, SOE had already begun to consider an operation against this site	**Alfriston**	Knaben molybdenum mines near Fjotland, approximately sixty miles inland from the southern tip of Norway.	Molybdenum was considered to be the most important war material that Germany obtained from Norway and therefore SOE, COHQ and RAF all showed interest in this site. It was eventually left to the RAF and USAAF, who launched attacks against the target in March, November, and December 1943, and again in 1944.
January 1941 (Air)	**Woodcock**	Proposed attack against Sola Airfield outside Stavanger.	The Air Ministry requested SOE to consider an attack against the Focke Wolfe aircraft and other heavy bombers. One unsuccessful sortie was made on the night of 3–4 May after which the operation was postponed and it does not appear to have ever been resurrected.
17 April 1942 (Sea)	**Redshank** (P. Deinboll, P. Getz, T. Grong)	The Baardshaug converter and transformer station which controlled power to the railway between the Orkla pyrite mine and the port of Thamshavn.	Successfully attacked on 4 May 1942. The transformer station was totally destroyed, which reduced the transport capacity of the line by 50 per cent for six months. Nevertheless, production at the mine was still 468,640 tons in 1942, only slightly down on the previous year. All escaped to Sweden.

Date	Operation	Objectives	Details
June 1942	**Seagull I** (Lt. Eskeland. 2.Lt. Skog, Sgt. Blindheim, J. Baalsrud, Sgt. Hanssen)	The disruption of supplies of blister copper, pyrites and zinc concentrate produced at the Sulitjelma mines in northern Norway through attacking Fagerli power station.	The original outline project was submitted for approval on 28 June. Postponed in October 1942 after Operation Musketoon led to an increase in security in the area and at the Sulitjelma plant.
September 1942	**Kestrel** (Lt. P. Getz, Sgt. T. Grong, Cpl. L. Bronn)	Fosdalen iron ore mines in north Trøndelag.	This plant had received machinery from Germany and 'full support for an increased rate of production'. It was successfully attacked on 5 October and production was reduced by 25 per cent for two months. The party escaped to Sweden.
November 1942	**Marshfield** (Lt. F. Normann, Sgt. K. Hennum)	Rodsand iron ore mines north of Åndalsnes.	First attempted in October. Eventually sailed on 8 November but the team disappeared after landing on the Møre coastline on 10 November 1942.
February 1943	**Seagull II** (Lt. P. Getz, Lt. T. Skog, Sgt. H. Hanssen, Sgt. T. Grong, Pte. S. Granlund, Gnr. E. Eriksen)	Sulitjelma mines.	Resurrected in December 1942. Party of six departed in the submarine *Uredd* on 5 February 1943 from Lunna Voe. The party never reached Norway. After the war it was discovered that the vessel had sailed into a German minefield close to Bodø.

Date	Operation	Objectives	Details
December 1943	**Granard** (Lt. P. Deinboll, 2.Lt. Bjørn Pedersen, O. Sættem)	Attack and destroy the loading tower, and sink a laden pyrites cargo vessel at the outer end of Thamshavn pier in order to dislocate the transport of sulphur pyrites from the Orkla mines.	Party sailed on 6 February 1942 and landed on the Norwegian coast two days later. It was several weeks before a German vessel of sufficient size came alongside the pier. On 26 February, limpet mines were placed on the S. S. *Nordfart*. Two holes were blown in the ship, which was then run aground. It only took a few months, however, before the ship was again in service, and therefore the operation had little long-term impact.
February 1943	**Gunnerside** (J. Rønneberg, K. Haukelid, K. Idland, F. Kayser, H. Storhaug, B. Strømsheim)	The storage and production plant for heavy water at Vemork so that present stocks and fluids in the course of production would be destroyed.	A first attempt to drop the team was made on 23 January, but it was the night of 16–17 February before it successfully landed in Norway. On 23 February, it joined up with the 'Swallow' group. The attack was carried out on the night of 27–28 February. The high-concentration cells and 500 kilograms of heavy water were destroyed. New high-concentration equipment was, however, brought from the Norsk Hydro sites at Notodden

Date	Operation	Objectives	Details
			and Såheim and 100 kilograms of heavy water brought back from Germany. Consequently, production recommenced only a few weeks later. Five of the party crossed to Sweden, while Haukelid remained in Norway.
February 1943	**Midhurst**	Proposed attack against the *frostfilet* factories in Hammerfest and Melbø.	The operation was abandoned in March 1943 owing to a number of local operational difficulties. Part of the operation was at one stage offered to OSS.
January 1943 (Air)	**Chaffinch** (T. Stenersen, O. Sandersen, M. Olsen)	One of the tasks of this three man party was to investigate the possibility of destroying enemy shipping in the Oslo and Drammen area.	The party took limpet mines with them to Norway and initially considered attacking shipping in Horten. On 19 May, however, the group attached a limpet mine to the *Sanev* while in dock at Moss. The boat sank the same day. A later attempt to attack shipping in Oslo harbour was abandoned. The party left Norway at the end of May.

Date	Operation	Objectives	Details
March 1943 (Air)	**Mardonius** (Max Manus, Gregers Gram)	To attack merchant shipping in Oslo fjord by means of limpet mines placed by single operators working from canoes. Local volunteers were to be trained.	The party made a number of contacts, including Sigurd Jacobsen from *Milorg*, who on 27–28 April helped them place limpets on several ships. The *Ortelsburg* was sunk, the *Tugela* and an Oil Lighter badly damaged and a harbour beacon destroyed. The team withdrew to Sweden on 4 May.
October 1943 (Air)	**Bundle** (M. Manus, G. Gram, E. Juden, C. Viborg)	To sink enemy shipping in Oslo Harbour and North Oslo fjord, with particular reference to enemy troop ships.	*Milorg*'s leadership was eventually made aware of this operation and agreed to arrange a supply of shipping intelligence. In early January, Manus arrived in Stockholm to try and get authority to develop and use 'baby' torpedoes, but without success. In February 1944, 'Bundle' sank a German patrol vessel, but from this point on the team took on the additional responsibility of propaganda under the title 'Derby'. Manus and Gram also began to work with the other NIC (1) teams in the Oslo area and became part of the 'Oslo Detachment' under Sønsteby. Ship sabotage was not, however, abandoned and in June 1944

Date	Operation	Objectives	Details
			six limpet mines were placed on the *Monte Rosa* but failed to cause major damage. In August, a German destroyer was attacked using a home-made torpedo and in January 1945 limpet mines were placed on the *Donau* and *Rolandsech*, damaging both.
October 1943 (Air)	**Feather I** (P. Deinboll, O. Nilssen, A. Wisløff, L. Bronn, T. Bjørnaas, P. Skjærpe, A. Hægstad)	To stop production at the Orkla pyrite mines by destroying the lift machinery in the lift shaft. If this proved to be too difficult, they should attack the railway between Orkanger and Thamshavn.	On 30 October a coordinated attack was carried out against the locomotives at Løkken, Thamshavn and Orkanger, which transported the materials from the mine to the point of shipment on the coast. Five locomotives were destroyed or put out of action. A further attack was carried out on 17 November and a rail car blown up. One of the team was killed, one captured, while the remaining men eventually escaped to Sweden.
November 1943 (Air)	**Goldfinch** (T. Stenersen, J. Allan, M. Olsen, O. Sandersen)	This was a continuation of the 'Chaffinch' operation and one of its tasks was to attack shipping on the west side of Oslo fjord.	Two operations were planned. In February 1944, the 'Goldfinch' team waited at Skien in readiness to attack the ship that was to transport the residues of heavy water from Vemork to Germany. It was never required. The second attack was to be against the *M/S Lappland* in Drammen at the beginning of May, but the ship sailed before the team was ready.

Date	Operation	Objectives	Details
November 1943 (Air)	**Company** (E. Tallaksen, B. Rasmussen, A. Trønnes)	To destroy the transformers at Arendal Smelteverk at Eydehavn near Arendal in southern Norway, which produced 4,000 tons of ferro-silicon yearly, all of which went to Germany.	The plant was attacked on 21 November and production was stopped for six months costing the Germans 2,500 tons of ferro-silicon.
April 1944	**'Swallow' and *Milorg*: the train ferry 'Hydro'**	A plan approved in February 1944 to stop the transportation of the remaining heavy water from Vemork to Germany by sinking the ferry carrying it across Lake Tinnsjø.	On the night of 19 February, an explosive charge was placed on the ferry 'Hydro' by Knut Haukelid, Knut Lier-Hansen from *Milorg* and Rolf Sørlie from B-org. The charge, 19 pounds of plastic explosive, went off the following morning as the ferry was crossing the lake, resulting in the loss of 500 kilos of 100 per cent heavy water and 14 Norwegian civilians. Four drums did, however, survive, and this along with a small amount of heavy water from Såheim, was shipped to Germany during the spring.
April 1944 (Stockholm)	**Feather II** (A. Hægstad, T. Bjørnaas, A. Wisløff)	To destroy the remaining electric locomotive on the Thamshavn railway.	The team of three entered from Sweden on 21 April. On 9 May, they blew up the locomotive and on 1 June the railway's last railcar was also destroyed. One of the locomotives had been sent to Oslo for repairs, but on 13 September this was attacked and damaged by the 'Oslo Detachment' under Gunnar Sønsteby.

Date	Operation	Objectives	Details
April 1944 (Sea)	**Albatross** (L. Skjold, P. Wegeland)	The aluminium plant at Saudasjøen was to be reconnoitred with a view to a possible future attack.	When production stopped at the plant due to lack of raw material, the plan was abandoned.
August 1944	**Docklow** (A. Hægstad, T. Bjørnaas, A. Wisløff)	To stop the export of pyrites and ores from the Sulitjelma mines by attacking the locomotives servicing the Sandnes to Skjønslua railway or by attacking the tug boats moving between Skjønslua and Finneid.	The 'Feather II' team left Stockholm for the field on 15 August but was quickly arrested by the Swedish authorities. On 3 September they made a second attempt, but on 11 September they were recalled after it became known that the transport of materials had ceased.
August/September 1944 (Stockholm – Air)	**Dodworth** (E. Sundseth)	Another attack on the Orkla pyrite mines.	On August 21, Sundseth was sent from Sweden to reconnoitre the area in readiness to receive a party that would be sent in from the UK. He returned on 6 September. On September 26, the Orkla attack was cancelled owing to the strong defences and a change in the general situation.

Appendix B

SEA-BORNE OPERATIONS INSTIGATED BY OR INVOLVING SOE ALONG THE NORWEGIAN SEABOARD, 1940-5[1]

Date	Operation	Objectives	Details
Autumn 1940	**Mandible** (formerly 'Castle')	To interrupt the supply of ilmenite from the A/S Titania mine at Sokndal by destroying the hydroelectric power station and loading appliances at the head of Jøssingfjord.	SOE had shown interest in this site as early as August 1940. From October, COHQ began to plan a raid against the target using a force that included three destroyers, 150 Special Service troops and Norwegian interpreters supplied by SOE. Ilmenite was considered to be a product of some importance, although it was pointed out that there were eleven months stocks in Germany. The raid would also provide practical experience, annoy the Germans and encourage Norwegians. The operation was eventually cancelled on the instructions of Churchill.
March 1941	**Almoner**	The Norwegian herring fleet in the North Sea.	This was a plan to attack the Norwegian herring fleet working between Haugesund and Egersund. SOE would provide Norwegian seamen who would operate as armed guards. The COS approved it in principle, but by mid-March it had been cancelled at the request of the Norwegian government.
4 March 1941	**Claymore**	The destruction of herring and cod oil plants on the Lofoten Islands, the arrest of local Quislings and enemy personnel and the securing of volunteers for the Norwegian navy.	Planned, organized and executed under the direction of COHQ in consultation with SOE. The operation included five destroyers, 500 commandoes from the Special Service Brigade and through SOE, 52 Norwegian men and officers were supplied along with guides and naval pilots. Altogether, eleven ships were sunk, factories and 800,000 gallons of oil destroyed, 213 enemy personnel captured and 314 Norwegian volunteers brought back to UK. Important Enigma equipment was also captured.
April 1941	**Maundy I**	Enemy shipping in the Norwegian leads.	By early March 1940, SOE had a mining squad in training and on 29 April 1940, the first Norwegian fishing boat left the Shetlands to lay mines in the inner leads. Eventually eleven out of eighteen 'R-Type' mines provided by the Royal Navy were laid in Norwegian coastal waters.

Date	Operation	Objectives	Details
April 1941	Hemisphere	Attack against a herring oil plant at Øksfjord in northern Norway.	The operation, conceived by Commander Frank Stagg of SOE, and consisting of ten Norwegian marines and one SOE agent, sailed on 8 April 1941. The plant was completely destroyed and the expedition returned to the UK on 15 April.
Spring 1941	Wallah	To establish a base in northern Norway from where operations could be launched with the aim of paralyzing German sea-borne traffic along the Norwegian coast.	By the end of July 1941, the Admiralty had approved 'Wallah'. The Norwegian naval staff and *Nortraship*, which provided a ship the SS-*Anderson* as a base for the operation, were both involved. The Admiralty also provided two 'Q' ships, heavily armed merchant vessels, which would be used to intercept German shipping. Local fishing boats would also be purchased and used to sail into harbours where explosives would be attached to enemy vessels. The possibility of using ski-troops to attack targets inland was also considered. In October 1940, the operation was placed under ACOS and in November under the C-in-C Home Fleet before it was eventually merged into 'Anklet'.
October 1941	Maundy II	To drop 'R-mines' in coastal waters north of Kristiansund.	The fishing boat M/V *Nordsjøen* left the Shetlands on 19 October with seven men and forty-two 'R-mines' on board. The mines were laid on 21 October but the boat encountered a major storm and had to be abandoned. All the men eventually got back to Britain, including a group of five led by Leif Larsen in the fishing boat 'Arthur'.
December 1941	Kitbag I	German-controlled shipping, cold storage plants, fish canning factories, herring oil factory, oil tanks, the capture of Quislings and the recruiting of Norwegian volunteers at Florø.	The force included approximately 250 men and officers from 6th Commando and thirty Norwegian men and officers provided by SOE under the leadership of Martin Linge. It eventually got underway on 11 December but was abandoned after reaching the Norwegian coast.

Date	Operation	Objectives	Details
December 1941	**Archery**	A raid on military and economic targets in the vicinity of Vågsøy with the objective of harassing the coastal defences of SW Norway and diverting enemy attention away from Operation Anklet.	Included almost 600 men and officers from No 3 and No 2 Commando plus six naval pilots and thirty-three Norwegian men and officers, including guides, provided by SOE and under the command of Martin Linge. The force sailed on 26 December and arrived off the Norwegian coast the following day. The RAF supported the British naval forces and a number of economic targets were destroyed.
December 1941	**Anklet**	The object was to cut enemy communications with the north of Norway. This evolved into an operation whereby a temporary defensive base would be established on the Lofoten Islands from where light naval forces could operate against German sea communications. The Norwegian fish industry was also a target.	Under the command of the commander-in-chief Home Fleet, a large naval and military force, including 300 men from No. 12 Commando, sailed on 22 December and arrived in the area on 26 December. The Norwegian navy provided two corvettes and over sixty naval ratings. An SOE contingent of seventy-seven men and officers also sailed with the main force. They were instructed to seize five local fishing boats and attack navigation lights along the Norwegian coast, while W/T operators aided communication and supplied intelligence. Seven fishing boats also sailed from the Shetlands to attack navigation lights in the area, although only three arrived in the Lofotens. The expedition withdrew on 28 December. Some local targets were destroyed and 266 Norwegians brought back, but little else was achieved.
January 1942	**Kitbag II**	To attack targets around Florø.	The naval force, which sailed in early January, included five Norwegian naval pilots supplied through SOE. A cargo ship and two trawlers were attacked before the force withdrew.

Date	Operation	Objectives	Details
January/February 1942	Q-Ships Operation	The Q-ships intended for Operation Wallah were taken over by C-in-C Home fleet to be used against enemy shipping.	The operation sailed from the Shetlands on 29 January but returned to Scapa Flow on 5 February after being spotted by enemy aircraft. SOE supplied intelligence, one officer, eight army and naval ranks, arms and explosives.
February 1942	Lark (Maundy) (O. K. Sættem, A. Christiansen)	To lay mines in the inner leads around Trondheim.	The plan was to send 'R-mines' with the Lark team to Norway and use rowing boats to lay the mines. It was never carried out.
October 1942	Title (L. Larsen, P. Bjornøy, R. Strand, J. Kalve)	This was a joint FOS/SOE operation. The plan was that a fishing boat would tow two submersible 'Chariots' and carry six Naval personnel into Trondheimfjord, where the attack against the Tirpitz would be launched.	The fishing boat 'Arthur' sailed on 26 October and arrived off the Norwegian coast on 29 October. The following day, in heavy seas, the two 'Chariots' were lost. The fishing boat was scuttled and the crew and naval personnel attempted to escape to Sweden. All except one, the seaman Bob Evans who was executed in January 1943, got back safely.
January 1943	Carhampton	The objective was to board and capture a convoy of merchant ships off the southern coastline of Norway and bring them back to the UK. The party was made up of forty-one men, including thirty from NIC (1) and ten from the RNN.	Attempts to sail were made in November but abandoned due to bad weather. The operation was then delayed until Operation Cabaret had been completed. It eventually left on 1 January 1943 in the Norwegian whale-catcher, the 'Bodø', which hit a mine on the way back and sank with the loss of thirty-three lives. Two attempts to capture ships were made in January but both failed and the party was forced to flee to the mountains. It was then decided that the group would assist Operation Yorker, a COHQ attack against the titanium mines in

Date	Operation	Objectives	Details
September 1943	**Vestige 1** (Harald Svindseth, Ragnar Ulstein, Nils Fjeld)	The objective of the 'Vestige' operations was to attack enemy shipping along the coast between Bergen and Ålesund.	Sogndal, but this was cancelled due to bad weather. Consequently, the party had to make their own way back. Sixteen captured the coastal steamer, 'Tromøysund', which was sunk in the North Sea, nineteen escaped to the UK in a fishing boat, two fled to Sweden, while four men remained in the country.
September 1943	**Vestige II** (L. Olsen, I Næss)	Kayaks would be used to get close to the vessel and limpet mines then attached to the ship's hull.	Landed on 3 September by MTB and on the night of 23 September attacked the *Hermut* in Gulenfjord, north of Bergen. The ship was grounded. The party was picked up by MTB on 17 November.
September 1943	**Vestige III** (S. Synnes, H. Hoel)	The aim was to attack shipping in Askvoll harbour.	Also landed on 3 September by MTB. Attempted an attack in Askvoll harbour but hampered by adverse weather. They moved to Ålesund and made contact with the 'Antrum' operation. Picked up on 17 November by subchaser as part of an SIS operation.
September 1943			Also landed by MTB on 3 September and on 6 October attacked the *Jantje Fritzen* in Ålesund using six limpets. The ship was, however, kept afloat and towed to Bergen for repairs. Picked up along with 'Vestige II'.
October 1943	**Chariot operation** (Karl Vilnes)	The object of the 'Barbara' operations was to sink enemy shipping in Norwegian coastal waters using 'Welmans', the one-man submersible craft.	An observer, Vilnes, was landed on Atløy, north of Bergen, to report the movements of shipping in Askvoll harbour to a nearby MTB that was carrying 'Chariots'. Owing to the absence of shipping nothing happened.

Date	Operation	Objectives	Details
November 1943	**Barbara I** (Lt. C. Johnsen, Lt. B. Pedersen. Lt. B. Marris RNVR, Lt. J. Holmes, RN)	The aim was to attack the anchorage at Askvoll.	On 20 November four 'Welmans' and two British and two Norwegian officers were transported to the west coast with the intention of sinking shipping or the floating dock in Bergen harbour. The 'Welmans' penetrated the inner harbour but the lead vessel was discovered and 2nd Lieutenant Pedersen captured. The other officers escaped after sinking their vessels and were eventually picked up on 5 February 1944.
December 1943	**Barbara II** The remaining Norwegians trained for Welman operations were 2./Lt. R. Larsen, Sgt. Ø. Hansen, Cpl. N. Olsen, Sgt. F. Kayser, Sgt. J. Akslen	The aim was to attack shipping in Gulenfjord.	A SOE observer was landed on the island of Atløy, and a second attempt was made to land another two observers further south. At the end of January 1944, however, after the operation had failed to get underway, both sets of observers were picked up and the operation abandoned.
February 1944	**Barbara III (Trace)** (Harald Svindseth, Ragnar Ulstein)	The overall aim was to attack shipping in Syvdefjord.	An advanced party, 'Trace', was landed on 6 February 1944 and began sending messages by W/T. The 'Welman' party sailed on 13 February but was forced back by bad weather. The operation was eventually abandoned, although the 'Trace' party continued to send messages until it was picked up on 16 March by subchaser.
February/March 1944	**Barbara IV**	To attack shipping around Egersund using limpet mines.	The initial objective was to supply intelligence using the 'Antrum Green' station in Ålesund, but the operation never took place.

Date	Operation	Objectives	Details
March 1944	**Vestige IV** (K. Idsand, A. Åkre, K. Endresen)	To attack shipping at Malm in North-Trøndelag.	The party initially failed to carry out any attacks, although later attempts were made against U-boats but with no success and a small vessel was sunk in Flekkefjord harbour. The party, however, remained in the field for the rest of the war. In early 1945, it was issued with new operation instructions and carried out acts of sabotage against German military camps in the area.
March 1944	**Vestige XII** (A. Torkildsen, A. Gade-Torp, F. Brandt)	To attack shipping loading pyrites at Sagvåg on the island of Stord.	On 16 March, a subchaser landed the party equipped with folding boats rather than kayaks. Conditions were so difficult that the party were eventually forced to flee to Sweden without carrying out any attacks.
March 1944	**Vestige V** (K. Vilnes, P. Ørstenvik)	To attack shipping in Frederickstad and other Østfold (eastern Norway) ports.	A subchaser dropped the party on 31 March 1944. Several attempts were made to attack shipping but weather difficulties again proved insurmountable and a subchaser recovered the party on 9 May. There were plans to revive 'Vestige V' in August 1944 but due to objections from SIS these were abandoned.
March 1944	**Vestige XIV** (R. Larsen, Ø. Hansen, B. Petersen)	An operation to attack shipping in Søderfjord.	The party was dropped by air on 31 March with folding boats and diving suits. On the way to carrying out an attack, the party was surprised and after an exchange of shots fled to Sweden. Although the party returned to the field at a later stage, no attacks were undertaken.

Date	Operation	Objectives	Details
April 1944	**Vestige VIII** (H. Hoel, I. Næss)	The party was instructed to lay mines north of Florø. Alternative targets were limpet attacks on shipping in Gulenfjord, the introduction of explosive charges into cases of salt herrings or sabotage of the automatic navigation lights in the fjord.	A subchaser landed the party at Skorpen on 12 April, but it failed to carry out any attacks due to the weather and short nights and was picked up on 1 May.
April 1944	**Maundy III/Dundee**	To introduce a party of four men to attack shipping in the Nordgulen and Florø area using the 'Sleeping Beauty'.	Despite four attempts, the first one on 16 April, bad weather and poor conditions meant that the operation never took place.
September 1944	**Salamander I** (R. Ulstein) (The 'Salamander' operations would use the 'Sleeping Beauty' – motorized submersible canoe)	To attack depot ships, U-boats and other vessels around Måløy using limpet mines.	SIS objected to the operation because it believed it threatened its 'Roska' station near Florø.
September 1944	**Salamander II** (F. Kayser, S. Synnes, A, Trønnes, K. Karlsen)	Target U-boat depot ships, U-boats and other shipping in Søvdefjord using limpet mines.	Landed by subchaser on 9 September but returned on 18 September with no success.

Date	Operation	Objectives	Details
September 1944	**Salamander III**	Target U-boat depot ships and U-boats at Hatvik using limpet mines.	SIS objected to the operation because of its station 'Frey' based at Guskøy south of Ålesund.
September 1944	**Salamander IV**	To attack workshop ships for U-boats, U-boats and other shipping at Vingvågen near Trondheim.	SIS objected to this operation because of its 'Reva' station near Bergen, but it was eventually cancelled because SOE agent in the area reported that the U-boat depot ship and U-boats were no longer at Hatvik.
September 1944	**Salamander V** (T. Lien, A. Fløisand, L. Olsen, I. Tønseth)	A plan to intercept a prison ship and release the thirty members of the resistance that were onboard. They were from the Narvik area and were being transferred via Trondheim to a concentration camp.	Left by fishing boat with two 'Sleeping Beauties' on 13 September. Returned on 30 September with no success.
Autumn 1944	**Cutlass** (H. Ryen, Cpl. Ratvik, seaman Ingebritsen)		Four MTBs would intercept the ship south of Rørvik. SOE agents would also go on board at Sandnesjøen to assist or to force the ship to sail for the UK if this failed. The operation was never carried out.

Appendix C

SOE LONG-TERM AND MISCELLANEOUS OPERATIONS IN NORWAY, 1940-5[1]

Date	Operation	Objectives	Details
November 1940 (sea)	**Unnamed** (M. Rasmussen, K. A. Lindberg, F. Pedersen Kviljo)	Contact resistance groups in Bergen and establish a W/T link with southern Norway.	The Abwehr had infiltrated the crew of the fishing boat *Urd 2* and all three SOE men were arrested after their arrival in Norway. They were executed on 11 August 1941.
January 1941 (submarine)	**Cheese I** (O. Starheim)	Contact resistance groups in southern Norway, collect intelligence, reconnoitre sabotage targets.	Starheim made contact with local groups and through Lt. Pål Frisvold, the central leadership of *Milorg*. He also sent back a significant volume of intelligence, before returning to Britain in July 1941.
September 1941 (sea)	**Letterbox** (K. J. Aarsaether, A. Wisløff)	To arrange weapons dumps, contact local resistance groups and commence instruction in the mountains near Ålesund. Wisløff would try and get work at Trondheim submarine base.	Both men returned early in November after making contact with groups around Ålesund.
October 1941 (sea)	**Arquebus** (S. Andersen, B. Haarvardsholm)	To organize resistance groups in the Haugesund area, establish W/T contact and investigate the possibility of importing explosives to attack the aluminium plant at Saudasjøen north of Stavanger.	Haarvardsholm was lost while returning to the UK on the *Blia* in November, but Andersen remained in Norway for the rest of the war. The radio was damaged and therefore contact was made in April 1942 with SIS station, 'Theta'. A new radio was eventually sent from Stockholm in October 1942 and contact established. Relations with *Milorg* were problematic until 1944 and the arrival of the 'Albatross' team.
December 1941 (sea)	**Antrum** (F. Aaraas, K. J. Aarsaether, followed by K. Aarsaether on 28 Jan 1942)	Set up W/T contact and develop groups in the Ålesund area.	Aaras trained a local radio operator and returned to the UK in January 1942. K. J. Aarsaether also returned in January and was replaced by his brother Knut, who returned to the UK in March. Radio contact with the area was problematic and by early 1943 had broken down.
December 1941 (sea)	**Archer** (I. Fosseide, B. Mathiesen, Lynghaul, R. Aarkvisla)	To organize a local intelligence service, reconnoitre possible sabotage targets, recruit and train local groups, establish radio contact.	In the short term, this operation was linked to Operation Anklet; in the longer term, it was the first of a series of operations sent into Nordland to establish a guerrilla organization. The group, however, never established radio contact and internal conflict between its members made it ineffective.

Date	Operation	Objectives	Details
January 1942 (air)	**Cheese II** (O. Starheim, A. Fasting)	To organize and instruct guerrilla bands in the Flekkefjord to Kristiansand area and receive arms.	Fasting carried out instruction while Starheim travelled to Oslo in January and met members of the central council of *Milorg*, including Rolf Palmstrøm, the head of communications, who asked for a wireless operator and set. It was agreed that Einar Skinnarland should travel to Britain to organize this, which he did along with the two SOE men on the 'Galtesund' in March. Three W/T sets were left behind for use by a local organization under Gunvald Thomstad.
February 1942 (Sea)	**Crow** (E. N. Stenersen, the organizer, and E. K. Jacobsen, the W/T operator, who followed on 27/3/42)	To establish W/T contact and organize guerrilla groups on the eastern side of Oslo fjord.	Stenersen went in first and made contact with the local *Milorg* organization and also with SL, which asked him to make his radio available. He found a sight for the W/T operator and in May fled to Stockholm. Jacobsen came on air the same month, but in July was taken by the Gestapo, who attempted to work his set. He escaped in December 1942.
February 1942 (sea)	**Anvil** (J. Gunleiksrud, the organizer, and W/T operator F. B. Johnsen, who followed on 12 March)	To establish W/T contact and organize guerrilla groups around Lillehammer. First attempt failed and Gunleiksrud eventually landed on 27 March	Gunleiksrud was arrested on arrival in February by the local *Milorg* organization on suspicion of being a provocateur. He also came into conflict with SL in Oslo. He left for Sweden in July. The W/T operator remained in Norway until the end of the war.

Date	Operation	Objectives	Details
February 1942 (sea)	**Lark** (Odd Sørli, A. Pevik, followed by O. K. Sættem and A. Christiansen [instructors] on 18 April. E. Hansen [W/T], H. Nygaard [organizer] also sailed on 18 April)	To establish radio contact, receive weapons and train and build up guerrilla groups in the area around Trondheim. Possible sabotage targets, such as submarine supply ships, would also be reconnoitred.	Sørli and Pevik made contact with groups in the Trondheim area. They were followed by the instructors and the W/T operator and organizer in April 1942. Nygaard took over from Sørli. Radio communication began in late May but contact was problematic during the summer. The W/T operator, Hansen, who had gone to Stockholm, was forced to return to Trondheim in autumn 1942 to help improve matters. His set was D/F d and on 16 December 1942 Nygaard and Hansen were arrested, although Nygaard escaped. This temporarily ended radio contact with the Trondheim area.
February 1942 (sea)	**Anchor** (T. Gulbrandsen, and E. Hvraal, the W/T operator who followed 17 April)	To establish W/T contact, instruct small groups in guerrilla warfare and prepare to receive arms drops in the area around Drammen, west of Oslo.	Gulbrandsen made contact with the leadership of *Milorg* in eastern Norway. He began instruction but in May was captured by the Gestapo. Hval was also captured soon after his arrival in Norway in April. Gulbrandsen escaped, with the help of the Gestapo in September and returned to Britain to work for the Germans: see below, Operation Omelette.
March 1942 (sea)	**Heron I** (A. Knudsen, O. Baarnes, H. Bugge, H. K. Hansen, A. Larsen, W/T operator)	Follow up to the 'Archer' party. The second of three parties that would organize and train a guerrilla force in the Vefsn district south of Mosjoen, receive arms dumps and establish W/T contact.	See below: **Heron II**

Date	Operation	Objectives	Details
March 1942 (air)	**Grouse I** (E. Skinnarland, organizer)	Skinnarland, who was originally sent to Britain by R. Palmstrøm, the head of signals in *Milorg*, was dropped in the county of Telemark to establish W/T contact and prepare the ground for the main 'Grouse' party, which was due to arrive at the end of April. The aim was to build an independent guerrilla organization in the Telemark/Rjukan area.	Skinnarland was dropped on the night of 27–28 March. He was instructed to deliver arms to *Milorg* and advise them that the organization in Telemark would operate independently. Skinnarland made contact with SL during June 1942. The second 'Grouse' party, under Jens Poulsson, was unable to leave Britain before the lighter nights began to take effect in May.
April 1942 (sea)	**Mallard** (E. Marthinsson and C. F. Aall)	The objective was to establish W/T contact and a guerrilla organization in the area just to the north of Bergen. Great care would be used in approaching *Milorg*.	The two men attempted to make contact with *Milorg* in Bergen, which eventually they managed to do. On 30 May, however, owing to information provided locally, the Gestapo captured the two SOE men and along with E. Hvaal they were shot. The arrest of the 'Mallard', 'Penguin' and 'Anchor' agents (see below) led to a series of arrests in the Bergen area and severely damaged local resistance groups.
April 1942 (sea)	**Heron II** (B. Sjoberg, E. Rustan, L. Langaas, R. M. Olsen, J. Kvarme, A. Gundersen)	Birger Sjoberg took over command of the 15-man party in the Vefsn district.	A considerable amount of weapons were imported into the area and the training of local groups began. Early in September 1942, however, owing to the work of a Norwegian agent, one of the 'Archer' group was arrested and led the Germans to a farm on Lake Majavatn where an SOE team was in hiding. An exchange of shots followed, which resulted in the death of two Germans. This contributed to a decision to declare a state of emergency in the area, the execution of thirty-four Norwegians and the break up of the Archer/Heron operation.

Date	Operation	Objectives	Details
April 1942 (sea)	**Penguin** (A. Værum organizer)	Sailed on the *Olaf* on 17 April with the 'Anchor' W/T operator E. Hvaal. Værum was instructed to work in the Haugesund to Egersund area, including Stavanger, organize local groups and consider sabotage of certain targets, including Sola aerodrome.	Landed at Nesvik near Telavåg on the island of Sotra outside Bergen on 21 April. Both 'Penguin' and 'Anchor' stayed with a contact man in Telavåg. On 26 April, six Germans and two Stapo men arrived at the agent's hideout and a shootout followed in which two Germans were killed. Værum was also killed while Hvaal was taken prisoner, tortured and later shot. As a result of this incident, all the houses in Telavåg were burnt down, all men between sixteen and sixty-five were sent to Sachsenhausen concentration camp in Germany, while the rest of the inhabitants were banished and interned in Norway.
April 1942 (air)	**Cockerel** (T. Hugo van der Hagen, E. Jensen)	To carry out instruction and training in the Kristiansand area.	In August 1941, Jensen left for Sweden followed by Hagen, who became part of Operation Carhampton in early 1943. After this operation was abandoned, he stayed behind in southern Norway to help F. Aaraas operate the 'Carhampton' W/T station. Aaraas was captured on 12 August 1943 but Hagen managed to escape.
April 1942 (Air)	**Raven** (W. Waage, L. Pettersen, C. Tønseth, G. Merkesdal, W/T operator)	To form guerrilla forces of approximately 300 men in the mountains around Voss and establish wireless contact with the UK. Tasks on an Allied invasion would be to block the Oslo-Bergen railway and control the aerodrome at Bomoen.	'Raven' soon came on air and transmitted until July, after which contact became problematic. In October 1942, Waage arrived in Stockholm and was sent back to the UK. Waage eventually returned in March 1943 as 'Pheasant'. In March 1943, Pettersen also arrived in Stockholm and was sent to the UK. Pettersen returned to Norway in September 1943 on Operation Redwing. In April 1943, the last two members of 'Raven' attempted to return to the UK, but only Tønseth was successful. Organization work continued in the area but there was no contact with the UK until September 1943. In the spring of 1944, a new group called 'Redstart' arrived.

Date	Operation	Objectives	Details
May 1942 (Catalina)	**Unnamed** (S. Granlund, E. Østgaard)	Two men landed by Catalina to establish an arms dump north of Folda in northern Norway.	
July 1942	**Ostrich** (B. Pedersen, P. Deinboll)	This was a plan to send two men into Norway to contact Norwegian workers and train them in undetectable sabotage.	It appears that the operation was never carried out because the two men were allocated to Operation Granard.
July 1942 (Catalina and fishing boat)	**Hawke/Kingfisher** K. (Aarsæther H. Sverdrup)	Plan to organize a small resistance group on the Lofoten Islands in contact with the UK by W/T. The group would receive arms and stores, which would then be distributed to parts of Norway in barrels of fish by fishing boat or by air.	Attempts were made to deliver Aarsæther to northern Norway first by Catalina and second by fishing boat but failed. The first trip to land Sverdrup with stores sailed on 11 December 1942 and eventually reached the Lofotens. An attempt early in January 1943 to establish Aarsæther as the W/T operator was a failure and he returned with Sverdrup. The plan was eventually abandoned.
August 1942 (Submarine)	**Swan** (G. Bråstad W/T operator, A. Fasting)	Establish W/T contact and provide arms instruction to guerrilla groups east of Kristiansand. Fasting was also to train small groups in disposing of dangerous denouncers by assassination.	Landed by the submarine 'Minerve' on the night of 20–21 August off the coast of western Norway. Established W/T contact from 24 September. This operation was troubled by difficulties between Fasting and local groups, including *Milorg*. Fasting, who had been part of Operation Cheese was unpopular with local SOE groups and his presence caused friction. He left for Stockholm in November 1942 and Bråstad followed in February 1943. The local *Milorg* organization was hit badly by a series of arrests in December 1942.

Date	Operation	Objectives	Details
August 1942 (Sea)	**Cygnet** (P. Blystad, M. Berge)	This was a trip that left the Shetlands in the 'Sjø' on 22 August for a fortnight's reconnaissance of the Bergen coastal district.	Operation lost at sea.
August 1942	**Peewit** (O. J. Gulbrandsen, A. Øvre)	Plan to send men to develop contacts in the Oslo shipyards.	Appears plan was never carried out.
September 1942 (via Stockholm)	**Plover** (P. Solnerdal)	Early in 1942 the Norwegian High Command made a request for direct wireless communication with SL. In May, an agreement was reached with the signals chief of *Milorg* to this effect. 'Plover' was the result of this agreement. He was also instructed to train a local person who could take over from him, if necessary.	Plover went in through Stockholm and was installed in Oslo by early September. With the help of Sønsteby, he made contact with SL and came on air on 23 September. However, after problems with his call sign and with the help of *Milorg*, Plover got in touch with SIS station, 'Beta', and used its crystals and signals plan to communicate with the UK. In mid-November, Solnerdal was instructed to train his successor Rolf Krohn, who began to transmit in December. On 19 December, Solnerdal was ordered to Østfold and he sent his last message on 28 December. Krohn, however, signalled through another SIS station 'Corona' that Solnordal had been caught on 6 January 1943, and that he would flee to Sweden. Harald Kvande was recruited to set up a new station, 'Plover Beta', and he made contact on 26 May. He eventually changed to the 'Plover Blue' signal plan before being instructed to close down in September 1943.
September 1942 (Stockholm)	**Penguin Primus** (C. Langeland, G. Setesdal)	The aim was to re-establish W/T contact with the Stavanger area after the arrest of Arne Værum.	Between September 1942 and April 1943, attempts were made through Stockholm to send an agent into the area to establish radio contact but ultimately with no success.

Date	Operation	Objectives	Details
October 1942 (Air)	**Bittern** (Jan Allen, Rubin Larsen, Erik Aasheim, Johannes Andersen (*Gulosten*)	Preparations began in June to train two Norwegians, including Johannes Andersen better known as *Gulosten*, to undertake assassinations. In March, Andersen had killed Raymond Colberg, an Abwehr agent, and his criminal background attracted him to SOE. The party, dropped on the night of 3–4 October, was instructed to train resistance groups in assassination, assist in the carrying out of assassination and help prisoners to escape.	The group had a list of informers with them but their operation, for security reasons, was not communicated to *Milorg* and owing to this, confusion over its role and because of the behaviour of its most notorious member, it ended without having carried out its primary task. By the end of the year, the whole team had fled to Stockholm.
October 1942 (Air)	**Grouse II** (J. Poulsson (leader), K. Haugland, A. Kjelstrup, C. Helberg).	In early 1942, Poulsson had been selected as part of a plan to sink the Tinnsjø ferry and later to place flares in the valley around Rjukan to help guide the bombers on Operation Clairvoyant. In February	The party was dropped on 18 October and its first telegram was sent on 9 November. Its instructions were that, after the completion of 'Freshman'; it should train local groups in guerrilla operations, and target 'Hirdmen' – the NS vigilante guard – and denouncers. The group was, however, told to emphasize that its work did not signify that an invasion was imminent. On 23 November, after the failure of 'Freshman' and for security reasons, it was renamed 'Swallow'.

Date	Operation	Objectives	Details
		1942, he presented a paper to Malcolm Munthe suggesting the establishment of guerrilla groups in Telemark. This led to 'Grouse'. The team was due to be dropped at the end of April, but this never occurred. In mid-September, it was decided the party could also act as advance party for the British Airborne troops on Operation Freshman as well as organizing guerrilla groups in Øvre (Upper) Telemark.	
23 November 1942	**Swallow** (J. Poulsson (leader) K. Haugland, A. Kjelstrup, C. Helberg, E. Skinnarland)	After the failure of 'Freshman', Operation Grouse was renamed 'Swallow'. After Operation 'Gunnerside', 'Swallow' was instructed to continue with its subsidiary task of organizing local guerrilla groups, although	After 'Gunnerside', Haukelid and Kjelstrup moved to the south-west part of Telemark, while Haugland worked on Skinnarland's W/T skills. Poulsson and Helberg both eventually crossed to Sweden, as did Kjelstrup in October 1943, and Haugland after helping Skinnarland, made contact with SL in Oslo and then fled to Sweden. By the summer of 1943, however, Haukelid and Skinnarland had joined up. 'Swallow' had two W/T sets and from the autumn of 1943 these operated as 'Swallow Blue' under Skinnarland and 'Swallow

Date	Operation	Objectives	Details
		members of the original party could decide whether they stayed in the country. At this point, 'Swallow' was also divided into two parts. The organization of western Telemark would be under Knut Haukelid, Eastern Telemark, under Einar Skinnarland, would continue under the name 'Swallow'. Haugland would help 'Swallow' and through cut-outs, 'Bonzo'.	Green' under Niels Krohg, a local man. Haukelid and Skinnarland worked together close to Rjukan and it was through the 'Swallow Blue' station that intelligence on heavy water production was supplied and instructions given to attack its transportation to Germany. In April 1944, 'Swallow Blue' became 'Brown'. Skinnarland eventually joined the 'Sunshine' operation while Haukelid worked with 'Varg' (see below).
November 1942 (Sea)	Petrel (G. Fougner)	Fougner was instructed to meet Home Front leaders and discuss the SOE/PWE and Norwegian proposals for operational propaganda.	He left on 30 November and eventually arrived in Oslo where he met Bjørn Helland Hansen and Eugen Johannessen. He then travelled to Stockholm. He initially indicated that the proposals had been favourably received. He returned to London on 10 February.

Date	Operation	Objectives	Details
November 1942 (Air)	**Thrush** (B. Fjelstad, N. Gabrielsen)	Dropped on the night of 25–26 November. The objective was to establish a wireless base in the Bykle District in southern Norway as well as arrange for the receipt of stores and equipment for the 'Cheese' area.	Fjelstad was instructed to contact the *Milorg* district leader (DL) and act as an arms instructor. He was also to set up a place for the W/T station, which came on air on 7 December, and reconnoitre landing places for the 'Carhampton' operation. In December, many local *Milorg* men were arrested and consequently in February 1943 both men fled to Sweden.
November 1942 (Air)	**Gannet** (T. K. Hoff, O. Dobloug)	The objective was to provide arms instruction and guerrilla training as well as prepare three 'Saccharine' squads – (assassination teams).	The team landed on 30 November and travelled through the Gudbrandsdal and then Østerdal areas training local instructors and forming a 'Saccharine' squad in both valleys to undertake assassinations. In a period of five weeks, working with a locally appointed leadership, they trained sixty new instructors before departing for Sweden in February 1943.
December 1942 (Sea)	**Chough** (Lt. Robberstad)	A plan to recruit men from the Bremnes area to work at the Shetlands Base.	Sailed on 12 December. Robberstad was picked up a few days later having achieved relatively little.
December 1942 (Stockholm)	**Martin** (G. Solberg)	Solberg was instructed to go to the county of Troms in northern Norway to establish contacts and set up a W/T base in preparation for Operation Martin, a plan to organize and assist local resistance groups in this area.	Solberg left Stockholm on 20 December with a courier while a W/T was sent separately to Trondheim. Both men were, however, arrested at the Swedish border and Solberg was not released until 5 March. He went to the UK to become the W/T operator for the main 'Martin' operation.

Date	Operation	Objectives	Details
Jan 1943 (Sea)	**Moorhen** (A. Martens-Meyer)	The intention was to establish W/T contact with the local resistance organization in Bergen, set up a radio link between the groups in the area, instruct a local W/T operator, examine the possibility of shipping sabotage and possibly revive an export organization.	Left on 6 January with Lt. Robberstad equipped with six radio transmitters. Meyer made contact with local groups, but as the radios lacked transformers, the plan for a local network was shelved. One transmitter fortunately did work and contact was made with the UK. The local groups, especially after Televåg, feared reprisals and were not very accommodating. Meyer did, however, set up a group in Bergen and left two radio sets before travelling back to the UK at the end of February. Contact was never made.
Jan 1943 (Air)	**Chaffinch** (T. Stenersen, O. Sandersen, M. Olsen)	To work in the area to the west of Oslo, establish W/T contact, provide instruction and training, investigate the possibility of local groups undertaking shipping sabotage and prepare a small local team to carry out assassinations.	Landed on 23 January. Contact was quickly made with SL. Extensive training and instruction was carried out in the area. In liaison with SL a group of six men, an 'X Group', was set up and trained in 'silent' killing. Just before they left three more 'X-Groups' were prepared. The group also attempted and undertook ship sabotage in Drammen and Moss, respectively, before leaving Norway at the end of May 1943.
Feb 1943 (Sea)	**Lark** (J. Pevik, N. U. Hansen)	This was an operation to land arms and equipment in the Trondheim area in preparation for the resurrection of this operation.	The party left on 22 February and returned on 1 March having delivered approximately 500 kilos of material to three sites around Trondheim.

Date	Operation	Objectives	Details
February 1943	**Omelette** (T. Gulbrandsen)	This was a plan to use Gulbrandsen as a double agent to deceive the Gestapo over SOE plans in Norway.	Gulbrandsen, the former 'Anchor' organizer, was captured in May 1942. He was allowed to escape in September and eventually returned to England. His story was initially accepted but after the 'Crow' W/T operator returned to the UK and told SOE that Gulbrandsen had been allowed to escape, the truth came out. In early 1943, Gulbrandsen revealed how his escape was fixed. Because of threats against his family, he agreed to send intelligence on SOE back to the Gestapo in Norway either through W/T contact or letters to cover addresses in Oslo that would be delivered by new SOE agents. The operation was never undertaken and Gulbrandsen was sent to work at STS 26 for the rest of the war.
March 1943 (Sea)	**Antrum Red/Blue** (K. J. Aarsæther)	The objective was to send an agent back to the Ålesund area with two wireless sets, crystals and signals plans: 'Red' and 'Blue'. One of the stations would be used to provide shipping intelligence.	K. J. Aarsæther sailed on 4 March. 'Antrum Red' came on air on 19 March. 'Antrum Blue' became an important contact and link for the 'Vestige' and 'Barbara' operations. He also contacted local organizations, trained a local telegraphist and contacted a group in the Molde area. Aarsæther eventually became sick and was returned to the UK in January 1944.
March 1943 (Sea)	**Lark Blue** (O. Sørli, E. G. Onstad)	The objective was to re-establish contact with and continue organizing groups in the Trondheim area as well as distribute arms dumps and prepare to receive Operation Source.	Landed on 14 March with two wireless sets. A third set had been landed a few weeks earlier. The Lark organization was still intact. Eventually two transmission sites were established in Trondheim and 'Lark Blue' came on air. Gjems-Onstad trained a local operator to replace him in Trondheim and attempted to set up a station in Kristiansund, 'Lark Brown'. In October 1943, both men left for Stockholm.

Date	Operation	Objectives	Details
March 1943 (Air)	**Pheasant** (W. Waage, J. Solberg Johansen, B. Iversen)	To establish a W/T contact with the UK and organize groups in the Valdres and northern Hallingdal area.	The party was dropped on 12 March 1943. On 23 April, the radio station came on air and continued to transmit until the end of the war. Contact was made with SL and a number of groups organized in the area. The first airdrop was not, however, received until April 1944 and therefore weapon training was delayed. Operation Firecrest arrived in May 1944 to relieve the 'Pheasant' party.
March 1943 (Sea)	**Heron (Red)** (O. Baarnes, A.E. Telnes, A. Gundersen)	To re-establish W/T contact with the 'Heron' organization and Lt. Sjøberg, deliver stores, inspect and provide information on local groups.	After the infiltration of the 'Heron' organization the previous September, radio contact with the UK was broken. The new team re-established contact on 7 April and Sjøberg was instructed to return to the UK. A Catalina aircraft picked him up at the beginning of May. Radio contact continued but was broken between September and December 1943.
March 1943 (Sea)	**Martin (Red)** (S. Eskeland, P. R. Blindheim, G. Solberg, J. S. Baalsrud)	The aim was to set up W/T contact between local groups in Troms and the UK, investigate and make contact with these groups and finally organize them into small units that could attack targets in support of an Allied landing.	Left on 23 March 1943 and arrived off the Norwegian coast on 28 March. A local tradesman, who the group had made contact with, contacted the authorities, which led to the arrival of the Gestapo. The only member of the team to survive was Jan Baalsrud, who made a remarkable journey to Sweden, which he reached towards the end of May.

Date	Operation	Objectives	Details
March 1943 (Air)	**Puffin** (W. Houlder, S. Blindheim)	To contact SL and train their groups in the Oslo area. Also to advise local groups on insaisissable sabotage in the Oslo shipyards.	*Milorg* were aware of the imminent arrival of this team before it landed on 17 April 1943. From early May until November, it trained groups in the area around Oslo. Both men were captured in November 1943 but escaped to Sweden. They returned in January 1944 and continued training until the summer, when both men travelled to Sweden. They then returned to help organize *Milorg* sabotage teams and actions in the area, often in collaboration with other SOE teams. Blindheim temporarily returned to Britain between January and April 1945.
April 1943 (Stockholm)	**Stonechat** (H. Lund)	To work as W/T operator in the vicinity of Rena in *Østerdal* and hold himself at the disposal of the DL.	W/T contact was made in September but there were many technical problems and by October 'Stonechat' was back in Stockholm. The following spring an attempt was made to set up 'Stonechat Green', but he was captured and replaced by 'Chicken', who came on air in September 1944.
June 1943 (Stockholm)	**Thrush Red** (B. Fjelstad, N. Gabrielsen)	Fjelstad was instructed to work as an instructor in the area to the east of Oslo while Gabrielsen would establish radio contact. They were also instructed to attempt to blow up the Prestebakke bridge in eastern Norway.	Plans to blow up the bridge were soon dropped. Fjelstad began training in the area. He then assisted SL by working as an instructor for the 'X-Groups'. Gabrielsen moved to Oslo to assist SL, training W/T operators and helping establish four new radio stations. He remained connected to SL helping them establish an internal communications network.

Date	Operation	Objectives	Details
September 1943 (Air)	**Redwing** (L. Pettersen, G. Wiig-Andersen)	The aim was to form a small group in the Voss-Bergen area that could work either as saboteurs or assist other teams from the UK, without endangering other groups in the area. Assassinations would also be undertaken in November as part of 'Ratweek'.	Dropped on 21 September, they made contact with local leaders and established a radio link with the UK. They also met the *Milorg* district leader for Bergen and established a relationship. No assassinations were undertaken due to the fear of reprisals. In early 1944, Pettersen was moved to the 'Pheasant' area but Andersen kept transmitting after receiving new crystals.
September 1943 (Air)	**Goshawke** (J. Gunleiksrud, O. Dobloug)	To provide further instruction for groups in Gudbrandsdal and Østerdal, which it was believed had been taken over by *Milorg*, and obtain fresh information on these groups. To arrange for assassinations during 'Ratweek' in November 1943.	Dropped on 21 September and carried out extensive training with local groups over the following weeks. Although they prepared for 'Ratweek', no assassinations were undertaken. In February 1944, they crossed the border into Sweden.

Date	Operation	Objectives	Details
September 1943 (Stockholm)	**Wagtail** (J. Pevik, K. Brodtkorp Danielsen, O. Halvorsen, F. Bekke)	The original objective was to reconnoitre the railway in Namdalen north of Trondheim with a view to cutting off the town at some future date. Before this was undertaken, however, both Pevik and Brodtkorp-Danielsen were instructed along with Ole Halvorsen and Frederick Brekke to attempt an assassination of the Norwegian informer, Henry Rinnan.	The team was led by Ole Halvorsen, a member of a Norwegian communist organization. An attempt against Rinnan was made on 7 October but failed. The Gestapo then arrested another member of the group, Brekke, which lead to the arrest of Johnny Pevik, who had by then moved on to commence his work in Namdalen. He was eventual executed in the cellars of the Mission Hotel in Trondheim.
October 1943 (Air)	**Grebe** (T Hoff, J. Beck, H. Løkken, H. Storhaug, A. Øvergård, A. Graven)	Instructed to establish independent of *Milorg*, a small force in the hills supplied direct from the UK. They were also directed to reconnoitre the Røros and Dovre railways in order, should the occasion arise, to prevent enemy troops movements.	Dropped on 10 October, three of the party were killed on landing and therefore the remaining three were forced to flee to Sweden, where they remained until the following January.

Date	Operation	Objectives	Details
October 1943 (Air)	**Lapwing** (R. Arnesen, L. Fosseide, S. Haugen, Lt. Kvaale)	The objective was to reconnoitre the Røros Railway, south of Trondheim, with a view to sabotage.	Dropped on 10 October. The W/T set was damaged but after several trips to Sweden radio contact was established in June 1944. During August, October and November 1944, an additional five men strengthened the party. It carried out its first action against the railway network on 10 December and again on 29 December 1944. Three men from the party were later killed in a clash with German forces.
November 1943 (Air)	**Curlew** (K. Haugland, G. Sønsteby)	To provide a wireless operator for *Milorg*, to advise *Milorg* on wireless matters and to instruct and equip the five wireless stations in the Oslo area.	Dropped on 17 November with the 'Goldfinch' party and containers of weapons and equipment. Haugland left for Kongsberg but was captured by the Gestapo, although he escaped and eventually began his work in Oslo. Sønsteby gathered the weapons and brought them to Oslo. In March, Haugland's transmissions were detected but he escaped capture and in April both men left for Stockholm.
November 1943 (Air and from Stockholm)	**Goldfinch** (T. Stenersen, J. Allan, M. Olsen, O. Sandersen)	The party was instructed to resume training in the area to the west of Oslo, liquidate dangerous informers as part of 'Ratweek', sabotage shipping on the west side of Oslo fjord and reconnoitre Gardemoen airport.	Stenersen and Allan were dropped on 17 November and met Olsen and Sandersen who had arrived from Sweden. The team always worked closely with SL. In December, two of the group were surprised by the Germans and Stenersen was shot and captured, while Olsen escaped. Olsen took over the party. Meanwhile Sandersen established W/T contact while Allen began weapons training. Olsen was joined by Edvard Tallaksen and Birger Rasmussen from the 'Company' team and began work. Reconnaissance of Gardemoen was undertaken and liquidations carried out. By May 1944, the team had been involved in the assassination of at least four informers. The team was also made ready to attack the ship that would transport heavy water to Germany and prepared an attack against shipping in Drammen. Members of the group also assisted in attacks against the Labour Service offices in Oslo.

Date	Operation	Objectives	Details
December 1943 (Air)	**Sandpiper** (J. Ropstad, A. Fosse, J. Eikanger, L. Tofte)	The group was instructed to make contact with existing organizations in southern Norway; establish W/T communication; provide instruction; reconnoitre and plan an attack against the aerodrome at Kjevik, north-east of Kristiansand; and prepare disruption or protection of communications if the Germans withdraw.	Dropped on 10 December, the group quickly made radio contact and at the end of December met local *Milorg* leaders. Over the coming months, training was carried out, some weapons delivered and in September the group was reinforced by the arrival of two instructors from Sweden. In October 1944, the 'Sanderling' team arrived.
December 1943 (Air)	**Osprey** (A. Espedal, K. Hetland, J. Weltzien, K. Kiærland)	Instructed to work in the Stavanger area, establish W/T contact, prepare local guerrilla groups, organize groups to sabotage or, if necessary, protect lines of communication, receive weapons and prepare a plan to neutralize Sola aerodrome.	Also dropped on 10 December, the group began organizational work in the area but did not receive a delivery of weapons until May 1944. Contact was quickly made with the *Milorg* district leader, who from February was in contact with SL in Oslo. From July 1944, the group began to instruct local *Milorg* groups. In autumn 1944, the area was hit by a series of arrests among SIS organization and 'Osprey' went into hiding. At the end of the year, the 'Avocet' team arrived.

Date	Operation	Objectives	Details
January 1944 (Sea)	**Falcon** (B. E, Sjøberg, A. E. Larsen)	To operate in the Mosjøen area reorganizing local groups, receive arms and equipment, reconnoitre and plan the destruction or defence of lines of communication, maintain order after a German withdrawal.	Landed late January. A further three parties were delivered to the area during March (see below) and after joining the 'Heron Red' team this meant that there was a party of sixteen working in the region. From April, however, German security police began a series of raids in the region and in June operations *Bärenfang I to III* commenced. This resulted in the breaking up of 'Falcon', including the death of Sjøberg in June, and by mid-August SOE operations in the area were at an end.
January 1944 (Stockholm)	**Throstle** (H. Hanson, A. Veda)	To work as weapons instructors for *Milorg* on the eastern side of Oslo under the command of the 'Thrush' party.	The team worked in D11, east of Oslo, and in the summer of 1944 helped in the sabotage of petrol and oil stores in the area.
January 1944 (Stockholm)	**Grebe Red** (A. Overgård, H. Storhaug, A. Graven)	A re-establishment of the original 'Grebe' party (see above).	Attempts to leave Sweden were initially hindered by the Swedish police and it was the end of February before the team crossed the border. W/T contact was made and in mid-April 'Goshawk' joined them. The group remained in situ for the rest of the year with some trips back and forth to Sweden. In December, J. Gunleiksrud took over the leadership and the team began its involvement in railway sabotage.

Date	Operation	Objectives	Details
January 1944 (Sea)	**Antrum Green** (K. Aarsæther)	Knut took over from his brother to continue W/T contact with the UK, provide intelligence, arrange sabotage of shipping and communications, form a group to carry out anti-sabotage and police the area in the event of a German withdrawal.	Remained in the area until September and organized guerrilla groups, weapons instruction, laid plans for demolishing ferries and began a whispering campaign aimed at mobilizing the Norwegian fishing fleet should an invasion occur.
February 1944 (Sea)	**Merlin** (H. Mowinkle-Nilsen, L. Dallard – W/T operator)	To organize and instruct groups in the Bergen area, establish W/T contact with the UK and prepare counter-scorch activities.	Three *Milorg* men returned to the UK on the boat. The Merlin W/T operator moved around the area until September 1944 when due to German raids he went undercover. Instruction was initially undertaken in Bergen and from May in the surrounding districts. In autumn 1944, the Merlin instructor moved back to Bergen where he remained until January 1945 when he joined the Bjorn West base.
February 1944 (Sea)	**Falcon (II)** (H. Lynghaug, L. Largass, A. Z. Solbakken)	See above.	
March 1944 (Air)	**Fieldfare** (J. Rønneberg, B. Strømsheim, O. Aarsæther)	To reconnoitre the Åndalsnes-Dombås railway, prepare weapons and explosives dumps near the railway, prepare counter-scorch plans for the railway.	Dropped on the night of 7–8 March. A bad landing so they lost much of their equipment. Received further supplies in July but had to survive until the liberation on meagre rations. Carried out their one and only action against the railway on 5 January 1945. In March 1945, Rønneberg travelled back to Britain but returned in May to help in the liberation of Ålesund

Date	Operation	Objectives	Details
March 1944 (Sea)	**Falcon (III)** (J. Kvarme, T. Valberg, E. Grannes)	See above.	Lt. Gausland went to Trondheim in January to rebuild contacts after a wave of arrests. Gjems-Onstad followed in March to take over the leadership and act as W/T operator. He built up local groups and returned to Stockholm in June. He returned to Trondheim in August with a new W/T operator, E. Løkse, 'Lark Yellow'. Løkse was arrested and Gjems-Onstad again returned from Stockholm, although his time was taken up with 'Durham' activities. Eventually, F. Beichman joined him as W/T operator followed by T. Bjørnas and A. Wisloff. In 1945, some railway sabotage was undertaken before Gjems-Onstad returned to Stockholm for the last time.
March 1944 (Stockholm)	**Lark/Durham** (E. Gjems-Onstad, I. Gausland, H. Larsen)	To establish W/T contact, reorganize Lark and build up the propaganda organization 'Durham'.	
March 1944 (Sea)	**Falcon Peregrine** (H. K. Hansen, L. Sandin, E. Rustan, R. Rogne)	See above.	
April 1944 (Sea)	**Albatross** (L. Skjøld, P. Wegeland)	To reorganize local groups if necessary; instruct them in arms, explosives and guerrilla tactics; and to prepare plans for the prevention of a German scorched-earth policy in the area north of Stavanger. Also to reconnoitre the aluminium plant at Saudasjøen.	Landed in the area on 17 April. Instruction continued through 1944 in cooperation with the local *Milorg* leadership in Haugesund. Weapons were delivered but in the autumn the Germans began a series of raids and the organization was under severe pressure. In November, the area was reinforced by the arrival of the 'Auk' team. Production at Saudasjøen had ceased due to a lack of raw materials.

Date	Operation	Objectives	Details
April 1944 (Air)	**Buzzard** (A. Aubert, H. Henriksen)	To assist SL in executing denouncers in the Oslo area.	Remained in the Oslo area for the rest of the war and was responsible for a number of assassinations. The most significant was the execution of Major-General Karl Marthinsen, the head of the Norwegian Stapo, in February 1945, which resulted in the execution of twenty-eight Norwegians.
April 1944 (Sea)	**Redstart** (W. Johannesen, F. Kvist, I. Birkeland)	To bring the organization in the Voss area into a state of readiness through instruction in guerrilla tactics and to prepare counter-scorch activities in case of a German withdrawal.	Landed on 30 April with the 'Firecrest' team. Joined the Merlin W/T operator and began training in the area. Made preparations to sabotage the Bergen railway to support an invasion and protect Dale power station from German destruction. In August, they moved to the Hardanger area to continue training but in September during a German raid they lost their W/T set.
April 1944 (Sea)	**Firecrest** (E. Madsen, B. Holth-Larsen, E. Lorentzen, G. Sætersday)	To relieve the 'Pheasant' team in the Hallingdal-Valdres area; reorganize groups; carry out instruction in weapons, explosives and guerrilla tactics; and prepare counter-scorch activities.	Landed 30 April and soon began to carry out weapons instructions. In the autumn, the men helped with the provision of supplies for the 'Elg' base. From summer of 1944, the team also began to undertake sabotage in the area, especially against oil and petrol supplies.
April 1944 (Air)	**Woodpecker** (O. Sættem)	To reconnoitre the Dovre railway and other forms of communication with a view to sabotage.	This was the leader of the party who was dropped with the 'Buzzard' team on the night of 28–29 April near Larvik and remained in the area until October.

Date	Operation	Objectives	Details
April/May 1944	**Goldcrest** (S. Sveinesen, R. Olsen)	To reinforce the DL and to increase the preparedness of District 14.1 around Drammen.	It is unclear whether this team ever went into Norway. The first radio message from 'Goldcrest' was, however, sent at the end of May, but this could have been done by a local operator.
May 1944 (Stockholm)	**Robin** (A. H. Pevik, A. Torp)	Another attempt to liquidate informers particularly Henry Rinnan and Ivar Grande whose activities had caused so much damage in the county of Trøndelag.	Left Stockholm on 20 May and stayed in Norway for one month without producing any results. Returned in early August and formed two groups to watch informers, but by mid-October both men had been recalled.
July 1944 (Stockholm)	**Crackle** (F. Brandt, A. Torhildsen)	Instruction in dealing with landmines.	Two visits were paid to the field and four courses held.
August 1944 (Air)	**Golden Eagle** (M. Olsen, O. Sandersen)	To make preliminary preparations for what became the 'Elg' base. To establish W/T contact, make ready to receive supplies and escapees from German mobilization orders.	Radio contact was made and in the next three month twenty supply drops were received. The main team arrived on 27 November.

Date	Operation	Objectives	Details
August/September 1944 (Stockholm)	**Sepals/Perianth** (Lt. Håkon Kyllingmark – commanding officer)	The plan was to set up two bases, 'Sepals' and 'Sepals I', with three operating units, 'Perianth', 'Perianth I & II', on Swedish territory close to Narvik under the cover of being intelligence operations. They would supply intelligence on the area, establish a W/T link and prepare attacks against targets, although nothing would be undertaken without authority from London. In November, permission was given to undertake sabotage.	By mid-September 1944, both bases were manned and had W/T contact but for the rest of the year they only supplied intelligence. In mid-January, preparations to set up a third base, 'Sepals III', began while the other two bases became 'Sepals I & II'. In March, another base 'Sepals Gorgon' was also set up. From mid-January sabotage was undertaken, initially from 'Sepals I' but primarily from 'Sepals III'. The bases were also a link, a source of supplies and an organizational point for *Milorg* groups around Narvik and in the county of Troms. The bases finally played an important role in the liberation of the area in May 1945 and in the protection of local sites.
September 1944	**Scale Operations:** Octave (Oslo), Minim (Stockholm), Quaver and Semi-Quaver (Nordland and Trondheim), Semi-Breve, Crotchet and Sharp that together were to cover Bergen and the Stavanger area	These Allied missions were to advise and assist the Home Front in organizing all available forces, to coordinate action within Norway with that taken by Allied forces outside, to help hinder German counter-scorch plans and assist in the arrival of military and civil supplies.	Only Quaver/Semi-Quaver and Minim were eventually undertaken. See below for details.

Date	Operation	Objectives	Details
September 1944 (sea)	**Woodlark** (H. Helgesen, O. Østgaard, O. Walderhaug)	To form a base from which the Nordland railway in Namdal north of Trondheim could be attacked.	Landed on 12 September, the three had by the end of September been joined by four additional men from Stockholm. The party established a base just inside the Swedish border but from an early stage it suffered from internal conflict and although a W/T operator arrived in November he was never able to make contact. Supplies were short and there were several trips to Stockholm. On 13 January, members of the party attacked the Jørstad Bridge resulting in the wrecking of a German troop train. From this point, however, the party gradually broke up, had new leadership and increasingly played a subsidiary role in the area, although it marched into Steinkjer as a separate unit at the liberation.
September 1944 (Sea)	**Razorbill** (H. Rasmussen, L. Pettersen)	To instruct groups in Bergen, receive weapons, arrange for the transfer of men to the Bjørn West base, reconnoitre chosen targets to be protected, carry out attacks against enemy oil supplies.	Arrived on 18 September. Another two arrived on 1 October. Training was carried out, weapons received, intelligence provided on the U-boat base. The group worked with both *Milorg* and the communist organization, *Saborg*. It also provided names of informers for liquidation, and two local men were assassinated. A steam ship and transformers at the ship works were also sabotaged. At the beginning of May 1945, it was 'Razorbill' that contacted the German Command in Bergen in order to help secure a peaceful liberation.
September 1944 (Sea)	**Antrum Yellow/Grey** (K. J. Aarsæther, K. Engelsen)	To organize and instruct groups in the Ålesund area, supply weapons and stores, prepare counter-scorch activities and plan sabotage against German communications during an invasion or withdrawal.	Sailed on night of 22/23 September and replaced Knut Aarsæther who returned to the UK. Work continued on building up the local organization and they were reinforced in October by the arrival of two more men. Antrum was instructed to work closely with the local *Milorg* leadership, which would be linked with SL in Oslo. At the end of October, a message was sent via the 'Antrum' radio that Ivar Grande, the informer, should be liquidated. He was killed on 11 December.

Date	Operation	Objectives	Details
September 1944 (Air)	**Sanderling** (K. Austad, T. Andersen, H. P. Armstrong, L. Eide)	The four were instructed to work in the counties of East and West Agder in southern Norway with the 'Sandpiper' team.	These four, including Percy Armstrong who had mixed British and Norwegian parentage, were dropped into southern Norway to reinforce the 'Sandpiper' team. Austad and Eide worked in the area around Kristiansand. Preparations were made to receive operation 'Varg I' but activities were badly hit by German raids and organization was difficult. Supplies also remained short and it was March 1945 before airdrops eased the situation and some training could commence.
October 1944 (Sea)	**Razorbill II** (E. N. Kvale, J. Nesheim)	See above.	
October 1944 (Sea)	**Lark** (Gjems-Onstad)	See above.	
October 1944 (Air)	**Sunshine, Moonlight, Starlight, Lamplight** (L. Tronstad, N. Lind, J. Poulsson, H. Nygaard, A. Kjelstrup, L. Bronn, E. Hagen, C. Helberg, G. Syverstad)	To protect the power stations in Telemark and Buskerud along with the Norsk Hydro industries in Rjukan and Notodden against any German attempt to initiate a scorched-earth policy. These power stations provided 60 per cent of the power in *Østlandet*, eastern Norway. Led by Leif Tronstad, who had been the central figure in the plans and preparations to disrupt heavy water	It was in many ways a reforming of the 'Gunnerside' team. The main party was dropped on 5 October. W/T contact was made with the UK and the operation worked closely with the management of Norsk Hydro, the local *Milorg* organization and through them with SL in Oslo. Training and a series of preparations were made to protect these sites over the coming months. On 11 March, Tronstad was tragically killed and Poulsson took over the leadership of the operation. On 9 May 1945, 'Sunshine' was ordered to mobilize. The district was brought under its control and the designated targets protected. Norwegian SS soldiers were imprisoned and Nazis arrested in collaboration with the local police.

Date	Operation	Objectives	Details
		production at Vemork. The plan was divided into three sections: 'Moonlight' with Rjukan at its core; 'Starlight' in Numedal, north-east of Rjukan; 'Lamplight' in the area around Notodden. Jens Poulsson led 'Moonlight' with Claus Helberg as W/T operator, Arne Kjelstrup led 'Starlight', while 'Lamplight' was the responsibility of Herluf Nygaard. Norman Lind, a British officer with Norwegian parents, acted as liaison officer. Einar Skinnarland became W/T operator at Tronstad's HQ.	
October 1944 (Air)	**Woodpecker** (K. Hellan, R. J. Johannesssen, Ø. Nilsen)	This party had originally been called 'Linnet'. They were instructed to reconnoitre the Dovre railway south of Trondheim with a view to carrying out sabotage.	Dropped on 4 October and joined their leader O. Sættem. In early March 1945, four additional men from Sweden reinforced the team. On 9 December, the party received orders to disrupt train traffic. They attacked the Stolan tunnel between Opdal and Bjerkinn and stopped traffic for three days. The party had W/T difficulties for a while and was short of supplies until further drops were made.

Date	Operation	Objectives	Details
October 1944 (Sea)	**Redstart** (F. Olsvik)	See above.	Olsvik was the new W/T operator. The Merlin operator moved to Bergen to serve the 'Redwing' team. At the beginning of December, the 'Redstart' team were told to prepare railway sabotage but as the Germans did not withdraw from the area this was never carried out. They continued with instruction until February when the priority became protection of key sites in the area, especially Bømoen aerodrome. Despite airdrops, the area lacked weapons and equipment and there was a series of raids that forced the team under cover. They eventually joined the Bjørn East base, which took over responsibility for the Hardanger area.
October 1944 (Sea)	**Siskin** (M. Olsen, R. Ulstein, H. Svindseth, N. Fjeld)	To instruct groups in the Sogn area, especially at important power stations in readiness to undertake preventative action. Also to receive supplies and establish W/T contact with the UK.	The team trained groups in the area and received supplies. Between 10 April and 1 May 1945, thirty-five tons of weapons and equipment were unloaded from subchasers and by mid-April around 480 men were organized in the Inner Sogn area alone. On 6 May, Captain Wendelbo Lysne arrived to take over all forces in the area. From 8 May mobilization began, and from 9 May members of NS and the Gestapo were disarmed and interned.
October 1944 (Sea)	**Bjørn West** (F. Kayser, S. Synnes)	The objective was to reconnoitre the area between Bergen and Sognefjord with a view to the possibility of establishing a guerrilla base and reception area.	Left the Shetlands on 15 October. This was the advance party, which would begin the preparatory work.

Date	Operation	Objectives	Details
October 1944 (Air)	**Quaver/Semi-Quaver** (J. Adamson, M. Watson, P. Dahl, Sgt. Lindsay)	To provide intelligence on enemy troop movements through the county of Nordland, assist local organizations, establish contact with *Milorg* and consider possibilities of railway sabotage between Mo and Mosjøen.	Dropped on 16 October this was the only operation sent to Norway that was predominately made up of British recruits, including an SOE officer. The strategically important area north of Trondheim had not had contact with the UK since the break-up of the 'Falcon' operation the previous August. The operation was a disaster as soon after landing the party was surprised by a group of German soldiers. This led to the capture of Adamson, his imprisonment in Norway and eventual transportation to Germany, although he survived the war. The other three recruits eventually escaped to Sweden.
October 1944 (Sea)	**Bjørn West II** (R. Tvinnerheim, K. Karlsen, A. Trones, M. Mathiesen)	See above. Also to establish radio contact, reconnoitre the billeting areas and dropping places and to report to London.	This was the rest of the preparatory group, which on 7 November received its first weapons drop.
October 1944 (Sea)	**Antrum** (H. Hoel, I. Næss)	See above.	See above.
November 1944 (Air)	**Varg I** (H. Sandvik, T. Abrahamsen, S. Heidenreich, E. Johnsen, H. Bugge)	To make preparations for the safe reception, billeting, maintaining, training and employment of men in the hills of Setesdal, north of Kristiansand. Once set up, the base would receive local *Milorg* forces that would be trained in weapons and explosives use, sabotage and anti-sabotage.	The team was dropped on the night of 1-2 November and met by J. Ropstad and 4 men from 'Sandpiper'. The leader was Harald Sandvik, and in addition to the original party four men from Milorg also joined the group. It was planned that the base would have 5 billeting areas.

Date	Operation	Objectives	Details
November 1944 (Air)	**Varg** (E. Vestre, T. Halvorsen)	See above.	Dropped on 7 November to reinforce the area.
November 1944 (Air)	**Woodlark** (Y. Øgarrd)	See above.	
November 1944 (Sea)	**Auk** (K. Vilnes, P. Ørstenvik, Capt. Sjø, Lt. Robberstad)	To reinforce the 'Arquebus' and 'Albatross' teams in the Haugesund area and reorganize the district. A W/T link would be established. The group's leader was responsible for all three teams and would be military adviser to the *Milorg* district leader. Local teams would organize preventative work and reconnoitre cutting points along local communications.	After the arrival of 'Auk' in early November contact with Milorg widened. The role assigned to local groups was a combination of counter-scorch activities and attempts to hinder German troop movements to the east should it be required.
November 1944 (Air)	**Dipford-Frinton** (P. Deinboll, A. Gjestland)	To work with SL as technical advisers on railways, telecommunications, information and propaganda.	The plane disappeared over the North Sea.

Date	Operation	Objectives	Details
November 1944 (Sea)	**Snowflake** (P. Ratvik, H. Svindseth to join him from 'Siskin')	To organize and instruct local groups around Nordfjord, south of Ålesund in arms, explosives, guerrilla warfare and counter-scorch activities in order to protect Svelgen Power and Transformer Station and Stryn Repeater Station.	Landed on 27 November and made W/T contact on 2 December. Had contact with a local SIS station, 'Roska', which during March 1945 sent messages on behalf of 'Snowflake'. By the time of the German surrender, 'Snowflake' had organized 400 men although they lacked weapons. On 13 May, it set up a HQ in Florø and was involved in the arrest of around seventy Nazis, informers and black marketers.
November 1944 (Air)	**Elg I** (P. Strande, P. Holst, A. Hagen, H. Christiansen)	To continue the work of 'Golden Eagle' by preparing for the safe reception, billeting, maintaining, training and employment of 1,200 men between Valdres and Hallingdal.	Dropped on 27 November, the four officers went to their billeting areas while Strand contacted the local *Milorg* organization.
November–January 1944	**Scapula**	This was a plan to send a whaleboat with two instructors, a W/T operator, arms and equipment to the island of Senja in the north of Norway to assist resistance groups in their efforts to resist the German evacuation of the local population.	In November 1944, SIS station 'Gudrun' on the island of Senja' (E. Johansen) telegraphed London asking for weapons to be supplied to local groups so that they could resist Germany's forced evacuation of the population. In the end, Johansen rejected the proposal and it was cancelled.

Date	Operation	Objectives	Details
November/ December 1944	**Husky** (Major Andrew Croft and Lt J. Baalsrud – a total party of five Norwegians and eight British officers)	To make contact with, supply and instruct detachments of *Milorg* behind the German lines in the north of Norway, with a view to operations against retreating enemy units.	The eventual plan was that the Royal Norwegian Navy would transport an SOE team to the north of Norway, while four fishing vessels would sail independently to the region to be at SOE's disposal. The operation was cancelled at the end of January 1945 due to the lack of protection from the enemy's small naval craft.
December 1944 (Air/Stockholm)	**Curlew** (G. Sønsteby)	In November, Sønsteby had been ordered to travel to London.	In mid-December, he returned to Norway via Stockholm with his 'Directive to nr 24', which set out his tasks as sabotage chief for SL.
December 1944 (Air to Stockholm)	**Minim** (Major H. A. Nyberg)	To represent SFHQ at SOE and OSS missions in Stockholm on all matters for which SFHQ was responsible to SHAEF. To assist in coordinating the activities of both missions.	Nyberg arrived in Stockholm on 16 December with the title of Honoury Assistant Military Attaché. Liaised on the preparation of the Norwegian police troops (Operation Beefeater) and sent regular reports on their progress, which also included intelligence on conditions in Norway. After the liberation, he accompanied the police troops into Norway.
December 1944 (Air)	**Cramlington** (H. Ryen)	The intention was to have a party of sixteen men working from a base on Swedish soil. The ultimate objective was to cut the railway between Grong and Majavatn in the Nordland. A base was to be set up in the neighbourhood of the target.	Dropped on 22 December. This was the preliminary reconnaissance by the leader of the party before he went on to Stockholm to meet the rest of the party.

Date	Operation	Objectives	Details
December 1944 (Sea)	**Bjørn East** (O. Berentsen, J. Akslen, K. Nordgron, L. Olsen)	As the area to be covered by Bjørn West base was so large, it was decided to divide it into two. Bjørn East would be close to Vossevangen.	This was a preliminary party of four under the leadership of Captain Berentsen.
December 1944 (Air)	**Elg II** (K. Poulssen, A. Thon)	See above.	Dropped on 28 December. From this point comprehensive instruction began and eventually many men returned to their hometowns to continue training. From September 1944 to May 1945 the base received 75 airdrops with equipment for 3000 men. W/T contact was maintained with London and the transmitters in 'Elg' were in contact with six other radio stations. In April 1945 the enemy began to show an interest in the base and on 26 April there was a clash between 120 Germans and 85 local men. Twenty-nine Germans were killed and thirty wounded, whilst 'Elg' lost six men and had two wounded.
December 1944 (Air)	**Farnborough I** (J. M. Neerland)	To cover the *Milorg* District D.11, this included part of Oslo and the area to the east of it. The aim of the Farnborough operations was to reinforce the district leadership and increase its preparedness, with special attention to preventative actions.	Dropped on 28 December, Neerland instructed the district's most important recruits, so-called 'Q-teams' that had formed cells and were hiding in the woods. He also examined and adjusted the protective plans that had been produced to cover this area.

Date	Operation	Objectives	Details
January 1944 (Air)	**Farnborough II** (E. Eng, J. Herman Linge)	To cover D.12, north-east of Oslo. Linge was also given the task of liquidating the Norwegian Nazi, Ole Utengen.	Dropped on the night of 31 December–1 January. Linge, son of Martin Linge, was captured and eventually transported to Germany. Meanwhile, Lt. Eng began instruction, organizing drop zones and selected those who would have responsibility for protecting key sites. He eventually became chief of staff in D.12 working closely with the district leader.
December 1944 (Air)	**Farnborough III** (E. Welle-Strand, K. E. Nordahl, O. Birknes, H. Engebretsen, A. Christiansen)	To cover the Oslo area. This was probably the best organized *Milorg* district, which by July 1944 had over 4,000 men in its ranks.	Dropped on the night of 31 December–1 January. Contact was quickly made with the district leader. The area had eight 'Foscott' priority targets, nine 'Carmarthen' targets and twenty-four smaller targets and therefore there was a significant amount of preparatory work to ensure that all these sites were protected. Instruction was also undertaken in both tactics and the use of weapons and explosives. To help training, a camp was set up outside Oslo. On 10 May, all the primary and secondary targets in Oslo were successfully taken over by protection units from D.13.
December 1944 (Air)	**Farnborough V** (K. Fossen, J. Opåsen)	To cover District 14.3, the area around Gjøvik north of Oslo.	Dropped on 29 December. Contact was quickly made with the district leader, but Opåsen was killed in a shooting accident during a training exercise. Nevertheless, over the following months, preparations to protect local targets, such as the Raufoss Ammunition Factory, continued along with the training of local recruits.
December 1944 (Air)	**Farnborough VI** (H. Stridsklev, G. Bjaali, K. Fjell)	District 15, the west side of Oslo fjord.	Dropped on the night of 28/29 December. (There is little information on this operation.)

Date	Operation	Objectives	Details
December 1944 (Air)	**Farnborough VII** (J. Irminger, J. Stensnes)	District 17, most of the county of Telemark in southern Norway.	Dropped on 1 January. *Milorg* men had formed cells in the hills and this was where early training began. Detailed plans were also drawn up for the protection of key sites such as Hauen Transformer Station.
December 1944 (Air)	**Avocet** (T. Lien, A. Floisand, J. Thu, I. Tonseth)	To reinforce 'Osprey' in the Stavanger area, organize sabotage cells along lines of communication, reconnoitre Sola aerodrome and dropping places, provide protection for vital plants.	It was dropped on 31 December and its radio station came on air on 9 January. The party was instructed to work with *Milorg*, although contact should be infrequent. A meeting with the DL for D19 was held but an instruction programme was delayed owing to a lack of weapons. There was only one drop in January, none in February and Stavanger had no weapons at all until a small amount was moved there at the end of March. At the liberation, 500 men were mobilized but only half had received weapons training. Protection of local sites also proved difficult.
November/December 1944 (Stockholm)	**Freethorpe** (F. Baarnes, I. Rogne, A. Solbakken, A. E. Larsen)	To protect the repeater station at Mo i Rana, attack railway communications and obtain intelligence on German troop movements using a group organized among the local railwaymen.	In September 1944, Odin Normann, a trades union courier, offered to build up an organization among the railwaymen in Mo i Rana. 'Quaver' was originally to contact Normann but after this failed a group was organized in Stockholm under 2nd Lt. Baarnes that through Normann and a Swedish contact formed a base just inside the Swedish border from where it was instructed to carry out its tasks. It would also have a W/T station 'Fulmar' to assist it. Eventually, attacks were carried out against the railway bridge north of Mo in February and the railway in April. At the liberation, 'Freethorpe' proceeded to Mo i Rana and assisted the local *Milorg* forces.

Date	Operation	Objectives	Details
January 1945 (Stockholm)	**Farnborough VIII** (P. Emblemsvåg, E. Boyesen, J. Elvestad)	To work in D.23, around Lillehammer and the Gudbrandsdal.	Crossed into Norway early in February and met the *Milorg* district leader at Tretten. They were instructed to plan protection of important sites in the area and instruct local groups in weapons and guerrilla tactics. Operating in this area, however, proved difficult, especially as the Wehrmacht had its HQ at Lillehammer. There were several confrontations with German patrols and in one of them Boyesen was killed. Nevertheless, in the early morning of 10 May, *Milorg* successfully took control of the important sites in the area.
January 1945 (Sea)	**Polar Bear VIII** (F. A. Søreida)	To protect the ports of Haugesund and Odda.	Sailed on 12 January and with the help of 'Arquebus' eventually arrived at Haugesund. He eventually undertook protective preparations at both ports.
January 1945 (Sea)	**Polar Bear III** (O. Drønen, J. Jensen)	To cover the port of Bergen.	Sailed on 16 January and eventually arrived at Bergen where they met the district leader for D20.2. It was discovered that the Germans had made preliminary preparations to demolish some quays. Two hundred men from *Milorg* were made ready to assist and preparations were made to protect the port. At the liberation, all the charges that the Germans had laid were disabled.
January 1945 (Sea)	**Polar Bear IV** (F. Åsmund Færøy)	To cover Stavanger.	Sailed on 16 January and landed on Bømlo north of Haugesund. Færøy was, however, arrested as he tried to get to Stavanger.
January 1945 (Stockholm)	**Polar Bear VI-W** (S. Skelfjord)	To cover Larvik, Sandefjord and Tønsberg on the west side of Oslo fjord.	He arrived in the area from Stockholm in January and worked closely with *Milorg*. In early March, he reported that he had completed his preparations.

Date	Operation	Objectives	Details
January 1945 (Stockholm)	**Polar Bear VI-Oslo** (S. Egede-Nissen, J. Helen)	To cover Oslo.	Arrived in the area on 19 January and at the end of the month made contacts with *Milorg* and harbour employees. Groups were trained but there were few signs that the Germans were preparing to destroy the quays. Nevertheless, training continued and on 8 May *Milorg* groups entered the harbour area and took up their positions. On 9 May, *Milorg* together with German guards began to patrol the harbour network.
January 1945 (Sea)	**Razorbill** (H. Rasmussen)	See above.	Rasmussen had returned to the UK to obtain equipment for Bjørn West. While in London it was agreed that targets in the Bergen area would be protected by B.org groups. Eventually, however, it was *Milorg* that organized protection of primary 'Foscott' targets in Bergen, while secondary targets were looked after by B.org.
January 1945 (Stockholm)	**Polar Bear VI-E** (I. Steensland)	To cover the harbours of Fredrikstad and Moss on the east side of Oslo harbour.	Arrived from Sweden on 23 January. The Germans had made preparations to destroy the harbour at Fredrikstad. Steensland was given a group of 120 men from *Milorg*. Contacts within the harbour were made, intelligence gathered and instruction commenced. In Moss, 100 men from *Milorg* were also trained in harbour protection. Early in February, Steensland assisted by *Milorg* organized the capture of a total of eleven tugboats from Moss and Fredrikstad and they were sailed to Sweden. He returned to Norway in early March and continued preparation, although his men lacked weapons. He then captured a cargo boat and small tanker and organized their disappearance to Sweden. He returned to Fredrikstad on 2 May and after the liberation, claiming he was from the Allied Commission in Oslo, persuaded the Germans to remove all their guards from the harbour.

Date	Operation	Objectives	Details
January 1945 (Stockholm)	**Coton** (A. Hegstad, L. Sandin, L. Langaas, J. Gundersen)	This was a plan, presented in early November 1944, to set up a base on Swedish territory from where the railway south of Mosjoen could be attacked. The main target was the Trolldal viaduct.	Hegstad travelled to reconnoitre the area around Atosstugan in Sweden at the end of January 1945 and the other men followed during February. By the middle of March, there were a total of fourteen living at the base, and on 21 April some of them cut the railway in two places north of Majavatn. At the liberation, the Coton party proceeded to Mosjoen and took over leadership of the resistance groups.
January 1945 (Sea)	**Corsham** (K. Stoltenberg, G. Berg, O. Bergh)	To protect Follafoss power station and Folden dam north of Trondheim.	Landed on 29 January and proceeded to the area of the targets. They were instructed to work independently but this proved impossible. Their radios were also damaged and eventually they decided to cross the border into Sweden, arriving in Stockholm on 6 March. They did not return to the area.
February 1945 (Stockholm)	**Polar Bear II** (L. Hauge, T. Renaas)	To cover the port of Trondheim.	The party arrived in Trondheim on 7 February. It was met by Gjems-Onstad who was coordinating the 'Lark' and 'Durham' operations. The Germans had made some preparations to blow up the quays but it was initially difficult to obtain recruits from within the harbour area to help. Eventually fifteen men from 'Lark' and fifty men from 'Durham' were transferred to 'Polar Bear' and training commenced. Unfortunately, weapons drops did not materialize. In April 1945, 'Polar Bear' was placed under the district leader for D.22, and on 9 May the team, consisting of 130, took over the harbour in Trondheim. Leif Hauge also took over the ports at Steinkjer and Namsos.

Date	Operation	Objectives	Details
Antrum (K. Aarsæther)	**Antrum** (K. Aarsæther)	To re-establish W/T contact with the UK, organize protection of certain 'Foscott' targets around Ålesund and provide arms instruction.	In January both K. J. Aarsæther and the *Milorg* district leader (DL) were brought back to the UK for conversations. It was decided that Knut Aarsæther would work better with the DL and he was sent back to the Ålesund area on 13–14 February. Radio contact was re-established on 17 February. Organization within the area continued and by mid-April there were 1,500 men prepared but without weapons, although in the final weeks of the occupation supplies did increase.
February 1945 (Sea)	**Diver** (P. Skram, T. Jørgen)	To act as military adviser to the district leader in Ålesund and in this role plan actions to protect local sites, assist the Allies in the event of an invasion or hamper a German withdrawal.	Sailed with the DL on 13 February. He had been given a new directive while in the UK. Contact would be established with SL in Oslo and the district, D.21, extended and divided into three subdistricts. *Milorg* groups would also be built up and trained. Contact was made with Oslo and approval given.
February 1945 (Sea)	**Crowfield** (B. Hasle, B. Lier, A. Vibe)	An operation to protect Moholt transformer station and Trondheim repeater station and to instruct and lead the local groups recruited for these tasks.	The operation commenced when Hasle and Lier were flown to Stockholm on 15 February. The group left for the border on 1 March but for various reasons this first attempt was abandoned. On 17 April, Hasle travelled via Oslo to Trondheim, arriving on 26 April. Vibe then left for Norway with another man and W/T contact was eventually established with Trondheim on 11 May. The targets were occupied on 9 May.

Date	Operation	Objectives	Details
February 1945 (Stockholm)	**Farnborough X** (E. Næss, N. Uri)	To cover D.25, centred on Hamar in eastern Norway.	The party arrived in Stockholm on 12 February and a few days later travelled to the district and met the DL. He had already received instructions to organize the protection of selected 'Foscott' targets, which the expedition was instructed to assist.
February 1945 (Air- Stockholm)	**Farnborough IX** (O. Berg)	To cover D.26, centred on Tynset and Alvdal in Hedemark in eastern Norway.	Arrived in Sweden on 19 January and reached the district on 14 February where he made himself available to the DL and assisted with preparations for the protection of 'Foscott' targets.
February 1945 (Air- Stockholm)	**Sparrow** (N. Gabrielsen)	To give *Milorg* W/T operators extra training and to assist them in ensuring a reliable communication service with the UK. If required to assist W/T operators outside Oslo.	Norman Gabrielsen had been working with SL since autumn 1943. This was a continuation of his earlier work.
February 1945 (Stockholm)	**Sepals III** (L. Schanche, B. Bjølseth, O. Mjeide)	To organize the despatch of operation 'Crofton', carry out certain sabotage activities, maintain contact with *Milorg*, provide instruction and, when possible, supply them with weapons.	Preparations began in January (see above). Several acts of sabotage were undertaken from this base.

Date	Operation	Objectives	Details
February 1945 (Stockholm)	**Dunkerton** (E. Jacobsen, S. Hårstad, M. Uglem, A. Aksnes)	To protect power stations at Nea, south-east of Trondheim.	All the men were recruited in Sweden and trained there. By 18 February, they were in Norway, meeting and developing contacts in the area. By mid-March, however, due to German activity the group was back in Stockholm. The whole group was back in Norway by the end of April
February 1945 (Stockholm)	**Chacewater** (S. Armtsen, A. Larsen, K. Stordalen)	To organize protection of 'Foscott' targets in D.16, in Telemark and Buskerud.	Dropped on 21 February, the group made contact with DL for D.16. Targets around Kongsberg were agreed and training of local cells began. German raids, however, soon followed and in clashes a number of enemy troops were killed, which led to further raids and the loss of equipment. Nevertheless, by the time of the liberation 'Chacewater' had 300 men under them and together they took over their targets intact.
February 1945 (Air)	**Redstart** (I. Birkeland, C. Johnsen)	See above.	In January, Birkeland returned to the UK. He returned to Norway on 21 February and the priority was to protect certain important sites in the area (see above).
February 1945 (Sea)	**Bjørn West** (B. Eliassen)	See above.	Further reinforcement.
February 1945 (Sea)	**Turkey** (A. Pevik, U. Axelsen)	To join the other SOE groups operating in the Oslo area and work with them under the authority of SL and the direct command of Gunnar Sønsteby.	Dropped on 22 February and became part of the 'Oslo Gang' operating under Sønsteby.

Date	Operation	Objectives	Details
February 1945 (Air)	**Polar Bear I** (L. Larsen, B. Rist)	To cover the port of Narvik.	Arrived at the 'Sepals II' base on 22 February and brought, with the help of Swedish soldiers, significant supplies. Contacts were made with *Milorg* in D.40 and with Kyllingmark, head of the 'Sepals' operation. Stores were moved closer to Narvik and training undertaken but activity by enemy troops meant that progress was slow.
February 1945 (Air-Stockholm)	**Farnborough IV**	To cover D14.1, Buskerud and Telemark.	Was due to be landed on 23 February but the operation was replaced by 'Chacewater'.
February 1945	**Griffon** (A. Ratche, A. Engebretsen)	To reinforce the 'Grebe' party and help undertake railway sabotage.	Both 'Griffon' and 'Guillemot' with two Norwegian army officers were dropped on 24 February and assisted 'Grebe' in its area.
February 1945 (Air)	**Guillemot** (B. Sevendal, K. Bredsen)	See above.	
February 1945 (Air)	**Cramlington** (Cpl. Y. Øgaard, 2. Lt. J. Kvarme, 2. Lt. H. Hansen),	To act as a reception party for Operation Waxwing (see below).	At the end of January, it was decided that H. Ryan (see above) and these three would act as a reception party for Operation Waxwing. There were problems with the Swedish authorities on the border and it was eventually the end of February before the party successfully crossed into Norway. The 'Waxwing' party was dropped on 24 March.
March 1945 (Stockholm)	**Clothall** (A. Johnsen, W. Hansen, J. Melsom, L. Aagard, B. Pettersen W/T operator from Sweden)	To provide protection for the power stations at Askim, south-east of Oslo, which supplied power to the capital.	Eventually dropped on 3 March and after a long march arrived in D.11. They began to reconnoitre the targets, draw up plans and organize local protection groups. Employees from within the targets were also trained in protection skills. By the end of April, these groups were made up of 4–500 men. From 7 May, 'Clothall' was mobilized and over the following days occupied its targets.

Date	Operation	Objectives	Details
March 1945 (Air)	**Crofton** (E. Juden, L. Schanke, O. Mjelde, B. Bjølset)	To protect power, repeater and telecommunications stations around Mo i Rana.	Left Stockholm in March to join up with the Sepals III base.
March 1945 (Stockholm)	**Caldy I** (2nd Lt. Songe-Møller)	The objective was to protect various power stations and repeater stations in D.18, in southern Norway. The party was instructed to work for the district leader and to have *Milorg* groups working for it.	This operation was instructed to take care of Høgefoss and Even Stadfoss power station, but little detail of this operation has survived.
March 1945 (Air)	**Cormorant I** (B. Stenseth)	To reinforce the district leadership and increase the preparedness of the D14.3.	Dropped on the night of 3 March. Stenseth carried out further training in the area.
March 1945 (Air)	**Sepals Gorgon**	See above.	See above.
March 1945	**Orm** (B. Hansen, B. Sætre)	To establish a reception base centred on Trysil in eastern Norway.	The first party was dropped on 3 March and included a W/T operator. Radio contact was made with the UK and a group of four with the base leader, Captain Aasen, arrived from Sweden. Supplies were initially limited and a strong German presence meant a lot of the work continued from across the Swedish border. Nevertheless, cooperation with *Milorg* was good and supplies and further teams arrived from Stockholm. At the German surrender, the Orm leadership with seventy-five men crossed the border. On 9 May, they accepted the surrender from the local German commandant.

Date	Operation	Objectives	Details
March 1945 (Air and Stockholm)	**Rook** (L. Petteresen, C. Tønseth)	This was partly a plan, originally called Operation Tiger, to kidnap a German naval officer, *Kapitan zur see*, Hans Roesing, who it was believed was the authority behind U-boat operations out of Bergen. The party was also instructed to organize sabotage and intelligence groups to undertake the work previously carried out by Saborg and BAR.	Arrived on 11 March but failed to locate its target. The team worked closely with the *Milorg* DL and at the beginning of May made contact with the German commander in Bergen. On 8 May, the Gestapo left the town and on 9 May around 1,100 local men were mobilized and occupied the important points in the locality.
March 1945 (Sea)	**Puffin** (S. Blindheim)	See above.	
March 1945 (Stockholm)	**Wren** (K. J. Aarsæther, T. Baakind, A. Øvre, E. Sem-Jacobsen)	The original objective was to carry out sabotage against communication lines south of Steinkjer.	The plan was to drop the party but this did not happen and eventually it was sent to Stockholm. Towards the end of April, the group, strengthened by six men trained in Sweden, went into Norway. By this stage, it had been decided that its role should change to a series of protective tasks. At the end of April, it was decided that Lt. G. Klem should join the party and its name was changed to 'Wren Antipodes' with the task of protecting Gudaa railway bridge. Whether or not Klem entered Norway is unclear.

Date	Operation	Objectives	Details
March 1945 (Air- Stockholm)	**Whinchat** (R. Holter)	To reinforce the DL and increase the preparedness of the district.	Holter was to be dropped on the night of 22 March.
March 1945 (Air)	**Chaffinch** (F. Solheim, O. Aas)	To work in D.17, in Telemark, to carry out instruction for *Milorg* groups in the area.	This was the last expedition to this district and training was undertaken over the following weeks.
March 1945 (Air)	**Waxwing** (twelve men from the Norwegian Parachute Company)	The objective was to help with attempts to delay German withdrawals from northern Norway by attacking the railway between Grong and Majavatn, north of Trondheim.	The original plan was to drop a group of twenty-four, but on the night of 24–25 March a party of only twelve was dropped under the command of Major Ole Jacob Bangstad. The 'Cramlington' party received them. On 15 April, they attacked the railway 50 kilometre north of Grong and destroyed 400 metres of line. On 21 April, the group raided Namskogen station, destroying crossings and switches. On 23 April, the group blew up 800 yards of rail north of Trongfors. Bangstad returned to Stockholm at the end of April and the group moved to a base across the Swedish border. The group carried out work in the area after the German capitulation.
March 1945 (Air)	**Rype** (OSS operation)	The party under the command of Major William Colby was instructed to help delay German withdrawals by attacking the railway south of Grong in the county of Trøndelag.	Eight B-24 liberators took off on 24 March carrying a total of thirty-six men. Only one Norwegian and sixteen Americans were, however, eventually dropped. One plane dropped its group in Sweden and three planes returned to Scotland with their loads intact. The team was met by a reception party and eventually 'Rype' consisted of sixteen Americans and seven Norwegians. They established a base at Gjevsjøen and prepared operations. On 15 April, the group blew up Tangen bridge, and on 25 April several sections of the railway in Lurudalen. The party left Gjevsjøen on 11 May and proceeded to Steinkjer, where they remained for several days.

Date	Operation	Objectives	Details
March 1945 (Air)	**Ibrox/Quail** (SAS team)	This was a plan to drop a party of 11 SAS soldiers and two Norwegians to attack the Snåsamoen bridge in north Trondelag. 'Quail' was the reception party that would be sent from Stockholm.	Due to bad weather, 'Ibrox' was cancelled at the beginning of April. The reception party had left Stockholm on 26 March and arrived at their destination on 30 March. They made radio contact but on 4 April they were forced back to Stockholm, where they arrived three days later.
April 1945	**Medley** (R. Larsen, K. Brodkorp-Danielsen)	To protect Bårdshaug substation and Berkåk repeater station in southern Trondelag.	This operation was initially given to the 'Dodsworth' team. This team of four units, however, never used and its job was eventually taken over by the team that was to act as the reception party for 'Widgeon', a group of three that would undertake railway sabotage between Støren and Opdal. 'Widgeon' never arrived and therefore its reception party was renamed 'Medley' and took over the role originally allocated to 'Dodsworth'. It carried out its tasks at the capitulation.
April 1945	**Antipodes**	This was a plan to keep open the major routes into Norway from Sweden by protecting the bridges over the River Glomma in eastern Norway. Seven expeditions were set up in Stockholm and six UK officers were selected to assist *Milorg* and groups that were already in Norway.	Of the seven expeditions, all but two reached their destinations. The 'Wren', 'Clothall' and 'Sepals II' operations were also given an 'Antipodes' role and reinforced by additional officers. At least three officers also arrived in D.11 to assist *Milorg* in preparing for bridge protection. *Milorg* also made preparations in the border districts to protect key bridges.

Date	Operation	Objectives	Details
April 1945	**Polar Bear IV** (D. Ånestad, B. Nilsen)	To protect Stavanger.	After the failure of the first operation, this team was dropped at Årdal in southern Norway on 25 April. With the help of 'Osprey', they eventually arrived in Stavanger.
April 1945	**Landrail** (Capt. R. Kvaal, I. Fosseide, R. Arnesen)	This group was instructed to take over command of the many military groups operating in Trondelag.	Crossed the border from Sweden on 5 May and reached Trondheim on the afternoon of 8 May.
April 1945 (Stockholm)	**Bjørn West** (A. Mathiesen)	See above.	Further reinforcement.
April 1945 (Sea)	**Varg II** (P. Vexels, O. Veraas, Capt. Christophersen)	See above.	This party was dropped on 17 April and included the British liaison officer Captain Christophersen.
April 1945 (Air)	**Dipper** (O. Walderhaug, H. Roald, R. Gathaw)	This group was instructed to organize and train local *Milorg* groups and lead the protection of power stations in subdistrict 21.3.	Landed on 21 April, but arrests in the area meant they returned and arrived back in the Shetlands two days later.
April 1945 (Sea)	**Chiffchaff I** (E. Johnsen)	To carry out instruction in D.12.	Instruction was carried out until the end of the war.
April 1945 (Air)	**Varg III** (M. Sonneland, D. Sjorestad)	See above.	The camp was eventually divided into four billeting areas. The first billeting area was eventually dropped because it had not received any supplies. The second billeting area was placed under Knut Haukelid. 'Varg' also became involved in counter-scorch operations, focusing on the power stations in the Arendal area. Significant weapons for up to 2,000 men were dropped but there was still a lack of provisions and therefore the camp never really got going.

Date	Operation	Objectives	Details
April 1945 (Air)	**Bjørn West VI** (M. Eikanger)	See above.	Further reinforcement.
April 1945 (Sea)	**Caldy II and III** (A. Fjeld, J. Stumpf)	See above.	The first operation was dropped on the night of 25–26 April and the second on 2–3 May to protect Skerka and Nomeland power stations, respectively.
April/May 1945 (Air)	**Ruff** (H. Brandt)	The objective was to set up a W/T station on the coast around Sognefjord to improve communication with the reception committees that were organizing the collection of supplies or pick-ups.	Landed on 4 May only a few days before the German capitulation.
May 1945 (Sea)	**Stork** (A. Rosenberg, J. Holvik, J. Heyerdahl-Larsen)	To organize and instruct groups around Sognefjord in weapons and guerrilla warfare, link up with existing groups, receive weapons and prepare protection of local power stations and telephone exchanges.	Landed on 4 May.
May 1945 (Sea)	**Skua** (J. Wright-Flood)	To provide radio contact between the 'Siskin' group and the UK.	Landed on 4 May.

Date	Operation	Objectives	Details
May 1945 (Sea)	**Redpoll** (G. Løken)	To establish a radio station on the coast in close to Bergen and in the vicinity of a suitable landing area in order to provide a speedy means of obtaining contact with reception committees.	Landed on 4 May.
May 1945 (Air- Stockholm)	**Polar Bear V** (G. Gundersen)	To cover the port of Kristiansand.	Gundersen was sent to Stockholm on 4 April from where he travelled by boat to Høvåg outside Kristiansand, arriving just before the capitulation. The Germans had made preparations to blow up the harbour but the local German commandant agreed that nothing would be carried out. Eventually, Gundersen with a group of eighty men took over the port.
May 1945	**Polar Bear VII** (H. Kristensen, I. Skielbred)	To cover the ports of Ålesund and Veblungnes.	This was cancelled.
May 1945 (Sea)	**Redbreast** (R. Mathiesen)	The objective was to send a W/T operator to maintain W/T communication between the Bremnes and Stord area and the UK	By the time Mathiesen was sent in, the German forces in Norway had capitulated.
	Barming (G. Klem, P. Ihlen, J. Andreassen)	To protect sites in Kristiansand.	Never carried out. *Milorg* protected the objectives.
	Bracknell and Reproach	To protect various power stations sites on the Lofoten Islands.	Never carried out.

NOTES

Introduction

1 The National Archives (henceforth TNA): 'Report on the visit to Allied land forces by MO 3 colonel, 14–18 June 1945' in WO 216/568.
2 Proclamation by Johan Nygaardsvold, on 9 June 1940, in A. Moland, *Over Grensen?* (Oslo: Orion forlag, 1999), pp. 24–5.
3 O. Riste, *London regjeringa: Norge i krigsalliansen 1940–1945*, 2nd edn, vol. I, 'prøvetid', 1940–1942, vol. II, 'vegen heim', 1942–1945 (Oslo: Det Norske Samlaget, 1995), p. 20.
4 TNA: WP (40) 27, SOE Charter, 19 July 1940, in CAB 66/10.
5 TNA: HS2/175, Norwegian Section History, HS8/280, 'British Military Aid to the Occupied Territories'.
6 M. R. D. Foot, *SOE in France* (London: HMSO, 1966); and M. R. D. Foot, *SOE in the Low Countries* (London: St. Ermin's Press, 2001).
7 Charles Cruickshank, *SOE in Scandinavia* (Oxford: Oxford University Press, 1986), pp. 169, 264–6; W. J. M. Mackenzie, *The Secret History of SOE: The Special Operations Executive 1940–1945* (London: St. Ermin's Press, 2000); M. R. D. Foot, *SOE: The Special Operations Executive 1940–1946*, 2nd edn (London: Pimlico, 1999).
8 For a definition of Home Front, see H. F. Dahl et al., *Norsk krigsleksikon 1940–1945* (Oslo: J.W. Cappelen, 1995), p. 175.
9 Sverre Kjeldstadli, *Hjemmestyrkene: hovedtrekk av den militære motstanden under okkupasjonen*, vol. I (Oslo: H. Aschehoug, 1959), and Riste, *London regjeringa*.
10 K. Jespersen, *No Small Achievement: Special Operations Executive and the Danish Resistance 1940–1945* (Odense: University of Press of Southern Denmark); Knut Haukelid, *Skis against the Atom* (London: William Kimber, 1954); Jomar Brun, *Brennpunkt Vemork 1940–1945* (Oslo: Universitetsforlaget, 1985); Jens Poulsson, *Aksjon Vemork: vinterkrig på Hardangervidda* (Oslo: Gyldendal, 1993). Three recent publications are the following: O. Njølstad, *Professor Tronstads Krig* (Oslo: Aschehoug, 2015); A. Ueland, *Tungtvannsaksjonen* (Oslo: Gyldendal, 2015); A. Ueland, *Shetlandsgjengen: Heltene i Nordsjøen* (Oslo: Kagge Forlag, 2017).

11 For a definition of strategy see: Colin S. Gray, *Modern Strategy* (Oxford: Oxford University Press, 1999), p. 17; and Basil H. Liddell-Hart, *Strategy: The Indirect Approach* (London: Faber and Faber, 1967), pp. 335-6, cited in Gray, *Modern Strategy*, p. 18.
12 Kjeldstadli, *Hjemmestyrkene*, p. 329.
13 D. Stafford, *Britain and European Resistance 1940-1945: A Survey of the Special Operations Executive, with Documents* (Toronto: University of Toronto Press, 1980); J. R. M. Butler (ed.), 'Grand Strategy', vols. I-VI, in *History of the Second World War* (London: HMSO, 1957 and 1964); M. Matloff, 'Allied Strategy in Europe 1939-1945', in P. Paret (ed.), *Makers of Modern Strategy from Machiavelli to the Nuclear Age* (Oxford: Oxford University Press, 1986), pp. 677-90.
14 TNA: memorandum entitled, 'Subversive Activity in the Occupied Territories', by A. F. Brooke, Chairman, Chiefs of Staff Committee, 2 June 1942, in HS7/2.
15 See Chapter 4, pp. 71-4. Riste, *London regjeringa*, vol. I., p. 20, 72-94.
16 Gray, *Modern Strategy*, p. 163.

Chapter 1

1 D. A. T. Stafford, *Britain and European Resistance 1940-1945: A Survey of the Special Operations Executive with Documents* (Toronto: University of Toronto Press, 1980), pp. 1-50; D. Stafford, 'The Detonator Concept: British Strategy, SOE and European Resistance after the Fall of France', *Journal of Contemporary History*, vol. 10, no. 2, April 1975, pp. 185-217; Mackenzie, *The Secret History of SOE: The Special Operations Executive* (London: St. Ermin's Press, 2000), pp. 56-71.
2 Mackenzie, *Secret History of SOE*, p. 69 & note 4.
3 TNA: WP (40) 271, 19 July 1940, in CAB 66/10.
4 Stafford, *Churchill & Secret Service* (London: Abacus, 1997), pp. 14-16, 21-2, 148-61, 163-65, 219; C. Andrew, 'Churchill and Intelligence', *Intelligence and National Security*, vol. 3, no. 3, July 1988, pp. 181-93.
5 TNA: COS (40) 315 (JIC), 2 May 1940, in CAB 80/10. Stafford, *Churchill & Secret Service*, pp. 204-20. D. Stafford, 'Britain Looks at Europe, 1940: Some Origins of SOE', *Canadian Journal of History*, vol. 10, no. 2, August, 1975, p. 233.
6 P. Wilkinson and J. Bright Astley, *Gubbins and SOE*, 2nd edn (London: Leo Cooper, 1997), pp. 69-74.
7 TNA: paper entitled 'Guerrilla Warfare', 4 July 1940, in CAB 63/92. Stafford, 'Britain Looks at Europe, 1940', p. 235.
8 Stafford, 'Britain Looks at Europe, 1940', p. 239.
9 Mackenzie, *Secret History of SOE*, pp. 4-11, 38-55; M. R. D. Foot, *SOE: The Special Operations Executive 1940-1946*, 2nd edn (London: Pimlico, 1999), pp. 1-16.

10 Stafford, *Britain and European Resistance*, p. 23.
11 TNA: Hand-written account of Section D by Lawrence Grand in HS7/5.
12 COS minutes, 21 January 1937, in WO193/685, and COS 843, 20 February 1939 in CAB16/183A, in B. P. Farrell, *The Basis and Making of British Grand Strategy* (New York: Edwin Mellen Press, 1998-9), book 1, p. 50; T. Imlay, 'Allied Economic Intelligence and Strategy during the "Phoney War"', *Intelligence and National Security*, vol. 13, no. 4, October 1998, p. 107.
13 TNA: WP (40) 168, in CAB 66/7, and discussed at WM (40) 141, 27 May 1940, in CAB 65/7. Farrell, *Basis and Making of British Grand Strategy*, pp. 47-8.
14 Mackenzie, *Secret History of SOE*, pp. 56-71; Stafford, *Britain and European Resistance*, pp. 24-27.
15 TNA: COS (40) 305 (JIC), JIC (40) 36, 26 April 1940, in CAB 80/10; Mackenzie, *Secret History of SOE*, pp. 56-60, 748.
16 H. Dalton, *The Fateful Years* (London: Frederick Muller, 1957), p. 366; W. Medlicott, *The Economic Blockade*, vol. I (London: HMSO, 1952 and 1959), pp. 13-6; Stafford, *Britain and European Resistance*, pp. 11, 26, 39.
17 Dalton, *Fateful Years*, p. 367; Stafford, *Britain and European Resistance*, pp. 29-30.
18 TNA: WP (40) 271, 19 July 1940, in CAB 66/10.
19 TNA: COS (40) 27 (0), 'Subversive Activities in Relation to Strategy', 25 November 1940 in CAB 80/56. COS (42) 133 (0), 'SOE Collaboration in Operations on the Continent', 12 May 1942, in CAB 80/62; COS (43) 142 (0), 'Special Operations Executive Directive for 1943', 20 March 1943, in CAB 80/68; COS (44) 957 (0), 'Directive to Special Operations Executive', 9 November 1944, in CAB 80/89.
20 TNA: COSSAC (43) 58 (final), 2 October 1943, in WO 219/40B; SHAEF/17240/13/Ops (A), 23 March 1944, 'Operational Directive to SFHQ', in WO219/4967, which states that at the COS (43) 237th meeting (0) on 15 October 1943, SOE activities were finally placed under COSSAC.
21 Stafford, *British and European Resistance*, p. 153.
22 Mackenzie, *Secret History of SOE*, pp. 75-84.
23 TNA: 'Personnel Employed by SOE', and 'Comparison of Total RAF Bomber Command Sorties from UK with those carried out for SOE', in HS7/1.
24 M. R. D. Foot, *SOE in France* (London: HMSO, 1966), p. 16.
25 Mackenzie, *Secret History of SOE*, p. 83; M. R. D. Foot, *Resistance: An Analysis of European Resistance to Nazism, 1940-1945* (London: Eyre Methuen, 1976), p. 139.
26 TNA: paper by H. T. N. Gaitskell, 31 July 1940, in HS8/271
27 S. Kjeldstadli, *Hjemmestyrkene: hovedtrekk av den militære motstanden under okkupasjonen*, vol. I (Oslo: H. Aschehoug, 1959), pp. 56, 89.

28 Appendix C, 'A History of the Shetlands Base Autumn 1939 to May 1945', in I. Herrington, *SOE in Norway*, PhD thesis, De Montfort University, 2004, pp. 319–22.
29 TNA: paper by G. T. N. Gaitskell, 31 July 1940, in HS8/271; memo from Sir Frank Nelson to Gladwyn Jebb, 5 November 1940, in HS8/334; biographical details on Charles Hambro supplied by SOE adviser, 25 July 2001; B. Brivati, *Hugh Gaitskell* (London: Richard Cohen, 1996), pp. 43–62.
30 Biographical details on Charles Hambro supplied by SOE adviser, 25 July 2001.
31 Ibid.
32 B. Bramsen and K. Wain, *The Hambros, 1779–1979* (London: M. Joseph, 1979); H. F. Dahl et al., *Norsk Krigsleksikon, 1940–1945* (Oslo: J.W. Cappelen, 1995), p. 155.
33 T. Lie, *Med England i ildlinjen, 1940–1942* (Oslo: Tiden Norsk Forlag, 1956), p. 61.
34 FO 837/24, as cited in C. Goulter, *A Forgotten Offensive* (London: Frank Cass, 1995), p. 116.
35 TNA: 'Diary of Scandinavian Tour', summer 1945, by J. S. Wilson, in HS9/ 1402/6. Medlicott, *The Economic Blockade*, vol. I, pp. 152–61. Statement of Thorry Kiær, director of the Orkla Mining Co., 18 July 1945, in Kjeldstadli, *Hjemmestyrkene*, p. 354. Appendix A, 'SOE *Coup de Main* Operations in Norway: 1940–1944', pp. 207–18.
36 TNA: 'Minutes of the First and Second Meetings of the Board of Directors, 30 August and 10 September 1940', in HS8/194; memo from Sir Frank Nelson to D, Lawrence Grand, August 1940, and memo from Lt. J. L. Chaworth-Musters to Sir Frank Nelson in August 1940, in HS2/238.
37 'Norwegian Expedition' (probably early May 1940), in HS2/ 241, and 'Log of V.2.S – Aberdeen to Norway and Return', 17 June 1940, in HS2/242.
38 Appendix A, 'SOE *Coup de Main* Operations in Norway: 1940–1944', pp. 207–18.
39 TNA: hand-written account of Section D by Lawrence Grande, in HS7/5.
40 Ibid. A. Haga, *Skygger over Utvær* (Oslo: J. W. Cappelens, 2001), pp. 15–27.
41 Letter from 'SOE Adviser', 29 November 2000, including information from the personal file of Frank Stagg. A. Judd, *The Quest for C: Sir Mansfield Cumming and the foundation of the British Secret Service* (London: Harper-Collins, 1999), p. 326.
42 *Norges Hjemmefront museum*, henceforth (NHM): 'Paralysing of Ship Movement on Norway's West Coast', 14 December 1940, from F. Stagg to Lt. Col. H. N. Sporborg; 'Proposals for Raids on Northern Norway from Iceland', 17 December 1940, from F. Stagg to Lt. Col. H. N. Sporborg, both in SOE archive, Boks 1.
43 Appendix B, 'Sea-Borne Operations Instigated by or Involving SOE, along the Norwegian Seaboard 1940–1944', pp. 219–28.

44 TNA: 'Report of No. 13 Military Mission to Norway', in HS8/261; Wilkinson and Astley, *Gubbins and SOE*, pp. 50–68.
45 Foot, *SOE: The Special Operations Executive, 1940–1946*, pp. 8–11; Stafford, *Britain and European Resistance*, p. 31.
46 Wilkinson and Astley, *Gubbins and SOE*, pp. 50–68.
47 TNA: personal file of John Skinner Wilson, in HS9/1605/3; IWM: J. S. Wilson, *Memories of a Varied Life*, Documents 16849, pp. 4, 70–1, 73.
48 TNA: 'War Diary and Intelligence Summary – MIR War Office Commanding Officer, Lt. Col. J. C. F. Holland DFC RE', in HS8/263; A. Croft, *A Talent for Adventure* (London: Hanley Swan, 1991), pp. 140–4; M. Munthe, *Sweet Is War* (London: Duckworth, 1954).
49 TNA: handwritten record by J. M. Addis of a meeting with C. Hambro, 4 February 1941, in FO371/29408; Munthe, *Sweet Is War*, pp. 53–114; C. G. Mckay, *From Information to Intrigue: Studies in Secret Service Based on the Swedish Experience, 1939–1945* (London: Frank Cass, 1993), p. 76.
50 McKay, *From Information to Intrigue*, pp. 76–8.
51 TNA: handwritten record by J. M. Addis of a meeting with C. Hambro, 4 February 1941, letter from Victor Mallet to Henry Hopkinson in the British Foreign Office dated 5 February 1941, note by J. Addis, 5 March 1941, all in FO371/29408
52 TNA: draft letter to Mr Victor Mallet in Stockholm from Charles Hambro, 15 September 1941; letter from H. N. Sporborg to Peter Loxley, Foreign Office, 27 September 1941; draft note for a meeting with Sir Charles Hambro, 15 October 1941, all in FO371/29697; letter from Lt. Col. J. S. Wilson to E. Nielsen, 23 January 1944, in HS2/128.
53 Linge was injured in the leg and evacuated to England on 30 April. The often-cited claim that appears to have originated from the Norwegian Section history that Linge arrived in Britain in September 1940 is incorrect. TNA: memo from Lt. J. L. Chaworth-Musters to Colonel G. F. Taylor, 17 August 1940, in HS2/240; HS7/174, 'History of the Norwegian Section'; E. Haavardsholm, *Martin Linge, min morfar* (Oslo: Gyldendal, 1993), pp. 98–135; Kjeldstadli, *Hjemmestyrkene*, p. 59.
54 TNA: note headed 'Section D', 7 August 1940; memo from J. L. Chaworth-Musters to Colonel G. F. Taylor, 17 August 1940; note from J. L. Chaworth-Musters to Sir Frank Nelson, 16 September 1940; and paper headed 'Norway', 1 September 1940, all in HS2/240; paper entitled, 'Norwegian Project', 3 November 1940, in HS2/128; H. Koht, *For fred og fridom i krigstid, 1939–1940* (Oslo: Tiden Norsk Forlag, 1957), pp. 265–6.
55 TNA: 'Norwegian Project', 3 November 1940, in HS2/128; note headed 'Section D', 7 August 1940, in HS2/240.
56 NHM: 'Consolidated Progress reports of S Section', weeks ending 28 January, 4 and 25 February 1941, in SOE archive, Boks 3a; TNA: 'SOE Executive Committee Weekly Progress Reports', weeks ending 30 January and 6 March 1941, in HS8/216.

57 NHM: 'Consolidated Progress reports of S Section' during the months of January to April in SOE archive, Boks 3a; TNA: HS7/174, 'History of the Norwegian Section'.
58 TNA: 'SOE Executive Committee Weekly Progress Reports', report for week ending 29 October 1941, in HS8/218.
59 Not all of those trained went on to work for SOE. TNA: HS7/175, 'Norwegian Section-History Appendices', Appendix B – 'A Short History of the Linge Company'; HS7/51, 'History of SOE's Training Section'.
60 NHM: 'Consolidated Progress reports of S Section', week ending 8 March in SOE archive, Boks 3a; information from the London archive of *E-kontoret*, cited in R. Ulstein, *Englandsfarten*, vol. II (Oslo: Det Norske Samlaget, 1965 and 1967), p. 375; J. W. Irvine, *The Waves Are Free: Shetland/Norway Links, 1940–1945* (Lerwick: Shetland, 1988), p. 34.
61 TNA: file HS2/238; NHM: 'Consolidated Progress reports of S Section', week ending 18 February in SOE archive, Boks 3a; *Den Norske regjerings virksomhet: fra 9 April til 22 Juni 1945*, vol. IV, *forsvarsdepartementet* (Oslo: Aschehoug, 1948), pp. 101–2; Haavardsholm, *Martin Linge, min morfar*, pp.148–86.
62 TNA: HS7/175, 'Norwegian Section-History Appendices', Appendix B – 'A Short History of the 'Linge Company'; and O. Riste, *London regjeringa: Norge i krigsalliansen, 1940–1945*, vol. 1, 2nd edn (Oslo: Det Norske Samlaget, 1995), p. 119.
63 TNA: minutes of ANCC of 4 March 1942 and of a special meeting held on 13 May 1942, in HS2/138; HS7/174, 'Norwegian Section-History'; NHM: replies by Colonel J. S. Wilson to a joint note by Major Helle and Major Hampton of STS 26, 31 March 1942, in FOIV archive, Boks 31; Kjeldstadli, *Hjemmestyrkene*, p. 63; Haavardsholm, *Martin Linge, min morfar*, p. 197; Mackenzie, *Secret History of SOE*, p. 198.
64 TNA: HS7/175, 'Norwegian Section – History', Appendix B – 'A Short History of the Linge Company'.
65 David Stafford, *Secret Agent: Britain's Wartime Secret Service* (London: BBC, 2002), p. 46.
66 D. Howarth, *The Shetlands Bus* (Lerwick: Shetland Times, 1998); F. Sælen, *Shetlands Larsen* (Oslo: J.W. Eides, 1948); Sir Brooks Richards, 'Britain and Norwegian Resistance: Clandestine Sea Transport', in P. Salmon (ed.), *Britain and Norway in the Second World War* (London: HMSO, 1995), pp. 161–6.
67 For example, see details of the 'Maundy', 'Vestige', 'Barbara' and 'Sleeping Beauty' operations in Appendix B, 'Sea-Borne Operations Instigated by or Involving SOE along the Norwegian Seaboard', pp. 219–28.
68 NHM: list of Shetland sea-sorties in SOE archive, Boks 9; A. Ueland, *Shetlandsgjengen: Heltene i Nordsjøen* (Oslo: Kagge Forlag, 2017), pp. 333, 337, 414–43.

69 Nagell: Beretning om E-kontorets virksomhet, 1.1.41–1.7.44, cited in Riste, *London regjeringa*, vol. I, p. 111; Irvine, *The Waves Are Free*, p. 34.
70 According to Berit Nøkleby, SIS's first sailing from Peterhead was in July 1941 and the last in November 1943. TNA: HS2/182, 'Shetlands Base'; HS2/175, 'Norwegian History – Appendices', Appendix A – 'A Short History of the Shetlands Base'; Nøkleby, *Pass godt på Tirpitz* (Oslo: Gyldendal, 1988), pp. 61–70.
71 NHM: list of Shetland-sea sorties in SOE archive, Boks 9; TNA: HS7/182, 'Shetlands Base – a Summary of Operations'; SOE Executive Committee Weekly Progress reports, weeks ending 21 January and 25 March 1942, in HS8/220; note from Major F. W. Ram to Lt. Col. J. S. Wilson, 23 January 1942 and letter from Finn Nagell, 18 December 1941, in HS2/139; Ueland, *Shetlandsgjengen*, p. 444–5.
72 Appendix B, 'Sea-Borne Operations Instigated by or Involving SOE along the Norwegian Seaboard 1940–1945', pp. 219–28.
73 NHM: SOE archive, Boks 11, Wilson's file, Appendix K, 'Summary of Air Operations to Norway 1942–1945'; list of Shetland sea-sorties, in Boks 9.
74 TNA: JP (41) 649, 'Special Operations Executive', report by JPS, 9 August 1941, in CAB79/13.
75 TNA: file HS7/4- D Section; Ueland, *Shetlandsgjengen*, pp. 59–62.
76 TNA: 'Operations in Scandinavia', 14 April 1940, in HS2/239.
77 TNA: 'Log of V.2.S – Aberdeen to Norway and Returning', 17 June 1940, in HS2/242; Ulstein, *Etterretningstjenesten*, vol. 1, pp. 92–5.
78 TNA: 'Log of V.2.S – Aberdeen to Norway and returning', 17 June 1940, in HS2/242; A. Haga, *Natt på norske kysten: den hemmelige militære nordsjøtrafikk, 1940–1943* (Oslo: J.W. Cappelen, 1979), pp. 27–39. Riste, *London regjeringa*, vol. 1, pp. 99–101.
79 Bickham Sweet-Escott claims that 'in the summer of 1940 the Balkan section of "D" was the only really operative part of the organisation'. No mention is made of Scandinavia; B. Sweet-Escott, *Baker Street Irregular* (Fakenham: Cox & Wyman, 1965), pp. 34, 39.
80 TNA: 'Norwegian Project', 3 November 1940, in HS2/128; 'Rebellion in Norway', undated in HS2/218; note headed 'Section D', 7 August 1940, in HS2/240; note on a conference held on 24 October 1940, in HS2/240; HS7/182-Shetlands Base; Letter from Charles Hambro to Admiral R. J. P. Brind, A.C.N.S. (H), 9 February 1943, with attached memo dated 8 February 1943, in HS8/827; Nøkleby, *Pass godt på Tirpitz*, p. 59; Lie, *Med England i ildlinjen*, p. 284.
81 TNA: HS7/175, Norwegian Section-History, Appendix A – 'A Short History of the Shetlands Base'.
82 TNA: Letter from Charles Hambro to Admiral R. J. P. Brind, A.C.N.S. (H), 9 February 1943, with attached memo dated 8 February 1943, in HS8/827.
83 NHM: SOE archive, Boks 11, Wilson's file, Appendix 'Q', 'Norwegian Liaison with Naval Authorities'.

84 Berit Nøkleby refers to four trips in the 1940–1 season that have the reference 'SS'. This was SOE's cryptogram for John Rognes and *Milorg* and does not stand for Secret Services. NHM: List of Shetland sea-sorties in SOE archive, Boks 9; Nøkleby, *Pass godt på Tirpitz*, pp. 59–60, 166.
85 TNA: HS7/175, Norwegian Section-History, Appendix A – 'A Short History of the Shetlands Base'.
86 NHM: SOE archive, Boks 11, Wilson's file, Appendix 'Q', 'Norwegian Liaison with Naval Authorities'.
87 TNA: HS7/175, Norwegian Section-History, Appendix A – 'A Short History of the Shetlands Base'; HS7/182, Shetlands Base.
88 B. Hafsten et al., *Flyalarm, luftkrigen over Norge, 1939–1945* (Oslo: Sem & Stenersen, 1991), p. 294; W. Mohr, 'The Contribution of the Norwegian Air Forces', in Salmon (ed.), *Britain and Norway in the Second World War*, pp. 94–5.
89 TNA: HS2/151, Operation Cheese, 1942–1945; NHM: Boks 11, Wilson's file, Appendix K, 'Summary of Air Operations to Norway, 1942–1945'; Nøkleby, *Pass godt på Tirpitz*, p. 17.
90 Foot, *SOE: The Special Operations Executive*, pp. 132–3; Foot, *SOE in France*, p. 75.
91 Stafford, *Britain and European Resistance*, p. 61.
92 Foot, *SOE in France*, p. 473; NHM: SOE archive, Wilson's file, Appendix K, 'Summary of Air Operations to Norway'.
93 NHM: Boks 11, Wilson's file, Appendix K, 'Summary of Air Operations to Norway, 1942–1945'.
94 A. F. Egner and S. W. Aasland, *BBC: Kanonen spiller Chopin: Flybårne forsyninger til Milorg i Norge 1940–1945* (Lysaker: A. F. Egner, 1997), p. 38.
95 Twelve operations were flown on behalf of SIS. Nøkleby, *Pass godt på Tirpitz*, p. 166, 174; for details of the SOE operations, see Appendix C, 'SOE Long-Term and Miscellaneous Operations in Norway, 1940–1945', pp. 229–79.
96 TNA: COS (43) 142 (0); Nøkleby, *Pass godt på Tirpitz*, p. 166.
97 Hafsten et al., *Flyalarm*, p. 275; B. Balchen, *Come North with Me* (London: Hodder & Stoughton, 1959), pp. 268–73.

Chapter 2

1 William Mackenzie and George Cruickshank make only scattered references to the series of policy documents on Norway. Norwegian publications are much better, although without access to SOE files in Britain they missed some important papers, especially early documents produced prior to December 1940. W. J. M. Mackenzie, *The Secret History of SOE: The Special Operations Executive* (London: St. Ermin's Press, 2000), pp. 205–6, 215, 671; C. Cruickshank, *SOE in Scandinavia*

(Oxford: Oxford University Press, 1986), pp. 172, 176, 241–2;
S. Kjeldstadli, *Hjemmestyrkene: hovedtrekk av den militære motstanden under okkupasjonen*, vol. I (Oslo: H. Aschehoug, 1959), pp. 91–3, 95–105, 174–90; O. Riste, *London regjeringa: Norge i krigsalliansen, 1940–1945*, vol. I, 2nd edn (Oslo: Det Norske Samlaget, 1995), pp. 108, 114–5.
2 A. Danchev and D. Todman (eds), *War Diaries 1939–1945: Field Marshall Lord Alanbrooke* (London: Weidenfield & Nicolson, 2001), p. 438.
3 See B. P. Farrell, *The Basis and Making of British Grand Strategy*, book I (New York: Edwin Mellen Press, 1998–9), pp. 47–8.
4 T. Imlay, 'Allied Economic Intelligence and Strategy during the "Phoney War"', *Intelligence and National Security*, vol. 13, no. 4, October 1998, p. 107.
5 H. P. Willmott, *June 1944* (Poole: Blandford Press, 1984), pp. 19–20.
6 TNA: WP (40) 168, 'British Strategy in a Certain Eventuality', in CAB 66/7, and discussed at WM (40) 141, 27 May 1940, in CAB 65/7.
7 The MI (R) files refer to a number of British staff papers on this matter such as COS (40) 454 (JP) and JP (40) 238, 13 June 1940; TNA: papers entitled 'Aide -Memoir on the Co-ordination of Subversive Activities in the Conquered Territories', 6 July 1940, and 'Organisation of Rebellions in Enemy Occupied Territory', 5 July 1940, both in HS8/259; 'Appreciation of the Possibilities of Revolt in Certain Specified Countries by March 1941', 25 July 1940, in HS8/259.
8 TNA: 'Rebellion in Norway', 7 June 1940, in HS2/240; 'Rebellion in Norway', 6 August 1940, in HS2/128; 'Norway', 1 September 1940, in HS2/128; 'Norwegian Project', 3 November 1940, in HS2/128.
9 TNA: WP (40) 362, 'Future Strategy', and 'Appreciation by the Chiefs of Staff Committee', 4 September 1940, in CAB 66/11; COS 647 (JP), 'Future Strategy', note by the Joint Planning Sub-Committee, 21 August 1940, in CAB 80/16; COS minutes, 31 August 1940, in CAB 79/6, cited in Farrell, *Basis and Making of British Grand Strategy*, book I, p. 55; D. A. T. Stafford, *Britain and European Resistance, 1940–1945: A Survey of the Special Operations Executive with Documents* (Toronto: University of Toronto Press, 1980), p. 31.
10 TNA: COS (40) 27 (0), 'Subversive Activities in Relation to Strategy', 25 November 1940, in Cab 80/56; Stafford, *Britain and European Resistance*, pp. 42–9.
11 The first directive has been criticised 'as reflecting little more than the aspirations of SOE itself'. See: N. Wylie, 'An Amateur Learns His Job? Special Operations Executive in Portugal 1940–1942', *Journal of Contemporary History*, vol. 36, no. 43, July 2001, p. 443; Stafford, *Britain and European Resistance*, pp. 46–7.
12 TNA: 'German Import Trade', document of Department of Overseas Trade (IIC), 20 December 1938, in FO 837/427; C. Goulter, *A Forgotten Offensive* (London: Frank Cass, 1995), p. 304; Mackenzie, *Secret History of SOE*, p. 5.

13 TNA: Ferroy Alloys-First Report, April 1940, in FO837/108; COS (40) 334, 'Irregular Activities in Norway', report by ISPB, 9 May 1940, in CAB 80/10.
14 TNA: COS (40) 323, 5 May 1940, letter dated 3 May from the MEW to the Admiralty, in CAB 80/10; 'Norwegian Expedition', early May 1940, in HS2/ 241; and 'Log of V.2.S – Aberdeen to Norway and Return', 17 June 1940, in HS2/242; letter from A/S Bjølvefossen, 8 June 1970, cited in Riste, *London regjeringa*, vol. I, p. 100.
15 TNA: 'Rebellion in Norway', 6 August 1940, in HS2/ 128.
16 TNA: 'Norwegian Policy', 11 December 1940, signed by Lt. Col. H. N. Sporborg, in HS2/128; Kjeldstadli, *Hjemmestyrkene*, pp. 91–3; Riste, *London regjeringa*, vol. I, p. 108; I. Kraglund and A. Moland, 'Hjemmefront', vol. 6, in M. Skodvin (ed.), *Norge i krig: fremmedåk & frihetskamp, 1940–1945* (Oslo: Aschehoug, 1987), p. 26.
17 WP (40) 352, 3 September 1940, in CAB 66/11, as cited in Farrell, *Basis and Making of British Grand Strategy*, book I, pp. 62–3.
18 TNA: 'Norwegian Policy', 11 December 1940, in HS2/128.
19 TNA: letter from Gladwyn Jebb to Major General Sir H. L. Ismay, 19 February 1941, in HS8/272. See also Chapter 1, pp. 18–19.
20 TNA: 'The Prospects of Subversion: A Country by Country Analysis', 21 April 1941, in HS8/272.
21 Note from Churchill to Eden, 3 April 1941, in CAB69/2, cited in Farrell, *Basis and Making of British Grand Strategy*, book I, p. 120.
22 TNA: 'A Study of Requirements for the Organisation of Insurrection in German-Occupied territories', 21 May 1941, by Colin McV. Gubbins; 'Comments on M's Paper', note from Col. A. M. Anstruther to AD/Z, 6 June 1941; 'SO2 Programme', paper by Colonel A. M. Anstruther, 9 June 1941, all in HS8/272; COS (41) 147 (0), memo from Hugh Dalton to Winston Churchill entitled 'Outline Plan of SO2 Operations', in CAB 80/58.
23 COS minutes, 12 March 1941, in CAB 79/9; JPS minutes, 15 March 1941, in CAB84/3; COS (41) 115 (0), 22 June 1941, in CAB 80/58, all cited in Farrell, *Basis and Making of British Grand Strategy*, book I, pp. 140–3; JP (41) 444, 13 June 1941, in Cab 79/12 and JP (41) 649, 'Special Operations Executive', 9 August 1941, in CAB 79/13, cited in Stafford, *Britain and European Resistance*, pp. 59–65.
24 Stafford, *Britain and European Resistance*, pp. 58–68; and Farrell, *Basis and Making of British grand Strategy*, book I, pp. 140–57.
25 COS (41) 115 (0), 22 June 1941, in CAB 80/58, cited in Farrell, *Basis and Making of British Grand Strategy*, book one, pp. 141–3.
26 TNA: JP (41) 649, 'Special Operations Executive', 9 August 1941, in CAB 79/13, cited in Stafford, *Britain and European Resistance*, pp. 59–65; Stafford, *Britain and European Resistance*, pp. 64–6.
27 TNA: memo from L (Col. A. M. Anstruther), to AD/Z, 2 April 1941, and memo from Lt. Col. H. N. Sporborg to Charles Hambro, 30 May 1941, both in HS8/272.

28 TNA: JP (41) 388, 'Operation Dynamite', 19 May 1941, in CAB121/443; FO *arkiv boks* 196, 'Staff Study on the Establishment of Our Forces in Northern Norway', 1 July 1941, cited in Riste, *London regjeringa*, vol. I, pp. 132–3.
29 TNA: memo from Churchill to the Joint Planning Staff (JPS), 21 September 1941, in PREM 3/328/6; JP (40) 515, dated 4 October, also in PREM 3/328/6 refers to the suitability of the 'climate for operations in southern Norway during March and April'; Danchev and Todman, *War Diaries, 1939–1945*, p. 187; Riste, *London regjeringa*, vol. I, p. 107.
30 TNA: JP (41) 609, 'A Campaign in Norway', 30 July 1941; JP (41) 735, 'Operations in the North', 9 September 1941; JP (41) 763, 'Operations in Northern Norway', 17 September 1941, in CAB 121/443; CAB 98/54, 'Operation Ajax', and WO193/805, 'Operation Ajax'; note ref. D255/1, 12 September 1941, from Churchill for COS Committee, in PREM3/328/11.
31 Farrell, *Basis and Making of British Grand Strategy*, book I, pp. 162–79; TNA: COS (41) 237, 8 July 1941, minute from Churchill to COS, in CAB 121/443. For details of these operations, see Appendix B, 'Sea-Borne Operations Instigated by or Involving SOE along the Norwegian Seaboard 1940–1945', pp. 219–28.
32 A. Danchev, 'God Knows: Civil Military Relations with Allies', in A. Danchev (ed.), *On Specialness: Essays in Anglo-American Relations* (Basingstoke: Macmillan, 1998), p. 54.
33 A. Danchev, 'Great Britain: The Indirect Approach', in D. Reynolds, W. F. Kimball and A. O. Chubarian (eds), *Allies at War: The Soviet, American and British Experience, 1939–1945* (Basingstoke: Macmillan, 1994), p. 8; Farrell, *Basis and Making of British Grand Strategy*, book I, pp. 162–79.
34 TNA: 'Scandinavian Policy', 16 April 1940, in HS2/10.
35 TNA: 'Directive to the Military Organisation in Norway in Reply to Their Report dated 10 June 1941 and addressed to HM King Haakon', 17 July 1941, in HS2/231 and 232.
36 TNA: letter from Lt. Col. H. N. Sporborg to Brigadier Colin McV; Gubbins, 28 November 1941, in HS8/237.
37 D. A. T. Stafford, *Churchill & Secret Service* (London: Abacus, 1997), p. 244.
38 Churchill opposed both Operations Mandible and Claymore. TNA: a note to the prime minister from H. L. Ismay, entitled 'Operation Castle', 7 January 1941, in PREM3/328/11A. For details of these operations, see Appendix B, 'Sea-Borne Operations Instigated by or Involving SOE along the Norwegian Seaboard 1940–1945, pp. 219–28.
39 The letter was eventually sent to only Gladwyn Jebb, the chief executive officer of SOE. TNA: letter from Sir Frank Nelson to Charles Hambro, 25 March 1941 and 'Scandinavian Policy', 16 April 1941, in HS2/10; Kjeldstadli, *Hjemmestyrkene*, pp. 62–3.
40 TNA: COS (41) 217, minute from Winston Churchill, 8 July 1941, in CAB 121/443.

41 TNA: 'Directive to the Military Organisation in Norway' in reply to their report dated 10 June 1941 and addressed to HM King Haakon, 17 July 1941, in HS2/231 and 232; 'Anglo-Norwegian Collaboration Regarding the Military Organisation', 24 November 1941, in HS2/127.
42 Farrell, *Basis and Making of British Grand Strategy*, book I, pp. 273–4; M. Matloff, 'Allied Strategy in Europe 1939–1945', in P. Paret (ed.), *Makers of Modern Strategy from Machiavelli to the Nuclear Age* (Oxford: Oxford University Press, 1986), p. 685.
43 Paret, *Makers of Modern Strategy*, p. 682.
44 These were 'Arcadia', in Washington, 22 December 1941–6 January 1942; 'Symbol' at Casablanca, 14–24 January 1943; 'Trident' in Washington, 12–25 May 1943; 'Quadrant' in Quebec, 14–24 August 1943; 'Sextant' at Cairo, 22–25 November 1943; 'Eureka' at Tehran, 28 November–1 December 1943; 'Second Cairo', 3–6 December 1943. Soviet representatives attended the Tehran conference.
45 W. S. Churchill, 'The Grand Alliance', vol. III, in *The Second World War* (London: Cassell, 1948–54), pp. 574–85.
46 Appendix I, 'Memorandum by the United States and British Chiefs of Staff (WW I)', cited in M. Howard, 'Grand Strategy', vol. IV, in J. R. M. Butler (ed.), *History of the Second World War* (London: HMSO, 1972), pp. 597–9; Stafford, *Britain and European Resistance*, pp. 81–2.
47 Farrell, *Basis and Making of British Grand Strategy*, book I, pp. 285–333.
48 W. S. Churchill, 'The Hinge of Fate', vol. IV, in *The Second World War* (London: Cassell, 1948–54), pp. 303–4; Farrell, *Basis and Making of British Grand Strategy*, book I, pp. 303, 312, 323; M. C. Mann, 'British Policy and Strategy towards Norway, 1941–1945', PhD diss., University of London, pp. 143–55; Danchev and Todman, *War Diaries, 1939–1945*, pp. 261, 263, 281, 321, 333, 338, 348. G. Till, 'Naval Power', in C. McInnes and G. D. Sheffield (ed.) *Warfare in the Twentieth Century: Theory and Practice* (London: Unwin Hyman, 1988), p. 11; H. P. Willmott, 'Operation Jupiter and Possible Landings in Norway', in P. Salmon (ed.), *Britain and Norway in the Second World War* (London: HMSO, 1995), pp. 102, 105, 106.
49 In October 1941, the COS agreed to the establishment of a deception section under a 'Controller', Colonel Oliver Stanley. The first proposal for 'Hardboiled' was sent to the COS in December 1941. TNA: NID/00502/42, Operation Hardboiled, 27 January 1942, in ADM223/481; Mann, 'British Policy', pp. 217–18.
50 Deception planning was now under Lt. Col. John Bevan and the London Controlling Section (LCS). On 27 July 1942, the COS instructed LCS to provide cover for 'Torch'. The eventual plan had two parts: 'Passover', designed to contain forces in Western Europe, and 'Solo', including 'Solo I', to provide actual cover for 'Torch'. See Mann, 'British Policy', pp. 221–4.
51 TNA: COS (42) 133(0), 'SOE Collaboration in Operations on the Continent', 12 May 1942, in CAB80/62.

52 Danchev and Todman, *War Diaries 1939–1945*, p. 187.
53 TNA: 'Norway – Future Planning: Some General Observations', by Lt. Col. J. S. Wilson, 5 June 1942, in HS2/128.
54 TNA: 'The Re-conquest of Norway: SOE's Role', by Lt. Col. J. S. Wilson, 6 April 1942, in HS2/218.
55 TNA: 'Norway – Future Planning: Some General Observations', by Lt. Col. J. S. Wilson, 5 June 1942, in HS2/128.
56 TNA: letter from H. N. Sporborg, to E. O. Coote (Foreign Office), 23 September 1942, in FO898/241.
57 E. Grannes, 'Operation Jupiter: A Norwegian perspective', in P. Salmon (ed.), *Britain and Norway in the Second World War* (London: HMSO, 1995), pp. 109–18.
58 TNA: 'Norway – Future Planning: Some General Observations', 5 June 1942, in HS2/128.
59 TNA: 'Operation Instructions for Crow', 1 January 1942, in HS2/152; 'Lt. B. E. Sjøberg's Report', in HS2/148. For details of operations, see Appendix C, 'SOE Long-Term and Miscellaneous Operations in Norway, 1940–1945', pp. 231–3.
60 TNA: 'The Re-conquest of Norway: SOE's Role', 6 April 1942, in HS2/218.
61 TNA: 'Present Situation in Norway and Directive as to Future Policy', from Brigadier Colin McV. Gubbins to Lt. Col. J. S. Wilson, 26 August 1942, in HS2/232.
62 TNA: memo from Brigadier Colin McV. Gubbins to Charles Hambro, in HS2/232.
63 Danchev and Todman, *War Diaries, 1939–1945*, p. 348; Appendix III (A), COS (42) 466 (0) Final, 'American-British Strategy in 1943', 31 December 1942, cited in Howard, 'Grand Strategy', vol. IV, in Butler, *History of the Second World War*, pp. 602–13.
64 Matloff, 'Allied Strategy in Europe 1939–1945', in Paret *Makers of Modern Strategy*, pp. 691–2.
65 Mann, 'British Policy', pp. 155–62; note from prime minister to General Ismay, for COS Committee, 18 April 1943, cited in Churchill, 'Hinge of Fate' vol. IV, in *The Second World War*, pp. 847–8.
66 TNA: COS (43) 214mtg (0), 13 September 1943, and COS (43) 578 (0), report by COSSAC on preparations for an operation against Norway, 25 September 1943, both cited in CAB 122/1190; Directive to COSSAC, 29 September 1943, signed by W. S. Churchill, cited in CAB 120/656; 'Operation "Atlantis" Directive for Planning', from HQ COSSAC, G-3 (ops) Division, to AC of S, G-3, in WO219/1861; F. Morgan, *Peace and War: A Soldiers Life* (London: Hodder & Stoughton, 1961), p. 175.
67 Mann, 'British Policy', pp. 230–4.
68 C. Barnett, *Engage the Enemy More Closely* (London: Penguin, 1991), pp. 729–44; Andrew Lambert, 'Seizing the Initiative: The Arctic Convoys

1944–1945', in N. A. M. Rodgers (ed.), *Naval Power in the Twentieth Century* (London: Macmillan, 1996), pp. 151–2.
69 TNA: COS (43) 142 (0), 'Special Operations Executive Directive for 1943', 20 March 1943, in CAB80/68; COS (44) 957 (0), SOE's Fourth Directive, 9 November 1944, in CAB 80/89.
70 NHM: 'Consolidated Progress Reports of S Section', no. 5, 26 February to 13 March 1943, in SOE archive, Boks 3a, TNA: paper entitled 'Chiefs of Staff Directive to SOE for 1943', 30 March 1943, in HS8/330.
71 TNA: 'Directive for Future Sabotage Policy in Norway', from Brigadier E. E. Mockler-Ferryman to Lt. Col. J. S. Wilson, 31 May 1943, in HS2/233; 'Resume of SOE Activities in Various Theatres of War', 25 June 1943, in HS8/199.
72 TNA: 'SOE Outline Plan for Joint Activities in Norway 1943/44', 26 June 1943 in HS2/218.
73 FO arkiv (NHM), rapport om konferanse i Scotco 14.6.44., cited in Riste, *London regjeringa*, vol. II, p. 182.
74 Danchev and Todman, *War Diaries, 1939–1945*, p. 486; and Stafford, *British and European Resistance*, p. 146.
75 M. R. D. Foot, *SOE in France* (London: HMSO, 1966), p. 236; PRO: COSSAC (43) 58 (Final), 'Proposal for Control of SOE/SO Activities in North-West Europe', 2 October 1943, cited in WO219/40B.
76 TNA: SHAEF/17240/13/Ops (A), 'Operational Directive to SFHQ', 23 March 1943, in WO219/4967.
77 Ibid.
78 TNA: 'SOE/SO Directive Fortitude – Deception Plan, Extracts from Plan "Fortitude"' (SHAEF [44]), 23 February 1944, in HS2/1; Mann, 'British Policy', pp. 234–48; M. Howard, 'Strategic Deception in the Second World War', vol. V, in F. H. Hinsley et al. (eds), *British Intelligence in the Second World War: Its Influence on Strategy and Operations* (London: HMSO, 1990), 105–17.
79 F. E. Morgan, *Overture to Overlord* (London: Hodder & Stoughton, 1950), pp. 115–16.
80 Riste, *London regjeringa*, vol. II, pp. 113–274; Mann, 'British Policy', pp. 280–312.
81 Morgan, *Overture to Overlord*, pp. 89, 112–29; Riste, *London regjeringa*, vol. II, pp. 150–6, 181–8, 237–47; Mann, 'British Policy', pp. 281–366.
82 Sir Peter Thorne, 'Andrew Thorne and the Liberation of Norway', in P. Salmon (ed.), *Britain and Norway in the Second World War*, pp. 209–11.
83 Morgan, *Overture to Overlord*, p. 129; Riste, *London regjeringa*, vol. II, p. 154.
84 Morgan, *Overture to Overlord*, p. 116.
85 Riste, *London regjeringa*, vol. II, pp. 150–6, 181–8, 237–47.
86 Ibid., pp. 237, 243.
87 NHM: paper entitled 'Actions against German Controlled Norwegian State railways' in SOE archive, Boks 5.

88 TNA: 'SOE/SO Directive to the Scandinavian Region', 1 April 1944, in HS2/1.
89 NHM: 'Consolidated Progress Reports of S Section', no. 29, June 1944, in SOE archive, Boks 3a.
90 TNA: 'Outline Plan for Joint SOE/SO-FO IV Activities in Norway from August 1944', from Lt. Col. J. S. Wilson to Brigadier E. E. Mockler-Ferryman, 31 July 1944, in HS2/235.
91 TNA: 'Directive on the Employment and Development of Resistance in Norway', 3 September 1944, signed by Brigadier E. E. Mockler-Ferryman and memo from Anti-U-boat division, Naval Staff, Admiralty, to NID (Q) (SOE) 25 August 1944, in HS2/234; J. Chr. Hauge, *Rapport om mitt arbeid under okkupasjonen* (Oslo: Gyldendal, 1995), pp. 184–7.
92 TNA: Note from Lt. Col. J. S. Wilson to Brigadier E. E. Mockler-Ferryman, 1 August 1944, in HS2/235.
93 TNA: paper entitled, 'The Present Situation in Norway' from Lt. Col. J. S. Wilson to Brigadier E. E. Mockler-Ferryman, 13 August 1944, with another paper entitled, 'Co-ordination of Resistance Planning and Activities with Projected Military Operations', by Major C. S. Hampton, in HS2/236.
94 Norwegian historians based on Hauge's recollections have claimed that SHAEF issued a draft directive to SOE in June 1944 exactly along the lines that this meeting called for. There appears to be no record of a June directive in the SHAEF files at TNA or in SOE files in Oslo. TNA: 'Minutes of the Thirty-Second Meeting of the Anglo-Norwegian Collaboration Committee', 17 August 1944, in HS2/138; Kjeldstadli, *Hjemmestyrkene*, pp. 324–5; and Hauge, *Rapport om mitt arbeid under okkupasjonen*, pp. 184–6.
95 Brigadier E. E. Mockler-Ferryman was in charge of SFHQ, which reported through a special staff branch direct to General Eisenhower. This is the document that Norwegian historians claim was issued as a draft in June 1944. TNA: 'Directive on the Employment and Development of Resistance in Norway', ref. MUS/2210/1899, 3 September 1944, signed by E. E. Mockler-Ferryman, in HS2/234.
96 TNA: telegram from SHAEF G-3 Division to Scottish Command HQ, subject 'Rankin Case B-Norway', 3 October 1944, in WO219/2380. Memo from SHAEF to Scottish Command HQ, 'Rankin Case B- Norway', October 1944, in WO219/2381.
97 TNA: memo from SFHQ (Brigadier E. E. Mockler-Ferryman) to G-3 Division, SHAEF, 18 October 1944 and telegram from SHAEF to Scottish Command, 26 October 1944, in WO219/2380.
98 TNA: internal SHAEF communication to AC of S, G-3 Division, 7 November 1944, in WO219/2380; memo from SHAEF, G-3 Division, to Chief of Staff, Allied Naval Expeditionary Force, 8 November 1944 and memo from Lt. Col. J. S. Wilson to Brigadier E. E. Mockler-Ferryman, 30 November 1944, in HS2/235.

99 E. F. Ziemke, *The German Northern Theatre of Operations 1940–1945* (Washington, DC: US Government Printing Office, 1976), pp. 301–2; H. Sandvik, *Frigjøringen av Finnmark 1944–1945* (Oslo: Gyldendal, 1975), pp. 19–32; K. O. Solhjell and F. Traphagen, *Fra krig til fred: fokus på Snåsa og nord-Trøndelag* (Ål: Boksmia, 2001), pp. 61–2.
100 TNA: JIC SHAEF (44) 16 (Revised), 25 November 1944, and telegram from SHAEF Main, signed by Eisenhower, to Scotco G (ops), 2 December 1944, in WO219/2381.
101 TNA: internal SHAEF communication from Chief Plans Section, K. G. McLean, to Chief Ops Section, Col. Alms, 1 December 1944, in WO219/2381.
102 TNA: memo from SHAEF G-3 Division to ANXF (SHAEF) Air Staff, 16 April 1945, in HS2/235.
103 Willmott, *Operation Jupiter and possible landings in Norway*, p. 98.

Chapter 3

1 'Factors Governing SOE operations', 21 April 1943, COS (43) 212 (0), in CAB80/69, cited in D. A. T. Stafford, *Britain and European Resistance 1940–1945: A Survey of the Special Operations Executive with Documents* (Toronto: University of Toronto Press, 1980), p. 33.
2 O. Riste, *London regjeringa: Norge i krigsalliansen, 1940–1945*, vol. I, 2nd edn (Oslo: Det Norske Samlaget 1995), pp. 17–94.
3 To quote Sverre Kjeldstadli, 'The British scepticism towards Norwegians and the Norwegian authorities meant that the leadership within SOE insisted that a military underground movement in Norway had to be built up outside and independent of the Norwegian authorities.' Later historians have also pointed to the British attitude towards Norwegians as a factor that made early relations difficult. See S. Kjeldstadli, *Hjemmestyrkene: hovedtrekk av den militære motstanden under okkupasjonen*, vol. I (Oslo: H. Aschehoug, 1959), p. 90; Riste, *London regjeringa*, vol. I, p. 21; F. Kersaudy, *Vi stoler på England* (Oslo: Cappelen, 1991), p. 66.
4 M. R. D. Foot, *SOE: The Special Operations Executive 1940–1946*, 2nd edn (London: Pimlico, 1999), pp. 34–5, 44.
5 TNA: paper entitled 'Norwegian Expedition', in HS2/241; A. Ueland, *Shetlandsgjengen: Heltene i Nordsjøen* (Oslo: Kagge Forlag, 2017), pp. 14, 35, 36
6 Riste, *London regjeringa*, vol. I, pp. 17, 20.
7 V. Krosby, 'Host to Exiles: The Foreign Office and the Norwegian Government in London 1940–1945', *London School of Economics*, 1979, p. 31.

8   TNA: 'Suggested Collaboration between Section D and the Norwegian Authorities', June 1940, and file note, 'Suggestions from "D"' (Lawrence Grand), probably June 1940, in HS2/240.
9   TNA: file note, 'Section D', 7 August 1940 and memo from Lt. J. L. Chaworth-Musters, 17 August 1940, in HS2/240; 'Norwegian Project', 3 November 1940, in HS2/218; H. Koht, *For fred og fridom i krigstid, 1939–1940* (Oslo: Tiden Norsk Forlag, 1957), p. 265; W. J. M. Mackenzie, *The Secret History of SOE: The Special Operations Executive* (London: St. Ermin's Press, 2000), p. 198.
10 TNA: file note on meeting between J. L. Chaworth-Musters and B. Ljungberg, 26 August 1940, in HS2/240; 'Norwegian Project', 3 November 1940, in HS2/218.
11 TNA: 'Norway', 1 September 1940, in HS2/240.
12 NHM: 'Consolidated Progress report of S Section', week ending 7 December 1940 in SOE archive, Boks 3a; TNA: 'Suggested Collaboration between Section D and the Norwegian Authorities', date unknown but probably June 1940, and 'Norway', 1 September 1940, in HS2/240; 'Norwegian Project', 3 November 1940, in HS2/128.
13 Koht, *For fred og fridom i krigstid*, p. 265.
14 Bridges to Selborne, with a copy to Sporborg, top secret, 3 May 1945, in Selborne papers, 21, cited in M. R. D. Foot, *SOE in the Low Countries* (London: St. Ermin's Press, 2001), p. 74.
15 O. Riste, 'Relations between the Norwegian Government in Exile and the British Government', in P. Salmon (ed.), *Britain and Norway in the Second World War* (London: HMSO, 1995), p. 44; Koht, *For fred og fridom i krigstid*, pp. 265–6.
16 TNA: 'Norway', 1 September 1940, in HS2/240; paper entitled 'Norway-Future Planning', by Lt. Col. J. S. Wilson, 5 June 1942, in HS2/128; Riste, *London regjeringa*, vol. I, p. 21; Kersaudy, *Vi stoler på England 1939–1949*, p. 66.
17 J. R. Lowell, 'On a Certain Condescension in Foreigners', in H. S. Commager (ed.), *Britain Through American Eyes* (London: Bodley Head), pp. 426–43, cited in A. Danchev, 'Great Britain: The Indirect Strategy', in D. Reynolds, W. F. Kimball and A. O. Chubarian (eds), *Allies at War: The Soviet, American and British Experience 1939–1945* (Basingstoke: Macmillan, 1994), p. 5; Foot, *SOE in the Low Countries*, p. 43.
18 TNA: paper entitled, 'Norway', 1 September 1940, in HS2/240.
19 NHM: 'Consolidated Progress report of S Section', week ending 7 December 1940, in SOE archive, Boks 3a; TNA: letter from Hugh Dalton to the Prime Minister, 8 January 1941, in HS8/306.
20 Riste, *London regjeringa*, vol. I, pp. 113, 154, and vol. II, p. 29.
21 O. Riste, 'Utefront', vol. VII, in M. Skodvin (ed.), *Norge i Krig: fremmedåk og frihetskamp* (Oslo: Aschehoug, 1987), p. 50.

22 Two hundred forty-one vessels were tankers. At the time, Nortraship was the largest ship-owning company in the world. See Atle Thowsen, 'Business Goes to War: The Norwegian Navy in Allied War Transport', in P. Salmon (ed.), *Britain and Norway in the Second World War* (London: HMSO, 1995), pp. 51–66.
23 Riste, 'Utefront', vol. VII, in Skodvin (ed.), *Norge i Krig*, p. 49; Krosby, 'Host to Exiles', p.43.
24 TNA: 'Report on the Norwegian Troops at Dumfries by Major C. P. D. Legard M12 d', 20 June 1940, in FO371/24838.
25 Article entitled '17 May 1940', by Johan Scharffenberg from the paper *Arbeiderbladet* (Oslo), published on 10 May 1940, cited in Kjeldstadli, *Hjemmestyrkene*, p. 22.
26 TNA: letter from M. Colban (Norwegian ambassador to Britain) to Viscount Halifax, 7 July 1940, including a copy of the address from the Presidential Board of the Storting to the King of Norway, 27 June 1940, and the King's answer dated 3 July 1940, in FO371/24828.
27 Riste, *London regjeringa*, vol. I, pp. 95, 154; and Koht, *For fred og fridom i krigstid 1939–1940*, p. 263.
28 On 19 November 1940, Halvdan Koht was granted three months' leave. Lie took over in London and on 27 January 1941, Koht handed in his formal letter of resignation. On 19 February, Lie became Norway's foreign minister. See Krosby, 'Host to Exiles', p. 74.
29 Riste, *London regjeringa*, vol. I, *Bilag* (enclosure) II, pp. 249–58.
30 TNA: enclosure no. 9, 'note from Mr. C. Hambro', 6 January 1941, in HS8/306.
31 T. Lie, *Med England i ildlinjen, 1940–1942* (Oslo: Tiden Norsk Forlag, 1956), p. 61; TNA: note from L. Collier 17 December 1940, in FO371/24828.
32 TNA: note from Cecil Dormer (British ambassador to the Norwegian government), 20 November 1940, and letter from Cecil Dormer to the Foreign Office, 16 December 1940, in FO371/24828. Letter from Hugh Dalton to Winston Churchill, 8 January 1941, in HS8/306; Lie, *Med England i ildlinjen 1940–1942*, p. 114.
33 *Den norske regjerings virksomhet under krigen fra 9 april til 22 juni*, vol. IV, *forsvarsdepartementet*, p. 102.
34 TNA: 'Interview with Captain Nagell', 21 November 1940, in HS2/238; NHM: 'Consolidated Progress Reports of S Section', weeks ending 21 December 1940, 21 January and 18 February 1941, in Boks 3a; Riste, *London regjeringa*, vol. I, p. 111; Haavardsholm, *Martin Linge, min morfar* (Oslo: Gyldendal, 1993), pp. 175, 186, 204–5.
35 Lie later denied any involvement in 'Claymore', although SOE and the COHQ files appear to undermine this. TNA: files DEFE2/141, Operation Claymore and HS/224, Operation Claymore; NHM, 'Consolidated Progress Report of S Section', weeks ending 21 January, 11 and 18

February 1941, in SOE archive, Boks 3a; 'Øksfjord Operation', in SOE archive, Boks 44. For details of these operations, see Appendix B, 'Sea-Borne Operations Instigated by or Involving SOE along the Norwegian Coastline, 1940–1945', pp. 219–28; Lie, *Med England i ildlinjen, 1940–1942*, p. 140.

36 Lie, *Med England i ildlinjen, 1940–1942*, p. 140.
37 John Rognes' account to the *undersøkelskommisjon*, 24 January 1947, cited in Kjeldstadli, *Hjemmestyrkene*, note 24, p. 377.
38 NHM: 'Consolidated Progress Report of S Section', week ending 25 February 1941 in SOE archive, Boks 3a; TNA: notes headed 'report on interview with SS (Rognes) on 19 February 1941', 'interview with SS, Frank Stagg and J. L. Chaworth-Musters 24 February 1941' and memo from A. A. Flygt to Charles Hambro, 5 March 1941, in HS2/228.
39 TNA: 'Directive to the Military Organisation in Norway in Reply to Their Report Dated 10 June 1941 and Addressed to HM King Haakon', 17 July 1941, in HS2/231 and 232; letter from General Fleischer to Harry Sporborg, 19 July 1941, in HS2/231; Lie, *Med England i ildlinjen, 1940–1942*, pp. 249–50.
40 See Chapter 4, pp. 90–116.
41 A. Moland, *Milorg 1941–1943: Fremvekst, Ledelse og Organisajon* (Oslo: NHM, 1991), pp. 10–15; Grimnes, *Hjemmefrontens Ledelse* (Oslo: Universitetsforlaget, 1979), pp. 213–27.
42 TNA: 'Report to the King from the Military Council in Norway, 10 June 1941', in HS2/231.
43 TNA: letter from Captain Schive to Lt. Col. H. N. Sporborg, 12 November 1941, in HS2/127.
44 Lie, *Med England i ildlinjen, 1940–1942*, p. 251.
45 TNA: letter from Charles Hambro to Oscar Torp, 25 November 1941, including paper entitled 'Anglo-Norwegian Collaboration Regarding the Military Organisation in Norway', in HS2/127.
46 TNA: letter from Charles Hambro to Major-General Sir H. L. Ismay, 30 November 1941, and letters from Major-General Sir H. L. Ismay to Anthony Eden, 24 January 1942, and to Oscar Torp, 22 February 1942, in CAB121/452.
47 TNA: letter from Charles Hambro to Major General H. L. Ismay, 30 November 1940, in HS2/127.
48 TNA: file CAB 121/452; Appendix B, 'Sea-Borne Operations Instigated by or Involving SOE along the Norwegian Seaboard, 1940–1945', pp. 219–28.
49 TNA: letter from Hambro to Lie, 15 December 1941, in HS2/127; memo from Lt. Col. H. N. Sporborg to Brigadier Colin McV. Gubbins, 15 January 1942, and 'Report on Conduct of "Anklet"' by J. W. Torrance, 10 January 1942, in HS2/199; FD 1326, LIE-TORP, 17 December 1941, med *bilag*, cited in Riste, *London regjeringa*, vol. I, p. 145; Kjeldstadli, *Hjemmestyrkene*, note 64, p. 361.

50 TNA: letter from Charles Hambro to Oscar Torp, 14 January 1942, in HS2/127; letter from Lt. Col. H. N. Sporborg to Brigadier Colin McV. Gubbins, 15 January 1942, in HS2/199.
51 Lie, *Med England i ildlinjen, 1940–1942*, pp. 114, 118–19.
52 J. Nygaardsvold, *Norge i krig-London, 1940–1945* (Oslo: Tiden Forlag, 1983), p. 92; Riste, *London regjeringa*, vol. I, p. 156.
53 FD 13-H, Torp-H.M. Kongen 20.3.42, cited in Riste, *London regjeringa*, vol. I, p. 164; TNA: letter from L. Collier, British ambassador to Norway, to Anthony Eden, Foreign Secretary, 10 November 1943, in FO371/29422.
54 Riste, *London regjeringa*, vol. I, pp. 156–84.
55 See Riste, *London regjeringa*, vol. I, pp. 186, 188, 266.
56 TNA: paper entitled 'Re-conquest of Norway', an extract from a survey made by a committee under the Royal Norwegian Ministry of Defence, 19 January 1942, in HS2/218; Riste, *London regjeringa*, vol. I, pp. 165–6; *Regjeringa og hjemmefronten under krigen: akstykker utgitt av stortinget* (henceforth ROH), document no. 9, pp. 64–8.
57 TNA: 'Minutes of ANCC Meetings from 16 February 1942 to 26 April 1945', in HS2/138.
58 Kjeldstadli, *Hjemmestyrkene*, p. 174.
59 Riste, *London regjeringa*, vol. I, p. 216.
60 NHM: reply by J. S. Wilson to a paper by Major Hampton and Major Helle at STS 26, 13 April 1942, in FO IV archive, Boks 31; TNA: minutes from the first to the fifth meetings of the ANCC, 16 February to 24 April 1942, in HS2/138.
61 TNA: 'Minutes of ANCC Meetings from 16 February 1942 to 26 April 1945', in HS2/138; NHM: paper entitled 'Principles of Service in Nor.I.C. (I)', (undated) in FOIV archive.
62 Kjeldstadli, *Hjemmestyrkene*, pp. 175, 407 (footnote 7).
63 TNA: 'Re-conquest of Norway: The Norwegian "Home Front" and the Norwegian Army in UK', 26 March 1942, extract from a survey made by a Committee under the Royal Norwegian Ministry of Defence, 19 January 1942, in HS2/218.
64 TNA: letter from Charles Hambro to General Hansteen, 3 April 1942, in HS2/127; Papers entitled 'Training of the Norwegian Land Forces in UK', 28 February 1942, and 'Introduction', 17 February 1942, in HS2/218.
65 TNA: 'Re-conquest of Norway: The Norwegian "Home Front" and the Norwegian Army in UK', 26 March 1942, in HS2/218.
66 TNA: memo from Lt. Col. H. N. Sporborg to Brigadier Colin McV. Gubbins, 28 November 1941, in HS8/237.
67 TNA: 'The Re-conquest of Norway: SOE's Role', 6 April 1942, in HS2/218.
68 TNA: minutes of the first, third and fourth meetings of ANCC, 16 February, 20 March and 8 April 1942, respectively, in HS2/138.

69 TNA: letter from Lt. Col. H. N. Sporborg to E. O. Coote (Foreign Office), 23 September 1942, in FO898/241; letter from Lt. Col. J. S Wilson to E. Nielsen in Stockholm, 23 January 1944, in HS2/128.
70 TNA: note from Lt. Col. J. S. Wilson to Col. A. M. Anstruther, copy to Lt. Col. H. N. Sporborg, and including list of industrial targets for Norway, in HS2/129.
71 TNA: letter from MEW to A. H. B. Schofield at the British Foreign Office, 8 January 1942, in FO371/32827; Riste, *London regjeringa*, vol. II, pp. 47–8.
72 For example, see details on Operation Clairvoyant in Appendix A, 'SOE *Coup de Main* Operations in Norway 1940–1944', p. 209.
73 TNA: paper entitled 'Norwegian Policy', 11 December 1940, in HS2/128.
74 TNA: memo from Brigadier Colin McV. Gubbins to AD/Z, accompanied by paper entitled, 'Notes on the Organisation of a Sabotage System', 11 April 1941, in HS8/272.
75 TNA: 'Anglo-Norwegian Collaboration Regarding the Military Organisation in Norway', by Lt. Col. H. N. Sporborg, 24 November 1941, in HS2/127; memo from Lt. Col. H. N. Sporborg to Brigadier Colin McV. Gubbins, 28 November 1941, in HS8/237.
76 Olav Riste argues that SOE had a short-term 'action' policy for Norway and a long-term 'preparation' policy. The long-term responsibility of preparing a secret army was eventually passed to *Milorg*. Meanwhile, SOE continued with its own organization that could undertake sabotage in Norway in the period prior to a reoccupation. According to Riste, SOE held to this policy throughout 1942; Riste, *London regjeringa*, vol. II, p. 27.
77 T. A. Barstad, 'Norsk motstand fra Svensk grunn', in S. Ekman and O. K. Grimnes (eds), *Brøderfolk i ufredstid – Norsk forbindelser under annen verdenskrig* (Oslo: Universitetsforlaget, 1991), pp. 228–61; Kjeldstadli, *Hjemmestyrkene*, note 16, p. 425.
78 TNA: note from Malcolm Munthe to Frank Stagg, undated in HS2/231; Munthe, *Sweet Is War* (London: Duckworth, 1954), pp. 120–52.
79 TNA: letter to Munthe from SOE HQ, 17 April 1941, in HS2/231.
80 TNA: telegram for Munthe from SO2, 21 April 1941; telegram from Munthe, 1 May 1941; letters from Daniel Ring in Stockholm to Colonel Ljungberg and John Rognes, 12 June 1941; note from Frank Stagg to A. A. Flygt, undated in HS2/228; note from Lt. Col. H. N. Sporborg to John Rognes, 8 August 1941, in HS2/231.
81 TNA: letter from Frisvold to Rognes, 8 September 1941, in HS2/228.
82 TNA: memo from A. A. Flygt to Lt. Col. H. N. Sporborg, 10 December 1942; NHM: Kja, Boks 14mp, *Stockholmsmøtet* – Instructions for Daniel Ring, 1 June 1942, cited in Barstad, 'Norsk Motstand fra Svensk grunn', p. 231.
83 TNA: telegram from Lt. Col. H. N. Sporborg to E. Nielsen, 18 February 1942, letter from SOE HQ to Nielsen, no. 23, 3 March 1942, in HS2/232;

report from Ring to Rognes, no. 31, 10 June 1942, in HS2/129; 'The Re-conquest of Norway: SOE's Role', by J. S. Wilson, 6 April 1942, in HS2/218.

84 TNA: letter from Lt. Col. J. S. Wilson to General Hansteen, 29 October 1942, in HS2/232.
85 TNA: letter from General Hansteen to Lt. Col. J. S. Wilson, 3 November 1942, in HS2/232.
86 Why this was the case is unclear. See TNA: paper from FO IV, unsigned, 4 March 1943, in HS2/233.
87 TNA: telegram to Stockholm for Mrs Bernardes, no. 0258, 1 March 1943, and letter to Lt. Col. Bjarne Øen from Lt. Col. J. S. Wilson, 30 March 1943, in HS2/233; NHM: FOIV, Boks 34, letter from SOE Stockholm to SOE HQ, cited in Barstad, 'Norsk motstand fra Svensk grunn', p. 245.
88 TNA: letter from Nielsen to SOE HQ, N5, 7 January 1943, and letter from Nielsen to Lt. Col. J. S. Wilson, 12 February 1944, in HS2/233; J. Chr. Hauge, *Rapport om mitt arbeid under okkupasjonen* (Oslo: Gyldendal, 1995), p. 126; Kjeldstadli, *Hjemmestyrkene*, p. 324.
89 See Appendix C, 'SOE Long-Term and Miscellaneous Operations in Norway 1940–1945', pp. 229–79.
90 An example was Operation Wagtail. TNA: HS2/212, Operation Wagtail; A. Moland, *Over grensen?* (Oslo: Orion forlag, 1999), p. 214; Appendix C, 'SOE Long-Term and Miscellaneous Operations in Norway 1940–1945', p. 246.
91 TNA: 'Minim' (undated) in HS2/215; history of the Stockholm Mission, written by Miss Janet Gow in December 1945, in HS7/190; E. Welle-Strand, *Vi vil verne vårt land: antisabotasje i Norge, 1944–1945* (Oslo: NHM, 2000), p. 52.
92 O II was situated in the department FO III, which was responsible for land and air operations. See FO arkiv boks 45, *Foreløbig arbeidsprogram for III kontor*, utarbeidet av Bjarne Øen 19.3 og approbert 31.3.42, cited in Riste, *London regjeringa*, vol. I, pp. 189–90.
93 TNA: 'Liaison between Norwegian High Command and SOE', by Lt. Col. J. S. Wilson to General Hansteen and Colonel Christophersen, 1 July 1942.
94 NHM: *Arbeidsprogram for IV kontor*, 5 December 1942, signed by Bjarne Øen in FO IV archive, boks 32; TNA: minutes of the 13th meeting of ANCC, 11 December 1942, in HS2/138.
95 NHM: *Administrasjonen samarbeid med andre norske kontorer og SOE*, and letter from Lt. Col. Bjarne Øen (FO IV), 4 July 1944, in FO IV archive, Boks 32.
96 TNA: memo headed 'Joint Staff in Norwegian Section', from Lt. Col. J. S. Wilson to Brigadier E.E. Mockler-Ferryman, June 1944, in HS2/235.
97 There were altogether eighteen Norwegians to be moved into joint offices, including Lt. Col. Øen.
98 TNA: 'Liaison between Norwegian High Command and SOE', for the information of General Hansteen and Colonel Christophersen, by Lt. Col. J. S. Wilson, 1 July 1942, in HS2/127.

99   TNA: memo from Lt. Col. J. S. Wilson to Brigadier E. E. Mockler-Ferryman, including 'SOE Outline Plan for Joint Activities in Norway 1943/44', in HS2/218.
100 TNA: copy of internal FO IV paper, untitled, 4 March 1943, in HS2/233.
101 TNA: 'SOE in Norway and the Secret Military Organisation', by Lt. Col. J. S. Wilson, 25 June 1942, in HS2/129.
102 TNA: paper entitled, 'Re-conquest of Norway', 26 March 1942, an extract from a survey made by a Committee under the Royal Norwegian Ministry of Defence, 19 January 1942, in HS2/218.
103 Riste, *London Regjeringa*, vol. II, p. 29.
104 TNA: 'SOE Long-Term Policy in Norway', 21 September 1942, in HS2/128.
105 TNA: 'Report from a Conference in Stockholm in March 1944' (translation), 14 April 1944, in HS2/233; Kjeldstadli, *Hjemmestyrkene*, p. 320.
106 TNA: 'Directive on the Employment and Development of resistance in Norway', 3 September 1944, in HS2/235.
107 TNA: letter from 'Kretsen' to the Norwegian Government in HS2/129; Riste, *London regjeringa*, vol. II, pp. 30–4; A. Moland, *Sabotasje i Norge under 2. Verdenskrig*, 2nd edn (Oslo: NHM, 1987), pp. 4–5.
108 TNA: letter from L. Collier to A. Eden, no. 49, 3 September 1942, in HS2/129.
109 Riste, *London regjeringa*, vol. II, p. 32.
110 ROH, document nr. 30, cited in Riste, *London regjeringa*, vol. II, p. 32.
111 TNA: letter from Lt. Col. H. N. Sporborg to E. O. Coote (Foreign Office), ref. F/5357/130/17, 23 September 1942, in FO898/241.
112 Kjeldstadli, *Hjemmestyrkene*, pp. 163–7.
113 Leif Tronstad's *dagbok* (diary), 9 March 1943, and ROH, dok. Nr. 85, cited in Riste, *London regjeringa*, pp. 36–37; O. Njølstad, *Professor Tronstads Krig* (Oslo: Aschehoug, 2015), pp. 220–3.
114 TNA: letter from L. Collier to A. Eden (Foreign Office), ref. N5230/40/30, in HS2/129.
115 TNA: memo from Lt. Col. J. S. Wilson to D/Plans, 26 April 1943, in HS2/128.
116 TNA: letter from Nielsen to SOE HQ, 10 June 1943, including copy of the minutes from the meeting in May in Sweden between FO and *Milorg*, in HS2/233.
117 TNA: letter from SOE HQ (Lt. Col. J. S. Wilson) to Nielsen, 23 January 1944, in HS2/128.

Chapter 4

1   Norwegian historiography tends to follow Sverre Kjeldstadli's claim that SOE set out to build up a 'military underground movement' in Norway outside and independent of 'those men in Norway that

had begun to organise military resistance from Oslo'. S. Kjeldstadli, *Hjemmestyrkene: hovedtrekk av den militære motstanden under okkupasjonen*, vol. I (Oslo: H. Aschehoug, 1959), p. 90.

2 Kjeldstadli, *Hjemmestyrkene*; I. Kraglund and A. Moland, 'Hjemmefront', vol. VI, in M. Skodvin (ed.), *Norge i krig: fremmedåk & frihetskamp 1940-1945* (Oslo: Aschehoug, 1987); M. Skodvin, *Striden om okkupasjonsstyret i Norge fram til 25 september 1940* (Oslo: Det Norske Samlaget, 1956); T. C. Wyller, *Nyordning og motstand* (Oslo: Universitetsforlaget, 1958); Kraglund, *Holdningskampen, 1940-1942* (Oslo: NHM, 1993); Moland, *Milorg, 1941-1943: fremvekst, ledelse og organisasjonen* (Oslo: NHM, 1991); B. Nøkleby, 'Holdningskamp' and 'Nyordning', vols. IV and III in Skodvin (ed.), *Norge i krig*; T. Gjelsvik, *Norwegian Resistance, 1940-1945* (London: Church, 1979); A. Moland, 'Norway', in B. Moore (ed.), *Resistance in Western Europe* (Oxford: Berg, 2000).

3 Nøkleby, 'Nyordning', vol. III, in Skodvin (ed.), *Norge i krig*, p. 22; Kraglund, *Holdningskampen, 1940-1942*, p. 3.

4 O. Hoidal, *Quisling: A Study in Treason* (Oslo: Universitetsforlaget, 1989); H. F. Dahl, *Quisling: A Study in Treachery* (Cambridge: Cambridge University Press, 1999), pp. 70-109.

5 Kraglund, *Holdningskampen, 1940-1942*, p. 4.

6 Kraglund, *Holdningskampen, 1940-1942*, p. 3; Moland, 'Norway', in Moore (ed.) *Resistance in Western Europe*, p. 240; H. F. Dahl, 'Norsk politikk, 1940-1945: Kontinuitet eller brudd?', in Dahl (ed.) *Krigen i Norge* (Oslo: Pax Forlag, 1974), p. 20.

7 ROH, pp. 50-9; Kraglund, *Holdningskampen, 1940-1942*, p. 12.

8 Moland, 'Norway', in Moore, *Resistance in Western Europe*, pp. 223-40.

9 Kraglund, *Holdningskampen, 1940-1942*, pp. 2-3, 16-7; Wyller, *Nyordning og motstand*; Nøkleby, 'Nyordning' and 'Holdningskamp', vols III and IV, in Skodvin (ed.), *Norge i krig*; Moland, 'Norway', in Moore (ed.), *Resistance in Western Europe*, pp. 223-48; O. K. Grimnes, 'Litt om Kretsen og om Hjemmefrontledelsen' in *Norge og den 2. verdenskrig: motstandskamp strategi og marinepolitikk* (Oslo: Universitetsforlaget, 1972), pp. 118-35; T. Halvorsen, 'Okkupasjonshistorien og de besværlige kommunistene', in S. Ugelvik Larsen (ed.), *I krigens kjølvann* (Oslo: Universitetsforlaget, 1999), p. 71.

10 Moland, 'Norway', in Moore (ed.), *Resistance in Western Europe*, p. 225; Kjeldstadli, *Hjemmestyrkene*, pp. 66-89.

11 O. Grimnes, *Hjemmefrontens Ledelse* (Oslo: Universitetsforlaget, 1979), pp. 10-7, 302-420.

12 Grimnes, *Hjemmefrontens Ledelse*, pp. 14-7; Moland, 'Norway', in Moore (ed.), *Resistance in Western Europe*, pp. 232-3; L. Borgersrud, 'Wollweber-Organisasjonen i Norge' (PhD thesis in history at the University of Oslo, 1994); T. Halvoresen, 'Okkupasjonshistorien og de besværlige kommunistene', in Ugelvik Larsen (ed.), *I krigens kjølvann*, pp. 59-75.

13 Moland, *Milorg, 1941–1943*, pp. 5–6.
14 Grimnes, *Hjemmefrontens Ledelse*, pp. 44, 215–8; Kraglund and Moland, 'Hjemmefront', vol. VI, in Skodvin (ed.), *Norge i krig*, p. 23; Kjeldstadli, *Hjemmestyrkene*, p. 73.
15 H. F. Dahl et al., *Norsk Krigsleksikon, 1940–1945* (Oslo: J.W. Cappelen, 1995), p. 339.
16 Instilling VI fra Undersøkelseskommisjonen (UK) av 1945, cited in Kjeldstadli, *Hjemmestyrkene*, p. 75; ROH, document no 11, 'Promemoria by Professor Johan Holst', 10 October 1941, p. 71; report by Johan Holst to UK in 1945, cited in Kraglund and Moland, 'Hjemmefront', vol. VI, in Skodvin (ed.), *Norge i krig*, p. 24.
17 L. Borgersrud, 'Militære veivalg 1940–1945', in Larsen (ed.), *I krigens kjølvann*, pp. 149–50; D. G. Thompson, 'From Neutrality to NATO: The Norwegian Armed Forces and Defence Policy 1905–1955' (PhD thesis: Ohio State University, 1996), p. 87; R. R. Eriksen and A. Moland, *Hvor uforberedt var vi 9. April?* (Oslo: NHM, undated), pp. 13–15.
18 Grimnes, *Hjemmefrontens Ledelse*, p. 44.
19 Kraglund and Moland, 'Hjemmefront', vol. VI, in Skodvin (ed.) *Norge i krig*, pp. 30, 35.
20 Report by Ole Berg to UK, cited in Moland, *Milorg, 1941–1943*, p. 11.
21 During 1944 the *Råd* gradually became superfluous and in 1945 was reorganized. Moland, *Milorg, 1941–1943*, pp. 10–11.
22 ROH, document no. 9, report from 'Johan Holst til general Fleischer', 28 October 1941, pp. 64–8, and no. 11, 'Promemoria ved professor Johan Holst', 10 November 1941, pp. 71–6; O. Riste, *London regjeringa: Norge i krigsalliansen, 1940–1945*, vol. I (Oslo: Det Norske Samlaget, 1995), p. 166.
23 TNA: 'Rebellion in Norway', 7 June 1940, in HS2/240; 'Rebellion in Norway', 6 August 1940, in HS2/128; 'Norway', 1 September 1940, in HS2/240; draft entitled, 'The Planning of Revolutionary Activities', in HS8/255.
24 TNA: 'Log of V.2.S – Aberdeen to Norway and Return', 17 June 1940, 'Extract from Diary – Summary of Achievements of the Norwegian Expedition' (undated) and report dated 6 August 1940, all in HS2/242; 'Rebellion in Norway', 6 August 1940, in HS2/218.
25 TNA: HS7/174, Norwegian Section History; NHM: report entitled 'Lark', July 1945, in SOE archive, Boks 35b; M. Munthe, *Sweet Is War* (London: Duckworth, 1954), pp. 123, 124, 147, 148; A. Croft, *A Talent for Adventure* (London: Hanley Swan, 1991), p. 141.
26 TNA: COS (40) 27 (0), 'Subversive Activities in Relation to Strategy', 25 November 1940, in CAB 80/56.
27 TNA: 'Norwegian Policy', 11 December 1940, in HS2/128.
28 NHM: List of Shetland sea-sorties, in SOE archive, Boks 9; Appendix C, 'SOE Long Term and Miscellaneous Operations in Norway 1940–1945', pp. 268–70.

29 TNA: report from Arne Ekornes, 12 April 1940, in HS2/228; NHM: List of Shetland sea-sorties, in SOE archive, Boks 9.
30 TNA: 'Subversive Operations in Scandinavia', a minute for the Minister, 16 December 1940, in HS2/128; Paper entitled, 'The Prospects of Subversion: A Country by Country Analysis', in HS8/272.
31 TNA: telegram from SO2 to Malcolm Munthe, 28 April 1941, in HS2/231.
32 See above, Chapter 3, pp. 55–6.
33 SOE were aware that Rognes was closely associated with Colonel Olaf Helset in *Milorg*. NHM: 'Consolidated Progress reports of S Section', week ended 25 February 1941, in SOE archive, Boks 3a; report on interview with SS (Rognes), 19 February 1941, in HS2/228.
34 TNA: memo to Charles Hambro from A. A. Flygt, 5 March 1941, and telegram from Lerwick to London, 16 April 1941, in HS2/228; NHM: 'Consolidated Progress Reports for S Section', weeks ending 4 and 11 March 1941, in SOE Archive, Boks 3a.
35 TNA: report on Arne Ekornes to the Royal Norwegian Minister of Defence, London, April 12 1941, in HS2/228.
36 TNA: interview with Rognes, F. Stagg and Lt. Chaworth-Musters, 24 February 1941, memo from A. A. Flygt to Charles Hambro, 5 March 1941, and report on Arne Ekornes to the Royal Norwegian Ministry of Defence, London, 12 April, 1941, in HS2/228; NHM: List of Shetland sea-sorties, in SOE archive, Boks 9.
37 TNA: note from A. A. Flygt to SY, 27 June 1941, in HS2/231.
38 TNA: telegram to Munthe from SO2, 21 April 1941, and telegram to 4301, 1 May 1941 in HS2/228.
39 TNA: Report on Arne Ekornes to the Royal Norwegian Minister, London, 12 April and telegram 0100 to Munthe from SO2, 27 June 1941, in HS2/228; J. Schive, *Tyve år etter* (Oslo: Gundersen, 1960), p. 11; NHM: List of Shetland sea-sorties, in SOE archive, Boks 9.
40 TNA: 'Report to His Majesty the King' (translation), 10 June 1941, in HS2/231; Schive, *Tyve år etter*, p. 12.
41 TNA: 'Directive to the Military Organisation in Norway in Reply to Their Report Dated 10 June 1941 and Addressed to H. M. King Haakon', in HS2/231; Schive, *Tyve år etter*, p. 14.
42 Schive replied to SOE directive, although he claims that it never reached Britain. A document in the SOE archives in London appears to suggest that at least a draft of Schive's communication eventually reached SOE. Trygve Lie also claims that further communications were sent to London; TNA: document headed both, 'Rough Draft of Report by JacobSchive', and copy of hand-written letter headed 'From R (Rådet) to the Government and Norwegian General', signed by Schive, in HS2/231; Schive, *Tyve år etter*, p. 17; T. Lie, *Med England i ildlinjen, 1940–1942* (Oslo: Tiden Norsk Forlag, 1956), p. 250.
43 Moland, *Milorg, 1941–1943*, pp. 12–13.

44 ROH: document no. 8, report by 'Jakob Schive til General Fleischer', 28 October 1941, pp. 60–4, and No. 9, report by 'Johan Holst til general Fleischer', 28 October 1941, pp. 64–8.
45 FD 1325, cited in Riste, *London regjeringa*, vol. I, p. 163.
46 TNA: letter from Jacob Schive to Lt. Col. H. N. Sporborg, 12 November 1941, in HS2/127.
47 TNA: memo from Sir Charles Hambro to Oscar Torp, 25 November 1941, with 'Anglo-Norwegian Collaboration Regarding the Military Organisation in Norway', 24 November 1941, in HS2/127.
48 TNA: memo from SOE HQ to E. Nielsen, 3 March 1942, in HS2/232.
49 See footnote 76, p. 62.
50 Kjeldstadli, *Hjemmestyrkene*, pp. 126–7.
51 TNA: memo 'Reference M's memo of 24 November 1941', from Major R. C. Holme to George Wiskeman, 26 November 1941, in HS2/23
52 TNA: memo from D/S (Lt. Col. H. N. Sporborg) to Brigadier Colin McV. Gubbins, 28 November 1941, in HS8/237; 'SOE Operations in Norway', 27 March 1942, in HS2/128.
53 It is claimed that instructions were sent to *Milorg* through the Norwegian government at this time asking them to revert to a more decentralized structure. TNA: memo from Lt. Col. H. N. Sporborg to Brigadier Colin McV. Gubbins, 25 November 1941, in HS8/237; 'The Re-conquest of Norway: SOE's Role', 6 April 1942, in HS2/218.
54 TNA: memo from Lt. Col. H. N. Sporborg to Brigadier Colin McV. Gubbins, 25 November 1941, in HS8/237; memo from SOE HQ to Nielsen, 3 March 1942, and letter from SOE HQ to SOE Stockholm, 13 May 1942, in HS2/232; 'SOE Operations in Norway', 27 March 1942 and 'The Re-conquest of Norway', 6 April 1942, in HS2/218.
55 TNA: 'The Re-conquest of Norway: SOE's role', 6 April 1942, in HS2/218.
56 TNA: minutes of a 'Special Meeting of Anglo-Norwegian Collaboration Committee', 13 May 1942, in HS2/138.
57 TNA: 'Norway – Future Planning: Some General Observations', 5 June 1942, in HS2/128.
58 TNA: 'Re-conquest of Norway: The Norwegian "Home Front" and the Norwegian Army in UK', extract from a survey made by a Committee under the Royal Norwegian Ministry of Defence, 19 January 1942, in HS2/218.
59 TNA: 'Duties and Activities of MIR', by J. C. F. Holland, 22 July 1940, in HS8/256.
60 TNA: 'Norway – Future Planning: Some General Observations', 5 June 1942, in HS2/128.
61 TNA: 'The Re-conquest of Norway: SOE's Role', 6 April 1942, in HS2/218.
62 TNA: 'Norway – Future Planning: Some General Observations', 5 June 1942, in HS2/128.

63 TNA: 'SOE in Norway and the Secret Military Organisation', 25 June 1942, in HS2/232.
64 TNA: 'SOE in Norway and the Secret Military Organisation, 25 June 1942, in HS2/232.
65 TNA: hand-written note from Brigadier Colin McV. Gubbins, 3 July 1942, in HS2/232.
66 Moland, *Milorg, 1941–1943*, pp. 19–22.
67 See map entitled '*Milorg* Districts', pp. xi–xii.
68 Altogether it issued twenty directives, the last one dated 6 May 1945. See Kraglund and Moland, 'Hjemmefront', vol. VI, in Skodvin (ed.), *Norge i krig*, p. 120.
69 Kjeldstadli, *Hjemmestyrkene*, p. 193.
70 TNA: memo from Lt. Col. J. S. Wilson to Brigadier Colin McV. Gubbins, 8 September 1942, including paper entitled, 'The Norwegian Home Front: General Directive'; memo from Lt. Colonel J. S. Wilson to Brigadier Colin McV. Gubbins, entitled 'Recent Mission to Secret Military Organisation Headquarters, Oslo', 15 August 1942, both in HS2/232.
71 TNA: letter to SOE Stockholm for Mr. P. Falk from SOE HQ, signed by Lt. Col. J. S. Wilson, 14 August 1942, in HS2/232.
72 TNA: memo entitled, 'Recent Mission to Secret Military Organisation Headquarters, Oslo' from Lt. Colonel J. S. Wilson to Brigadier Colin McV. Gubbins, 15 August 1942, in HS2/232.
73 TNA: paper entitled 'Present Situation in Norway and Directive as to Future Policy', from Brigadier Colin McV. Gubbins to Lt. Col. J. S. Wilson, 26 August 1942, in HS2/232.
74 TNA: 'SOE Long-Term Policy in Norway', 21 September 1942, in HS2/218; note from Brigadier Colin McV. Gubbins to Charles Hambro, 1 October 1942, in HS2/232; Kjeldstadli, *Hjemmestyrkene*, p. 184; and Riste, *London regjeringa*, vol. II, p. 28.
75 FA, *hylle* 21, FO-H, mappe, 'Telegrams from Stockholm, November 42–March 43', dok, der av 15 October 1942, SL til FO, cited in Kjeldstadli, *Hjemmestyrkene*, p. 303.
76 TNA: 'Present Situation in Norway and Directive as to Future Policy', from Brigadier Colin McV. Gubbins to Lt. Col. J. S. Wilson, 26 August 1942, in HS2/232.
77 TNA: letter from Lt. Col. H. N. Sporborg to E. O. Coote at the British Foreign Office, 23 September 1942, in HS2/129.
78 TNA: document entitled, 'Direction for Groups with Special Tasks in Norway', 25 September 1942, in HS2/232.
79 J. Chr. Hauge, *Rapport om mitt arbeid under okkupasjonen* (Oslo: Gyldendal, 1995), pp. 40–5; Kjeldstadli, *Hjemmestyrkene*, pp. 167–8; Appendix C, 'SOE Long-Term and Miscellaneous Operations in Norway, 1940–1945', pp. 233–7.

80 Ole Berg i sin forklaring til UK 1945 av 7 February 1947, cited in Kjeldstadli, *Hjemmestyrkene*, pp. 171–2.
81 Hauge, *Rapport om mitt arbeid under okkupasjonen*, p. 31; Appendix C, 'SOE Long-Term and Miscellaneous Operations in Norway, 1940–1945', pp. 271–2.
82 TNA: copy of internal FO IV memo, 3 March 1943, in HS2/233; internal SOE paper entitled 'Précis-Bittern Operation', 3 February 1943, in HS2/200.
83 TNA: minutes of ANCC meetings of 8 January and 12 February 1943, in HS2/138.
84 Riste, *London regjeringa*, vol. II, pp. 37–8.
85 TNA: memo from Brigadier Colin McV. Gubbins to Sir Charles Hambro, 1 October 1942, in HS2/232.
86 Kjeldstadli, *Hjemmestyrkene*, pp. 310–2, 316–17, 320–1.
87 TNA: HS7/174 Norwegian Section History; Poulsson, *Aksjon Vemork: vinterkrig på Hardangervidda* (Oslo: Gyldendal, 1993), p. 144.
88 Ole Berg and Lasse Heyerdahl Larsen were sent from the Norwegian Legation in Stockholm, while Olaf Helset, Jens Chr. Hauge and Carl Semb represented *Milorg*. Lieutenant Bjarne Øen and Captain Jacob Schive represented FO IV and FO-H. TNA: letter from Nielsen in Stockholm to SOE HQ, 10 June 1943, including paper entitled 'Translation of Minutes from 8633', in HS2/233.
89 TNA: memo from Lt. Col. J. S. Wilson to Brigadier E. E. Mockler-Ferryman, 26 June 1943, with attached paper, 'SOE Outline Plan for Joint Activities in Norway 1943/44', in HS2/218.
90 NHM: 'Consolidated Progress Reports of S Section', nos. 24 and 28, January and May 1944, in SOE archive, Boks 3b; Kjeldstadli, *Hjemmestyrkene*, p. 229.
91 TNA: memo from Lt. Col. J. S. Wilson to Brigadier E. E. Mockler-Ferryman, 26 June 1943, with attached paper, 'SOE Outline Plan for Joint Activities in Norway 1943/44', in HS2/218.
92 Kjeldstadli, *Hjemmestyrkene*, p. 314.
93 ROH, document no. 183, letter 'To the Prime Minister from the military committee, police leadership and the civil leadership, 15 November 1943', p. 331; Kjeldstadli, *Hjemmestyrkene*, pp. 314–18.
94 NHM: 'Report on the Wireless Service between SL and UK and in Districts 11–16 and 24 and 25, from the Autumn of 1943 to April 1944', by Lt. K. Haugland in SOE archive, Boks 22; 'Operation Instructions for Curlew', 6 October 1943, in SOE archive, Boks 14.
95 TNA: 'Report from a Conference in Stockholm in March 1944' (translation), April 1944, in HS2/233.
96 TNA: memo from Lt. Col. J. S. Wilson to Brigadier E. E. Mockler-Ferryman, 26 February 1944, in HS2/235.

97 TNA: 'Minutes of the Thirty Second Meeting of the Anglo-Norwegian Collaboration Committee', held on Thursday, 17 August 1944, in HS2/138, which Hauge attended; Memo from AD/X.1 to A/CD, ref. ADX/97, concerning Hauge's visit to London during November 1944, in HS6/619; Hauge, *Rapport om mitt arbeid under okkupasjonen*, pp. 187, 219.

98 F. Færøy, *Frigjøringen* (Oslo: NHM, undated), p. 20.

99 TNA: 'Directive from the Central Leadership (SL) to the District Leadership (DS) Regarding the Norwegian Home Forces (HS)', September 1944, in HS2/235; NHM: 'Directive to the District Leaders (DS) from *Milorg's* Central Leadership (SL)', December 31 1944, in SOE Archive, Boks 5.

100 See Chapter 2, pp. 46–7.

101 TNA: 'Directive for Future Sabotage Policy in Norway', from Brigadier E. E. Mockler-Ferryman to Lt. Col. J. S. Wilson, 31 May 1943, in HS2/128; Appendix A, 'SOE *Coup de Main* Operations in Norway: 1940–1944', pp. 213–15; see operations such as 'Goldfinch' and 'Chaffinch'.

102 ROH, document no. 183, letter 'To the Prime Minister from the military committee, police leadership and the civil leadership, 15 November 1943', p. 331; Kjeldstadli, *Hjemmestyrkene*, pp. 314–8; Riste, *London regjeringa*, vol. II, p. 41; Hauge, *Rapport om mitt arbeid under okkupasjonen*, pp. 193–8; TNA: letter from T. E. Bromley and P. N. Loxley, British Foreign Office, 8 June 1944, in HS2/235; letter from Lt. Col. J. S. Wilson to H. A. Nutting, Northern dept. of the Foreign Office, March 1944, in HS2/234.

103 TNA: 'Report from a Conference in Stockholm in March 1944' (translation), 14 April 1944, in HS2/233; Kraglund and Moland, 'Hjemmefront', vol. VI, in Skodvin (ed.), *Norge i krig*, p. 136; A. Moland, *Over grensen?* (Oslo: Orion forlag, 1999), pp. 49–50.

104 ROH, document no. 183, p. 331; Grimnes, *Hjemmefrontens Ledelse*, pp. 308–10.

105 TNA: 'Report from a Conference in Stockholm, March 1944' (translation), April 1944, in HS2/233.

106 A. Moland, *Kampen mot mobiliserings-trusselen i Norge, 1943–44* (Oslo: NHM, 1987), pp. 20–8.

Chapter 5

1 Combined Operations changed its title on several occasions during the war. By March 1942, its head Lord Mountbatten was given the title Chief of Combined Operations (CCO), made a vice admiral and permitted to attend meetings of the COS Committee. In December 1943, Major-General R. E. Laycock replaced Mountbatten and remained CCO until the end of the war. See TNA: DEFE2/697 and 1773, 'History of the Combined Operations'.

2 TNA: COS (41) 166, Directive to the Director of Combined Operations, 14 March 1941, in DEFE2/1773.
3 To avoid the confusion over the various titles that Combined Operations went under from 1940, the acronym COHQ will be used throughout.
4 TNA: WP (40) 362, 'Future Strategy', an appreciation by the Chiefs of Staff Committee, 4 September 1940, in CAB 66/11; COS (40) 468, 'Raiding Operations Directive to General Bourne', 17 June 1940, in DEFE2/1773.
5 TNA: COS (40) 27 (0), 'Subversive Activities in Relation to Strategy', 25 November 1940, in CAB 80/56.
6 TNA: 'Norway', 1 September 1940, in HS2/240.
7 TNA: 'Winter Policy for Norway', by F. Stagg, 25 November 1940, in HS2/128.
8 TNA: 'Norwegian Policy', 11 December 1940, in HS2/128.
9 TNA: 'Raiding Parties: Relationship between DCO & SO2', 14 December 1940, in HS8/818; W. J. M. Mackenzie, *The Secret History of SOE: The Special Operations Executive* (London: St. Ermin's Press, 2000), pp. 94, 361.
10 Initially, until February 1941, Commander Fletcher was the COHQ liaison officer with SOE. Later in 1941, Major D. A. Wyatt was appointed SOE's liaison officer with COHQ. He retained this position until his death in the Dieppe raid in August 1942. TNA: minutes of 42nd Meeting held at DCO's office at 15.30 hrs, 16 December 1940, in HS8/818.
11 The raids were 'Mandible' (formerly 'Castle'), 'Claymore', 'Hemisphere', 'Kitbag I', 'Archery', 'Anklet' and 'Kitbag II'. For details see, Appendix B, 'Sea-Borne Operations Instigated by or Involving SOE along the Norwegian Seaboard 1940–1945', pp. 219–28.
12 O. Riste, *The Neutral Ally: Norway's Relations with Belligerent Powers in the First World War* (Oslo: Universitetsforlaget, 1965), p. 98.
13 TNA: document of the Industrial Intelligence Centre (IIC) entitled 'German Import Trade', 20 December 1938, in FO837/427; C. Goulter, *A Forgotten Offensive* (London: Frank Cass, 1995), p. 118.
14 W. N. Medlicott, *The Economic Blockade*, vol. I (London: HMSO, 1952 and 1959), pp. 153, 158–9; TNA: minutes of the second meeting of the Special Operations Board of Directors held on 10 September 1940, in HS8/194; Memo to Lt. J. Chaworth-Musters from D/C, 20 August 1940, in HS2/201.
15 TNA: letter from Charles Hambro to F. Stagg and S2, 21 December 1940, in HS2/201; operation instructions for Operation Castle, in DEFE2/353.
16 TNA: a summary of Operation Castle, 27 December 1940, in DEFE2/353; letter from Charles Hambro to Harry Sporborg, Frank Stagg, and telegrams from Charles Hambro to Malcolm Munthe in Stockholm, 21 and 28 December 1940, respectively, in HS2/201.
17 TNA: DEFE2/201, and a note to the prime minister from H. L. Ismay, 17 January 1941, in PREM3/328/11A; M. Gilbert, *Finest Hour: Winston Churchill, 1939–1941* (London: Heinemann, 1983), p. 325.

18 See, Appendix B, 'Sea-Borne Operations Instigated by or Involving SOE along the Norwegian Seaboard 1940–1945', pp. 219–28; TNA: letter from Hugh Dalton to W. S. Churchill, in CAB121/447; hand-written appreciation by the DDCO, 10 January 1941, in DEFE2/141.
19 TNA: letter from L. C. Hollis to W. Churchill, 21 January 1941; letter from Churchill to General Ismay and COS Committee, 22 January 1941; and a further letter from L. C. Hollis to Churchill, 27 January 1941, all in PREM3/328/7; see Chapter 2, pp. 36–7.
20 None of the authors provide contemporaneous evidence to support their claim; E. Thomas, 'Norway's Role in British Wartime Intelligence', in P. Salmon (ed.), *Britain and Norway in the Second World War* (London: HMSO, 1995), p. 123; D. A. T. Stafford, *Churchill & Secret Service* (London: Abacus, 1997), p. 244; H. Sebag-Montefiore, *Enigma: The Battle for the Code* (London: Phoenix, 2001), p. 132; Rolf Dahlø, *Skjebnetråder: En historie om de ukjente krigerne* (Oslo: Schibsted forlag, 2001), p. 136.
21 TNA: appreciation written by the DDCO, 10 January 1941, in DEFE2/141; minutes of a meeting held at DCO's office, 27 January 1941, to discuss Operation Claymore, in HS2/224.
22 TNA: 'A Winter Policy for Norway', by Frank Stagg, 25 November 1940, in HS2/128; letter from Hugh Dalton to Winston Churchill, 17 January 1941, in CAB 121/447; NHM: A series of papers produced by Stagg on proposed operations in northern Norway, in SOE archives, Boks 1.
23 TNA: report by Brigadier J. C. Haydon, consolidated results of Operation Claymore, 4 March 1941, in DEFE2/140; letter from Lt. Col. H. N. Sporborg to Capt. J. Knox, 3 January 1941, in DEFE2/141; Sebag-Montefiore, *Enigma*, pp. 132–6; and D. Kahn, *Seizing the Enigma* (London: Arrow, 1992), pp. 127–36.
24 TNA: letter from L. C. Hollis to Churchill, 27 January 1941, in Premier/3/328/7; Sebag-Montefiore, *Enigma*, p. 132.
25 B. Nøkleby, 'Nyordning', vol. II, in M. Skodvin (ed.), *Norge i krig: fremmedåk & frihetskamp 1940–1945* (Oslo: Aschehoug, 1985), p. 167; Dahlø, *Skjebnetråder, p. 135*.
26 Nøkleby, 'Nyordning', vol. II, in Skodvin (ed.), *Norge i krig*, p. 163; OKW/KIB I/346 and 247 (entries of 6 and 8 May 1941), and OKW/KTB 2/1007 sq., cited in K. J. Muller, 'A German Perspective on Allied Deception Operations in the Second World War', *Intelligence and National Security*, vol. 2, July 1987, p. 317; report by the C-in-C, Navy, to the Fuehrer on March 18, 1941, cited in *Fuehrer Conferences on Naval affairs 1939–1945* (London: Greenhill, 1990), p. 183.
27 TNA: answer to a series of questions from DCO on Operation Claymore, provided by SO2, 3 February 1941, in HS2/224; 'Enclosure no. 9', including 'Note from Mr C. Hambro', dated 6 January 1941, in HS8/306; O. Riste, *London regjeringa: Norge i krigsalliansen, 1940–1945*, vol. I (Oslo: Det Norske Samlaget, 1995), p. 118.

28 TNA: 'Scandinavian Policy', 16 April 1940, in HS2/10.
29 TNA: file DEFE2/697; Mann, 'British Policy and Strategy towards Norway, 1941–1945', PhD diss., University of London, 1998, p. 103.
30 See Chapter 2, p. 35.
31 TNA: COS (41) 240 (0), 'Raids on the Coast of Norway', directive to C-in-C Home Fleet, C-in-C Home Forces, and the Adviser on Combined Operations (ACO), 24 October 1941, cited in DEFE2/80; Riste, *London regjeringa*, vol. I, pp. 142–50.
32 For details, see Appendix B, 'Sea-Borne Operations Instigated by or Involving SOE along the Norwegian Seaboard 1940–1945', pp. 219–28.
33 Ibid.
34 Ibid.
35 TNA: 'Operation Instructions No. 1 for Archer', December 1941, in HS2/147.
36 TNA: COS (42) 31st Meeting, 28 January 1942, 'Raids on Norway', in CAB79/17.
37 KTB der OKW 1942, vol. I, pp. 124–5, cited in Riste, *London regjeringa*, vol. I, p. 210; Kjeldstadli, *Hjemmestyrkene: hovedtrekk av den militære motstanden under okkupasjonen*, vol. I (Oslo: H. Aschehoug, 1959), pp. 131–2; *Fuehrer Conferences on Naval Affairs 1939–1945*, pp. 246–9, 257, 259–62.
38 Muller, 'German Perspective on Allied deception Operations in the Second World War', p. 317.
39 TNA: COS (40) 27 (0), 'Subversive Activities in Relation to Strategy', 25 November 1940, in CAB 80/56.
40 In February 1942, Mountbatten proposed two major raids on the Norwegian coast: 'Audacity', an attack on Ålesund with 1,500 commandoes, and 'Centaur', an attack on the Glomfjord factory in northern Norway using 500–700 commandoes. Both were rejected, 'Audacity' was called off because of the strength of the German Air Force (GAF), and attempts to resurrect it again at the end of 1942 were rejected due to opposition from the C-in-C Home Fleet. TNA: COS (42) 35 (0), 7 February 1942, COS (42) 482 (0), 27 December 1942, COS (42) 360th meeting, 30 December 1942, all cited in CAB121/445; Mann, 'British Policy', p. 164.
41 TNA: HS7/174, SOE's Norwegian Section History.
42 Operation Musketoon and Operation Freshman were the two COHQ-led operations. Operations Redshank, Kestral and Marshfield were SOE-led. For details of SOE operations, see Appendix A, 'SOE *Coup de Main* Operations in Norway 1940–1944', pp. 207–18.
43 TNA: letter from Louis Mountbatten to Charles Hambro, 5 March 1942, in HS2/127.
44 TNA: letter from Trygve Lie to Charles Hambro, 17 December 1941, and letter from the MEW to A. H. B. Schofield at the Foreign Office regarding Herring Oil factories, 8 January 1942, in FO371/32827.

45 At the time it was estimated the plant had a capacity to produce 5,000–9,000 tons per annum and was being expanded. TNA: DEFE2/364 and 5 and NHM: FOIV archive, Boks 56, 'Knotgrass/Unicorn'.
46 A. S. Milward, *The Fascist Economy in Norway* (Oxford: Oxford University Press, 1972), p. 264; H. Paulsen, 'Tysk økonomisk politikk i Norge 1940–1945', in H. F. Dahl (ed.), *Krigen i Norge* (Oslo: Pax Forlag, 1974), p. 84.
47 See TNA: DEFE2/122, Operation Cartoon, and NHM: FO IV archive, Boks 56, 'Cartoon/Barter'.
48 TNA: paper entitled 'Attack on the Pyrite Mines etc. on Stord Island in Southern Norway on the night of 23/24 January 1943', in DEFE2/122; Kjeldstadli, *Hjemmestyrkene*, p. 215.
49 TNA: a note with enclosed report from Ottar Grundvig to Mr Hysing Olsen in Notraship, to Charles Hambro from the Ministry of War Transport, 1 April 1942, in HS2/180; Appendix B, 'Sea-Borne Operations Instigated by or Involving SOE along the Norwegian Seaboard 1940–1945', pp. 223–4.
50 It was estimated that this mine produced between 150 and 200,000 tons of raw ore, as well as ilmenite and magnetite concentrate. TNA: memo to COS to ACOS from Colonel R. M. Neville CCO, 4 February 1943, in DEFE2/627; Appendix B, 'Sea-Borne Operations Instigated by or Involving SOE along the Norwegian Seaboard 1940–1945, pp. 219–28.
51 OKW/KTB 5/79, and OKW/KTB 5 129, cited in Muller, 'German Perspective on Allied Deception Operations in the Second World War', p. 319.
52 P. F. Dahl, *Heavy Water and the Wartime Race for Nuclear Energy* (Bristol: IOP, 1999), pp. 24–7; TNA: 'Appendix A to SX's memorandum on "Clairvoyant"', 20 December 1941, attached to a note headed 'Lurgan', 30 July 1942, in HS2/184.
53 R. Wiggan, *Operation Freshman* (London: William Kimber, 1986); Mann, 'British Policy', pp. 172–80; J. A. Poulsson, *Aksjon Vemork: vinterkrig på Hardangervidda* (Oslo: Gyldendal, 1993), pp. 52–67; A. Ueland, *Tungtvannsaksjonen* (Oslo: Gyldendal, 2015).
54 TNA: letter from Mr. A. Webster (Ministry of Supply) to Lt. J. Chaworth-Musters, 10 August 1940, in HS2/238.
55 TNA: letter to Air Vice Marshal C. E. H. Medhurst, from SOE, 2 January 1942, including paper entitled, 'Clairvoyant', 1 January 1942, in HS2/218; NHM: 'Consolidated Progress reports of S Section', weeks ending 27 January and 10 February 1942, in SOE archive, Boks 3a.
56 TNA: letter from H. J. Phelps, Enemy Resources department at the MEW, to M. W. Perrin (DSIR), 29 March 1942, in HS8/955; M. Howard, 'Grand Strategy', vol. IV, in J. R. M. Butler (ed.), *History of the Second World War* (London: HMSO, 1956–7), p. 586.
57 Britain's atomic bomb project was set up on Churchill's instructions and ministerial responsibility was entrusted to Sir John Anderson; Howard,

'Grand Strategy', vol. IV, in Butler (ed.), *History of the Second World War*, p. 586.
58 TNA: memo from SN (Lt. Col. Wilson), to DSIR, 7 May 1942, in HS2/184.
59 TNA: COS (42) 292nd meeting, 19 October 1942, cited in DEFE2/219.
60 TNA: letter from Major Nicholls (MO1-SP) to Lt. Col. Henniker, Air Borne Division, ref. D/CCO/658, 27 October 1942, in DEFE2/ 219. HQ, No 38 Wing, RAF, Operation Order No 5, ref. 38W/MS 10/15/AIR, 16 November 1942, in DEFE2/224.
61 J. Brun, *Brennpunkt Vemork 1940–1945* (Oslo: Universitetsforlaget, 1985), pp. 28–35.
62 E. Welle-Strand, *Vi vil verne vårt land: anti-sabotasje i Norge, 1944–1945* (Oslo: NHM, 2000), pp. 13–14.
63 TNA: letter to Lt. Col. M. C. A. Henniker, CRE Airborne Division, ref. SR1149/42, 16 November 1942, in DEFE2/219.
64 Vestfjord links Østlandet (eastern Norway) and Vestlandet (western Norway); O. Njølstad, *Professor Tronstads Krig* (Oslo: Aschehoug, 2015), pp. 130/1; N. Bascombe, *The Winter Fortress* (London: Head of Zeus, 2017), p. 331.
65 The operational instructions for 'Grouse I & II' in March and August 1942, respectively, make no mention of an operation against heavy water. TNA: paper entitled 'SOE Operation "Gunnerside"' (undated but probably March 1943), in HS2/190; NHM: Operation Grouse I, 28 March 1942, and Operation Instructions for Grouse II, 31 August 1942, in SOE archive, Boks 22.
66 TNA: communication to the prime minister from CCO (Lord L. Mountbatten) by telephone, 22 November 1942, in DEFE2/ 219, and note to Lt. Col. J. S. Wilson from D/CE, 23 November 1942, in HS2/172; R. Wiggan, *Operation Freshman*, p. 97.
67 TNA: letter from Lt. Col. H. N. Harry Sporborg from D/CCO, 4 February 1942, suggesting a list of targets in Norway; minutes of a meeting held on 22 August to discuss the coordination of COHQ and SOE attacks on targets in Norway; memo from CD (Sir Charles Hambro), 5 September 1942, advising directors and section heads to liaise directly with their counterparts at COHQ, all in HS2/226; for details of 'Seagull', see Appendix A, 'SOE *Coup de Main* Operations in Norway 1940–1945', p. 211.
68 TNA: COS (42) 146th meeting (0), 13 October 1942, cited in a paper entitled, 'Small Scale Raiding', 16 December 1942, in HS2/10.
69 TNA: letter from the Admiralty to ACOS, the C-in-C Rosyth, CCO and the Admiral (Submarines), 4 November 1942, in DEFE2/616.
70 TNA: COS (43) 3rd meeting (0), 4 January 1943, in CAB 70/59.
71 TNA: minutes of a meeting held in the war room, Admiralty House, 28 May 1943, in HS2/226.
72 TNA: memo from Lt. Col. J. S. Wilson to Brigadier Colin McV. Gubbins, entitled 'CCO and ACOS', 3 February 1943, in HS2/276.

73 TNA: 'Notes', 8 January 1943, and letter to Group Captain G. T. Jarman, RAF Kinloss, from CAP, 25 February 1943, in DEFE2/522; memo from Lt. Col. H. N. Sporborg to Charles Hambro, 18 February 1943, in HS2/218.
74 TNA: letters from Lt. Col. J. S. Wilson to Commander Ryder, COHQ, 12 and 16 December 1942, and memo from Lt. Col. J. S. Wilson to MG, 29 November 1942, all in HS2/226.
75 NHM: letter from General Hansteen, Norwegian C-in-C, to Lord Louise Mountbatten, CCO, 30 December 1942, in FOIV archive, mappe 17-C-4.
76 TNA: memo from Rear Admiral Brand, ACNS (H), to CCO, 'C' (SIS), and Sir Charles Hambro, 19 January 1943, in HS2/226.
77 TNA: 'Report on Combined Operations North Force 1942/43 by Force Commanders', 9 May 1943, and memo from Lt. Col. J. S. Wilson to Brigadier E. E. Mockler-Ferryman, 30 May 1943, in HS2/226.
78 TNA: memo from Lt. Col. J. S. Wilson to Brigadier C. McV. Gubbins, 29 December 1942.
79 C. Messenger, *The Commandos 1940–1946*, pp. 246–51; Mann, 'British Policy', pp. 201–2; H. K. Svensholt, *Norske Torpedobåter gjennom 125 år 1873–1998* (Oslo: Norsk Tidsskrift for Sjøvesen, 2001); Kjeldstadli, *Hjemmestyrkene*, p. 216 and notes 8, 9 and 10, pp. 419–20.
80 See Appendix A, 'SOE *Coup de Main* Operations in Norway 1940–1944', pp. 207–18.
81 D. Garnett, *The Secret History of PWE: The Political Warfare Executive 1939–1945* (London: St. Ermin's Press, 2002), pp. ix, 1.
82 Garnett, *Secret History of PWE*, pp. x–xii.
83 Mackenzie, *Secret History of SOE*, pp. 6–7; E. Howe, *The Black Game: British Subversive Operations against the Germans during the Second World War* (London: Michael Joseph, 1982), pp. 36–53.
84 TNA: COS (40) 27 (0), 'Subversive Activities in Relation to Strategy', 25 November 1940, in CAB80/56.
85 Garnett, *Secret History of PWE*, pp. 75–81.
86 Lockhart was appointed director general in March 1942 and remained in position until the end of the war; ibid., p. 124.
87 The first regional director for Scandinavia was Thomas Barman; ibid., p. 86.
88 Mr Jebb's minute of 5 September in SOE archive file (AD/S.1) CD/p.5/23, cited in Mackenzie, *Secret History of SOE*, p. 101.
89 Appendix J, SOE and PWE (Agreement of September 1942), cited in Mackenzie, *Secret History of SOE*, pp. 772–3.
90 TNA: 'Norwegian Policy', 11 December 1942, in HS2/128.
91 Riste, *London regjeringa*, vol. I, p. 122.
92 Sibs were rumours disseminated either through the clandestine radio stations or through agents in the field that were designed to subvert the authority or morale of the German authorities across occupied Europe. Riste, *London regjeringa*, vol. I, pp. 151–2, vol. II, pp. 99–100; H. F. Dahl,

'Dette er London': NRK i krig 1940–1945 (Oslo: J.W. Cappelen Forlag, 1978), Garnett, *Secret History of PWE*, pp. 211–15.
93 TNA: COS (40) 27 (0), 'Subversive Activities in Relation to Strategy', 25 November 1940, in CAB80/56; JP (41) 649, 'Special Operations Executive', report by the Joint Planning Staff (JPS), 9 August 1941, in CAB 79/13; COS (43) 142 (0), 'Special Operations Directive for 1943', 20 March 1943, in CAB 80/68; COS 957 (0), 'SOE's Fourth Directive', 9 November 1944, in CAB80/89; 'Operational Directive to SFHQ', ref. SHAEF/17240/13/Ops, 23 March 1944, in WO 219/4967.
94 TNA: 'Fifth Column in Scandinavia and Holland', 31 July 1940; 'Underground Propaganda to Scandinavia', 29 September 1940; 'Subversive Propaganda for Norway', 4 October 1940, all by T. G. Barman, in FO898/240; Riste, *London regjeringa*, vol. I, p. 151; T. Barman, *Diplomatic Correspondent* (London: Hamish-Hamilton, 1968); Dahl, *Dette er London*, pp. 162, 206.
95 TNA: 'Propaganda and Political Warfare-Norway', attached to a memo from Mr Kenney to Capt. Hackett, 11 April 1942, in FO898/73.
96 TNA: letter to Lt. Col. J. S. Wilson from Capt. H. A. Nyberg, 7 September 1942, in FO898/73.
97 TNA: 'A Survey of Training, Preparation of and Planning for the "Operational Propaganda Field-Work Scheme" for Norway, as well as the Reasons for Abandoning the Scheme', from Capt. H. A. Nyberg to Lt. Col. J. S. Wilson, 10 March 1943; memo from Sir Charles Hambro to SY, 6 April 1942, in FO898/73.
98 TNA: letter from SY (K) to George Wiskeman, 16 April 1942, in FO898/73.
99 TNA: 'Plan of Political Warfare against Scandinavia', 18 February 1942, in FO898/240.
100 UK Innst. VI, p. 145, cited in Riste, *London regjeringa*, vol. I, p. 122.
101 At the end of August 1940, the Norwegian authorities reached agreement with BBC and Ministry of Information over broadcasts to Norway, which satisfied Norwegian demands and provided a framework within which both sides worked with little conflict for the rest of the war; Riste, *London regjeringa*, vol. I., p. 151; and Dahl, *Dette er London*, pp. 153–5.
102 TNA: memo from Rowland Kenney (PWE) to Capt. Hackett, 11 April 1942, including a draft paper entitled 'Propaganda and Political Warfare-Norway', in FO898/73.
103 TNA: minutes of the ANCC 24 April, 13 May, 29 May, 10 July, 14 August, 11 September, 9 October and 13 November 1942, cited in FO898/73.
104 TNA: 'Extracts from the minutes of ANCC of 29 May 1942 and internal PWE memo from Mr R. Kenney to Thomas Barman, 10 July 1942, in FO898/73.
105 Olav Riste suggests this project was the result of a Norwegian response to a British wish to intensify Allied propaganda in occupied Europe in light

of a fear that people were losing patience with the failure to establish a 'Second Front'. TNA: 'A survey of the "Operational Propaganda Scheme for Norway" as well as the Reasons for Abandoning the Scheme', 10 March 1943, from Capt. H. A. Nyberg SOE to Lt. Col. J. S. Wilson, in FO898/73; Riste, *London regjeringa*, vol. II, p. 99.

106 Fougner met Bjørn Helland Hansen and Eugen Johannessen while in Oslo. A meeting was held on 28 February 1943 in London, which included members of SOE, PWE and Norwegian representatives, to discuss the letter from the Home Front; TNA: internal PWE memo from Mr Brinley Thomas to Mr K. Kenney, 1 March 1943 (written 28 February 1943), and 'A Survey of the "Operational Propaganda Field-Work Scheme for Norway" as well as Reasons for Abandoning the Scheme', from Capt. H. A. Nyberg to Lt. Col. J. S. Wilson, 10 March 1943, all in FO898/73; Riste, *London regjeringa*, vol. II, pp. 99–100.

107 TNA: reply from the Home Front on the issue of Allied propaganda, sent to Trygve Lie, June 1943, in HS2/234.

108 TNA: minutes of the 20th meeting of the ANCC, 1 July 1943, in HS2/234.

109 TNA: notes of a discussion between Lt. Col. J. S. Wilson and Mr R. Kenney, 11 August 1943, in FO898/73.

110 TNA: 'PWE preliminary working plan for Norway', 19 November 1943, produced in response to a joint PWE/OWI (the American Office of War Information), and SOE/OSS political warfare plan, 9 October 1943, in FO898/73.

111 TNA: minutes of the 27th meeting of the ANCC, 10 February 1944, in HS2/138; telegram from Capt. H. A. Nyberg to E. Nielsen, 24 February 1944, in HS2/234.

112 Appendix A, 'SOE *Coup de Main* Operations in Norway 1940–1945', pp. 207–18.

113 TNA: memo from Capt. H. A. Nyberg to Nielsen in Stockholm, 16 February 1944, in HS2/192.

114 TNA: report entitled 'Impressions from the "Homefront" from a visit to the Oslo District during the period 12 March 1943 to 3 May 1943', in HS2/191. The report is also in the PWE file, FO898/74.

115 From SOE, there was Lt. Col. J. S. Wilson, H. A. Nyberg, and G. Wiskeman and from PWE, Brinley Thomas and Mr. K. Kenney. TNA: letter from Lt. Col. H. N. Sporborg to Brinley Thomas (PWE), ref. F/488/130/17, 24 August 1943, in HS2/234.

116 TNA: paper entitled, 'SOE Outline Plan for Joint Activities in Norway 1943/44' attached to memo from Lt. Col. J. S. Wilson to E. E. Brigadier Mockler-Ferryman, 26 June 1942, in HS2/218.

117 TNA: letter from J. C. Adamson (SOE) to 2nd/Lt. Gram, ref. 517, 9 October 1943, in HS2/192.

118 The material arrived in London on 3 February and was immediately passed to PWE. Gram and Manus requested that a printing press be supplied to

help in the production of their illegal newspaper *Aftonbladet*; TNA: file note headed 'Max Manus and Gregers Gram'; letter from Lt. Col. J. S. Wilson to J. Galsworthy (Northern Dept. Foreign Office), 19 August 1944; letter from SOE HQ to Nielsen, 16 February 1944, all in HS2/192.

119 TNA: letter from SOE HQ (Lt. J. S. Col. Wilson) to Nielsen Stockholm, 24 March 1944; letter from Nielsen to SOE HQ, 7 February 1944, citing a letter by Wilson, 22 January 1944, all in HS2/192.

120 TNA: letters from Leif Tronstad in FO IV to J. C. Adamson, 20 January 1944; letter from Bjarne Øen FO IV to Lt. Col. J. S. Wilson, 27 January 1944; Operation Orders for Bundle/Derby, 28 March 1943, all in HS2/192; NHM: 'Rapport til FO fra Fenrik Max Manus ang. Derby', 24 September 1945, in FO IV archive, Boks 78.

121 According to Manus, the organization totalled 490 men. NHM: 'Rapport til FO fra Fenrik Max Manus ang. Derby' in FO IV archive, Boks 78; M. Manus, *Underwater Saboteur* (London: William Kimber, 1953), p. 175.

122 NHM: report entitled 'Durham', 17 July 1945, interrogation of Lt. Arthur Pevik, 14 June 1945, and report on 'Lark' by E. Gjems-Onstad, Stockholm, 12 July 1944, in SOE archive, Boks 35b; E. Gjems-Onstad, *Durham: Hemmelige operasjoner i Trøndelag mot tysk okkupasjonsmakt 1943–1945* (Oslo: Sollia Forlag, 1981).

123 TNA: 'Joint PWE/OWI and SOE/OSS Political Warfare Plan. Regional Summary – Norway', 26 November 1943, in FO898/242.

124 TNA: letter from Mr Brinley Thomas to Director of Plans, 12 April 1944, in FO898/242.

125 TNA: FO898/243, and memo no. 22, from SHAEF, Psychological Warfare Division, 1 July 1944, in FO898/382.

126 TNA: memo no. 22 from SHAEF, Psychological Warfare Division, 1 July 1944, in FO898/382.

127 TNA: minutes of a meeting at 64 Baker St., 29 December 1944, in FO898/382.

128 The American Office of Strategic Services was an agency of the US government directly responsible to the Joint Chiefs of Staff (JCS). TNA: 'Notes on OSS/SOE Liaison', in HS8/4; B. F. Smith, *The Shadow Warriors: OSS and the Origins of the CIA* (London: Deutsch, 1983), pp. 160–3; I. Dear, *Sabotage and Subversion: The SOE and OSS at War* (London: Cassell Military, 1996), pp. 12–13; Mackenzie, *Secret History of SOE*, pp. 388–93.

129 TNA: note from Lt. Col. J. S. Wilson to Brigadier Colin McV. Gubbins, 24 October 1942, in HS2/134; NHM: letter from Lt. Col. J. S. Wilson to Leif Tronstad, 30 November 1942, in FO IV archive, Boks 32.

130 TNA: 'Summary of Proposed Psychological Warfare Undertaking in Norway', 23 December 1942, in HS2/134.

131 TNA: 'Précis of Meeting Held at Kingston House on 11 January 1943 to Discuss OSS Activities in Norway'; letter from Sir Charles Hambro to Colonel Huntingdon – SO), 14 January 1943, in HS2/218.

132 TNA: COS (43) 117 (0), OSS proposals and the agreement with SOE regarding operations in Norway, and letter from Sir Charles Hambro to Lt. Col. Bruce OSS, 26 March 1943, in HS2/219.
133 TNA: HS7/174, SOE's Norwegian Section-History.
134 TNA: history of the 'Stockholm Mission', by Miss Janet Gow, December 1945, in HS7/190.
135 TNA: paper entitled 'Project Westfield', 23 October 1943, addressed to Brigadier E. E. Mockler-Ferryman (SOE) and Lt. Col. J. F. Haskell (SO), in HS2/134; history of the 'Stockholm Mission', by Miss Janet Gow, December 1945, in HS7/190.
136 TNA: 'Interview with Admiral Stark, ISA', 24 August 1943', in HS8/790; See C. Barnett, *Engage the Enemy More Closely* (London: Penguin, 2000), p.773, for details of Stark.
137 B. Balchen, *Come North with Me* (London: Hodder & Stoughton, 1959), pp. 258–68; Riste, *London regjeringa*, vol. II, p. 172–5; B. H. Heimark, *The OSS Norwegian Special Operations Group in World War II* (London: Praeger, 1994), p. 16.
138 TNA: memo from J. F. M Whiteley (GS DAC of S, G-3) to COS, 30 November 1944, in WO219/2381.
139 TNA: internal memo from OSS HQ, European Theatre of Operations, to Commanding General, United States Strategic Air Force, 18 March 1945, in HS2/6.
140 TNA: telegram from W. J. Keswick to Col. Frank, 20 October 1942, in HS2/134.
141 TNA: memo from Major General Colin McV. Gubbins to MG, 13 February 1943; minutes of a meeting held in room 362, Norgeby House, 20 February 1943, to discuss Operation Midhurst; memo from Lt. Col. J. S. Wilson to MG, 28 February 1943, all in HS2/196; letter from Major General Colin McV. Gubbins (date unknown), in HS2/219; J. Jakub, *Spies and Saboteurs: Anglo-American Collaboration and Rivalry in Human Intelligence Collection and Special Operations 1940–45* (London: Macmillan Press, 1999), pp. 94–5.
142 Smith, *The Shadow Warriors*, p. 162; Dear, *Sabotage and Subversion*, p. 168.
143 Heimark, *OSS Norwegian Special Operations Group in World War II*, pp. 5–8; NHM: B. Langeland, '*Rype*': *The Norwegian Special Operations Group* (Unpublished, 1975), in FO IV archive, Boks 144.
144 In February 1943, Lt. Col. Stromholtz was attached to the OSS in Washington. In July, Colonel Munthe-Kaas replaced him. Between August 1943 and February 1944, three Norwegian officers were attached to NORSO; NHM: note from Lt. Col. B. Øen to Major G. Brewer, 15 February 1943; Letter from General Hansteen to Lt. Col. J. S. Wilson, 7 July 1943, and note from Captain L. Tronstad to Lt. Col. J. S. Wilson, 15 July 1943, all in FO IV archive, Boks 32.

145 TNA: memo from SOE/SO HQ London to G-3 (Ops Div SHAEF), 25 April 1944, in WO219/2380. Heimark, *OSS Norwegian Special Operations Group in World War II*, pp. 13, 15.
146 TNA: letter from Lt. Col. J. S. Wilson to Brigadier E. E. Mockler-Ferryman, 6 January 1944, in HS2/234.
147 TNA: memo from Brigadier E. E. Mockler-Ferryman to Major General Colin McV. Gubbins, copy to Lt. Col. J. S. Wilson, 4 February 1944; draft letter to W. Donovan from Lt. Col. H. N. Sporborg, February 1944 and W. Donovan's reply, February, all in HS2/234.
148 TNA: SHAEF staff minute sheet, 11 May 1944; memo from W. B. Smith COS, to GOC-in-C Scottish Command, 15 July 1944; memo to GOC-in-C Scottish Command, 19 August 1944, all in WO219/2380.
149 G. Pedersen, *Militær motstand i nord 1940–1945* (Tromsø: Universitetsforlaget, 1982), p. 126.
150 NHM: memo from Lt. Cmdr. F. W. G. Unger-Vetlesen, via Major Brewer (copy for Lt. Col. J. S. Wilson), 17 June 1944; memo to Lt. Cmdr F. W. G. Unger-Vetlesen, via Major Brewer (copy for Lt. Col. J. S. Wilson), 14 July 1944; orders to Lt. Håkon Kyllingmark, 29 July 1944, all in SOE archive, Boks 46.
151 NHM: note from Hans Ericksen to Lt. Cmdr. F. W. G. Unger-Vetlesen, 10 August 1944, in SOE archive, Boks 46; Pedersen, *Militær motstand i nord 1940–1945*, p. 131.
152 TNA: 'Directive for Sabotage Operations' to Commanding Officer, Sepals Groups, from SFHQ, 16 November 1944, in HS2/235.
153 FOIV/154, Sepals 1 Op. 10, report dated London 13 November 1942, cited in Pedersen, *Militær motstand i nord*, p. 156.
154 Pedersen, *Militær motstand i nord*, p. 134.
155 TNA: paper from OSS to Commanding General United States Air Forces, attention Chief of Staff, 7 December 1944, in HS2/235. Two squadrons were later provided by 492 BG to supply *Milorg* further south; see p. 33.
156 Note marked 'Bases' and memo to G. Vetlesen from Brøgger, 10 March 1945, in SOE Boks 46, cited in Pedersen, *Militær motstand i nord*, pp. 156–8.
157 Pedersen, *Militær motstand i nord 1940–1945*, pp. 159–62, 163–5, 177.
158 Langeland, 'Rype', in FO IV archive, Boks 144; and Heimark, *The OSS Norwegian Special Operations Group in World War II*, p. 61.
159 TNA: memo from Lt. Gen. Thorne to SHAEF, 12 September 1944, in WO219/2380; memo from SFHQ (Lt. Col. J. S. Wilson and Lt. Cmdr F. W. G. Unger-Vetlesen) to Colonel Joseph F. Haskell, Commanding Officer SO, OSS, ETOUSA, 16 September 1944, in HS2/235.
160 TNA: telegram from SHAEF to SCOTCO, 25 October 1944, in HS2/234.
161 TNA: memo to AC of S, G-3 Division SHAEF Main, from SFHQ, 29 December 1944, in HS2/235; memo from SFHQ to AC of G-3 Division, SHAEF, 14 December, in HS2/234.

162 TNA: minutes of meeting held at SFHQ, 16 January 1945, on Norwegian Resistance, in HS2/235.
163 NHM: SFHQ Report on dispatch of NORSO Group on Operational Missions to Chief, Scandinavian Section, SO Branch, OSS, and memo to Lt. Cmdr. F. W. G. Unger-Vetlesen from Hans Ericksen, 5 April 1945, in SOE archive, Boks 144; Langeland, 'Rype', in FOIV archive, Boks 144.

Chapter 6

1 M. R. D. Foot, *SOE: The Special Operations Executive 1940–1946*, 2nd edn (London: Pimlico, 1999), pp. 31–2; D. A. T. Stafford, *Britain and European Resistance 1940–1945: A Survey of the Special Operations Executive with Documents* (Toronto: University of Toronto Press, 1980), p. 40.
2 C. Barnett, *Engage the Enemy More Closely* (London: Penguin, 2000), pp. 253, 394.
3 Stafford, *Britain and European Resistance 1940–1945*, p. 130.
4 F. H. Hinsley et al., *British Intelligence in the Second World War: Its Influence on Strategy and Operations*, vol. 1 (HMSO: London, 1979–88), pp. 16–7.
5 B. Nøkleby, *Pass godt på Tirpitz* (Oslo: Gyldendal, 1988), pp. 183, 165.
6 TNA: HS2/174, the Norwegian Section History.
7 R. Ulstein, *Etterretningstjenesten 1940–1945* (Oslo: NHM, 1994), pp. 32–40.
8 TNA: letter from J. K. Cordeaux (SIS) to Col. R. Neville (COHQ), 23 March 1943, in DEFE2/449; Nøkleby, *Pass godt på Tirpitz*, pp. 218–20.
9 Ulstein, *Etterretningstjenesten 1940–1945*, p. 13.
10 JIC (43) 517, 22 December 1943, cited in Stafford, *Britain and European Resistance*, pp. 137–9.
11 J. G. Beevor, *SOE: Recollections and Reflections 1940–1945* (London: Bodley Head, 1981), p. 73.
12 TNA: JIC (42) 156 (0), 29 April 1942, in CAB 84/85, and COS (42) 142 (0), 'Special Operations Executive Directive for 1943', 20 March 1943, in CAB 80/68.
13 Nøkleby, *Pass godt på Tirpitz*, pp. 30–1.
14 *Den Norske regjerings virksomhet fra 9 april 1940 til 22 juni 1945*, vol. IV, *Forsvarsdepartementet*, p. 102.
15 TNA: interview with Captain Finn Nagell, 21 November 1940, in HS2/238.
16 K. Jeffery, *MI6: The History of the Secret Intelligence Service 1909–1949* (London: Bloomsbury, 2010), p. 374.
17 TNA: report entitled 'Military Organisation in Norway' from J. B. Newill, in HS2/228. FKA, Nagells arkiv 88.2, cited in O. Riste, *London*

regjeringa: *Norge i krigsalliansen, 1940–1945*, vol. I (Oslo: Det Norske Samlaget, 1995), p. 111.
18 NHM: 'Consolidated Progress Reports of S Section', nos 33 and 34, weeks ending 16 and 23 July 1941, in SOE archive, Boks 3a.
19 M. Smith, *Foley: The Spy Who Saved 10,000 Jews* (London: Coronet), p. 180.
20 TNA: memo from Major F. W. Ram to Charles Hambro, 2 May 1942, in HS2/136.
21 Ibid.; for details, see A. Ueland, *Shetlandsgjengen: Heltene i Nordsjøen* (Oslo: Kagge Forlag, 2017), pp. 230–4.
22 TNA: 'Report on Operation Anchor and Penguin', from Malcolm Munthe to Lt. Col. H. N. Sporborg, in HS2/136; S. Kjeldstadli, *Hjemmestyrkene: hovedtrekk av den militære motstanden under okkupasjonen*, vol. I (Oslo: H. Aschehoug, 1959), pp. 156–8.
23 TNA: HS7/174, the Norwegian Section History.
24 TNA: 'SOE Long-term Policy in Norway', 21 September 1942, in HS2/128.
25 Notes from the Personal File of J. L. Chaworth-Musters supplied by SOE Adviser at the Foreign Office; P. L. Johns, *Within Two Cloaks* (London: William Kimber, 1979).
26 B. A. Rørholt, *Amatørspionen 'Lerken'* (Oslo: Hjemmenes, 1985), p. 178; R. Ulstein, *Etterretningstjenesten i Norge 1940–1945*, vol. I (Oslo: Cappelen, 1987–92), pp. 92–3, 106–7; TNA: letter from Lt. Col. J. S. Wilson to Major John Rognes, 2 July 1942, in HS2/139.
27 K. Haukelid, *Skis against the Atom* (London: William Kimber, 1954), pp. 39–42, 54–5; S. Midtskau, *London svarer ikke* (Oslo: E.G. Mortensens, 1968), p. 111.
28 TNA: HS7/174, the Norwegian Section History.
29 TNA: memo from Charles Hambro to D/T, 17 March 1941, and telegrams from 'Cheese', 1 June and 10 June 1941, in HS2/150; File 1/470/14 cited in W. J. M. Mackenzie, *The Secret History of SOE: The Special Operations Executive* (London: St. Ermin's Press, 2000), p. 95.
30 The accounts of Rørholt and Jones are contradictory. Jones claims that he reacted to a telegram from Norway about heavy water, while Rørholt, a member of the 'Skylark B' team, claims that it responded to a request from the Home Station for information on heavy water. The contact for the 'Skylark B' team was Professor Leif Tronstad, who at the time was a leading figure in the emerging military resistance in Trøndelag; Rørholt, *Amatørspionen 'Lerken'*, p. 83; R. V. Jones, *Most Secret War* (London: Wordsworth Editions, 1998), pp. 205–6; Ulstein, *Etterretningstjenesten i Norge 1940–1945*, vol. I, p. 152; J. Brun, *Brennpunkt Vemork 1940–1945* (Oslo: Universitetsforlaget, 1985), p. 14.
31 Welsh had worked in Norway prior to the outbreak of war. At the end of April 1940, he returned to England and in May 1941 became head of the Norwegian section of SIS. TNA: letter from DSIR (Michael Perrin) to

Gorell Barnes (Privy Council Office), 1 December 1942, in CAB126/171; letter to Nielsen in SOE Stockholm from Lt. Col. J. S. Wilson, 4 October 1943, in HS2/187; Brun, *Brennpunkt Vemork*, p. 37; Jones, *Most Secret War*, pp. 307–9, 472–4; FO II's London arkiver, Welsh til Nagell, 20 October 1943, in Section V's arkiv, cited in Nøkleby, *Pass godt på Tirpitz*, pp. 34–5.

32 TNA: memo from Lt. Col. J. S. Wilson, 20 April 1943, in HS2/186.
33 TNA: letter from Lt. Col. J. S. Wilson to Broadway (SIS), ref. JSW/296, 23 October 1943, in HS2/187; letter from Lt. Col. J. S. Wilson to Lt. Cdr. E. Welsh, 28 March 1944, in HS2/188.
34 TNA: telegrams from 'Theta' and note from Lt. Col. J. S. Wilson to LB (someone within SIS), 5 May 1942, in HS2/136; K. Ottosen, *Theta Theta* (Oslo: Universitetsforlaget, 1983), p. 56.
35 TNA: message from 'Upsilon', telephoned 10 April from 'C', in HS2/161.
36 The final report of the only survivor of 'Martin', Jan Baalsrud, was also passed to SIS; TNA: letter ref. NS/215, 26 March 1943, in HS2/161.
37 TNA: memo from Lt. Col. J. S. Wilson to Brigadier E. E. Mockler-ferryman, 26 June 1943, with paper entitled, 'SOE Activities in Norway during 1943/1944', 26 June 1943, in HS2/218.
38 NHM: minute to SN (Lt. Col. J. S. Wilson), ref. SA/85, 18 October 1942, in SOE archive, Boks 14; TNA: memo to DC/E from Lt. Col. J. S. Wilson, 11 January 1943, in HS2/245.
39 TNA: telegram to 'Swan', 6 January 1943, cited in HS2/280, SOE war diary, November 1942–March 1943.
40 Ulstein, *Etterretningstjenesten i Norge 1940–1945*, vol. III, p. 429.
41 TNA: minute received from SIS, 4 November 1943, in HS2/139; 'Report on Operational Plans for Meeting of ANCC', 9 September 1943', in HS2/236.
42 TNA: memo headed 'Notes re. Martin', from Captain P. F. S. Douglas to SN/A.1, 10 April 1943, in file HS2/161; Ulstein, *Etterretningstjenesten i Norge 1940–1945*, vol. I, p. 240.
43 Nøkleby, *Pass godt på Tirpitz*, p. 184.
44 TNA: paper entitled 'Trondheim Organisations', 6 October 1941, in HS2/231; Ulstein, *Etterretningstjenesten i Norge 1940–1945*, vol. II, p. 137, vol. III, pp. 344–5; O. Reed-Olsen, *Two Eggs on My Plate* (London: Companion Book Club, 1954).
45 Stafford, *Britain and European Resistance*, p. 130.
46 TNA: letter from the Admiralty to ACOS, the C-in-C Rosyth, CCO, and the Admiral (Submarines), 4 November 1942, in DEFE2/616.
47 TNA: COS (43) 3rd meeting, 4 January 1943, in CAB 70/59.
48 See Chapter 5, p. 162; TNA: minutes of a meeting held in the war room, Admiralty House, 28 May 1943, in HS2/226.
49 Kenneth Macksey uses the term 'C-ban' to describe SIS objections to operations on Norway's coast; K. Macksey, *Commando Strike: The Story of*

Amphibious Raiding in World War II (London: Secker & Warburg, 1985), p. 158.
50 TNA: 'Report on Operational Plans for Meeting of ANCC', 12 August 1943, in HS2/236.
51 TNA: 'Report on Operational Plans for Meeting of ANCC', 9 December 1943, in HS2/236.
52 TNA: Telegram to Lerwick, 22 February 1944, in HS2/209.
53 TNA: letter to Broadway, 3 March 1944, in HS2/209.
54 TNA: letter to Broadway with enclosed intelligence, 22 May 1944, in HS2/209.
55 TNA: report on Vestige V and minute from SIS, 28 July 1944, in HS2/209.
56 SIS raised objections to 'Salamander' I, III and IV. Operations I and III never went ahead, IV was cancelled due to operational reasons, while II and V went ahead in September 1944; TNA: paper entitled, 'Salamander Operations', 6 September 1944, and letter from J. K. Cordeaux (SIS) to the Director of Naval Intelligence, 23 September 1944, in ADM223/481.
57 TNA: COS (43) 142 (0), 'Special Operations Directive for 1943', 20 March 1943, in CAB 80/68; 'Directive for Future Sabotage Policy in Norway', 31 May 1943, in HS2/233; see also Appendix A, 'SOE *Coup de Main* Operations in Norway 1940–1944', pp. 207–18.
58 T. Pryser, *Hitlers hemmelige agenter: Tysk etteretning I Norge 1939–1945* (Oslo: Universitetsforlaget, 2001), pp. 112–19.
59 B. Christophersen, *Norsk militær innsats ute og hjemme 1940–1945* (Bergen: John Greig, 1981).
60 W. N. Medlicott, *The Economic Blockade*, vol. I (London: HMSO, 1952 and 1959), p. 153.
61 KTB der OKW 1942, I, pp. 124–5, cited in Riste, *London regjeringa*, vol. I, p. 210.
62 Nøkleby, *Pass godt på Tirpitz*, pp. 219–20.
63 Defence Committee no 7, 2 March 1942, in CAB 69/4, cited in M. Gilbert, *Road to Victory: Winston S. Churchill 1941–1945* (London: Heinemann, 1989), p. 70; C. Barnett, *Engage the Enemy More Closely* (London: Penguin, 2000), p. 695.
64 Appendix C, 'A History of the Shetlands Base Autumn 1939 to May 1945', in I. Herrington, 'The SIS and SOE in Norway 1940–1945: Conflict or Co-operation?', *War in History*, vol. 9, no. 1, January 2002, pp. 82–110.
65 NHM: 'Staff of Norwegian Section, SOE: 1942–1945', in SOE archive, Boks 10.
66 TNA: letters to the First Sea Lord, 22 and 26 December, and the First Sea Lord's reply on 24 December, in PREM 3/328/6; W. S. Churchill, 'The Gathering Storm', vol. I, in *The Second World War* (London: Cassell, 1948–54), pp. 420–33.
67 TNA: 'Report on Position of Plans and Projects' as at 5 March 1941, in HS8/231.

68 NHM: 'Consolidated Progress Reports of S Section', weeks ending 29 April, 7 May, 15 May 1941, in SOE archive Boks 3a; 'Operational Diary, August 1943–June 1944', in SOE archive, Boks 5; TNA: 'Repetition of Operation Maundy', in ADM223/481; message from Lt. Col. Ram, SOE to Major L. H. Mitchell, 24 February 1942, in HS2/159.
69 See Chapter 5, p. 97.
70 TNA: a minute from Mr Brittain to the British Treasury, 23 September 1941, in HS2/244.
71 TNA: SOE Executive Committee – weekly progress reports, May–August 1941, in HS8/217; SOE Executive Committee – weekly progress reports, September–November 1941, in HS8/218; NHM: 'Consolidated Progress Reports of S Section', 6 August 1941–25 November 1941, in SOE archive, Boks 3b.
72 TNA: paper entitled, 'Services Rendered by SOE to CCO: October 1941 to March 1942', attached to a note from C. H. Hambro to J. C. Haydon, 27 March 1942, in HS8/818.
73 TNA: naval cipher from the Admiralty to C-in-C Home Fleet, 22 February 1941, in PREM3/328/7; reports, various – directives and heads of sections plans and projects, 5, 8 and 18 March 1941, in HS8/231.
74 NHM: 'Interview with Lt. Col. H. N. Sporborg, Frank Stagg, Captain Danielsen and Captain Ullstrup of the Norwegian Destroyer "Mansfield"', in SOE archive, Boks 44; TNA: note by Hugh Dalton on 'Hemisphere', in HS8/ 367.
75 See Chapter 5, pp. 97–8.
76 In August 1943, RNorN MTB Flotilla became the 54th (N) MTB Flotilla and was expanded to twelve vessels; TNA: memo from ACOS to the Secretary for the Admiralty, 18 October 1942, in DEFE2/616; M. C. Mann, 'British Policy and Strategy towards Norway, 1941–1945', PhD diss., University of London, 1998, pp. 188–190.
77 TNA: COS (43) 142 (0), 'Special Operations Directive for 1943', 20 March 1943, in CAB 80/68; 'Directive for Future Sabotage Policy in Norway', from Brigadier E. E. Mockler-Ferryman to Charles Hambro, 31 May 1943, in HS2/233.
78 NHM: Appendix Q, 'Norwegian Section: Liaison with Naval Authorities', in SOE archive, Boks 11, Wilson's file.
79 TNA: paper entitled, 'Attacks on Enemy Coastal Shipping', from Brigadier E. E. Mockler-Ferryman to D/Plans, 6 July 1943, in HS8/284.
80 NHM: '*Coup de Main* Operations – Shipping', in SOE archive, Boks 9; TNA: papers on Vestige I, II and III and memo from ACOS (Vice-Admiral Wells) to Lt. George Pollock, 2 September 1943, in HS2/208; for details, see Appendix B, 'Sea-Borne Operations Instigated by or Involving SOE Along the Norwegian Seaboard 1940–1945', pp. 219–28.
81 TNA: 'History of the Welman', in PREM3/191/1; 'History of the Welman Craft', by Professor D. M. Newitt (SOE), in DEFE2/958; P. Kemp, *Underwater*

Warriors: The Fighting History of Midget Submarines (London: Cassell, 1996), pp. 158–64.
82 TNA: 'Minutes of a Meeting on Welman Craft Held at Northways on 9 February 1943', in DEFE2/958.
83 TNA: telegram from Lerwick, ref. local 916, 9 June 1943, in HS8/800.
84 TNA: SOE Executive Committee – weekly progress reports, weeks commencing 19 July and 16 August, in HS8/225.
85 TNA: message from FOC, submarine sta., 3 August 1943, in HS8/800.
86 NHM: 'Operational Diary, August 1943–June 1944', in SOE archive, Boks 5; Appendix B, 'Sea-Borne Operations Instigated by or Involving SOE Along the Norwegian Seaboard 1940–1945', pp. 219–28.
87 There is at least one case of a 'Chariot' coming loose in heavy seas and having to be cut loose and dropped over board. See Kemp, *Underwater Warriors*, p. 122; Kjeldstadli, *Hjemmestyrkene*, p. 215; J. W. Irvine, *The Waves Are Free: Shetland/Norway Links, 1940–1945* (Lerwick: Shetland, 1988), p. 142.
88 C. Goulter, *A Forgotten Offensive* (London: Frank Cass, 1995), p. 309.
89 ADM223/172 & 315, cited in Ulstein, *Etterretningstjenesten*, vol. III, pp. 391–9; Barnet, *Engage the Enemy More Closely*, pp. 844, 852–3.
90 A. D. Lambert, 'Seizing the Initiative: The Arctic Convoys, 1944–45', in N. A. M. Rodgers (ed.), *Naval Power in the Twentieth Century* (London: Macmillan, 1996), p. 151.
91 TNA: paper entitled 'Salamander Operations', 6 September 1944, in ADM233/481; NHM: Operation Instructions for Salamander in FO IV archive, Boks 122; Ulstein, *Etterretningstjenesten 1940–1945*, pp. 32–40; Appendix B, 'Sea-Borne Operations Instigated by or Involving SOE Along the Norwegian Seaboard 1940–1945', pp. 219–28.
92 NHM: Appendix Q, 'Norwegian Section Liaison with Naval Authorities', in SOE archive, Boks 11, Wilson's file; TNA: note from the Director of Operational Research, Admiralty, to Admiral (Submarines), 11 February 1947, and from Flag Officer Submarines, Fort Blockhouse, Gosport, to Director of Operational research, 25 April 1947, in ADM 199/1890; Kemp, *Underwater Warriors*, pp. 168, 175.
93 Christine Goulter, in her history of Coastal Command, argues that its anti-shipping campaign in north-west Europe was clearly successful in terms of tonnage sunk; Goulter, *Forgotten Offensive*, pp. 316–7; Irvine, *The Waves Are Free*, p. 131.
94 *Den norske regjerings virksomhet: fra 9 april til 22 juni 1945*, vol. IV, *forsvarsdepartementet*, p. 31.
95 Christine Goulter also argues that the Coastal Command offensive made a major contribution through diverting German manpower and war materials to defend shipping; Goulter, *Forgotten Offensive*, pp. 316–17.

96 In November 1941, Hitler decided to move the *Tirpitz* to Norway. Report of the C-in-C Navy to the Fuehrer, 13 November 1941, and 29 December 1941, cited in *Fuehrer Conferences on Naval affairs*, pp. 237, 248.
97 See Nøkleby, *Pass godt på Tirpitz*, pp. 75, 81.
98 TNA: telegrams nos. 985 and 956, dated 21 February and 7 March 1942, in HS2/141.
99 I can find nothing in SOE archives to support this theory. NHM: 'Lark Notes', in SOE archive, Boks 33, and Boks 38; TNA: files HS2/159 and 160; R. Dahlø, *Skjebnetråder: En historie om de ukjente krigerne* (Oslo: Schibsted forlag, 2001), p. 165.
100 TNA: HS2/179, Operation Frodesley.
101 Although the first craft was complete by end of June 1942, it was September before preliminary trials began. TNA: memo from Lt. Col. J. S. Wilson to Malcolm Munthe, 7 May 1942, in HS2/202; 'History of the Welman', in PREM 3/191/1; Kemp, *Underwater Warriors*, p. 158.
102 TNA: memo to Malcolm Munthe from Lt. Col. J. S. Wilson, 7 May 1942, in HS2/202.
103 TNA: HS2/202, Operation Title.
104 The 'Lark' organization approached a local man, Johan Utseto, who owned a fishing boat called the *Monitor*. He rejected their approach and therefore a boat from the Shetlands had to be used. A courier was sent to Trondheim from the British legation in Stockholm to collect certain papers, including a certificate for the *Arthur*, which had been organized by the 'Lark' organization. At the beginning of October 1942, Odd Sørli flew to Scotland with these papers. He was also able provide information on the area around Trondheim before the operation sailed. TNA: 'Orders for Operation Title', issued by the office of Admiral (Submarines), 22 September 1942; letter from SOE to captain, the Lord Ashbourne RN, 1 October 1942; paper entitled 'Title', by Lt. Col. J. S. Wilson, 16 November 1942, all in HS2/202.
105 TNA: paper entitled 'Title' by Lt. Col. J. S. Wilson, 16 November 1942, in HS2/202.
106 TNA: letter from Commander D. C. Ingram RN to Lt. Col. J. S. Wilson, 19 October 1942, in HS2/206.
107 TNA: HS2/206, Operation Source.
108 See Mann, 'British Policy', pp. 75–6.
109 C. Webster and N. Frankland, *The Strategic Air Offensive against Germany 1939–1945* (London: HMSO), vol. I, p. 141, note 2, and vol. II, part 4, pp. 66, 292; W. F. Craven and J. L. Cate (eds), *The Army Air Forces in World War II*, vol. II (Washington DC: Office of Air Force History, 1983), pp. 674–6, 851.
110 Goulter, *Forgotten Offensive*.
111 Stafford, *Britain and European Resistance*, pp. 61–2, 111–12, 116–17; Foot, *SOE: The Special Operations Executive 1940–1946*, pp. 31–2.

112 TNA: 'Norwegian Policy', 11 December 1940, in HS2/128.
113 TNA: JP (41) 649, 'Special Operations Executive', report by the Joint Planning Staff, 9 August 1941, in CAB79/13; Farrell, *The Basis and Making of British Grand Strategy*, book I (New York: Edwin Mellen Press, 1998-9), p. 142.
114 In August 1941, the Butt Report after examining hundreds of photographs and flight reports concluded that of all aircraft recorded as having hit their targets, only one-third got within five miles of them. See Webster and Frankland, *Strategic Air Offensive against Germany 1939-1945*, vol. IV, pp. 205-13, cited in Denis Richards, *RAF Bomber Command in the Second World War: The Hardest Victory* (London: Penguin, 2001), p. 96.
115 Sverre Kjeldstadli argues that the Norwegian view was that sabotage was the preferred alternative as it avoided unnecessary damage to property and casualties. He continues that for the Allies, after the Casablanca Conference in 1943, bombing became a necessity, but with regard to Norway the Norwegian view eventually prevailed. Riste disputes this. He argues that each target was judged on its merits and that sabotage or bombing was chosen on the basis of suitability. Both the British and Norwegians were prepared to accept either means and therefore neither bombing nor sabotage was the choice of one nation. Kjeldstadli, *Hjemmestyrkene*, pp. 210-11; Riste, *London regjeringa*, vol. II, pp. 61-2.
116 TNA: AIR15/491, Operations against Naval and Industrial Targets – Norway and Denmark.
117 The meeting that led to these operations was held on 29 November. Finn Nagell claims that there was more than one meeting and Hambro certainly suggested weekly meetings with Coastal Command. TNA: Report from Air Chief Marshal, Commander-in-Chief, Coastal Command, on operations against military industrial targets, Norway, 4 January 1941, and letter from Charles Hambro to Group-Captain Lloyd, 27 December 1940, in AIR15/491; KKA, Nagell's arkiv, mappe 77, and conversations with Nagell in 1970, cited in Riste, *London regjeringa*, vol. I, p. 108.
118 TNA: 'Rebellion in Norway', 6 August 1940 and 'Norwegian Project', 3 November 1940', in HS2/128; Riste, *London regjeringa*, vol. I, p. 108.
119 See Chapter 5, pp. 149-50.
120 B. Hafsten et al., *Flyalarm: Luftkrigen over Norge 1939-1945* (Oslo: Sem & Stenersen, 1991), p. 126; *Den norske regjerings virksomhet fra 9 april 1940 til 22 juni 1945*, vol. IV, *forsvarsdepartementet*, p. 125; Riste, *London regjeringa*, vol. II, p. 47.
121 Bomber Command undertook several operations against Norwegian airfields during the campaign in Norway, but by spring 1941 the focus had moved to dropping mines. At this time Britain also took delivery of twenty B-17s, some of which undertook two raids against Norway

in September 1941. Up until June 1941, Germany was still dropping a heavier payload on Britain than it received. H. P. Willmott, *The Great Crusade* (London: M. Joseph, 1989), pp. 277–84; Farrell, *Basis and Making of British Grand Strategy*, book I, p. 186; Hafsten et al., *Flyalarm: Luftkrigen over Norge 1939–1945*, pp. 79–82, 109–17, 129.

122 J. A. Poulssen, *Aksjon Vemork: vinterkrig på Hardangervidda* (Oslo: Gyldendal, 1993), p. 38; see Chapter 5, p. 159.

123 NHM: 'Consolidated Progress Reports of S Section', nos. 61 and 62, 27 and 10, February 1942, in SOE archive, Boks 3a.

124 TNA: internal COHQ note from A.P.1 to C.A.P., 31 October 1942, and letter from Brigadier C. McV. Gubbins (SOE) to Major General J. C. Haydon (COHQ), 30 October 1942, in DEFE2/219.

125 TNA: 'Report with Reference to Attacks at Rjukan and Vemork' (translation), from Leif Tronstad to General Hansteen, 30 November 1943, in HS8/955; Riste, *London regjeringa*, vol. II, pp. 50, 53.

126 Brun, *Brennpunkt Vemork*, p. 70.

127 TNA: telegram from 'Swallow', 8 July, in HS2/187.

128 TNA: 'Report with Reference to Attacks at Rjukan and Vemork' (translation), from Leif Tronstad to General Hansteen, 30 November 1943, in HS8/955; memo from Captain L. Tronstad to Lt. Col. J. S. Wilson, 5 August 1943, in HS2/187; Kjeldstadli, *Hjemmestyrkene*, p. 206; O. Njølstad, *Professor Tronstads Krig* (Oslo: Aschehoug, 2015), pp. 250–66.

129 TNA: memo from Lt. Col. J. S. Wilson to Air Commodore A. R. Boyle, 10 August 1943, in HS2/187.

130 TNA: paper entitled, 'TA Project: Enemy Intelligence', from M. W. Perrin and Major R. R. Furman to the Chancellor of the Exchequer and Major General Groves, 28 November 1944, in CAB126/244; Hinsley et al., *British Intelligence in the Second World War*, vol. II, p. 128; Brun, *Brennpunkt Vemork*, pp. 65, 74; P. F. Dahl, *Heavy Water and the Wartime Race for Nuclear Energy* (Bristol: IOP, 1999), p. 248; A. Kramish, *The Griffin* (Boston: Houghton Mifflin, 1986); Jones, *Most Secret War*, pp. 472–3.

131 TNA: paper entitled, 'Norway – Production of Heavy Water', by Michael Penn (this is probably M. W. Perrin), 20 August 1943, in HS8/ 955.

132 TNA: memo from Lt. Col. J. S. Wilson to Air Comdr. A. R. Boyle, 10 August 1943; memo from Lt. Col. H. N. Sporborg to Brigadier E. E. Mockler-Ferryman, 5 October 1943; note from Brigadier E. E. Mockler-Ferryman to Lt. Col. H. N. Sporborg, 15 October 1943, and letter from H. N. Sporborg to W. L. Gorell-Barnes, 16 October 1943, all in HS2/187.

133 TNA: letter from L. C. Hollis (secretary to the COS Committee) to CAS (Chief of the Air Staff, Sir Charles Portal), 18 October 1943, in AIR8/1767.

134 TNA: note from the Chief of the Air Staff, Sir Charles Portal, to Brigadier Hollis, 20 October 1943, in AIR8/1767.

135 TNA: Operation 131, Provisional Main Reports, 18 November, in AIR40/481.
136 Kjeldstadli, *Hjemmestyrkene*, p. 221; Brun, *Brennpunkt Vemork 1940–1945*, p. 78.
137 TNA: letter from L. Collier, British Ambassador to Norway to Trygve Lie, Norwegian Foreign Minister, 4 January 1944, and note to Anthony Eden, British Foreign Minister from L. Collier, ref. N235/24/G, 7 January 1944, in HS2/234; Riste, *London regjeringa*, vol. II, pp. 54–6.
138 Kjeldstadli claims that SOE was not advised of the operation until it was over. Riste claims that SOE shared the Norwegian view that the heavy water site was more suited to sabotage than bombing. Kjeldstadli, *Hjemmestyrkene*, pp. 205–7; Riste, *London regjeringa*, vol. II, p. 58; see Njølstad, *Professor Tronstads Krig*, pp. 250–90.
139 TNA: Paper headed, 'List of Selected Targets', no 2, Knaben Molybdenum Mines, 5 September 1942, in HS8/131.
140 Small amounts also came from northern Norway and Finland. TNA: Memo from Lt. Col. H. N. Sporborg to Brigadier Colin McV. Gubbins, 28 November 1942, in HS8/237; paper entitled 'Knaben Molybdenum Mine: Appreciation of Importance to Germany', in AIR20/8179; Goulter, *Forgotten Offensive*, p. 310; F.D. 5359/45, RK., Abt., 'Delivery Programme for the Norwegian Economy, 1 September 1942 to 31 August 1943', cited in A. S. Milward, *The Fascist Economy in Norway* (Oxford: Oxford University Press, 1972), pp. 61, 264.
141 TNA: 'Reports to the COS, March 1942–December 1942', month ending 14 May 1942, in HS8/244; NHM: 'Consolidated Progress Report of S Section', week ending 31 March, in SOE archive, Boks 3a; ANCC Meetings, 1–20, no 5, 24 April 1942, in FOIV archive, Boks 32.
142 TNA: 'Consolidated Progress Reports of S Section', weeks ending 21 July, 21 August and 27 September 1942; paper entitled 'Projected Operations', 12 August 1942, in HS2/226; meeting of 'search committee' at COHQ, 24 October 1942, in DEFE2/4.
143 TNA: 'Reports on Operational Plans for Meetings of ANCC', 12 February 1943, in HS2/236.
144 NHM: 'Mosquito Attack on Knaben, 3 March 1943', in SOE archive, Boks 9; TNA: Paper entitled, 'Knaben Molybdenum Mine', in AIR20/8179; 'Operation 131', in AIR/481; Webster and Frankland, *Strategic Air Offensive against Germany*, vol. II, part 4, p. 292; Kjeldstadli, *Hjemmestyrkene*, note 38, p. 415.
145 TNA: memo from Lt. Col. J. S. Wilson to E. E. Mockler-Ferryman, 13 December 1944, in HS2/235; FA, hylle 20, mappe 'Samarbeidet med SOE: Generelt', cited in Kjeldstadli, *Hjemmestyrkene*, p. 208; C. Gunnfeldt, *Bomb Gestapo Hovedkvarteret* (Oslo: Wings Forlag, 1995).
146 NHM: FO IV archive, Boks 9, 'Bombing'; Hafsten et al., *Flyalarm: Luftkrigen over Norge 1939–1945*, pp. 238–9.

147 TNA: minutes of meeting held at SFHQ, 16 January 1945, in HS2/234; internal memo from SHAEF (G-3 Division) to SFHQ, 25 January 1945, in HS2/235.
148 TNA: paper entitled 'SOE', 10 April 1942, in HS8/898.

Chapter 7

1 TNA: COS (40) 27 (0), 'Subversive Activities in Relation to Strategy', 25 November 1940, in CAB 80/56.
2 TNA: COS (43) 142 (0), 'Special Operations Directive for 1943', 20 March 1943, in CAB 80/68; paper entitled, 'The Prospects of Subversion: A Country by Country Analysis', 21 April 1941, in HS8/272.
3 TNA: COS (40) 27 (0), 'Subversive Activities in Relation to Strategy', 25 November 1940, in CAB 80/56.
4 NHM: 'Consolidated Progress Report of S Section', week ending 28 January 1941, in SOE archive, Boks 3a,
5 Appendix A, 'SOE *Coup de Main* Operations in Norway 1940–1944', pp. 207–18.
6 TNA: 'Norwegian Policy', 11 December 1940, in HS2/128.
7 For full details on the training of Norwegian recruits, see Chapter 1, pp. 19–23.
8 Appendix A, 'SOE *Coup de Main* Operations in Norway 1940–1944', pp. 207–18; TNA: note from Lt. Col. J. S. Wilson to Lt. Col. H. N. Sporborg, 27 February 1941, telegram from Lerwick, 8 March 1941, and telegram from Lerwick to SO2, 5 April 1941, all in HS2/207.
9 W. J. M. Mackenzie, *The Secret History of SOE: The Special Operations Executive* (London: St. Ermin's Press, 2000), pp. 729–36.
10 TNA: 'The Organisation and Control of Special Duty (SD) Operations in Northwest Europe 1940–1945', in AIR20/8224; SOE Executive Committee – weekly progress reports, week ending 21 January 1942, in HS8/220.
11 See Chapter 2, pp. 36–7.
12 See Chapter 3, pp. 62–3.
13 M. Munthe, *Sweet is War* (London: Duckworth, 1954), pp. 129, 132, 149.
14 TNA: 'Reports, Various – Directives and Heads of Sections Plans and Projects', as at 5 March 1941, in HS8/231; letter from W. S. Churchill to the First Sea Lord, 26 December 1940, in PREM 3/328/6.
15 NHM: 'Consolidated Progress Report of S Section', week ending 4 March 1941, in SOE archive, Boks 3a.
16 William Mackenzie mentions 'Clairvoyant' in passing but incorrectly states that not a single party was dispatched. Mackenzie, *Secret History of SOE*, p. 206.

17 TNA: letter from Lt. H. N. Sporborg to Air Vice Marshal C. E. H. Medhurst (Air Ministry), including paper entitled 'Clairvoyant', 2 January 1942, in HS2/218; Appendix A, 'SOE *Coup de Main* Operations in Norway, 1940-1944', pp. 207-18.
18 A. S. Milward, *The Fascist Economy in Norway* (Oxford: Oxford University Press, 1972), p. 173; H. Paulsen, 'Tysk økonomisk politikk i Norge 1940-1945', in H. F. Dahl (ed.), *Krigen i Norge* (Oslo: Pax Forlag, 1974), pp. 77-86.
19 NHM: 'Consolidated Progress Reports of S Section', weeks ending, 4 March, 29 April, 24 September 1941, in SOE archive, Boks 3a; TNA: SOE Executive Committee – weekly progress reports for months of November and December 1941, in HS8/219.
20 TNA: COS (42) 27th meeting, 24 January 1942, cited in CAB121/306; SOE Executive Committee – weekly progress report, for 21 January 1942, in HS8/220.
21 TNA: COS (42) 27th meeting, 24 January 1942, COS (42) 89, 4 February 1942, COS (42) 55, 18 February 1942, cited in CAB121/306; SOE Executive Committee – weekly reports, week ending 28 January, and fortnight ending 14 October 1942, in HS8/220 and 221; NHM: 'Consolidated Progress Reports of S Section', January and February 1942, in SOE archive, Boks 3a; Milward, *Fascist Economy in Norway*, p. 61.
22 See Chapter 6, p. 216.
23 NHM: paper entitled, 'Redshank', in SOE archive, Boks 9; information supplied by J. A. Holmen at the Orkla *Industrimuseum* (Industrial museum) in Norway; Paulsen, 'Tysk økonomisk politikk i Norge 1940-1945', in Dahl (ed.), *Krigen i Norge*, p. 84; Milward, *Fascist Economy in Norway*, pp. 58, 86; C. Goulter, *A Forgotten Offensive* (London: Frank Cass, 1995), pp. 303, 305.
24 TNA: 'Reports, Various – Directives and Heads of Sections, Plans and Projects', report as at 10 June 1941, in HS8/231; SOE Executive Committee – weekly progress reports, weeks commencing 13 and 20 August 1941, in HS8/217.
25 Appendix A, 'SOE *Coup de Main* Operations in Norway 1940-1944', pp. 207-18; TNA: 'Minutes of ANCC Meetings 16 February 1942 – 26 April 1945', in HS2/138; report on operational plans for ANCC, 9 September 1943, in HS2/236; NHM: paper entitled 'Redshank', in SOE archive, Boks 9, and Boks 36, 'Dodsworth'; S. Kjeldstadli, *Hjemmestyrkene: hovedtrekk av den militære motstanden under okkupasjonen*, vol. I (Oslo: H. Aschehoug, 1959), p. 222; A. Moland, *Sabotasje i Norge under 2. Verdenskrig* (Oslo: NHM, 1987), p. 12.
26 Kjeldstadli, *Hjemmestyrkene*, p. 222; TNA: memo from SN (Lt. Col. J. S. Wilson) to D/CD (0) (Brigadier Colin McV. Gubbins), ref. SN/1775, 1 October 1942, in HS2/129.

27 TNA: minutes of 1st meeting of ANCC, in HS2/138; O. Njølstad, *Professor Tronstads Krig* (Oslo: Aschehoug, 2015), pp. 112–13.
28 TNA: report on operational plans for the ANCC, 9 September 1943, in HS2/236.
29 Information supplied by J. A. Holmen at the Orkla *Industrimuseum* (Industrial museum) in Norway; NHM: paper entitled 'Redshank', in SOE archive, Boks 9; Fd 5217/45, Rk Haupt, cited in Milward, *Fascist Economy in Norway*, p. 269.
30 Information supplied by J. A. Holmen at the Orkla *Industrimuseum* (Industrial museum) in Norway; statement by Thorry Kiær, Managing Director of Løkken mines, 18 July 1945, in HS7/178.
31 Appendix A, 'SOE *Coup de Main* Operations in Norway 1940–1944', pp. 207–18; NHM: paper entitled 'Kestrel', in SOE archive, Boks 9; letter from SOE HQ to Nielsen, 14 November 1943 and letter from Nielsen to Lt. Col. J. S. Wilson, 26 September 1944, both in SOE archive, Boks 19; Kjeldstadli, *Hjemmestyrkene*, p. 223.
32 Appendix A, 'SOE *Coup de Main* Operations in Norway 1940–1944', pp. 207–18; NHM: paper entitled 'Marshfield' in SOE archive, Boks 9.
33 Sulitjelma could also produce 30,000 tons of copper concentrate and 9,000 tons of zinc concentrates per annum; Appendix A, 'SOE *Coup de Main* Operations in Norway 1940–1944', pp. 207–18; TNA: Operation Seagull, 'operation instruction no. 1', 14 September 1942, in HS2/177; NHM: SOE archive, Boks 36, Operation Docklow.
34 Appendix A, 'SOE *Coup de Main* Operations in Norway 1940–1944', pp. 207–18.
35 Ibid.; TNA: 'Reports to COS', month ending 15 June 1942, in HS8/244; C. Barnett, *Engage the Enemy More Closely* (London: Penguin, 2000), pp. 200, 254, 262.
36 This is just a sample of the many publications that narrate the operational details of 'Gunnerside'; Kjeldstadli, *Hjemmestyrkene*, pp. 220–1; J. A. Poulsson, *Aksjon Vemork: vinterkrig på Hardangervidda* (Oslo: Gyldendal, 1993), pp. 80–104; Haukelid, *Skis against the Atom* (London: William Kimber, 1954), pp. 70–102; T. Gallacher, *Assault in Norway: The True Story of the Telemark Raid* (London: Purnell, 1975), A. Ueland, *Tungtvannsaksjonen* (Oslo: Gyldendal, 2015).
37 Until recently, publications that examine the attacks against heavy water production in Norway have excluded 'Clairvoyant'. For example, see O. K. Grimnes, 'The Allied Heavy Water Operations at Rjukan', *Insttutt for Forsvarsstudier (IFS) Info*, vol. 4, 1995, pp. 7–12. More recently though it has become recognized. See Ueland, *Tungtvannsaksjonen*.
38 It is important to emphasize that this was a joint SOE/FO operation as the British histories tend to undervalue the Norwegian contribution. Mackenzie, *Secret History of SOE*, p. 654.
39 TNA: 'Appendix A to SX's memorandum on "Clairvoyant"', 20 December 1941, attached to a note headed 'Lurgan', 30 July 1942, in HS2/184.

40 TNA: letter from W. Hansteen (Norwegian commander-in-chief) to Vice Admiral Lord Louis Mountbatten, 21 November 1942, including a memo on 'the effect of the different alternatives of execution upon the production possibilities as a whole', in DEFE2/219; Operation Instructions No 1, 'Gunnerside', 15 December 1942, in HS2/185.
41 TNA: paper entitled, 'SOE Operation "Gunnerside"', in HS2/190; J. Brun, *Brennpunkt Vemork 1940–1945* (Oslo: Universitetsforlaget, 1985), pp. 28, 31, 35–7.
42 Appendix A, 'SOE *Coup de Main* Operations in Norway 1940–1944', pp. 207–18.
43 Kjeldstadli, *Hjemmestyrkene*, p. 220; Brun, *Brennpunkt Vemork*, pp. 37–8.
44 TNA: Operation Gunnerside, 'Outline Project for Approval', 24 November 1942, in HS2/185; memo from Lt. Col. J. S. Wilson to Brigadier Colin McV. Gubbins, 3 March 1943, in HS2/190.
45 M. R. D. Foot claims that 'Gunnerside' scuppered Hitler's advance towards an atomic bomb. Publications on Germany's atomic research suggests otherwise and show that Germany never made available the huge resources that would be required to produce an atomic bomb. M. R. D. Foot, *SOE in the Low Countries* (London: St. Ermin's Press, 2001), p. 74; See P. F. Dahl, *Heavy Water and the Wartime Race for Nuclear Energy* (Bristol: IOP, 1999), pp. 191–2; Grimnes, 'The Allied Heavy Water Operations at Rjukan', pp. 9–10; J. Cornwell, *Hitler's Scientists: Science, War and the Devil's Pact* (London: Penguin, 2003), pp. 318, 319, 320, 321, 335, 403–4; T. Powers, *Heisenberg's War: The Secret History of the German Bomb* (Boston: Da Capo Press, 2000), p. 478.
46 TNA: memo from Lt. Col. J. S. Wilson to A/CD, ref. SN/1469, 10 August 1943, in HS2/187; Brun, *Brennpunkt Vemork*, p. 74; A. Olsen, *Norsk Hydro gjennom 50 år: Et eventyr for realitetens verden* (Oslo: Norsk Hydro Kvælstofaktieselskap, 1955), p. 417.
47 TNA: paper entitled 'Chiefs of Staff Directive to SOE for 1943', attached to a note from Lt. Col. J. S. Wilson to D/Plans, 30 March 1943, in HS8/330.
48 TNA: 'Resume of SOE Activities in Various Theatres of War', 25 June 1943, in HS8/199; Kjeldstadli, *Hjemmestyrkene*, pp. 220–1; information provided by J. A. Holmen at the Orkla *Industrimuseum* (industrial museum).
49 SOE *coup de main* teams did receive help from local people who often belonged to the local resistance. The 'Grouse' team received local help with food and supplies. Poulsson, *Aksjon Vemork*, pp. 57–9.
50 TNA: 'SOE Weekly Progress Reports', week ending 18 May 1942, in HS8/220; memo from Lt. Col. J. S. Wilson to Brigadier Colin McV. Gubbins, 3 March 1942, in HS2/190; Poulsson, *Aksjon Vemork*, p. 84.
51 NHM: paper entitled 'Kestrel', in SOE archive, Boks 9; TNA: letter from SOE HQ Lt. Col. J. S. Wilson to Nielsen, 23 January 1944; information provided by J. A. Holmen at the Orkla *Industrimuseum* (industrial museum); Kjeldstadli, *Hjemmestyrkene*, pp. 165–7, 220–1.

52　TNA: paper entitled, 'Directive for Future Sabotage Policy in Norway', from AD/E (Brigadier E. E. Mockler-Ferryman) to SN (Lt. Col. J. S. Wilson), ref. ADE/20, in HS2/128.
53　Appendix A, 'SOE *Coup de Main* Operations in Norway 1940–1944', pp. 207–18.
54　See Chapter 2, pp. 41–2; TNA: paper entitled 'Chiefs of Staff Directive to SOE for 1943', attached to a note from Lt. Col. J. S. Wilson from D/Plans, 30 March 1943, in HS8/330; COS (43) 142 (0), 'Special Operations Executive Directive for 1943', 20 March 1943, in CAB80/68; NHM: paper entitled 'Actions against German Controlled Norwegian State Railways', in SOE archive, Boks 5.
55　Appendix C, 'SOE Long Term and Miscellaneous Operations in Norway 1940–1944', pp. 246–50; NHM: paper entitled 'Actions against German Controlled Norwegian State Railways', in SOE archive, Boks 5.
56　TNA: 'Directive for Future Sabotage Policy in Norway', from Brigadier E. E. Mockler-Ferryman to Lt. Col. J. S. Wilson, 31 May 1943, in HS2/233; Chapter 4, p. 91.
57　Appendix A, 'SOE *Coup de Main* Operations in Norway 1940–1944', pp. 207–18; NHM: 'Operation Instructions for Redwing', in SOE archive, Boks 29; 'Operation Instructions for Chaffinch', part II, in SOE archive, Boks 20; TNA: reports from and interrogations of Tor Stenersen, 7 June 1943, 23 August and 23 September 1943, in HS2/243.
58　M. Manus, *Underwater Saboteur* (London: William Kimber, 1953), pp. 41, 54; Appendix A, 'SOE *Coup de Main* Operations in Norway 1940–1944', pp. 207–18.
59　Kjeldstadli, *Hjemmestyrkene*, pp. 221–2; Haukelid, *Skis against the Atom*, pp. 155–70.
60　TNA: memo from Lt. Col. Wilson to Major-General Colin McV. Gubbins, 1 March 1944, memo from BSS/A to BSS, 23 March 1944, memo from AD/P to A/CD, 20 May 1944, telegram from Swallow Brown, 18 September 1944, all in HS2/188; D. Irving, *The Virus House: Germany's Atomic Research and Allied Counter-Measures* (London: W. Kimber, 1967), pp. 181–93; Olsen, *Norsk Hydro gjennom 50 år*, pp. 421–2; 'The Real Heroes of Telemark', a documentary about the 'Grouse' and 'Gunnerside' operations, broadcast by BBC Bristol, September/October 2003.
61　TNA: note from Leif Tronstad to DS Lt. Col. Wilson, 7 February 1944, in HS2/188.
62　TNA: memo from Lt. Col. Wilson to CD Major General Colin McV. Gubbins, 1 March 1944, and report by G. Syverstad, 25 March 1943 (made in Stockholm), both in HS2/188; Haukelid, *Skis against the Atom*, pp. 155–70.
63　Letter from Ole Berg to the Norwegian minister of defence, 22 June 1943, cited in Moland, *Sabotasje i Norge under 2. Verdenskrig*, p. 7.
64　Appendix C, 'SOE Long-Term and Miscellaneous Operations in Norway 1940–1945', pp. 229–79.

65 TNA: 'Report from Munthe in Stockholm', 31 September 1940, in HS2/228; 'Some Notes on the German Occupation of Bergen and the Return to England', by A. Croft, April 1940, in HS8/261; file note dated 6 August, in HS2/242; NHM: report entitled 'Lark', in SOE archive, Boks 35b; Munthe, *Sweet Is War*, p. 123; A. Haga, *Natt på Norskekysten: den hemmelige militære nordsjøtrafikk, 1940–1943* (Oslo: J.W. Cappelen, 1979), pp. 27–39.
66 TNA: 'Rebellion in Norway', 6 August 1940, in HS2/128; 'Norway', 1 September 1940, in HS2/240.
67 Appendix C, 'SOE Long-Term and Miscellaneous Operations in Norway 1940–1945', pp. 229–79; TNA: 'Report on Melancton Rasmussen and Frithof Pedersen' (undated), in HS2/242; NHM: list of Shetland sea-sorties in SOE archive, Boks 9; T. Pryser, *Hitler's hemmelige agenter: Tysk etterretning i Norge 1939–1945* (Oslo: Universitetsforlaget, 2001), pp. 60–1.
68 TNA: 'Norwegian Policy', 11 December 1940, in HS2/128.
69 Unfortunately the 'Claribel' files for Norway appear to have disappeared. Nevertheless, the 'Claribel' files for Denmark and the Headquarter files provide some guide to plans for Norway. TNA: file HS2/82, 'Claribel' (Denmark); 'Reports, Various – Directives and Heads of Section – Plans and Projects' as at 5 March 1941 and 8 March 1941, in HS8/231; D. A. T. Stafford, *Britain and European Resistance 1940–1945: A Survey of the Special Operations Executive with Documents* (Toronto: University of Toronto Press, 1980), p. 81.
70 There is no specific file on 'Cockfight' in SOE archives in London or Oslo. In progress reports, it is described as a project for 'the establishment of a Secret Army in Norway'. NHM: 'Consolidated Progress Reports of S Section', during 1941 and 1942, in SOE archive, Boks 3a; TNA: 'Reports, Various – Directives and Heads of Sections Plans and Projects', as at 15 November 1941, in HS8/231.
71 For details see Chapter 4, pp. 78–9; NHM: 'Consolidated Progress Reports of S Section' during 1941, in SOE archive, Boks 3a; list of Shetland sea sorties, in SOE archive, Boks 9.
72 TNA: 'Norwegian Policy', 11 December 1940, in HS2/128; paper entitled 'Directive to the Military Organisation in Norway', 17 July 1941, in HS2/231.
73 Appendix C, 'SOE Long-Term and Miscellaneous Operations in Norway 1940–1945', pp. 229–79.
74 Ibid.
75 TNA: 'SOE Executive Committee – Weekly Progress Reports', weeks commencing 3 December 1941 and 17 December, in HS8/219.
76 Appendix C, 'SOE Long-Term and Miscellaneous Operations in Norway 1940–1945', pp. 229–79. I have considered 'Archer' and 'Heron' to be two separate operations. TNA: COS (40) 27 (0), 'Subversive Activities in Relation to Strategy', 25 November 1940, in CAB 80/56.

77 Appendix C, 'SOE Long-Term and Miscellaneous Operations in Norway 1940–1945', pp. 229–79; TNA: Operation Instructions for 'Crow', 1 January 1942, in HS2/152; Operation Instructions for 'Raven', 3 April 1942, in HS2/162; Operation Instructions for 'Lark' W/T Operator and two Instructors in Mines, Arms and Devices, 7 March 1942, in HS2/159.
78 NHM: list of Shetland sea sorties, in SOE archive, Boks 9; A. F. Egner and S. W. Aasland, *BBC: Kanoner spiller Chopin: Flybårne forsyninger til Milorg i Norge 1940–1945* (Lysaker: A. F. Egner, 1997), p. 38.
79 TNA: letter from Lt. Col. J. S. Wilson to Major John Rognes, 2 July 1942, in HS2/139; Appendix C, 'SOE Long-Term and Miscellaneous Operations in Norway 1940–1945', pp. 229–79.
80 TNA: 'SOE Long-Term Policy in Norway', 21 September 1942, in HS2/128.
81 These were operations: 'Archer/Heron', 'Crow', 'Lark', 'Anchor', 'Mallard' and 'Penguin'. Appendix C, 'SOE Long-Term and Miscellaneous Operations in Norway 1940–1945', pp. 229–79.
82 Pryser, *Hitlers hemmelige agenter*, pp. 102, 256; Kjeldstadli, *Hjemmestyrkene*, pp. 156–8; Appendix C, 'SOE Long-Term and Miscellaneous Operations in Norway 1940–1945', pp. 229–79.
83 In August 1942, Didrik Nilsen, the *Milorg* district leader for eastern Norway, arrived in Stockholm and advised SOE of Jacobsen's capture. Appendix C, 'SOE Long-Term and Miscellaneous Operations in Norway 1940–1945', pp. 229–79; TNA: KV2/828 – MI5 file on Ernst Jacobsen.
84 Why 'Omelette' was never undertaken is not revealed in the files. Gulbrandsen worked at STS26 for the rest of the war. Appendix C, 'SOE Long-Term and Miscellaneous Operations in Norway 1940–1945', pp. 229–79; TNA: KV2/829, Gulbrandsen's MI5 file; *Avhør* (interrogation) av Fehmer, 11 June 1945, ved *kriminalbetjentene* Nytrøen og Biltvedt, p. 9, cited in T. Pryser, *Hitler's hemmelige agenter: Tysk etterretning i Norge 1939–1945* (Oslo: Universitetsforlaget, 2001), p. 206.
85 NHM: 'Anvil Operation Instructions' (undated) and 'Anvil Messages', in SOE archive, Boks 39.
86 See Chapter 4, pp. 229–79.
87 Sverre Kjeldstadli argues that SOE teams were instructed to avoid 'contact and co-operation with *Milorg*'. The operational instructions issued at the time do not appear to confirm this. NHM: 'Anvil Operation Instructions' (undated), in SOE archive, Boks 39; TNA: 'Operation Instructions for Crow', 1 January 1942, in HS2/152; paper headed 'Crow', ref. DCE/G.2., 1 January 1943, in HS2/153; Kjeldstadli, *Hjemmestyrkene*, p. 182.
88 Operations 'Anvil', 'Crow', 'Mallard', Cheese II', 'Anchor' and 'Grouse' all had some contact with *Milorg* HQ or the local leadership of *Milorg*. Appendix C, 'SOE Long-Term and Miscellaneous Operations in Norway 1940–1945', pp. 229–79; TNA: 'SOE in Norway and the Secret Military organisation', 25 June 1942, in HS2/232; report by 'Crow' organizer E. N. Stenersen, on meetings with SMO (*Milorg*), 28 May 1942, in HS2/152.

89 Lt. Col. J. S. Wilson appears to accept that SOE operations had at least created an expectation of a landing in Norway. TNA: 'Norway-Future Planning', 5 June 1942, in HS2/128. FA, FO IV, hylle 15, mappe 'Tyske kontraspionasje: Sydlige', sak nr. 3, cited in Kjeldstadli, *Hjemmestyrkene*, p. 171.
90 After the incident at Telavåg and Majavatn, many resistance members had to flee the country or were arrested, and local *Milorg* groups were badly hit. See J. Chr. Hauge, *Rapport om mitt arbeid under okkupasjonen* (Oslo: Gyldendal, 1995), p. 16; Kjeldstadli, *Hjemmestyrkene*, pp. 158–67.
91 NHM: note from Lt. Col. J. S. Wilson to Lt. Col. Øen, 3 August 1943, in FO IV archive, Boks 93.
92 TNA: memo from Lt. Col. J. S. Wilson to Lt. Col. Roche, 11 November 1943, in HS2/245; NHM: 'Report on the Wireless Service between SL and UK from the Autumn of 1943 to April 1944' by Lt. K. Haugland, in SOE archive, Boks 22; Appendix C, 'SOE Long-Term and Miscellaneous Operations in Norway 1940–1945', pp. 229–79; Pryser, *Hitlers hemmelige agenter*, p. 130.
93 TNA: 'SOE Long-Term Policy in Norway', 21 September 1942, in HS2/128; 'Direction for Groups with Special Tasks in Norway', 25 September 1942, in HS2/232.
94 NHM: 'Consolidated Progress Reports of S Section', weeks ending 4 November and 4 December 1942, in SOE archive, Boks 3a.
95 Appendix C, 'SOE Long-Term Operations in Norway 1940–1945', pp. 229–79; TNA: paper entitled 'Norway – Future Planning', 5 June 1942, in HS2/128; NHM: 'Falcon' reports in SOE archive, Boks 44.
96 TNA: 'Norway – Future Planning: Some General Observations', 5 June 1942, in HS2/128.
97 TNA: 'Operation Instructions for Grouse', 31 August 1942, in HS2/172; NHM: 'Consolidated Progress Reports of S Section', 26 February to 13 March 1943, in SOE archive, Boks 3a; see Chapter 2, pp. 51–2.
98 NHM: 'Air Transport Operations', Appendix K, in SOE archive, Boks 11, Wilson's file; M. R. D. Foot, *SOE in France* (London: HMSO, 1966), p. 474.
99 The operations 'Chaffinch' and 'Puffin' were sent into the Oslo region in January and April 1942, respectively, to work with the central leadership of *Milorg*; NHM: 'Operation Instructions for Puffin', 10 April 1943, in SOE archive, Boks 14; 'Operation Instructions for Chaffinch, Part II', November 1942, in SOE archive, Boks 20.
100 For example, see details of Operations Martin and Osprey in Appendix C, 'SOE Long-Term Operations in Norway 1940–1945', pp. 229–79; NHM: 'Operation Instructions for Martin', 20 March 1943, in SOE archive, Boks 43; 'Details on Operation Osprey', in SOE archive, Boks 27.
101 TNA: paper entitled 'SOE Outline Plan for Joint Activities in Norway 1943/44', attached to a memo from SN (Lt. Col. J. S. Wilson) to AD/E

(Brigadier E. E. Mockler-Ferryman), ref. SN/1202, 26 June 1943, in HS2/218; Njølstad, *Professor Tronstad's Krig*, p. 332.
102 NHM: 'Operation Instructions for Sandpiper', 2 December 1943, in SOE archive, Boks 24; 'Operation Instructions for Merlin', 8 February 1944, Boks 29.
103 An assassination within this context was a secret execution to remove someone who was seen as a threat to the local resistance or SOE. A. Moland, *Over grensen?* (Oslo: Orion forlag, 1999), pp. 17–18.
104 Kjeldstadli, *Hjemmestyrkene*, pp. 105–27; B. Nøkleby, 'Nyordning', vol. II, in M. Skodvin (ed.), *Norge i krig: fremmedåk & frihetskamp 1940–1945* (Oslo: Aschehoug, 1985), pp. 45–80; Pryser, *Hitlers hemmelige agenter*, pp. 180–4.
105 Kjeldstadli, *Hjemmestyrkene*, p. 124; Moland, *Over grensen?*, pp. 41–2, 209–26.
106 Pryser, *Hitlers Hemmelige Agenter*, pp. 19–56.
107 Kjeldstadli, *Hjemmestyrkene*, p. 117.
108 Moland, *Over grensen?*, p. 45.
109 Kjeldstadli, *Hjemmestyrkene*, pp. 118–19, 168–9.
110 J. Andenæs, *Det vanskelige oppgjøret* (Oslo: Tano-Aschehoug, 1998), p. 63.
111 Munthe, *Sweet Is War*, pp. 145–8.
112 NHM: report by Gunvald Tomstad, 19 April 1943, in SOE archive, Boks 25.
113 NHM: 'Consolidated Progress Report of S Section', week ending 12 May 1942, in SOE archive, Boks 3a.
114 NHM: 'Operation Instructions for Bittern', in SOE archive, Boks 14.
115 TNA: 'Operation Instructions for Swan', 13 August 1942, in HS2/176.
116 TNA: telegram from 'Swan', 11 December 1942, in HS2/176; NHM: 'MI5 Report on Rolf Ellingsen', 10 April 1943, and 'Report from Swan', 19 February 1943, in SOE archive, Boks 25; Kjeldstadli, *Hjemmestyrkene*, p. 171.
117 The operations were 'Bittern', 'Grouse', 'Gannet', 'Chaffinch' and 'Thrush'; Appendix C, 'SOE Long-Term and Miscellaneous Operations in Norway 1940–1945', pp. 229–79.
118 TNA: memo from Lt. Col. J. S. Wilson to E unknown, 24 September 1942; 'Précis: Bittern Operation', 3 February 1943, both in HS2/200; Pryser, *Hitlers hemmelige agenter*, pp. 104–6.
119 Riste, *London regjeringa*, vol. II, pp. 33–4, 36–7; Moland, *Over Grensen?*, pp. 60–4.
120 TNA: letter from Lt. Col. J. S. Wilson to Nielsen, 17 November 1942, in HS2/200; NHM: 'Report from Jacob Schive on the Majavatn Affair and Bittern', 9 February 1943, in FO IV archive, Boks 78.
121 NHM: 'Gannet: Short Preliminary Survey of Situation in Anvil Area', February 1943, from Capt. P. F. S Douglas to Lt. Col. J. S. Wilson, 19 March 1943, in SOE archive, Boks 40.

122 Moland, *Over grensen?*, p. 56.
123 NHM: 'Operation Instructions for Chaffinch, Part II', November 1942, in SOE archive, Boks 20; 'Report from Chaffinch Group', from Karl Iversen (Tor Stenersen) to FO, 3 June 1943, in SOE archive, Boks 21; TNA: 'Report Concerning "Liquidating" Groups', from 2/Lieutenant Tor Stenersen to FO 4, 23 August 1943, in HS2/243.
124 See Moland, *Over grensen?*, pp. 108–12.
125 Arnfinn Moland argues that the fundamental reason was the differences in the nature of the occupation and the development of resistance between Denmark and Norway. See Moland, *Over grensen?*, pp. 46, 326–8.
126 TNA: paper entitled, 'SOE Outline Plan for Joint Activities in Norway 1943/44', attached to a memo from Lt. Col. J. S. Wilson to Brigadier E. E. Mockler-Ferryman, 26 June 1943, in HS2/218.
127 These were Miss Elsa Kristoffersen, Yngvar Løvdok, Richard Jensen and Harald Falchenberg. NHM: 'Operation Instructions for 'Goldfinch', 6 October 1943, in FO IV archive, Boks 77; Redwing Operation Instructions, 7 September 1943, in SOE archive, Boks 29; Goshawk Operation Instructions, 10 September 1943, in SOE archive, Boks 39; 'Rapport fra Goshawk til Major Douglas *angående* (concerning) Rat Week' in SOE archive, Boks 40; TNA: 'Short Review of Goldfinch Work', from H.14 (Martin Olsen), Goldfinch leader, to Lt. Col. J. S. Wilson and Lt. Col. Øen, 1 June 1944, in HS2/243; E. Jensen et al., *Kompani Linge*, vol. II (Oslo: Gyldendal, 1948), p. 149; Moland, *Over grensen?*, pp. 69, 114–23.
128 NHM: report by acting 2/Lieut. Per Berg (B. Fjelstad), 11 May 1944, in SOE archive, Boks 25; FO IV (SPA), skuff 2, Boks 54, 24 February 1944, Goldfinch, 'Oversikt fra 1/12-43 til 21/2-44', cited in Moland, *Over grensen?*, p. 72.
129 TNA: 'Report from a Conference in Stockholm in March 1944' (translation), 14 April 1944, in HS2/233.
130 NHM: Operation Instructions for Buzzard (undated) and memo from Major Jens Henrik Nordlie to SOE, 30 March 1944, in FO IV archive, Boks 19; NHM, Mi IV (SPA), skuff I, mp 104, cited in Moland, *Over grensen?*, p. 71.
131 TNA: 'Directive on the Employment and Development of Resistance in Norway', 3 September 1944, in HS2/234; Hauge, *Rapport om mitt arbeid under okkupasjonen*, p. 186.
132 TNA: paper entitled, 'Targets Which Are Released for Attack', in HS2/204.
133 NHM: letter from Lt. Col. J. S. Wilson to Edgar Nielsen in Stockholm, 14 November 1943, in SOE archive, Boks 19; TNA: telegram from 'Goldfinch', 26 April 1944, in HS2/192; 'Short Review of Goldfinch Work', from H.14 (Martin Olsen) to Lt. Cols. Wilson and Øen, 1 June 1944, in HS2/243.

134 Pryser, *Hitlers hemmelige agenter*, pp. 253, 254, 327.
135 NHM: 'General Reports – Operations', Oct–Dec 1944, in SOE archive, Boks 30; Jensen et al., *Kompani Linge*, vol. II, p. 166.
136 TNA: telegram to Antrum Yellow, 29 October 1944, telegram from Antrum Grey, 30 October 1944, telegram from Antrum Grey, 16 December 1945, all in HS2/144.
137 Moland, *Over grensen?*, pp. 71, 73.
138 NHM: memo from Major Jens Henrik Nordlie to Lt. Col. J. S. Wilson, 17 February 1945, in FO IV archive, Boks 19; TNA: letter from Lt. Col. H. N. Sporborg to C. F. A. Warner (Foreign Office), 28 February 1945, in HS2/234; Moland, *Over Grensen?*, pp. 165–8.

Chapter 8

1 TNA: 'Outline Plan for Joint SOE/SO-FO IV Activities in Norway from August 1944', from Lt. Col. J. S. Wilson to Brigadier E. E. Mockler-Ferryman, 31 July 1944, in HS2/235.
2 NHM: SOE archive, Boks 36, operations 'Docklow' and 'Dodworth'; Appendix A, 'SOE *Coup de Main* Operations in Norway 1940–1944', pp. 207–18; S. Kjeldstadli, *Hjemmestyrkene: hovedtrekk av den militære motstanden under okkupasjonen* (Oslo: H. Aschehoug, 1959), p. 223.
3 TNA: letter from Lt. Col. J. S. Wilson to Nielsen, 23 January 1944, in HS2/128.
4 TNA: extracts from Plan 'Fortitude' (SHAEF [44] 13), 23 February 1944, and 'Plan Fortitude', including 'SOE/SO Directive to Scandinavian Region', in HS2/1.
5 TNA: letter from Lt. Col. J. S. Wilson to Nielsen, 23 January 1944, in HS2/128.
6 TNA: paper entitled, 'A.T. Mobilisation in Norway', attached to minutes of the 30th meeting of the ANCC, 8 June 1944, in HS2/138; A. Moland, *Kampen mot mobiliserings-trusselen i Norge, 1943–1944* (Oslo: NHM, 1987), pp. 21–2.
7 TNA: 'Report from a Conference in Stockholm in March 1944' (translation), 14 April 1944, in HS2/233.
8 NHM: 'Interrogation of Capt. Gunnar Sønsteby', 2 July 1945, in SOE archive, Boks 16; G. Sønsteby (i samarbeid med J. B. Gundersen), *Bak rapportene* (Oslo: Aventura, 1985), pp. 140–208.
9 Sønsteby, *Bak rapportene*, p. 152.
10 NHM: report from 24 (Sønsteby), typed on 20 September 1944, in FO IV archive, Boks 13; SOE archive, Boks 16, the 'Oslo Group'; Moland, *Kampen mot mobiliserings-trusselen i Norge, 1943–1944*, p. 21.
11 TNA: memo from Bjarne Øen to Lt. Col. J. S. Wilson, headed 'Directive to no 24', 6 December 1944, in HS2/204.

12 Lt. Colonel J. S. Wilson was in Norway in June and July 1945, met members of the Oslo Detachment and visited many of the sites that they had attacked. TNA: 'Diary of Scandinavian Tour' by J. S. Wilson, in HS9/1605/3.
13 NHM: SOE archive, Boks 11, Wilson's file, Appendix J, 'Local Acts of Sabotage'; R. Berg and P. Lindhjem, *Norge og den 2. verdenskrig: Militær motstand i Rogaland og Vestfold* (Oslo: Universitetsforlaget, 1972), pp. 90–5; T. A. Barstad, *Sabotasjen i Oslo området 1944–1945* (Oslo: Universitetsforlaget, 1991), pp. 40–2.
14 TNA: 'Directive on the Employment and Development of Resistance in Norway', 3 September 1944, in HS2/234.
15 The Communists group working around Oslo caused some of the damage listed. NHM: paper entitled, 'Damage Done by Sabotage to Industrial Plants in 1944' from the Norwegian Economic Intelligence Office, 16 April 1945, in FO IV archive, Boks 14, 'Sabotasje Oversikt'.
16 NHM: document entitled 'Undersøkelse vedr. Sabotasjeskader', 20 July 1945, in FO IV archive, Boks 14.
17 A. Moland, *Sabotasje i Norge under 2. Verdenskrig* (Oslo: NHM, 1987), p. 28.
18 TNA: 'Directive on the Employment and Development of Resistance in Norway', 3 September 1944, in HS2/234.
19 Barstad, *Sabotasjen i Oslo området*, pp. 38–45.
20 TNA: 'Report from 24 (Gunnar Sønsteby)', 20 September 1944, in FO IV archive, Boks 13; report on the 'Operation against the Verpen Svovelsyrefabrikk', 16 August 1944, in SOE archive, Boks 19.
21 NHM: telegram to 'Firecrest', 26 July 1944, in SOE archive, Boks 20.
22 NHM: SOE archive, Boks 11, Wilson's file, Appendix J, 'Oil and Petrol Sabotage'.
23 Ibid.; NHM: 'General Reports' – operations, in SOE archive, Boks 30; A. D. Lambert, 'Seizing the Initiative', in N. A. M. Rodgers (ed.), *Naval Power in the Twentieth Century* (London: Macmillan, 1996), pp. 151–2.
24 NHM: SOE archive, Boks 11, Wilson's file, Appendix J, 'Local Acts of Sabotage'.
25 Ibid.; Barstad, *Sabotasjen i Oslo området*, pp. 92–3, 96; T. A. Barstad, *Pelle-gruppa: sabotører på Østlandet 1944–1945* (Oslo: J. Cappelen, 1987), p. 105.
26 Moland, *Sabotasje i Norge under 2. verdenskrig*, p. 29.
27 NHM: 'Report on the Wireless Service between SL and the UK and in the Districts 11–16 and 24 & 25 from the Autumn of 1943 to April 1944', by Lt. K. Haugland in SOE archive, Boks 22, mappe 15/3/1.
28 Barstad, *Sabotasjen i Oslo området*, pp. 97–101.
29 NHM: telegram to 'Firecrest', 26 July 1944 in SOE archive, Boks 20; telegram to Chiffchaff, nr B 1412, 28 July 1944, in Boks 15.
30 See Chapter 7, p. 155.

31 See Chapter 2, pp. 47–8.
32 TNA: memo from SFHQ, Brigadier E. E. Mockler-Ferryman to G-3 Division, SHAEF, 18 October 1944, and telegram from SHAEF to Scottish Command, 26 October 1944, in WO219/2380.
33 See Chapter 2, p. 48; see Appendix C, 'SOE Miscellaneous and Long-Term Operations in Norway', pp. 229–79.
34 See Appendix C, 'SOE Long-Term and Miscellaneous Operations in Norway, 1940–1945', pp. 229–79; Moland, *Sabotasje i Norge under 2. Verdenskrig*, pp. 24–7.
35 NHM: paper entitled 'Actions against German Controlled Norwegian State Railways', in SOE archive, Boks 5; Moland, *Sabotasje i Norge under 2. Verdenskrig*, p. 25.
36 Ibid.; Moland, *Sabotasje i Norge under 2. Verdenskrig*, p. 26.
37 TNA: 'Appreciation – on the Action Which Can Be Taken to Interfere with the Movement of German Forces Throughout and Out of Norway', 10 January 1945, in HS2/235.
38 TNA: 'Report on the Value of SOE Operations in the Supreme Commander's Sphere', from SHAEF G-3 Division to the COS, July 1945, cited in WO219/40B; W. J. M. Mackenzie, *The Secret History of SOE: The Special Operations Executive* (London: St. Ermin's Press, 2000), p. 671; Sir C. Gubbins, 'Resistance Movements in the War', *Journal of the Royal United Services Institute*, vol. 93, 1948; I. Kraglund and A. Moland, 'Hjemmefront', vol. 6, in M. Skodvin (ed.), *Norge i krig: fremmedåk & frihetskamp 1940–1945* (Oslo: Ascheoug, 1987), p. 236.
39 K. J. Muller, 'A German Perspective on Allied Deception Operations in the Second World War', *Intelligence and National Security*, vol. 2, no. 3, July 1987, pp. 318–1.
40 See K. O. Solhjell and F. Traphagen, *Fra krig til fred: fokus på Snåsa og Nord-Trøndelag* (Ål: Boksmia, 2001), pp. 194–5.
41 See Solhjell and Traphagen, *Fra krig til fred*, pp. 120–2, 196; Moland, *Sabotasje i Norge under 2. Verdenskrig*, pp. 24–7.
42 TNA: 'Monthly SOE/SO Reports, Nos. 13–20, Oct 1944–May 1945', No. 17, 10 February 1945, in WO219/90.
43 Solhjell and Traphagen, *Fra krig til fred*, pp. 196–7.
44 See Chapter 3, pp. 65–7.
45 For details, see Chapter 1, pp. 26–7.
46 A. F. Egner and S. W. Aasland, *BBC: Kanonen spiller Chopin: Flybårne forsyninger til Milorg i Norge 1940–1945* (Lysaker: A. F. Egner, 1997), p. 18.
47 TNA: 'The Military Home Front. Survey Par December 1st 1944', compiled by FO IV, in HS2/230; Kjeldstadli, *Hjemmestyrkene*, p. 229; A. Moland, 'Norway', in B. Moore (ed.), *Resistance in Western Europe* (Oxford: Berg, 2000), p. 230.
48 TNA: transcripted notes taken by Lt. Cdr. Sir George Pollock, while visiting Norway during June and July 1945, in HS2/213; J. Birkenes, *Milorg*

i D 17 1940–1945 (Nedre Telemark) (Skien: Selskapet for Skien byvel, 1982), p. 210; O. Njølstad, *Professor Tronstads Krig* (Oslo: Aschehoug, 2015), p. 378.
49 E. Jensen et al., *Kompani Linge*, vol. II (Oslo: 1948), pp. 304, 324–31.
50 TNA: 'Diary of a Scandinavian Tour', by Lt. Col. J. S. Wilson, in HS9/1402/6.
51 According to Arnfinn Moland, by the spring of 1945 the *Milorg* men were 'equipped, trained and well disciplined' and 'prepared for the worst alternative, a German last stand in Norway'. Moland, '*Milorg* and SOE', in P. Salmon (ed.), *Britain and Norway in the Second World War* (London: HMSO, 1995), p. 149; Moland, 'Norway', in Moore (ed.), *Resistance in Western Europe*, p. 230.
52 NHM: SOE archive, Boks 11, Wilson's file, Appendix M, 'Radio Communications – General Survey' and Appendix I, 'Wireless Stations in Norway'.
53 TNA: minutes of the 31st and 32nd meetings of the ANCC on 20 July and 17 August 1944, respectively, in HS2/138.
54 See Appendix C, 'SOE Long-Term and Miscellaneous Operations in Norway 1940–1945', pp. 229–79; NHM: 'Farnborough Operational Instructions', in SOE archive, Boks 1; E. Welle-Strand, *Vi vil verne vårt land: anti-sabotasje i Norge, 1944–1945* (Oslo: NHM, 2000), pp. 10–1, 21–35.
55 See Appendix C, 'SOE Long-Term and Miscellaneous Operations in Norway 1940–1945', pp. 229–79.
56 NHM: 'Operation Instructions for Siskin', 11 October 1944, in SOE archive, Boks 31; 'Consolidated Progress Reports of S Section', 1–31 May 1944, in SOE archive, Boks 3a; Jensen et al., *Kompani Linge*, vol. II, pp. 94–106.
57 See Chapter 7, pp. 169–70.
58 Moland, *Kampen mot mobiliserings trusselen i Norge 1943–1944*, pp. 19–20, 22–3; T. A. Barstad, 'Norsk motstand fra svensk grunn', in S. Ekman and O. K. Grimnes (eds), *Broderfolk i ufredstid – Norsk forbindelser under annen verdenskrig* (Oslo: Universitetsforlaget, 1991), pp. 272–6; J. Birkenes, *Milorg i D17 1940–1945 (Nedre Telemark)* (Skien: Selskapet for Skien byvel, 1982), pp. 171–200; Welle-Strand, *Vi vil verne vårt land*, p. 23.
59 TNA: paper entitled 'Chiefs of Staff Directive to SOE for 1943', attached to a note from Lt. Col. J. S. Wilson to D/Plans, 30 March 1943, in HS8/330.
60 NHM: 'Bjørn West Reports', in SOE archive, Boks 30.
61 NHM: 'Golden Eagle Operation Instructions', 28 August 1944, in SOE archive, Boks 20, 'Golden Eagle Telegrams'.
62 NHM: memo from Lt. Col. J. S. Wilson to Brigadier E. E. Mockler-Ferryman, 21 September 1944, in SOE archive, Boks 5; 'Bjørn West Reports' in Boks 30; 'Bjørn East Reports', in FO IV archive, Boks 125;

TNA: HS7/175 – Norwegian Section History – Appendix 'N', 'Formation of *Milorg* Bases'; Appendix C, 'SOE Long-Term and Miscellaneous Operations in Norway 1940–1945', pp. 229–79.

63 For details, see Chapter 7, pp. 163–4; Appendix C, 'SOE Long-Term and Miscellaneous Operations in Norway', pp. 229–79.

64 TNA: 'Report from a Conference in Stockholm in March 1944' (translation), 14 April 1944, in HS2/233.

65 TNA: 'Minutes of the Thirty-Second Meeting of the Anglo-Norwegian Collaboration Committee', 17 August 1944, in HS2/138; Welle-Strand, *Vi vil verne vårt land*, pp. 6–10.

66 TNA: 'Directive on the Employment and Development of Resistance in Norway', 3 September 1944, in HS2/234.

67 Welle-Strand, *Vi vil verne vårt land*, pp. 6–9.

68 TNA: files HS2/170 and 171, Operation Sunshine; HS2/156 Operation Moonlight; HS2/168 & 169, Operation Starlight; NHM: 'Ekspedisjonen "Sunshine" Personell', in SOE archive, Boks 23b; 'Starlight', 'Lamplight', 'Moonlight' rapporter, in FO IV archive, Boks 93; J. A. Poulsson, *Aksjon Vemork: vinterkrig på Hardangervidda* (Oslo: Gyldendal, 1993), pp. 113–40; Welle-Strand, *Vi vil verne vårt land*, pp. 13–21; Appendix C, 'SOE Long-Term and Miscellaneous Operations in Norway 1940–1945', pp. 229–79.

69 NHM: memo from Lt. Col. J. S. Wilson to Nielsen, 31 October 1944 and including a list of 'Foscott' and 'Carmarthen' objectives, in SOE archive, Boks 6; Welle-Strand, *Vi vil verne vårt land*, pp. 21–35.

70 Appendix C, 'SOE Long-Term and Miscellaneous Operations in Norway 1940–1945', pp. 229–79; NHM: SOE archive, Boks 6, list of 'Foscott' and 'Carmarthen' targets.

71 Appendix C, 'SOE Long-Term Operations in Norway 1940–1945', pp. 229–79; NHM: 'Outline of Projected Projects for Norway', from Lt. Col. J. S. Wilson to Brigadier E. E. Mockler-Ferryman, 21 September 1944, in SOE archive, Boks 5; 'Consolidated Progress Reports of S Section', No. 32, 1–30 September 1944, in Boks 3a; TNA: file HS2/205, 'Polar Bear IV'; *Den norske regjerings virksomhet: fra 9 april til 22 juni 1945*, vol. IV, *forsvarsdepartementet*, p. 124; Welle-Strand, *Vi vil verne vårt land*, pp. 45–51.

72 NHM: Operation Instructions for 'Snowflake', 'Avocet' and 'Diver', in SOE archive, Boks 31, 27 and 32.

73 TNA: 'Direction on the Employment and Development of Resistance in Norway', September 1944, in HS2/234.

74 TNA: 'Directive from the Central Leadership (SL) to the District Leaders (DS) Regarding the Norwegian Home Forces (HS)', September 1944, in HS2/235.

75 F. Færøy, *Frigjøringen* (Oslo: NHM, 1995), pp. 18–21.

76 J. Chr. Hauge (translated by M. Hauge), *The Liberation of Norway* (Oslo: Gyldendal, 1995), p. 99.

77 O. K. Grimnes, *Et flyktningesamfunn vokser fram: Nordmenn i Sverige 1940–1945* (Oslo: H. Aschehoug, 1969), pp. 244–80; Færøy, *Frigjøringen*, pp. 14–6, 37.
78 NHM: SOE archive, Boks 11, Wilson's file, Appendix P, 'Special Force Detachment, Force 134'.
79 TNA: 'Operation Doomsday' – Joint Plan by DCOS, Planning Staff, Commander-in-Chief Rosyth, Military Commander Joint Task Force, 13 Group RAF (Plans), April 1945, in WO106/4401.
80 TNA: 'Proposals for a Military Mission', by C. K. Squires (Scottish Command), 28 August 1944, in HS2/215.
81 TNA: paper entitled, 'Scale Missions', 15 September 1944, in HS2/215; NHM: paper entitled, 'Outline of Projected Plans for Norway', from Lt. Col. J. S. Wilson to Brigadier E. E. Mockler-Ferryman, 21 September 1944, in SOE archive, Boks 5.
82 TNA: paper entitled 'Norway: Provision of SOE/SO Missions', 10 September 1944, in HS2/234; paper entitled 'Scale Missions', 15 September 1944, in HS2/215.
83 Mackenzie, *Secret History of SOE*, p. 659.
84 Other SOE operatives with mixed British/Norwegian parentage were also sent into Norway, such as Percy Armstrong (Operation Sanderling) and Norman Lind (Operation Sunshine). The failure of SOE activity was not down to bad luck, as Mackenzie claims, but the effectiveness of German security forces. See Appendix C, 'SOE Long-Term and Miscellaneous Operations in Norway 1940–1945', pp. 229–79; TNA: memo from Lt. Col. J. S. Wilson to Nielsen, 22 October 1944, and memo from Lt. Col. J. S. Wilson to DPS, 26 October 1944, both in HS2/215; Kjeldstadli, *Hjemmestyrkene*, pp. 270–2; Mackenzie, *Secret History of SOE*, p. 659.
85 TNA: paper entitled 'Scale Missions: Minim', and 'Minim' reports, in HS2/215.
86 Appendix C, 'SOE Long-Term and Miscellaneous Operations in Norway 1940–1945', pp. 229–79; NHM: SOE archive, Boks 1, 'Antipodes', 23 April 1945; Welle-Strand, *Vi vil verne vårt land*, pp. 52–3.
87 Færøy, *Frigjøringen*, p. 27; H. Sandvik, *Frigjøringen av Finnmark 1944–1945* (Oslo: Gyldendal Norsk Forlag, 1975), p. 42; Riste, *London regjeringa: Norge i krigsalliansen, 1940–1945*, vol. II (Oslo: Det Norske Samlaget, 1995), pp. 157–236.
88 Appendix C, 'SOE Long-Term and Miscellaneous Operations 1940–1945', pp. 229–79; TNA: file HS2/195, Operation Husky; memo from Lt. Col. J. S. Wilson to Brigadier E. E. Mockler-Ferryman, 7 December 1944; memo from Lt. Col. J. S. Wilson to Brigadier E. E. Mockler-Ferryman, 21 December 1944; memo from Wilsin to Mockler-Ferryman, 26 December 1944; memo from Mockler-Ferryman to Wilson, 29 December 1944; memo from Mockler-Ferryman to Wison, 17 January 1941, all in HS2/235; Riste, *London regjeringa*, vol. II, p. 212; G. Pedersen, *Militær motstand i nord 1940–1945* (Tromsø: Universitetsforlaget, 1982), pp. 142–4.

89 J. Chr. Hauge, *Frigjøringen* (Oslo: Gyldendal, 1970), pp. 108–9; Riste, *London regjeringa*, vol. II, p. 270; Færøy, *Frigjøringen*, p. 35.
90 Pedersen, *Militær motstand i nord*, pp. 172–5; M. C. Mann, 'British Policy and Strategy towards Norway, 1941–1945', PhD diss., University of London, 1998, p. 345.
91 TNA: 'Abstract of General Thorne's letter to General Bedell-Smith' (Chief of Staff to General D. D. Eisenhower), 27 May 1945, in WO106/1987.
92 Hauge, *Frigjøringen*, p. 146.
93 TNA: memo from AD/X.1 to Lt. Col. H. N. Sporborg, 28 November 1944, and paper entitled 'Draft', 17 November, in HS6/169; T. Pryser, *Hitler's hemmelige agenter: Tysk etterretning i Norge 1939–1945* (Oslo: Universitetsforlaget, 2001), pp. 162–4.
94 *Den norske regjerings virksomhet: fra 9 april til 22 juni 1945, bind IV, forsvarsdepartementet*, p. 125; TNA: transcription of notes taken by Sir George Montagu-Pollock, during his visit to Norway in 1945, in HS2/213; paper entitled, 'Norwegian Home Front', written by General Andrew Thorne in October 1945, in WO106/1984.
95 Hauge, *Frigjøringen*, pp. 134–5.
96 PRO: paper entitled, 'Norwegian Home Front', by General Sir Andrew Thorne, October 1945, in WO106/1984.
97 Hauge, *Frigjøringen*, p. 135.
98 At the liberation the German forces in Norway possessed 131 tanks, and although considered obsolete they were still in good condition. TNA: letter from General Sir Andrew Thorne, Commander Allied Land Forces, to CIGS (GOW 73), 15 July 1945, in WO106/1983; report on the visit to Allied Land Forces Norway by MO3 Colonel, 14–18 June 1945, in WO216/568.
99 On 3 May, the only first-line troops under the control of Scotco were two SAS regiments still fighting in Germany. The 1st Airborne Division, minus the 1st Parachute brigade, was assigned for Norway at the last moment. 'Doomsday' began on 9 May and up until end of that month over 7,000 men were airlifted into Oslo and Stavanger. The first 'Doomsday' sealift arrived in mid-May and in early June the American 474 Infantry Regiment (Reinforced) arrived in Drammen and Oslo. See Mann, 'British Policy', pp. 325–366; Riste, *London regjeringa*, vol. II, pp. 271–4; B. Hafsten et al., *Flyalarm: Luftkrigen over Norge 1939–1945* (Oslo: Sem & Stenersen, 1991), pp. 290–4.
100 NHM: SOE archive, Boks 11, Wilson's file, Appendix P, 'Special Force Detachment Force 134'.
101 Mann, 'British Policy', pp. 358–66; Færøy, *Frigjøringen*, pp. 45–6.

Conclusion

1 O. Riste, *London regjeringa*, vol. I (Oslo: Det Norske Samlaget, 1995), p. 109.

2 H. P. Willmott, 'Operation Jupiter and Possible Landings in Norway', in P. Salmon (ed.), *Britain and Norway in the Second World War* (London: HMSO, 1995), p. 98.
3 M. Milner, *Battle of the Atlantic* (Stroud: Tempus, 2003), pp. 23, 235, 236.
4 This is largely a synthesis of the views expressed by S. Kjeldstadli in *Hjemmestyrkene: hovedtrekk av den militære motstanden under okkupasjonen* (Oslo: H. Aschehoug, 1959) and Riste in *London regjeringa*, vols. I and II.
5 D. A. T. Stafford, *Britain and European Resistance 1940–1945: A Survey of the Special Operations Executive with Documents* (Toronto: University of Toronto Press, 1980), pp. 7–8.
6 O. Riste, *The Norwegian Intelligence Service 1945–1970* (London: F. Cass, 1999), pp. 34–54.

Appendix A

1 Compiled from the following sources: TNA: HS2, HS7, HS8, DEFE2, PREM3, CAB files; NHM: SOE archive; S. Kjeldstadli, *Hjemmestyrkene: hovedtrekk av den militære motstanden under okkupasjonen* (Oslo: H. Aschehoug, 1959); P. F. Dahl, *Heavy Water and the Wartime Race for Nuclear Energy* (Bristol: IOP, 1999).

Appendix B

1 Compiled from the following sources: TNA: HS2, HS7, HS8, DEFE2, PREM3, ADM and CAB files. NHM: SOE and FO IV archives.

Appendix C

1 This information is compiled from the following sources: TNA: HS2, HS7, and HS8 files. NHM: SOE and FO IV archives. S. Kjeldstadli, *Hjemmestyrkene: hovedtrekk av den militære motstanden under okkupasjonen* (Oslo: H. Aschehoug, 1959); E. Jensen, [*et al*], *Kompani Linge*, vols I and II, (Oslo: Gyldendal, 1948); J. Birkenes, *Milorg i D17, 1940–1945, (Nedre Telemark)* (Skien: Selskapet for Skien byvel, 1982); R. Berg and P. Lindhjem, *Militær motstand i Rogaland og Vestfold*, (Oslo: Universitetsforlaget, 1972); E. Welle-Strand, *Vi vil verne vårt land: antisabotasje I Norge, 1944–1945* (Oslo: NHM, 2000); G. Pedersen, *Militær motstand i nord 1940–1945* (Tromsø: Universitetsforlaget), 1982.

BIBLIOGRAPHY

Primary sources

(1) The National Archives, Kew, England.
The files of the Special Operations Executive
German Section: HS6/217, HS6/619.
Headquarters Papers: HS7/1-HS7/66, HS7/174–182.
Headquarters Papers: HS8/1-HS8/1043.
Norwegian Section: HS2/126–252.
Personal Files: HS9.
Scandinavian Region: HS2/1–12.
Scandinavian War Diaries: HS7/279–282.
Swedish Section: HS2/253–272.

Records of the Ministry of Defence

Combined Operations Headquarters records: DEFE2.

Records of the Admiralty, Naval Forces, Royal Marines, Coastguard and Related Bodies

Admiralty and Ministry of Defence Navy Department:
   Correspondence and Papers: ADM/1.
Naval Intelligence and Operational Intelligence Centre: ADM223.
War History Cases and Second World War: ADM199.

Records of the Air Ministry and RAF

Bomber Command: AIR14.
Coastal Command and Ministry of Defence: AIR15.
Department of the Chief of Air Staff: AIR8.
Directorate of Operations and Intelligence and Directorate of Plans: AIR9.
Directorate of Intelligence and Related Bodies: AIR20.
Judge Advocate General's Office: AIR18.

War Office Files

Directorate of Military Operations and Intelligence: WO106.
Directorate of Military Operations and Intelligence: WO208.
Directorate of Military Operations and Plans: WO193.
Office of the CIGS: WO216.
SHAEF: WO219.

Records of the Cabinet Office

Cabinet Office: Ministry of Defence Secretariat: CAB120.
Cabinet Office: Secret Information Centre: CAB121.
Cabinet Office Private Collections: CAB127.
Chiefs of Staff Memoranda: CAB80.
Chiefs of Staff Minutes: CAB79.
Defence Committee (Ops): CAB69.
Defence Committee (Supply): CAB70.
Joint Planning Committee – later Joint Planning Staff – memos and minutes: CAB84.
Tube Alloys Consultative Council minutes and papers: CAB126.
War Cabinet and Cabinet memos: CAB66.
War Cabinet and Cabinet minutes: CAB65.
War Cabinet and Cabinet Office: British Joint Staff Mission, Washington: CAB122.
War Cabinet and Cabinet Offices: Lord Hankey papers: CAB63.

Records of Prime Minister's Office

Operational Correspondence and Papers: PREM3.
Records of the Ministry of Economic Warfare and
   Successors: FO837.

Foreign Office Records

Embassy and Consulate Sweden: General Correspondence: FO188.
Political Departments: General Correspondence: FO371.
Private Office: Papers of Sir Anthony Eden 1935–46: FO954.

Political Warfare Executive and Foreign Office Records

Political Intelligence Department papers: FO898.

The Secret Service (MI5)

Personal Files 1914–79: KV2.

The SOE Adviser, Records and Historical Department, the Foreign & Commonwealth Office, London

Documents and information from the SOE personal files of:
Captain H. J. Marks.
E. Skinnarland.
E. J. Jacobsen.
E. M. Nielsen.
G. O. Wiskeman.
Lt. Col. J. S. Wilson.
Lt. Commander F. N. Stagg RN.
Lt. J. L. Chaworth-Musters RNVR.
Major P. W. T. Boughton-Leigh.
T. Gulbrandsen.

(2) Norges Hjemmefrontmuseum, Askerhus Festning, Oslo, Norway

FO IV archives, boks 1–167.
SOE archives, boks 1–48.

Private papers

The Liddell Hart Centre for Military Archives: The papers of Brigadier E. E. Mockler-Ferryman (1896–1978).
The National Army Museum, Chelsea, London: The papers of General Sir Andrew Thorne.

Oral interviews

The Imperial War Museum Sound Archive, All Saints Annexe, Austral St., London.
A. Croft, ref. 8686/9748.
A. Kjelstrup, ref. 8311.
B. Rasmussen, ref. 8314.
D. Howarth, ref. 12309.
G. Sønsteby, ref. 8310.
J. C. Adamson, ref. 12295.
K. Haukelid, ref. 8316.

Unpublished sources

Information supplied by J. A. Holmen at the Orkla Industrimuseum (Industrial Museum), Pb 23,7331, Løkken Verk, Norway.
Proceedings from a Conference on Britain and European Resistance 1939–1945, at St. Antony's College, Oxford, December 1962.

Published sources

Aanensen, E., *Når vi kommer inn fra havet: historien om den Norske brigade i Skottland 1940–1945*, Oslo: Dreyer, 1974.

Abelsen, F., *Marinens fartøyer 1939-1945 og deres skjebne*, Oslo: Sem & Stenersen, 1986.
Adamson, H. C., and P. Klem, *Blood on the Midnight Sun*, New York: W. W. Norton, 1964.
Andenæs, J., *Det vanskelige oppgjøret*, 3rd edn, Oslo: Tano-Aschehoug, 1998.
Andrew, C., 'Churchill and Intelligence', *Intelligence and National Security*, vol. 3, no. 3, July 1988, pp. 181-93.
Astley, J. B., *The Inner Circle: A View of War at the Top*, London: Hutchinson, 1971.
Astrup, H., *Oslo Intrigue: A Women's Memoir of Norwegian Resistance*, New York: McGraw-Hill, 1954.
Baden-Powell, D. T., *Operation Jupiter: SOE's Secret War in Norway*, London: R. Hale, 1982.
Balchen, B., *Come North with Me*, London: Hodder & Stoughton, 1959.
Barman, T., *Diplomatic Correspondent*, London: Hamish-Hamilton, 1968.
Barnett, C., *Engage the Enemy More Closely*, London: Penguin, 2000.
Barstad, T. A., *Pelle-gruppa: sabotører på Østlandet 1944-1945*, Oslo: J. Cappelen, 1987.
Barstad, T. A., 'Norsk motstand fra svensk grunn', in S. Ekman and O. K. og Grimnes (eds), *Broderfolk i ufredstid - Norsk forbindelser under annen verdenskrig*, Oslo: Universitetsforlaget, 1991.
Barstad, T. A., *Sabotasjen i Oslo området 1944-1945*, Oslo: Universitetsforlaget, 1991.
Bascombe, N., *The Winter Fortress*, London: Head of Zeus, 2017.
Baxter, C. F., 'Winston Churchill: Military Strategist?' *Military Affairs*, vol. 47, no. 1, February 1983, pp. 7-10.
Beesley, P., *Very Special Intelligence*, London: Greenhill, 2000.
Beevor, J. G., *SOE: Recollections and Reflections 1940-1945*, London: Bodley Head, 1981.
Ben-Moshe, T., 'Winston Churchill and the Second Front: A Reappraisal', *Journal of Modern History*, vol. 62, no. 3, September 1990, pp. 503-37.
Bennet, R., 'Fortitude, Ultra and the Need to Know', *Intelligence and National Security*, vol. 4, no. 3, July, 1989, pp. 482-502.
Berg, R., and P. Lindhjem, *Norge og den 2. verdenskrig: militær motstand i Rogaland og Vestfold*, Oslo: Universitetsforlaget, 1972.
Birkenes, J., *Milorg i D 17 1940-1945 (Nedre Telemark)*, Skien: Selskapet for Skien byvel, 1982.
Birkhaug, K., *Telavåg: fiskeværet som tyskerne slettet ut i 1942*, Oslo: Gyldendal, 1946.
Blindheim, S., *Nordmenn under Hitlers fane: dei norske front kjemparane*, 2nd edn, Oslo: Norges Boklag, 1977.
Blindheim, S., *Offiser i krig og fred*, Oslo: Det Norsk Samlaget, 1981.
Bond, B., *British Military Policy between the Two World Wars*, Oxford: Clarendon Press, 1980.

Boog, H., '"Josephine" and the Northern Flank', *Intelligence and National Security*, vol. 4, no. 1, January 1989, pp. 137–60.

Borgersrud, L., *Nødvendig innsats: sabotørene som skapte den aktive motstanden*, Oslo: Universitetsforlaget, 1997.

Boyce, F., and D. Everett, *SOE: The Scientific Secrets*, Stroud: Sutton, 2003.

Bramsen, B., and K. Wain, *The Hambros, 1779–1979*, London: M. Joseph, 1979.

Bruce-Lockhart, R., *Comes the Reckoning*, London: Putnam, 1947.

Brun, J., *Brennpunkt Vemork 1940–1945*, Oslo: Universitetsforlaget, 1985.

Burhans, R. D., *The First Special Services Forces*, Washington DC: Infantry Journal Press, 1947).

Butcher, H. C., *My Three Years with Eisenhower*, London: William Heinemann, 1946.

Butler, J. R. M., 'Grand Strategy', vol. II and vol. III, part II, in J. R. M. Butler (ed.), *History of the Second World War*, London: HMSO, 1957, 1964.

Cave-Brown, A., *The Last Hero: Wild Bill Donovan*, London: Joseph, 1982.

Chalou, G. C., *The Secrets War: The Office of Strategic Services in WW II*, Washington DC: National Archives and Records Administration, 1991.

Christensen, C., *De som heiste flagget*, Oslo: Cappelen, 1986.

Christensen, Chr. A. R., *Norge under okkupasjonen*, Oslo: Fabritius, 1964.

Christensen, D., *Hemmelig agent i Norge: Den utrolige beretning om Hugo Munthe-Kaas i britisk spesialtjeneste mot Tyskerne*, Oslo: Hjemmetsbokforlag, 1987.

Christensen, D., *Den skjulte hånd: historien om Einar Johansen*, Oslo: W.W. Damm, 1990.

Christophersen, B., *Norsk militær innsats ute og hjemme 1940–1945*, Bergen: John Greig, 1981.

Churchill, W. S., *The Second World War*, vols. I–VI, London: Cassell, 1948–54.

Cookridge, E. H., *Inside SOE: The Story of Special Operations in Western Europe 1940–1945*, London: A. Baker, 1966.

Cooper, D. F. (R.E), 'Operation "Freshman"', *Royal Engineers Journal*, vol. LX, March 1946, pp. 31–8.

Cornwall, J., *Hitler's Scientists: Science, War and the Devil's Pact*, London: Penguin, 2003.

Craven, W. F., and J. L. Cate (eds), *The Army Air Forces in World War II*, vols. I and II, Washington DC: Office of Air Force History, 1983).

Croft, A., *A Talent for Adventure*, London: Hanley Swan, 1991.

Cruickshank, C., *SOE in Scandinavia*, Oxford: Oxford University Press, 1986.

Cubbage, T. L., 'The Success of Operation Fortitude: Hesketh's History of Strategic Deception', *Intelligence and National Security*, vol. 2, no. 3, July 1987, pp. 327–46.

Cunningham, C., *Beaulieu: The Finishing School for Secret Agents*, London: Leo Cooper, 1998.

Dahl, H. F. (ed.), *Krigen i Norge*, Oslo: Pax Forlag, 1974.
Dahl, H. F., *'Dette er London': NRK i krig 1940–1945*, Oslo: J.W. Cappelen Forlag, 1978.
Dahl, H. F., G. Hjeltnes, B. Nøkleby, N. J. Ringdal and Ø. Sørensen, *Norsk krigsleksikon 1940–1945*, Oslo: J.W. Cappelen, 1995.
Dahl, H. F., *Quisling: A Study in Treachery*, Cambridge: Cambridge University Press, 1999.
Dahl, H. F. (ed.), *Danske Tilstander Norske Tilstander 1940–45*, Oslo: Forlaget, 2010.
Dahl, H. F., G. Hjeltnes, B. Nøkleby, N. J. Ringdal and O. Sørensen, *Norsk krigsleksikon, 1940–1945*, Oslo: J.W. Cappelen, 1995.
Dahl, P. F., *Heavy Water and the Wartime Race for Nuclear Energy*, Bristol: IOP, 1999.
Dahlø, R., *Skjebnetråder: En historie om de ukjente krigerne*, Oslo: Schibsted forlag, 2001.
Dalton, H., *The Fateful Years*, London: Frederick Muller, 1957.
Danchev, A., *Establishing the Anglo-American Alliance: The Second World War Diaries of Brigadier Vivian Dykes*, London: Brassey's, 1990.
Danchev, A., *On Specialness: Essays in Anglo-American Relations*, Basingstoke: Macmillan, 1998.
Danchev, A., and D. Todman (eds), *War Diaries 1939–1945: Field Marshal Lord Alanbrooke*, London: Weidenfield & Nicolson, 2001.
Davies, H. J., 'From Special Operations to Special Political Action: The "Rump SOE" and SIS Post-War Covert Action Capability 1945–1973', *Intelligence and National Security*, vol. 15, no. 3, October 2000, pp. 55–76.
Dear, I., *Sabotage and Subversion*, London: Cassell Military, 1996.
Dear, I., *Ten Commandos 1942–1945*, London: Grafton, 1987.
Denham, H. M., *Inside the Nazi Ring: A Naval Attaché in Sweden 1940–1945*, London: Murray, 1984.
Diesen, T., *Milorg i Stor-Oslo: distrikt 13s historie*, Oslo: Orion, 1997.
Dodds-Parker, D., *Setting Europe Ablaze: Some Accounts of Ungentlemanly Warfare*, Windlesham: Springwood, 1983.
Dorman Drummond, J., *But for These Men*, Morly: Elmfield Press, 1974.
Dunford-Slater, J., *Commandos*, London: William Kimber, 1955.
Edwards, G., *Norwegian Patrol*, Shrewsbury: Curliffe, 1985.
Egner, A. F., and S. W. Aasland, *BBC: Kanonen spiller Chopin: Flybårne forsyninger til Milorg i Norge 1940–1945*, Lysaker: A. F. Egner, 1997.
Ehrman, J., 'Grand Strategy', vols. V and VI, in J. R. M. Butler (ed.), *History of the Second World War*, London: HMSO, 1956–7.
Eisenhower, D. D., *Crusade in Europe*, New York: William Heinemann, 1948.
Elliot-Bateman, M. (ed.), *The Fourth Dimension of Warfare*, Manchester: Manchester University Press, 1970.
Ellis, Major L. F., 'Victory in the West', vols. I and II, in J. R. M. Butler (ed.), *History of the Second World War*, London: HMSO, 1966–8.

Eriksen, K. E., and T. Halvorsen, T., 'Frigjøringen', vol. 8, in M. Skodvin (ed.), *Norge i krig: fremmedåk og frihetskamp 1940-1945*, Oslo: Aschehoug, 1987.
Farrell, B. P., 'Symbol of Paradox: The Casablanca Conference 1943', *Canadian Journal of History*, vol. 28, no. 1, April 1993, pp. 21-40.
Farrell, B. P., 'Yes, Prime Minister: Barbarossa, Whipcord and the Basis of British Grand Strategy, Autumn 1941', *Journal of Military History*, vol. 57, no. 4, October 1993, pp. 599-625.
Farrell, B. P., *The Basis and Making of British Grand Strategy*, books I and II, New York: Edwin Mellen Press, 1998-9.
Ferris, J., 'The Intelligence-Deception Complex: An Anatomy', *Intelligence and National Security*, vol. 4, no. 4, October 1987, pp. 719-34.
Fjærli, E., *Den norske hær i Storbritannia 1940-1945*, Oslo: Tanum-Norli, 1982.
Foot, M. R. D., *SOE in France*, London: HMSO, 1966.
Foot, M. R. D. (ed.), *War and Society: Historical Essays in Honour and Memory of J.R. Western 1928-1971*, London: Paul Elek, 1973.
Foot, M. R. D., *Resistance: European Resistance to Nazism 1940-1945*, London: 1976.
Foot, M. R. D., 'Was SOE Any Good?' *Journal of Contemporary History*, vol. 16, no. 1, January 1981, pp. 167-81.
Foot, M. R. D., 'The OSS and SOE: An Equal Partnership?', in G. C. Chalou, *The Secrets War: The OSS in World War Two*, Washington, DC: National Archives Trust Fund Board, 1992.
Foot, M. R. D., *The Special Operations Executive 1940-1946*, 2nd edn, London: Pimlico, 1999.
Foot, M. R. D., *SOE in the Low Countries*, London: St. Ermin's Press, 2001.
Foot, M. R. D., and J. H. Langley, *MI9: Escape and Evasion 1939-1945*, London: Book Club Associates, 1979.
Freedman, L., P. Hayes and R. O'Neil, *War, Strategy and International Politics: Essays in Honour of Sir Michael Howard*, Oxford: Clarendon Press, 1994.
Anthony Martienssen (ed.), *Fuehrer Conferences on Naval Affairs 1939-1945*, London: Greenhill, 1990.
Færøy, F., *Frigjøringen*, Oslo: NHM, 1995.
Gallagher, T., *Against All Odds: Midget Submarines against the Tirpitz*, London: Macdonald, 1971.
Gallagher, T., *Assault in Norway: The True Story of the Telemark Raid*, London: Purnell, 1975.
Garnett, D., *The Secret History of PWE: The Political Warfare Executive 1939-1945*, London: St. Ermin's Press, 2002.
Gerhardsen, E., *Felleskap i krig og fred: erindringer 1940-1945*, Oslo: Tiden-Norsk Forlag, 1970.
Gibbs, N. H., 'Grand Strategy', vol. I, in J. R. B. Butler (ed.), *History of the Second World War*, London: HMSO, 1976.
Gilbert, M., *Finest Hour: Winston S. Churchill 1939-1941*, London: Heinemann, 1983.

Gilbert, M., *Road to Victory: Winston S. Churchill, 1941-1945*, London: Heinemann, 1989.
Gjelsvik, T., *Norwegian Resistance, 1940-1945*, London: Church, 1979.
Gjems-Onstad, E., *Durham: hemmelige operasjoner i Trøndelag mot tysk okkupasjonsmakt 1943-1945*, Oslo: Sollia Forlag, 1981.
Gjems-Onstad, E., *Lark: Milorg i Trøndelag 1940-1945*, Trondheim: Midt Norge Forlag, 1990.
Gleditsch, N., and K. Gleditsch, *Glimt fra kampårene*, Oslo: Dreyer, 1954.
Goulter, C., *A Forgotten Offensive*, London: Frank Cass, 1995.
Grannes, E., *I skyggen av Jupiter 1941-1944*, Oslo: Tiden-Norsk Forlag, 1989.
Gray, C., *Modern Strategy*, Oxford: Oxford University Press, 1999.
Grimnes, O. K., *Norge under okkupasjonen*, Oslo: Universitetsforlaget, 1969.
Grimnes, O. K., *Et flyktningesamfunn vokser fram: Nordmenn i Sverige 1940-1945*, Oslo: H. Aschehoug, 1969.
Grimnes, O. K., *Hjemmefrontens Ledelse*, Oslo: Universitetsforlaget, 1979.
Grimnes, O. K., 'Overfall', vol. I in M. Skodvin (ed.), *Norge i krig: fremmedåk & frihetskamp 1940-1945*, Oslo: Aschehoug, 1984.
Grimnes, O. K., 'Historieskrivingen om okkupasjonen: det nasjonale konsensus syndromets gjennomslagskraft', *Nytt Norsk Tidsskrift*, vol. 2, 1990, pp. 108-21.
Grimnes, O. K., 'The Allied Heavy Water Operations at Rjukan', *Institutt for Forsvarsstudier* (IFS Info), vol. 4, 1995, pp. 7-12.
Guhnfeldt, C., *Bomb gestapo hovedkvarteret*, Oslo: Wings Forlag, 1995.
Gwyer, J. M. A., 'Grand Strategy', vol. III, part I, in J. R. M. Butler (ed.), *The Second World War*, London: HMSO, 1964.
Haavardsholm, E., *Martin Linge, min morfar*, Oslo: Gyldendal, 1993.
Hafsten, B., U. Larsstuvold and S. Stenersen, *Flyalarm: Luftkrigen over Norge 1939-1945*, Oslo: Sem & Stenersen, 1991.
Haga, A., *Natt på norskekysten: den hemmelige militære nordsjøtrafikk, 1940-1943*, Oslo: J.W. Cappelen, 1979.
Haga, A., *Jernring rundt Bjørn West*, Oslo: Cappelen, 1982.
Haga, A., *Klar til storm: med de norske commandos i annen verdenskrig*, Oslo: Cappelen, 1984.
Haga, A., *Aksjon Telavåg*, Oslo: Cappelen, 1993.
Haga, A., *Skygger over Utvær*, Oslo: J.W. Cappelen, 2001).
Hamilton-Hill, D., *SOE Assignment*, London: New English Library, 1975.
Handel, M. I., 'Introduction: Strategic and Operational Deception in Historical Perspective', *Intelligence and National Security*, vol. 2, no. 3, July 1987, pp. 1-92.
Hansen, P. C., 'The Royal Norwegian Air Force in Canada 1940-1945', *Canadian Defence Quarterly*, vol. 17, no. 2, April 1987, pp. 61-6.
Harrison, G. A., *Cross Channel Attack: U.S. Army in World War II*, Washington DC: United States Army, 1951.
Hartmann, P., *Bak fronten*, Oslo: H. Aschehoug, 1955.
Harvey, J., *The Diplomatic Diaries of Oliver Harvey*, London: Collins, 1970.

Hauge, E. O., *Salt-Water Thief* (translated by M. Munthe), London: Gerald Duckworth, 1958.
Hauge, J. Chr., *Frigjøringen*, Oslo: Gyldendal, 1970.
Hauge, J. Chr., *The Liberation of Norway* (translated by Marius Hauge), Oslo: Gyldendal, 1995.
Hauge, J. Chr., *Rapport om mitt arbeid under okkupasjonen*, Oslo: Gyldendal, 1995.
Haukelid, K., *Skis against the Atom*, London: William Kimber, 1954.
Heimark, B. H., *The OSS Norwegian Special Operations Group in World War II*, London: Praeger, 1994.
Helle, B., *The Norwegian Navy in the Second World War*, Oslo: Naval Staff, 1997.
Helle, E., *Oscar Torp, arbeidergutt og statsmann*, Oslo: Gyldendal, 1982.
Herrington, I., 'The SIS and SOE in Norway 1940–1945: Conflict or Co-operation?', *War in History*, vol. 9, no. 1, January 2002, pp. 82–110.
Hesketh, R., *Fortitude: The D-Day Deception Campaign*, London: St. Ermin's Press, 1999.
Hinsley, F. H., E. E. Thomas, C. F. C. Ransom and R. C. Knight (eds), *British Intelligence in the Second World War: Its Influence on Strategy and Operations*, vols. 1–III, HMSO: London, 1979–88.
Hoidal, O., *Quisling: A Study in Treason*, Oslo: Universitetsforlaget, 1989.
Howard, M., *The Mediterranean Strategy in the Second World War*, London: Weidenfeld & Nicolson, 1968.
Howard, M., 'Grand Strategy', vol. IV, in J. R. M. Butler (ed.), *History of the Second World War*, London: HMSO, 1972.
Howard, M., *The Continental Dilemma: The Dilemma of British Defence Policy in the Era of Two World Wars*, London: Penguin, 1974.
Howard, M., 'Strategic Deception in the Second World War', vol. V, in F. H. Hinsley et al. (eds), *British Intelligence in the Second World War: Its Influence on Strategy and Operations*, London: HMSO, 1990.
Howarth, D., *We Die Alone*, London: Reprint Society, 1957.
Howarth, D., *The Shetland Bus*, London: Elmfield Press, 1976.
Howarth, P., *Undercover: The Men and Women of the Special Operations Executive*, London: Routledge & Kegan Paul, 1980.
Howe, E., *The Black Game: British Subversive Operations against the Germans during the Second World War*, London: Michael Joseph, 1982.
Hæstrup, J., *Europe Ablaze: An Analysis of the History of the European Resistance Movement*, Odense: Odense University Press, 1979.
Imlay, T., 'Allied Economic Intelligence and Strategy during the "Phoney War"', *Intelligence and National Security*, vol. 13, no. 4, October 1998, pp. 107–32.
Irving, D., *The Virus House: Germany's Atomic Research and Allied Counter-Measures*, London: W. Kimber, 1967.
Irvine, J. W., *The Waves Are Free: Shetland/Norway Links, 1940–1945*, Lerwick: Shetland, 1988.

Jakub, J., *Spies and Saboteurs: Anglo-American Collaboration and Rivalry in Human Intelligence Collection and Special Operations 1940-1945*, London: Macmillan, 1999.
Jensen, E., P. Ratvik and R. Ulstein, *Kompani Linge*, vols. I and II, Oslo: Gyldendal, 1948.
Jones, R. V., *Reflections on Intelligence*, London: Heinemann, 1989.
Jones, R. V., *Most Secret War*, 2nd edn, London: Wordsworth Editions, 1998.
Judd, A., *The Quest for C: Sir Mansfield Cumming and the Foundation of the British Secret Service*, London: HarperCollins, 1999.
Kahn, D., *Seizing the Enigma*, London: Arrow, 1992.
Kemp, A., *The SAS at War 1941-1945*, London: Penguin, 2000.
Kemp, P., *Underwater Warriors: The Fighting History of Midget Submarines*, London: Cassell, 1996.
Kennedy, L., *Menace: The Life and Death of the Tirpitz*, London: Sphere, 1979.
Kersaudy, F., *Vi stoler på England* (translated from French by Sidsel Mellbye), Oslo: Cappelen, 1991.
Kjeldstadli, S., *Hjemmestyrkene: hovedtrekk av den militære motstanden under okkupasjonen*, vol. I, Oslo: H. Aschehoug, 1959.
Koch, H. W., 'The Strategic Air Offensive against Germany: The Early Phase, May-September 1940', *The Historical Journal*, vol. 34, no. 1, January 1991, pp. 117-41.
Koht, H., *For fred og fridom i krigstid, 1939-1940*, Oslo: Tiden Norsk Forlag, 1957.
Kraglund, I., *Sikringstjenesten 1940-1945*, Oslo: NHM, 1990.
Kraglund, I., *Holdningskampen, 1940-1942*, Oslo: NHM, 1993.
Kraglund, I., and A. Moland, 'Hjemmefront', vol. 6, in M. Skodvin (ed.), *Norge i krig: fremmedåk & frihetskamp 1940-1945*, Oslo: Aschehoug, 1987.
Kramish, A., *The Griffin*, Boston, MA: Houghton Mifflin, 1986.
Kurzman, D., *Blood and Water: Sabotaging Hitler's Bomb*, New York: Henry Holt, 1997.
Laquer, W., *Guerrilla Warfare*, New Jersey: Transaction, 1998.
Leifland, E., 'Deception Plan Graffham and Sweden-Another View', *Intelligence and National Security*, vol. 4, no. 2, April 1989, pp. 295-315.
Leighton, R. M., 'Overlord Revisited: An Interpretation of American Strategy in the European War 1942-1944', *American Historical Review*, vol. LXVI, July 1963, pp. 919-37.
Lie, T., *Med England i ildlinjen, 1940-1942*, Oslo: Tiden Norsk Forlag, 1956.
Lie, T., *Hjemover*, Oslo: Tiden Norsk Forlag, 1958.
Lindsay, D., *Forgotten General: A Life of Andrew Thorne*, Salisbury: Michael Russell, 1987.
Lochen, E., 'Den Norske Stockholmslegation's Rettskontor under Krigen', *Nordisk Tidskrift for Vetenskap, Konst och Industri*, vol. 65, no. 1, January 1989, pp. 11-16.

Lorain, P., *Secret Warfare: The Arms and Techniques of the Resistance*, London: Orbis, 1984.
Ludlow, P., 'Great Britain and Northern Europe 1940–1945', *Scandinavian Journal of History*, vol. 4, no. 2, 1979, pp. 123–62.
Mackenzie, W. J. M., *The Secret History of SOE: The Special Operations Executive*, London: St. Ermin's Press, 2000.
Macksey, K., *The Partisans of Europe in World War II*, London; Hart-Davis Macgibbon, 1975.
Macksey, K., *Commando Strike: The Story of Amphibious Raiding in World War II*, London: Secker & Warburg, 1985.
Macksey, K., *Godwin's Saga: A Commando epic*, London: Brasseys Defence, 1987.
Manus, M., *Underwater Saboteur*, London: William Kimber, 1953.
Marks, L., *Between Silk and Cyanide: A Codemaker's War 1941–1945*, London: HarperCollins, 1998.
Marshall-Cornwall, J., *Wars and Rumours of Wars: A Memoir*, London: Leo Cooper, 1984.
Masterman, J., *The Double Cross System in the War of 1939–1945*, London: Pimlico, 1972.
Matloff, M., 'Allied Strategy in Europe 1939–1945', in P. Paret (ed.), *Makers of Modern Strategy from Machiavelli to the Nuclear Age*, Oxford: Oxford University Press, 1986).
Matloff, M., and E. M. Snell, *Strategic Planning for Coalition Warfare 1941–1942 and 1943–1944, in US Army in World War II*, Washington, DC: OCMHDA, 1953 and 1959.
McInnes, C., and G. D. Sheffield (eds), *Warfare in the Twentieth Century: Theory and Practice*, London: Unwin Hyman, 1988.
Mckay, C. G., *From Information to Intrigue: Studies in Secret Service Based on the Swedish Experience, 1939–1945*, London: Frank Cass, 1993.
Mclachlan, D., *Room 39: Naval Intelligence in Action 1939–1945*, London, Weidenfield & Nicolson, 1968.
Medlicott, W. N., *The Economic Blockade*, vols. I and II, London: HMSO, 1952 and 1959.
Messenger, C., *The Commandos 1940–1946*, London: Grafton, 1991.
Messenger, P. A., 'Fighting for Relevance: Economic Intelligence and Special Operations Executive in Spain 1943–1945', *Intelligence and National Security*, vol. 15, no. 3, Autumn 2000, pp. 33–54.
Michel, H., *The Shadow War: Resistance in Europe 1939–1945* (translated by R. Barry), London: Andre Deutsch, 1972.
Midtskau, S., *London svarer ikke*, Oslo: E.G. Mortensens, 1968.
Milner, M., *Battle of the Atlantic*, Stroud: Tempus, 2003.
Milward, A. S., *The Fascist Economy in Norway*, Oxford: Oxford University Press, 1972.

Milward, A. S., 'The Economic and Strategic Effectiveness of Resistance', in S. Hawes and R. White, *Resistance in Europe 1939-1945*, London: Allen Lane, 1975.
Moland, A., *Kampen mot mobiliserings-trusselen i Norge, 1943-1944*, Oslo: NHM, 1987.
Moland, A., *Sabotasje i norge under 2. verdenskrig*, 2nd edn, Oslo: NHM, 1987.
Moland, A., *Milorg, 1941-1943: fremvekst, ledelse og organisasjonen*, Oslo: NHM, 1991.
Moland, A., *Over grensen?* Oslo: Orion forlag, 1999.
Moore, B. (ed.), *Resistance in Western Europe*, Oxford: Berg, 2000.
Moorhead, A., *Eclipse*, New York: Harper & Row, 1945.
Morgan, F. E., *Overture to Overlord*, London: Hodder & Stoughton, 1950.
Morgan, F. E., *Peace and War: A Soldiers Life*, London: Hodder & Stoughton, 1961.
Munthe, M., *Sweet Is War*, London: Duckworth, 1954.
Muller, K. J., 'A German Perspective on Allied Deception Operations in the Second World War', *Intelligence and National Security*, vol. 2, no. 3, July 1987, pp. 301-26.
Murphy, C. J., 'SOE and Repatriation', *Journal of Contemporary History*, vol. 36, no. 2, April 2001, pp. 309-24.
Muus, F. B., *The Spark and the Flame* (translated by J. F. Burke), London: Museum Press, 1956.
Nielsen, T., *Bak de tyske linjer: Milorg basen Bjørn 1944-1945*, Oslo: Gyldendal, 1992.
Nissen, H. S. (ed.), *Scandinavia during the Second World War*, Oslo: Universitetsforlaget, 1983.
Njølstad, O., *Jens Chr. Hauge: Fullt og Helt*, Oslo: Aschehoug, 2008.
Njølstad, O., *Professor Tronstads Krig*, Oslo: Aschehoug, 2015.
Grimnes O. K., *Norge og den 2. verdenskrig: motstandskamp, strategi og marinepolitikk*, Oslo: Universitetsforlaget, 1972.
Nygaardsvold, J., *Norge i krig-London, 1940-1945*, Oslo: Tiden Forlag, 1983.
Nyquist, G., *99th Infantry Battalion*, Decorah: Amundsen, 1990.
Nøkleby, B., 'Nyordning', vol. II, in M. Skodvin (ed.), *Norge i krig: fremmedåk & frihetskamp 1940-1945*, Oslo: Aschehoug, 1985.
Nøkleby, B., 'Holdningskamp', vol. IV, in M. Skodvin (ed.), *Norge i krig: fremmedåk og frihetskamp*, Oslo, Aschehoug, 1986.
Nøkleby, B., *Pass godt på Tirpitz*, Oslo: Gyldendal, 1988.
O'Halpin, E., '"Toys" and "Whispers" in 16-Land: SOE in Ireland 1940-1942', *Intelligence and National Security*, vol. 15, no. 4, winter 2000, pp. 1-18.
Olsen, A. K., *Norsk Hydro gjennom 50 år: Et eventyr fra realitetens verden*, Oslo: Norsk Hydro Kvælstofaktieselskap, 1955.
Ottosen, K., *Theta Theta*, Oslo: Universitetsforlaget, 1983.
Paulsen, H. (ed.), *Norge og den 2. verdenskrig: mellom nøytrale og allierte*, Oslo: Universitetsforlaget, 1968.

Paulsen, H. (ed.), *Norge og den 2. verdenskrig: 1940 fra nøytrale til okkupert*, Oslo: Universitetsforlaget, 1969.
Pedersen, G., *Militær motstand i nord 1940–1945*, Tromsø: Universitetsforlaget, 1982.
Philby, K., *My Silent War*, St. Albans: Panther, 1973.
Pimlott, B., *Hugh Dalton*, London: Papermac, 1985.
Pimlott, B., *The Second World War Diary of Hugh Dalton*, London: Jonathan Cape, 1986.
Pogue, F. C., *George C. Marshall: Organiser of Victory*, New York: Viking, 1973.
Pogue, F. C., 'The Supreme Command', in K. R. Greenfield (ed.), *U.S. Army in the Second World War*, Washington, DC: OCMHDA, 1954.
Poulsson, J. A., *Aksjon Vemork: vinterkrig på Hardangervidda*, Oslo: Gyldendal, 1993.
Powers, T., *Heisenberg's War: The Secret History of the German Bomb*, Boston, MA: Da Capo Press, 2000.
Pryser, T., *Hitler's hemmelige agenter: Tysk etterretning i Norge 1939–1945*, Oslo: Universitetsforlaget, 2001.
Reed-Olsen, O., *Two Eggs on My Plate*, London: Companion, 1954.
Reynolds, D., W. F. Kimbell and A. O. Chubrarian, *Allies at War: The Soviet, American and British Experience 1939–1945*, Basingstoke: Macmillan, 1994.
Richards, D., *RAF Bomber Command in the Second World War: The Hardest Victory*, London: Penguin, 2001.
Riste, O., *The Neutral Ally: Norway's Relations with Belligerent Powers in the First World War*, Oslo: Universitetsforlaget, 1965.
Riste, O., 'Alliansepolitikk og brubygging', *Norsk Historisk Tidsskrift*, vol. 52, no. 3, 1973, pp. 261–7.
Riste, O., 'Utefront', vol. 7, in M. Skodvin (ed.), *Norge i Krig: fremmedåk og frihetskamp*, Oslo: Aschehoug, 1987.
Riste, O., 'Norway in Exile 1940–1945: The Formation of an Alliance Relationship', *Scandinavian Journal of History*, vol. 12, no. 4, 1987, pp. 317–29.
Riste, O., 'Forholdet mellom den Norske og den Svenske regjeringa under krigen', *Nordisk Tidskrift for Vetenskap, Konst och Industri*, vol. 65, no. 1, January 1989, pp. 1–10.
Riste, O., 'Norsk tryggingspolitikk fra isolasjonisme til atlantisk integrasjonen', *Norsk Historisk Tidsskrift*, vol. 72, no. 3, 1993, pp. 318–32.
Riste, O. (ed.), *Fredsgeneralen*, Oslo: Aschehoug, 1995.
Riste, O., *London regjeringa: Norge i krigsalliansen, 1940–1945*, 2nd edn, vol. I, 'prøvetid', vol. II, 'vegen heim', Oslo: Det Norske Samlaget, 1995.
Riste, O., *The Norwegian Intelligence Service 1945–1970*, London: F. Cass, 1999.
Riste, O., *Norway's Foreign relations*, Oslo: Universitetsforlaget, 2001.
Riste, O., and B. Nøkleby, *Norway 1940–1945: The Resistance Movement*, Oslo: J. Grundt Tanum Forlag, 1970.

Roberts, A., *Eminent Churchillians*, London: Weidenfield & Nicolson, 1994.
Rodgers, N. A. M. (ed.), *Naval Power in the Twentieth Century*, London: Macmillan, 1996.
ROH, Stortinget: *Regjeringen og hjemmefronten under krigen. Akstykker utgitt av stortinget*, Oslo: Aschehoug, 1948.
Roskill, S., *The Navy at War 1939-1945*, Ware: Wordsworth Editions, 1998.
Rustung Hegland, J., *Angrep i skjærgården: norske motortorpedobåters operasjoner fra Shetland 1941-1945*, Oslo: Dreyers, 1989.
Den norske regjerings virksomhet under krigen fra 9 april 1940 til 22 juni 1945. *Departementenes meldinger*, vol. IV, *forsvarsdepartementet*, Oslo: Aschehoug, 1948.
Rønneberg, J., 'Operation Gunnerside: Reminiscences of a Heavy Water Saboteur', *IFS Info*, vol. 4, 1995, pp. 13–16.
Rørholt, B., *Usynlige soldater: Nordmenn i secret service forteller*, Oslo: H. Aschehoug, 1990.
Rørholt, B., *Amatørspionen 'Lerken'*, Oslo: Hjemmenes, 1985.
Salmon, P. (ed.), *Britain and Norway in the Second World War*, London: HMSO, 1995.
Salmon, P., *Scandinavia and the Great Powers 1890-1940*, Cambridge: Cambridge University Press, 1997.
Sandvik, H., *Frigjøring av Finnmark 1944-1945*, Oslo: Gyldendal, 1975.
Sandvik, H., *Krigsår: med Kompani Linge i trening og kamp*, Oslo: Cappelen, 1979.
Seaman, M., 'Good Thrillers, but Bad History: A Review of Published Works on the Special Operations Executive's Work in France during the Second World War', in K. G. Robertson (ed.), *War, Resistance and Intelligence: Essays in Honour of M. R. D. Foot*, Barnsley: Leo Cooper, 1999.
Sebag-Montefiore, H., *Enigma: The Battle for the Code*, London: Phoenix, 2001.
Schive, J., *Tyve år etter*, Oslo: Gundersen, 1960.
Schjeldrup, F., *Over bakkekammen*, Oslo: Gyldendal, 1949.
Schofield, S., *Musketoon*, London: Jonathan Cape, 1964.
Skobba, I., *Krigen i Telemark 1940-1945: likvidasjoner og sabotasje - kommunister og milorg*, Oslo: Varsko Forlag, 1996.
Skodvin, M., *Striden om okkupasjonsstyret i Norge fram til 25 september 1940*, Oslo: Det Norske Samlaget, 1956.
Skodvin, M. (ed.), *Norge i krig: fremmedåk og frihetskamp 1940-1945*, vols. I - VIII, Oslo: H. Aschehoug, 1984-7.
Skodvin, M., *Norsk historie 1939-1945: krig og okkupasjon*, Oslo: Det Norske Samlaget, 1991.
Smith, B. F., *The Shadow Warriors: OSS and the Origins of the CIA*, London: Deutsch, 1983.
Solhaug, O., *Okkupasjonen i Finnmark*, Oslo: Båtsfjord, 1974.
Solhjell, K. O., and F. Traphagen, *Fra krig til fred: fokus på Snåsa og Nord-Trøndelag* (Ål: Boksmia, 2001).

Stafford, D. A. T., 'The Detonator Concept: British Strategy, SOE and European Resistance after the Fall of France', *Journal of Contemporary History*, vol. 10, no. 2, April 1975, pp. 185–217.
Stafford, D. A. T., 'Britain Looks at Europe, 1940: Some Origins of SOE', *Canadian Journal of History*, vol. 10, no. 2, August 1975, pp. 231–47.
Stafford, D. A. T., *Britain and European Resistance 1940–1945: A Survey of the Special Operations Executive with Documents*, Toronto: University of Toronto Press, 1980.
Stafford, D. A. T., *Churchill & Secret Service*, London: Abacus, 1997.
Stafford, D. A. T., *Secret Agent: Britain's Wartime Secret Service*, London: BBC, 2002.
Steen, S. (ed.), *Norges krig*, vols. I–III, Oslo: Gyldendal, 1947–50.
Svensholt, H. K., *Norske torpedobåter gjennom 125 år 1873–1998*, Oslo: Norsk Tidsskrift for Sjøvesen, 2001.
Sweet-Escott, B., *Baker Street Irregular*, Fakenham: Cox & Wyman, 1965.
Sønsteby, G., *Reports from Nr. 24*, London: Four Square, 1967.
Sønsteby, G., and J. B. Gundersen, *Bak rapportene*, Oslo: Aventura, 1985.
Sørensen, Ø., 'Forskningen om krigen i Norge: tradisjonelle og nye perspective', *Nytt Norsk Tidskrift*, vol. 1, 1989, pp. 40–58.
Sørhus, K., *Milorg D13 i kamp*, Oslo: Norsk Kunstforlag, 1972.
Sælen, F., *Shetlands Larsen*, Oslo: J.W. Eides, 1948.
Tennant, P., *Touchlines of War*, Hull: University of Hull Press, 1992.
Thompson, D., 'Norwegian Military Policy 1905–1940: A Critical Appraisal and Review of the Literature', *Journal of Military History*, vol. 61, no. 3, 1997, pp. 503–20.
Thorne, P., 'Andrew Thorne and the Liberation of Norway', *Intelligence and National Security*, vol. 61, no. 3, July 1992, pp. 300–17.
Till, G., 'Naval Power', in C. McInnes and G. D. Sheffield (eds), *Warfare in the Twentieth Century: Theory and Practice*, London: Unwin Hyman, 1988.
Townsend, C., 'The Irish Republican Army and the Development of Guerrilla Warfare 1916–1921', *English Historical Review*, vol. XCIV, April 1979, pp. 318–44.
Udgaard, N. M., *Great Power Politics and Norwegian Foreign Policy*, Oslo: Universitetsforlaget, 1973.
Ueland, A., *Tungtvannsaksjonen*, Oslo: Gyldendal, 2015.
Ueland, A., *Shetlandsgjengen: Heltene i Nordsjøen*, Oslo: Kagge Forlag, 2017.
Ugelvik Larsen, S. (ed.), *I krigens kjølvann*, Oslo: Universitetsforlaget, 1999.
Ulstein, R., *Englandsfarten*, vol. I and II, Oslo: Det Norske Samlaget, 1965 and 1967.
Ulstein, R., *Etterretningstjenesten i Norge 1940–1945*, vols. I–III, Oslo, Cappelen, 1987–92.
Ulstein, R., *Etterretningstjenesten 1940–1945*, Oslo: NHM, 1994.
Warner, C., and J. Benson, *Above Us the Waves*, London: White Lion, 1953.

Webster, Sir C., and A. N. Frankland, 'The Strategic Air Offensive', vols. I and II, in J. R. M. Butler (ed.), *History of the Second World War*, London: HMSO, 1961.
Welle-Strand, E., *Vi vil verne vårt land: anti-sabotasje i Norge, 1944–1945*, Oslo: NHM, 2000.
West, N., *Secret War: The Story of SOE, Britain's Wartime Sabotage Organisation*, London: Hodder & Stoughton, 1992.
Wheeler, M., 'The SOE Phenomenon', *Journal of Contemporary History*, vol. 16, no. 3, July 1981, pp. 513–9.
White, R., 'Teaching the Free Man How to Praise: Michael Foot on SOE Resistance in Europe', in K. G. Robertson (ed.), *War Resistance and Intelligence: Essays in Honour of MRD Foot*, Barnsley: Leo Cooper, 1999.
Widmark, F., *Kampen om Thamshavnbanen: SS Kommando Drontheim*, vol. II, Orkanger: F. T. Widmarks, 1974.
Wiggan, R., *Operation Freshman*, London: William Kimber, 1986.
Wilkinson, P., *Foreign Fields: The Story of a SOE Operative*, London: Taurus, 1997.
Wilkinson, P., and J. B. Astley, *Gubbins and SOE*, 2nd edn, London: Leo Cooper, 1997.
Willmott, H. P., *June 1944*, Poole: Blandford Press, 1984.
Willmott, H. P., *The Great Crusade*, London: M. Joseph, 1989.
Wilt, A. F., 'The Significance of the Casablanca Decisions, January 1943', *Journal of Military History*, vol. 55, no. 4, October 1991, pp. 517–29.
Wylie, N., 'An Amateur Learns His Job? Special Operations Executive in Portugal, 1940–1942', *Intelligence and National Security*, vol. 36, no. 3, July 2001, pp. 441–58.
Young, G. K., *The Diaries of Sir Robert Bruce Lockhart*, vol. II, 1939–1965, London: Macmillan, 1980.
Ziemke, E., *The German Northern Theatre of Operations 1940–1945*, Washington, DC: US Government Printing Office, 1976.
Ørvik, N., *Norsk Sikkerhets-Politikk 1920–1939*, Oslo: Universitetsforlaget, 1962.

Film and video

'Rapport fra Nr 24', documentary about Gunnar Sønsteby made by *Norges Rikskringkasting* (NRK: Norway's State Broadcasting Corporation), in 1994.
'I Kamp for Frihet', a documentary about Joachim Rønneberg, leader of the 'Gunnerside' operation, broadcast by *Norges Rikskringkasting* (NRK) on 26 May 2001.
'The Real Heroes of Telemark', a documentary about the 'Grouse' and 'Gunnerside' operations, produced by *BBC Bristol* and broadcast on September/October 2003.
'War at Sea', a documentary written by Professor Andrew D. Lambert, produced by the *BBC* and broadcast on April/May 2004.

PhD theses

Borgersrud, L., 'Wollweber-Organisasjonen i Norge', *University of Oslo*, 1994.
Gordon, Gerd Stray, 'The Norwegian Resistance during the German Occupation 1940–1945: Repression, Terror and Resistance: The West Country of Norway', *University of Pittsburgh*, 1978.
Goulter, C., 'A Forgotten Offensive, RAF Coastal Commands Anti Shipping Campaign, 1940–1945', *University of London*, 1993.
Krosby, V., 'Host to Exiles: The Foreign Office and the Norwegian Government in London 1940–1945', *London School of Economics*, 1979.
Mann, M. C., 'British Policy and Strategy towards Norway, 1941–1945', University of London, 1998.
Thompson, D. G., 'From Neutrality to NATO: The Norwegian Armed Forces and Defence Policy 1905–1955', *Ohio State University*, 1996.

INDEX

Abwehr (German intelligence) 166
Admiral Commanding the Orkneys and Shetlands (ACOS) 126, 128, 130–2
Admiralty, the 25–6, 47, 102–3, 119, 127–36
  SIS 112, 126
aircraft 27–8
airdrops 26–7
Alms, Col. J. H. 116
aluminium 149
amphibious raids 21, 58–9
ANCC see Anglo Norwegian Collaboration Committee
Andersen, Johannes 168
Anderson, Sir John 140
Anglo Norwegian Collaboration Committee (ANCC) 46, 57, 58, 59, 60
  coup de main attacks 151
  propaganda 106–7
Anstruther, Col. A. M. 35
'Arcadia' conference 38
Arctic convoys 38–9, 198
arms 159, 160, 180, 183
assassinations see liquidations
atomic bomb 140, 153
Auxiliary Units 9
Aviemore 21

Balchen, Bernt 27, 113
Barman, Thomas 105
Battle of the Atlantic 198
Baumann, Axel 64
Beichman, Lt. Col. Johan 75
Berg, Col. Ole 64
Berg, Lt. Col. Ole 75
Berg, Paal 72, 73
Bismarck (ship) 123–4
black markets 106
Böhme, Gen. 191
Bohr, Nils 140

Bomber Command 34
bombing see strategic bombing
Borge, Ivar 158
Bourne, Gen. 9
Boye, Thore 60
Brewer, Maj. George 112
Britain see Great Britain
British Army 46, 101, 102
Brooke, Gen. Sir Alan 35, 40–1
Bruce, Col. David 113
Brun, Jomar 101, 124, 140, 153

Carr, Frank 24
Central Leadership (SL) 76, 164, 168, 176
Chamberlain, Neville 8
Chariots (torpedoes) 132, 135
Chaworth-Musters, Lt. J. L. 15–16, 20, 51, 52, 122–3, 149
chemical factories 175
Chief of Staff to the Supreme Allied Commander (COSSAC) 43, 44
Chiefs of Staff (COS) 11, 35–6, 58, 96, 97
Christophersen, Col. 83
Churchill, Winston 8–9, 29, 35–7, 41, 128–9
  Jupiter 38–9, 40
  raids 95–6, 97
cipher material 95, 96
civilians 68–70, 73, 154–5, 160
  bombings 137, 140–1
Co-ordination Committee (KK) 73
coastal waters 127–36
COHQ see Combined Operations
Colby, Maj. William E. 116–17
Collier, Laurence 69
Combined Operations (COHQ) 1, 5, 94–104, 142
Combined Operations North Force (CONF) 130
Communists 74, 91
conscription 173–4, 183

COS *see* Chiefs of Staff
COSSAC *see* Chief of Staff to the
    Supreme Allied Commander
counter-scorch operations 184–5
coup de main operations 4, 40, 61–2,
    125–7, 146–57
Croft, Capt. Andrew 17, 18
Cromwell, Sir Frederic 112
Cruickshank, Charles 2

Dahl, Ørnulf 64
Dalton, Hugh 9, 11, 14, 31, 37, 53
    Ajax 35
    Hemisphere 55
    raids 94
Danielsen, Capt. E. C. 130
Defence High Command (FO) 59–60,
    61–2, 63, 66–7, 68
    coastal waters 128
    creation 200
    Milorg 80, 86, 87–9
    propaganda 106–7
    rat work 168
    secret army 161, 162, 163
Deinboll, Peter 151, 184
demography 6
Department of Scientific and Industrial
    Research (DSIR) 101
Devonshire (ship) 51
Diebner, Kurt 157
Director of Combined Operations
    (DCO) 93
Djupdraet, Sgt. Magnus Erling 99
Dollis, Astrid 166
Donovan, Gen. William 111, 113, 114

economic targets 93–4, 96, 99–100, 146
Eden, Anthony 51, 58, 121
Ekornes, Arne 78
Electra House (EH) 104
Ellingsen, Sverre 65
Enigma 95
equipment 113–14, 115–16, 180, 183
Ericksen, Hans 112

fascism 74
Fasting, Andreas 26, 141
FD-E *see* Norwegian Ministry of Defence
    Intelligence Office

Fehlis, Lt. Col. Heinrich 166
Finland 188–9
fish industry 130
fish oil 32, 96
fishing boats 23–6, 28, 78
Fleischer, Maj. Gen. 20, 51, 55, 56
flights 26–8
FO *see* Defence High Command
Foley, Maj. 121
Foreign Office 11, 18
Foreign Office Intelligence Office (UD/E)
    121
Forthun, Billy 26
'Fortitude North' 43–4, 45
Fougnar, Gunner 20, 107
France 3, 10, 30, 38, 45
Frisvold, Lt. Paal 64, 75, 78

Gabrielsen, Norman 163
Gaitskell, Hugh 14
Gerhardsen, Einar 73
German Army 178–9, 191–2, 194
    20th Mountain 47–8, 190
German navy 127, 198
Gestapo 165, 166, 167
government in exile *see* Norwegian
    government in exile
'Graffham' 43–4
Gram, Gregers 108–9, 156
Grand, Lawrence 9
Grande, Ivar 166, 170
Granland, Corp. Sverre 99
Great Britain 1, 3–4, 7, 8–9, 10
    Norway 29–30, 49, 54
    rebellions 30–1
    sabotage 176
    USA 37–8
    see also Chiefs of Staff; Royal
        Air Force; Royal Navy; Secret
        Intelligence Service; Special
        Operations Executive
Greece 4
Gubbins, Maj. Gen. Colin McVean 16,
    17, 40, 60, 122–3
    Milorg 83–4, 85–6
guerrilla warfare 8, 9, 40, 114, 186–7
    SOE policy 41–2, 81–3
Gulbrandsen, Torbjørn 161
Gunleiksrud, Jon 162

Haakon VII, King 1, 40, 51, 72, 194
Haavardsholm, Bernhard 123
Hackett, Capt. 106
Halifax, Edward Wood, Lord 51
Hambro, Sir Charles 14–15, 57–8, 59, 60, 112
 Milorg 61, 80, 81, 85
 Norwegian government in exile 52, 54
 propaganda 106
 RAF 137–8
Hammer, Rolf 160
Hammersen, Frithjof 192
Hampton, Lt. Col. C. S. 188
Hankey, Sir Maurice 9
Hansen, Knut Lier 157
Hansteen, Gen. Wilhelm 59, 61, 65, 98, 112
 liquidations 167
 Milorg 85
 RAF 143
Hartley, H. H. 10
Hauge, Jens Christian 65, 68, 73, 173–4, 181, 184
 liberation 191, 192, 193
 Milorg 87, 88, 89, 90
Haugland, Knut 163, 176
Haukelid, Knut 123, 156
heavy water 100–2, 124, 139–41, 152–4, 156–7
Helset, Maj. Olav 74–5
herring oil 15, 95
Heydrich, Reinhard 165
Heyerdahl-Larsen, Capt. Lasse 64, 65, 75
Himmler, Heinrich 167
Hitler, Adolf 96, 97–8, 100
HL *see* Homefront Leadership
Holdsworth, Gerald 24
Hole, Njål 140
Holland, Lt Col J. F. C. 9
Holst, Johan 56, 57, 75, 80
Homefront Leadership (HL) 73–4, 187
Horve, Cmdr. Thore 186
Howarth, Lt. D. A. 132
HS *see* Norwegian Home Forces
Huntingdon, Col. 112
hydroelectric plants 139–41

'Independent Companies' 16
Industrial Intelligence Centre (IIC) 32
industrial targets 14–15, 61–2
Ingebrigtsen, J. 51
Inter-Services Project Board (ISPB) 11, 32
iron ore 32, 151–2
Ismay, Maj. Gen. Sir H. L. 58

Jacobsen, Ernst Kirkeby 161
Jacobsen, Sigurd 156
Johns, P. L. 122–3
Jøssinglister (list of hostages) 58

Kaas, Finn 166
Keyes, Adm. 37
Keyes, Sir Roger 94
King-Hall, Cmdr. Stephen 9
KK *see* Co-ordination Committee
Knaben mines 141–2, 150
Koht, Halvdan 20, 51, 52
Kretsen 73
Krogvig, Bård 107
Kviljo, Fridjof Pedersen 20
Kyllingmark, Håkon 115

Labour Services 173–4, 183
Langmo, Rubin 20
Larsen, Alf 157
Lehmkuhl, H. K. 105
liberation 88–91, 145–6, 191–4
 preparation 179–91
Lie, Trygve 14, 22, 49, 53, 54–5
 amphibious raids 58, 59
 Claymore 97
 Milorg 55–6, 57
 sabotage 69–70
Lindberg, Konrad Alf 20
Linge, Martin 19–20, 21, 51
liquidations 165, 167–70, 201–2
Ljungberg, Col. Birger 20, 51, 55, 59

Mallet, Sir Victor 18
Manus, Max 108–9, 156
Marks, 2Lt. Hugh 18, 64
Marshall-Cornwall, Sir James 112
Marstrander, Lt. Cmdr. 60
Marthinsen, Maj. Gen. Karl A. 166, 170
Mediterranean, the 40–1
Menzies, Sir Stewart 9
MEW *see* Ministry of Economic Warfare

MI5 11
Midtskau, Sverre 26, 121, 123
Military Intelligence (Research) (MI [R])
    9–10, 12, 13, 16
Militærkontoret IV (MI IV) 63–4
Milorg ('official' military resistance) 3,
    5, 6, 61
  communication 63–4, 67–8
  government in exile 56–7
  heavy water 157
  leadership 181–2
  liberation 192–3, 194
  Norwegian Army High Command
    49–50
  protective force 185–6
  RAF 142–3
  rat work 168, 169–70
  resistance 73, 75, 76, 78–9, 159
  Rognes 55–6
  sabotage 172–3, 174–7, 204
  secret army 71–2, 161–3
  SIS 121–2, 124, 125
  SOE 80–92, 200–2
  training 180–1, 183–4
mining 14–15, 95
Ministry of Economic Warfare (MEW)
    14, 32, 62, 150
Mitchell, Capt. L. H. 122
Moe, Lt. Tycho 142
Moltke, Joachim von 192
molybdenum 141–2, 150
Morgan, Lt. Gen. Frederick 41
Mountbatten, Cmdr. Lord 58, 98
Munthe, Capt. Malcolm 17–18, 33, 64,
    148
  Milorg 57, 80, 85
  resistance 76, 79, 158

Nagell, Capt. Finn 21, 54, 121
Narvik 10, 39
Nasjonal Samling (NS) 2, 72, 142–3, 193
Neerland, Johan Møller 182
Nelson, Sir Frank 15
neutrality 52, 53, 59
Newill, J. B. 121
NIC I *see* Norwegian Independent
    Company No I
Nielsen, Edgar (Tom) 18, 65
Nilsen, Marino 166

NKP *see* Norwegian Communist Party
NKVD (People's Commissariat for
    Internal Affairs) 74
NNIU *see* Norwegian Naval Independent
    Unit
'No. 13 Military Mission' 16
Nordland, Nils 20
Normandy landings 45
NORSO *see* Norwegian Operational
    Group
North Sea 6, 7, 23–6
Norwegian Army High Command 49–50
Norwegian Communist Party (NKP) 74
'Norwegian Expedition' 15, 25, 51
Norwegian government in exile 5, 49–56,
    63–70, 80, 199
  collaboration 56–63
  propaganda 106, 107–8
Norwegian Home Forces (HS) 90, 192–3
Norwegian Independent Company No
    I (NIC I) 8, 19–20, 22, 60, 101–2
  coastal waters 131, 132
  coup de main attacks 156
  leadership 182
  sabotage 146, 173–4, 175, 177
  secret army 163, 164
  SOE 203
Norwegian Ministry of Defence
    Intelligence Office (FD-E) 21, 54–5,
    121
Norwegian Naval Independent Unit
    (NNIU) 26, 60
Norwegian Operational Group
    (NORSO) 114–15, 116
Norwegian War School 182
NS *see* Nasjonal Samling
Nyberg, Maj. H. A. 66, 190
Nygaardsvold, Johan 1, 59

Øen, Lt. Col. Bjarne 66, 68, 70, 87
Office of Strategic Services (OSS) 5, 67,
    93, 110–17
  bombing 142
  counter-scorch 184–5
oil 32, 175
operations:
  Ajax 35, 36, 97
  Almoner 130
  Anklet 21, 58–9, 97

Antipodes 190
Apostle 45
Archery 21, 58–9, 97
Arctic 148
Arquebus 160
Barbara 131–2, 147
Barter 115
Beauty 137–8
Bittern 168
Bodyguard 43–4
Bundle 109, 175
Cartoon 99
Chaffinch 156
Cheese 159
Clairvoyant 139, 148–9
Claribel 158
Claymore 37, 55, 96–7
Cobblestones 103
Cockade 41
Cockfight 159–60
Company 151
Derby 109
Docklow 152
Doomsday 45
Durham 109–10
Dynamite 35
Farnborough 182
Feather 126
Freshman 100–2, 203
Gunnerside 123, 124, 152–4, 203
Hardboiled 39
Hemisphere 55, 130
Heron 160
Husky 190–1
Jupiter 39, 40
Kestrel 151, 154–5
Kitbag 97
Mandible 95–6
Mardonius 108–9, 156
Marshfield 152
Maundy 129
Midhurst 114
Musketoon 69–70, 99
Nordlicht 47–8
Osprey 126
Overlord 4, 12, 43–8, 172, 198
Penguin 122
Performance 127
Pilgrim 97

Plover 87, 163
Polar Bear 186
Pullover 103
Rat Week 169
Redshank 61, 146–7, 150–1, 154
Redwing 156
Rype 116–17
Scale 189–90
Scapula 191
Seagull 152
Solo 39
Sonnie 113
Sunshine 185
Title 135
Torch 38
Vestige V 126, 131
Wallah 129
Youth 137–8
'Organisation' 72–3
Orkla Mining Company 14, 150–1
'Oslo Detachment' 174
OSS *see* Office of Strategic Services
'Osvald Group' 74
Ottar, Brynjulf 140

Palmer, Maj. 17
Palmstrøm, Rolf 163
Pelle Group 74
Petch, Lt. Col. 110
petrol 175
Pevik, Johnny 135, 158
Phillips, Rear Adm. T. S. 130
police 165–7, 182–3, 187–8, 190, 193
Political Warfare Executive (PWE) 93, 104–10
Pollock, Sir George Montagu 131
Portal, Sir Charles 140
Poulsson, Jens 139
propaganda 4, 9, 51, 82, 104–10
protective force 179–91, 184–6
PWE *see* Political Warfare Executive
pyrite ore 14, 126, 150–2

Quisling, Vidkun 72

RAF *see* Royal Air Force
raids 4, 9, 37, 94–104; *see also* amphibious raids
railways 42, 45, 47, 48, 116–17

bombing 138
coup de main attacks 155
Redshank 151
sabotage 176–8
Ram, Lt. Col. F. W. 66, 128
Ramsden, Col. 121
Rankin plans 44–5
rat work 165–70
rebellion 30–2
reception centres 183–4
Rediess, Frederick Wilhelm 165
Reed-Olsen, Oluf 125
refugees 19–20, 21, 113, 187–8
Reichskommissar 53–4
Reimers, Capt. J. H. 62, 66, 142, 184–5, 186
resistance movements 5, 72–9, 88–92, 166–7, 171–2, 190–1
  secret army 158, 159, 162
  see also Milorg
Riksrådforhandlinge 54
Ring, Daniel 64, 65
Rinnan, Henry 166, 170
RN see Royal Navy
Robsahm, Otto 126–7
Rognes, Capt. John 55, 60, 74–5, 78, 121
Rørholt, Lt. Col. Arnold 64
Rørholt, Bjørn 123
Rosbaud, Paul 140
Roscher-Lund, A. R. 64
Royal Air Force (RAF) 1, 5, 127, 180
  SOE 136–9, 141–3, 202
Royal Navy (RN) 1, 5, 119, 202
  coastal waters 127–8, 129–31, 132
Royal Norwegian Army see Norwegian Independent Company No I
Royal Norwegian Navy 55, 99, 128, 186
  30th MTB 130, 134
Rudolpho, Capt. 149
Ruge, Otto 75

Saborg 74
sabotage 2, 4, 8–9, 11, 62
  civilians 68–70
  collaboration 172–9
  economic targets 93–4
  intensification 203–4
  Milorg 80–1, 82, 85–6, 91, 201
  railways 45, 47, 48

SOE policy 33–4, 41–3
  see also coup de main operations; strategic bombing
'Salamander' operations 133
Scandinavian section 13–14
Scharnhorst (ship) 41, 136, 198
Schive, Capt. Jacob 56, 57, 75, 78–9, 80, 84
Scotland 23–4, 122; see also Shetlands Base
Scottish Command (Scotco) 44–5, 46, 47, 188, 191
secrecy 52
secret armies 4, 31–2, 71–2, 80–2, 145–6, 179–83
  Norway 34–5, 40, 41–3, 45–6
  SOE 157–65, 204, 205
Secret Intelligence Service (SIS) 1, 5, 11, 95, 120–7, 134
Section D 9–10, 12, 13, 51, 104
Selborne, Lord 12, 143
SFHQ see Special Force Headquarters
SHAEF see Supreme Headquarters, Allied Expeditionary Force (SHAEF)
Shetlands Base 2, 7, 19, 23, 25–6
  resistance 77–8
  SIS 122
Sipo 165–6
SIS see Secret Intelligence Service
Sivorg 73, 142
Skinnarland, Einar 102, 162, 163
'Skylark B' 123, 124
SL see Central Leadership
Smith-Kielland, Ingvald 64
smuggling 24–5
SOE see Special Operations Executive
SOE Mission 63, 64–6
Sola airfield 152
Solnørdal, Per 124, 163
Sønsteby, Gunnar 163, 170, 173–4
Sørli, Odd 158
Sørli, Rolf 157
sorties 26–8
Soviet Union 29, 34, 35, 69, 97
  Communism 74
  Finland 188–9
Special Force Headquarters (SFHQ) 12, 43, 46, 47

liberation 179, 180, 189–90
Special Operations Executive (SOE) 1–6,
    7–8, 13–18, 195–7, 204–5
  Admiralty 127–36
  air forces 136–43
  COHQ 94–104
  collaboration 56–63, 198–203
  coup de main operations 146–57
  liberation 46–7, 179–91, 194
  long-term objective 39–40
  military resistance 72–9
  military units 19–28
  Milorg 71–2, 80–92
  Norwegian government in exile 49–56
  'Norwegian Policy' 32–7
  origins 8–13
  OSS 110–17
  partnership 63–70
  PWE 104–10
  rat work 165–70
  resistance 73–4, 76–9
  Royal Navy 119
  sabotage 41–3, 172–9
  secret army 45–6, 157–65
  SIS 120–7
  subversion 31–2
Special Training School (STS) 21
spies 166
Sporborg, Lt. Col. Harry 14, 15, 16, 22,
    35
  amphibious raids 59
  ANCC 60
  Milorg 55, 57, 80
  Norwegian government in exile 52, 54
Stagg, Lt. Cmdr, Frank 16, 130
Starheim, Odd 20, 26, 123–4, 141, 167
Stenersen, Col. Tor 51, 162
Stockholm 17, 63, 64–6, 109–10
Storting (Parliament) 53–4
strategic bombing 4, 27, 119, 136–43
Strugstad, Oscar 64
submarine warfare 23, 24, 131–2, 133,
    135–6; *see also* U-boats
subversion 4, 8–10, 11, 31–2; *see also*
    propaganda
supplies 14–15, 16
Supreme Headquarters, Allied
    Expeditionary Force (SHAEF) 43,
    46, 47, 116

liberation 179, 180
  resistance 89–90, 171–2, 174
Sweden 17–18, 26, 115–16, 132–3
  coup de main attacks 147, 148
  iron ore 32, 128–9
  police forces 187–8
  see also Stockholm
Syverstad, Gunnar 157

Telavåg 122, 160
Temple, Col. 184–5
Terboven, Josef 72
Thomas, Brinley 110
Thorne, Lt. Gen. Sir Andrew 44, 192, 193
Tirpitz (ship) 41, 48, 98, 119
  and attacks 127, 128, 131, 134–6, 198
Torp, Oscar 57–8, 59
Torrance, Capt. J. W. 17, 58
transport 23–8, 147–8
Trondheim 39, 120–1
Tronstad, Leif 60, 62, 86, 184, 185
  atomic bomb 140
  Gunnerside 153
  heavy water 101, 124, 139
  Redshank 151

U-boats 133, 175
UD/E *see* Foreign Office Intelligence
    Office
Unger Vetlesen, Lt. Cmdr. F. W. G. 112
United States of America (USA) 4, 29,
    37–8; *see also* Office of Strategic
    Services
US Army 114–15
US Army Air Force (USAAF) 27, 28, 136,
    139–40, 140–1, 180

Værum, Arne 122
Valderhaug, Ingebrigt 26
Vemork 100–2, 139–41, 152–4, 156–7
Vilnes, Karl 132
volunteers 19–22, 147, 199

War Office 51
War-Trade agreement 14
weather conditions 6
Welle-Strand, Lt. 99
Wells, Vice Adm. L. V. 102–3
Welman one-man submarine 131–2, 135

Welsh, Eric 124
Wergeland, Harald 140
whale oil 32
Wilson, Lt. Col. John Skinner 16–17, 22, 42, 52–3, 98
   Milorg 82–3, 85, 86, 181
   Polar Bear 186
   propaganda 109

sabotage 70
secret army 162
SIS 123, 124
wireless stations 124–5
Wiskeman, George 14
Wollweber Organization 74

'X-Groups' 168, 169

www.ingramcontent.com/pod-product-compliance
Lightning Source LLC
Chambersburg PA
CBHW070009010526
44117CB00011B/1472